D0875286

CONFRONTING EVILS

In this new contribution to philosophical ethics, Claudia Card revisits the theory of evil developed in her earlier book *The Atrocity Paradigm* (2002), and expands it to consider collectively perpetrated and collectively suffered atrocities. Redefining the agency of evil as a secular concept and focusing on the inexcusability – rather than the culpability – of atrocities, Card examines the tension between responding to evils and preserving humanitarian values. This stimulating and often provocative book contends that understanding the evils in terrorism, torture, and genocide enables us to recognize similar evils in everyday life: daily life under oppressive regimes and in racist environments; violence against women, including in the home; violence and executions in prisons; hate crimes; and violence against animals. Card analyzes torture, terrorism, and genocide in the light of recent atrocities, considering whether there can be moral justifications for terrorism and torture, and providing conceptual tools to distinguish genocide from non-genocidal mass slaughter.

CLAUDIA CARD is Emma Goldman Professor of Philosophy at the University of Wisconsin–Madison. She is the author of *The Atrocity Paradigm: A Theory of Evil* (2002), *The Unnatural Lottery* (1996), *Lesbian Choices* (1995), and more than 100 articles and reviews. She has edited several books, including *The Cambridge Companion to Simone de Beauvoir* (Cambridge, 2003).

CONFRONTING EVILS

Terrorism, torture, genocide

CLAUDIA CARD

CAMBRIDGE
UNIVERSITY PRESS

CAMBRIDGE UNIVERSITY PRESS
Cambridge, New York, Melbourne, Madrid, Cape Town, Singapore,
São Paulo, Delhi, Dubai, Tokyo

Cambridge University Press
The Edinburgh Building, Cambridge CB2 8RU, UK

Published in the United States of America by Cambridge University Press, New York

www.cambridge.org
Information on this title: www.cambridge.org/9780521728362

First published 2010

Printed in the United Kingdom at the University Press, Cambridge

A catalogue record for this publication is available from the British Library

Library of Congress Cataloguing in Publication data
Card, Claudia.
Confronting evils : terrorism, torture, genocide / Claudia Card.
p.   cm.
Includes bibliographical references and index.
ISBN 978-0-521-89961-1 (hardback) – ISBN 978-0-521-72836-2 (paperback)
1. Good and evil.   2. Terrorism.   3. Torture.   4. Genocide.   I. Title.
BJ1401.C293 2010
170–dc22
2010022334

ISBN 978-0-521-89961-1 Hardback
ISBN 978-0-521-72836-2 Paperback

Cambridge University Press has no responsibility for the persistence or
accuracy of URLs for external or third-party internet websites referred to in
this publication, and does not guarantee that any content on such websites is,
or will remain, accurate or appropriate.

To my early philosophy teachers, in gratitude:

William H. Hay (1917–97)
Gerald C. MacCallum (1925–87)
Julius R. Weinberg (1908–71)
Robert R. Ammerman
Stanley Cavell

Contents

Contents   ix

Preface and acknowledgements

This book follows up on work that I began in *The Atrocity Paradigm: A Theory of Evil* (2002). There I began to develop a theory of evils intended to illuminate well-known atrocities that have occurred during my lifetime. The list is awesome. From my childhood, it includes Auschwitz, medical experiments by Japanese military unit 731 on prisoners and civilians in China, Stalin's gulags, and the firebombings of Japan by the United States. From my schooldays in Wisconsin it includes the Communist purges of Senator Joseph McCarthy and the murders of Ed Gein, said to be the inspiration for Alfred Hitchcock's film *Psycho* (1960). When I was in graduate school, President John F. Kennedy was assassinated, and the next year three civil rights workers were lynched in Mississippi. During the more than four decades that I have taught at the University of Wisconsin, Martin Luther King, Malcolm X, Robert Kennedy, and Harvey Milk were gunned down, and there were the Biafran war, Idi Amin's dictatorship in Uganda, apartheid in South Africa, the My Lai massacre, the killing fields of Cambodia, mass rape in war, the rise of factory farming in the US, massive destruction of rainforests, the Oklahoma City bombing of 1995, the terror bombings of September 11, 2001, and, closer to my home, the lethal protest bombing of the Army/Math Research Center on my campus in 1970, and the sex-crime murders by Caucasian Jeffrey Dahmer of Asian American youths in Milwaukee, followed by his own murder in 1994 in the prison at Portage, Wisconsin. These paradigms continue to inform my atrocity theory of evils. I now make sense of many of them under the headings of terrorism, torture, and genocide. This book aims also to make sense of evils less apt to make headlines, low-profile atrocities of domestic violence, prison rape, and other forms of terrorism and torture suffered daily by people whose names most of us will never know (although each of us probably knows some), and of the torture of animals.

The Atrocity Paradigm defined evils as reasonably foreseeable intolerable harms produced (maintained, aggravated, supported, tolerated, and so on) by culpable wrongdoing. Part I of this book modifies that theory and develops it further as background to taking up terrorism, torture, and genocide in Part II. Chapter 1 revisits enough of the main ideas of *The Atrocity Paradigm* that it is not necessary to read that book before this one. But chapter 1 is not mainly a review of *The Atrocity Paradigm*. It is mainly an attempt to refine, improve upon, and develop further some core ideas in the atrocity theory of evils.

Chapters in Part II apply, test, and extend ideas from Part I, and they explore the meanings of terrorism, torture, and genocide. Two themes run through Part II. The first is the danger of failing to preserve humanitarian values in responding to atrocities. Terrorism, torture, and even genocide have each been responses to perceived or alleged prior atrocities. Perpetrators seldom call those responses terrorism, torture, or genocide. The greatest moral challenges to those who respond to evils are, first, to recognize responses that would be evils and, second, to find or create alternative responses that are honorable. Initially, I had hoped to address both challenges. That goal proved too ambitious for one book. Part II of this book works on the first challenge: identifying evil responses. The second theme is more of a thesis: that appreciating the evils of international terrorism, political torture, and genocides, whether by governments or by political insurgents, enables us to recognize some of the same kinds of evils in more local, less publicized wrongs.

The writing of this book was facilitated by a Senior Fellowship at the Institute for Research in the Humanities in Madison, Wisconsin, from 2002 to 2007 (which, by agreement with university departments, releases fellows half-time from teaching duties), two semesters of sabbatical leave (2008–09) supported by the University of Wisconsin, and summer support from the University of Wisconsin Graduate School. Ancestors of several chapters had trial runs at Institute seminars, where I benefited from the expertise of international groups of colleagues in fields ranging from literature, history, and history of science to anthropology, Asian studies, and African languages and literatures. From those discussions I especially thank Paul Boyer, David Chan, Anne Enke, Nan Enstad, Johannes Heil, Robert Kingdon, Ullrich Langer, David Loewenstein, Florencia Mallon, David Morgan, Jack Niles, Tom Safely, Mike Shank, Frank Solomon, David Sorkin, and Lee Wandel for great suggestions, amazing references, and stimulating conversation.

Computer equipment and other research materials, as well as travel to present papers in Barcelona, Beijing, and Gothenburg and to many conferences in the US, were supported from 2001 to 2007 by a Wisconsin

Alumni Research Foundation professorship (named, at my choice, for Emma Goldman), for which I am most grateful. A warm thank you also to Christopher Feeney for expert editing of the manuscript.

In my home philosophy department, colleagues Paula Gottlieb, Lester Hunt, Steve Nadler, Russ Shafer-Landau, and Elliott Sober generously read and commented on ancestors of various chapters, as did my colleague in the law school, Leonard Kaplan. Paula Gottlieb gave me written comments on papers that preceded these chapters and directed me to relevant passages in Aristotle. Harry Brighouse heard an ancestor of chapter 1 and raised a point that led me to rethink what I wanted to say about the death penalty debate. Dan Hausman shared his own work on well-being and groups, and gave me helpful references. Philosophy graduate students and former graduate students contributed many helpful comments, especially Mohammed Abed, Jaime Ahlberg, Paraceve Atkin, David Concepcion, Sara Gavrell, Fred Harrington (who directed me to Shakespeare's *Titus Andronicus*), Holly Kantin, Matt Kopec, Kathryn Norlock, Tasia Persson, Alan Rubel, Andrea Veltman, and, from Beijing, Gao Shan, who did an oral paragraph-by-paragraph consecutive translation of papers I presented there. I thank all of them.

Colleagues from other universities and colleges in the US who read or heard and responded helpfully to ancestors of various chapters include Sharon Anderson-Gold, Bat-Ami Bar On, Sandra Lee Bartky, Ann Cudd, Howard Curzer, Victoria Davion, David Estlund, Marilyn Friedman, Thomas E. Hill, Jr., Alison Jaggar, Eva Kittay, Hilde Lindemann, Armen Marsoobian, James Nelson, Carol Quinn, John K. Roth, Robin Schott, Lissa Skitolsky, Elizabeth V. Spelman, Margaret Urban Walker, and a faculty member in the audience at Smith College who called to my attention the case of Beatrice Cenci.

It will be evident how much I have learned from other philosophers who are working on the concept of evil, especially Richard Bernstein, John Kekes, Berel Lang, Maria Pia Lara, Robin Schott, and Laurence Thomas. I learned much about the history of torture and questionable methods of intelligence-gathering from my colleague in the history department, Alfred McCoy, whose specialties include the Philippines, and from activists Hector Aristizabal and Jean Maria Arrigo, both torture survivors, at a symposium on torture at California State University in Fullerton. Reflections on collective evils were aided by tutorials over a two-year period with post-doctoral fellow Todd Calder. I continue to benefit from the work on collective wrongdoing by Margaret Gilbert, Christopher Kutz, Larry May, Arne Johan Vetlesen, and the late Iris Young.

Many chapters have early roots in conference presentations and shorter essays that are published in journals and anthologies. None of those materials is simply reproduced here. All have been rethought, heavily reorganized, rewritten, substantially expanded, and integrated into a continuous treatment of the themes of this book. A rough history of the evolution of the chapters is as follows. No chapter has been presented or published anywhere as it appears here.

Chapter 1 responds, in part, to concerns about the theory of *The Atrocity Paradigm* voiced by my former teacher Marcus G. Singer and by social psychologist Leonard Berkowitz. Both thought the agency component of my earlier conception of evils was too broad. I came to think some of their concerns well founded. Marilyn Frye thought the account of evils in *The Atrocity Paradigm* placed too much importance on intentions, and Alfred McCoy thought my account was not layered enough to do justice to political evils. I came to see issues underlying their concerns that I needed to address. That led me to attend more carefully to structural evils and to revise the agency component of my initial definition of evils to center moral indefensibility rather than culpability. No ancestor of this chapter has been published anywhere, although I read an early draft to an interdisciplinary audience at my university in the lecture series, "Focus on the Humanities."

Chapter 2 has roots in a paper presented at the conference "Moral Choices in the Age of Terrorism: Kant on Religion, Ethics, and Politics" that I co-organized in 2004 with my colleague Klaus Berghahn of the German department, at his invitation, to commemorate the 200th anniversary of Kant's death. Descendants of that paper were discussed at a Purdue University conference on evil (2005), the Chapel Hill Philosophy Colloquium (2005), Michigan State and St. Louis Universities, and the Universities of Victoria and Illinois-Urbana. An abbreviated version with a narrower focus appears in *Kant's Anatomy of Evil* (Anderson-Gold and Muchnik 2009).

Chapter 3 is mostly new. But it received jump-starts from a short response paper I wrote for the Eastern Division American Philosophical Association (APA) Convention in 2005 and a short panel discussion paper presented to the Canadian Society of Women in Philosophy in Saskatoon in 2006. One of those early short pieces is published in *Dancing with Iris*, a volume on the work of Iris Young (Ferguson 2009).

Chapter 4 includes a reworking, reorganizing, and substantial expansion of some material from a journal article, "Environmental Atrocities and Non-Sentient Life," that appeared in *Ethics and the Environment* (9:1;

2004). The discussion in that chapter of evils suffered by human groups, including the Murder, Inc. problem, is entirely new.

Chapter 5 has early roots in very short panel presentations at the International Association of Women Philosophers (IAPh) symposium in Barcelona (2002) and the Feminist Ethics and Social Theory (FEAST) conference in Tampa (2003). These panels led to a brief symposium piece, "Questions Regarding a War on Terrorism," published in the special issue of *Hypatia* edited by Robin Schott (18:1; 2003). A slightly expanded version of that symposium piece appears as "Making War on Terrorism in Response to 9/11" in *Terrorism and International Justice* (Sterba 2003), and a related essay with a different focus appears as "Responding to 9/11: Military Mode or Civil Law?" in *Feminist Philosophy and the Problem of Evil* (Schott 2007). Chapter 5 is more ambitious than any of these precursors.

Early drafts of chapter 6 were presented at the Rocky Mountain Philosophy Conference in Boulder (2006), the University of Victoria, and Washington University-St. Louis. An ancestor of parts of this chapter appears as "Recognizing Terrorism" in the *Journal of Ethics* (11:1; 2007).

The inspiration for chapter 7 was a short invited paper for a Central APA session on torture (2006), at which David Estlund pressed some helpful objections. A later version, presented at the 2007 British Academy symposium on criminal law and philosophy and to the Jowett Society at Oxford University, appears in *Criminal Law and Philosophy* (2:1; 2008). I am grateful for comments and questions in London and Oxford from John Tasioulas, Clare Chambers, Shlomit Harrosh, Douglas Husak, Onora O'Neill, and Ralph Wedgwood. Later drafts benefited from audience discussions at the University of Wisconsin at Stevens Point, Marquette University, Union College, Kent University in Canterbury, Westminster University in London, the University of Chicago Law School, and the symposium on torture at California State University in Fullerton (2007).

Some of the material on everyday torture in chapter 8 is reworked from an essay published in *Moral Psychology* (DesAutels and Walker 2004). Revised and expanded essays on everyday torture were discussed at the University of North Carolina-Charlotte, Texas Tech University, Pacific Division APA meetings, the Society for Analytical Feminism in Toronto (2004), the IAPh symposium in Gothenburg (2004), Santa Catarina University in Florianopolis, Brazil (2004), St. Mary's College of Maryland, Smith College, and the University of Oregon. The discussions in this chapter of "clean tortures" and torture at the dark sites are entirely new.

Some of the ideas for chapter 9 have roots in a very short IAPh paper, "Pernicious Injustice: The Case of Genocide" (Zurich 2000), which led to a panel discussion at a FEAST conference in Tampa (2001). An expanded version, "Genocide and Social Death," appears in Robin Schott's guest-edited special issue of *Hypatia* and in her book expanded from that issue (Schott 2007). The *Hypatia* version is reprinted in *Genocide's Aftermath: Responsibility and Repair*, which I co-edited with Armen Marsoobian (2007). Rewritten, rethought, and greatly expanded, that version evolved into chapter 9.

Some ideas for chapter 10 germinated in a short invited paper presented to the Society for the Philosophical Study of Genocide and the Holocaust at a convention of the Society for Phenomenological and Existential Philosophy in Philadelphia (2006). A rewritten and expanded version for the Spindel Conference in Memphis (2007) appears, together with comments by Ann Cudd, in the *Southern Journal of Philosophy* (46; Supplement 2008). A shorter version of that one was presented and discussed at the University of Southern Connecticut. Further work on the complexities of non-homicidal genocide and on ethnic cleansing led to chapter 10.

I dedicated *The Atrocity Paradigm* to five of my teachers from many stages of my education, including my undergraduate and graduate advisers Marcus G. Singer and John B. Rawls. The guidance and example of all of them produced turning points in my intellectual development. Their lives and work also embody the humanitarian values to which I aspire. This book is dedicated to more of my philosophy teachers who serve also as my models of humanitarian values. In alphabetical order, first is Robert R. Ammerman, whose skepticism, humor, and faith in the common sense of ordinary folk provide a counterbalance to philosophical speculations that threaten to lose touch with the real world. He introduced me to Ludwig Wittgenstein's idea of "family resemblance" concepts, of which I have made generous use in these chapters. Next is Stanley Cavell, also a Wittgensteinian, who, in the first year of his permanent appointment at Harvard (my second year of graduate school), set an inimitable example of generosity, receptivity, creativity, and synthesis in his lectures on the philosophy of religion. That course introduced me to the concept of demythologizing, which I also use in this work. The next three are no longer with us. William H. Hay was my first philosophy teacher and thereafter unfailing supporter. He had one of the most omnivorous minds and taught more philosophical subjects than anyone else I have known. Gerald C. MacCallum first grounded me in the classics of Western political philosophy and taught me patience and precision as well as (however inadvertently) never to be satisfied with my work. Julius R. Weinberg encouraged me with his own life story in the fall semester of my senior year when a graduate student informed me that no university would hire a woman to teach philosophy. To such teachers I owe so much of my enthusiasm for teaching and for philosophy, as well as my cautious optimism in the face of evil.

Acronyms and abbreviations

9/11	September 11, 2001
AI	Amnesty International
ALF	Animal Liberation Front
APA	American Philosophical Association
BWC	Biological Weapons Convention
CF	Coalition Forces
CIA	Central Intelligence Agency
CUP	Committee of Union and Progress
DOD	Department of Defense
EU	European Union
FACE	Freedom of Access to Abortion Clinic Entrances
FBI	Federal Bureau of Investigation
FEAST	Feminist Ethics and Social Theory
IAPh	International Association of Women Philosophers
ICC	International Criminal Court
ICRC	International Committee of the Red Cross
ICTY	International Criminal Tribunal for the Former Yugoslavia
ICTR	International Criminal Tribunal for Rwanda
IHL	International Humanitarian Law
IMT	International Military Tribunal
KGB	Russian abbreviation for Committee for State Security (Komityet Gosudarstvjennoj Biezopasnosti)
KKK	Ku Klux Klan
NGO	Non-Governmental Organization
PD	Prisoner's Dilemma
PETA	People for the Ethical Treatment of Animals
PHS	Public Health Service
POW	Prisoner of War
PTSD	Post-Traumatic Stress Disorder

SERE	Survival, Evasion, Resistance, and Escape
SLA	Symbionese Liberation Army
SPE	Stanford Prison Experiment
SPLC	Southern Poverty Law Center
SS	German abbreviation for Hitler's bodyguard (later, elite guard of the Third Reich) (*Schutzstaffel*)
STD	Sexually Transmitted Disease
UN	United Nations
US	United States
WAR	Women Against Rape
WMD	Weapons of Mass Destruction
WW I	World War I
WW II	World War II

PART I

The concept of evil

CHAPTER I

Inexcusable wrongs

A morally inexcusable action may fall anywhere on a continuum
from culpable ignorance or weakness to deliberately and knowingly
doing evil for its own sake. (Kekes 2005, p. 2)

The bombings of September 11, 2001 (hereafter 9/11), abuse of prisoners at
Abu Ghraib, and mass rapes and murders in Darfur have kept terrorism,
torture, and genocide in the global public eye through the first decade of
this century. Responses to atrocities are a continuing source of controversy within and without congress halls and university walls. Although
terrorism, torture, and genocide are today's paradigms of evil, each has
been itself a response to perceived or threatened evils. A motivation for
this book is the hope that atrocity victims and governments can learn
to respond without doing further evil and that they can model, instead,
humanitarian values. That hope takes seriously the concept of evil from a
secular moral point of view.

Increasingly since 9/11, philosophers are giving sustained attention to
that precise secular sense of "evil" in which it refers to especially heinous wrongs (Bernstein 2002, 2005; Grant 2006; Kekes 2005; Lara 2007;
Morton 2004). At the same time, others (such as Cole 2006) remain
skeptical of the value of rehabilitating the concept of evil after Friedrich
Nietzsche's critique (Nietzsche 1969, pp. 24–56). Many have worried about
its use as a political club and rallying tool that has the potential to stir
up mass hatreds. That worry was aggravated when former United States
President George W. Bush labeled Iran, Iraq, and North Korea an "axis of
evil," following the precedent of former President Ronald Reagan's labeling the Soviet Union an "evil empire" in 1983.[1]

---

[1] In his State of the Union Address on January 29, 2002, former President G. W. Bush coined the
term "axis of evil," naming those three countries. President Ronald Reagan used the term "evil
empire" in a 1983 speech to the National Association of Evangelicals, available online at: www.
youtube.com/watch?v=r5ZMeFXh4UI&feature=related.

The concern of many of us who are not persuaded to jettison the concept of evil is not with labeling individuals, countries, or alliances. It is more basic also than the classic theological conundrum of how a world that contains evils could have been created by a benevolent Supreme Being. Our concern is with certain logically more fundamental questions of philosophical ethics: What distinguishes evils from lesser wrongs? What kinds of evils are there and how are they related to each other? How are evils perpetrated, especially on a massive scale? Who is vulnerable to them and how? What responses to evils are honorable? Such are the questions addressed in this book's chapters.

This book continues the project of *The Atrocity Paradigm: A Theory of Evil* (Card 2002) to develop and deepen a secular understanding of evils that captures major evils of my lifetime, which spans nearly seven decades. My intent is to present a conception that is not vulnerable to Nietzsche's charge that the judgment "evil" embeds slavish values (Nietzsche 1969, pp. 15–56). Another aim is to provide a conception that is less vulnerable to political abuse. Chapter 2 rejects the Manichean fantasy of good and evil forces that eventually divide humanity into good and evil camps. Taking issue with the widely shared view of Immanuel Kant that nothing lies between good and evil (Kant 1996b, pp. 70–71), that chapter defends the possibility that many who are complicit in real evils are as individuals neither positively good nor downright evil. Kant discusses evil in terms of maxims defining individual intentions. Yet many evils are produced by collective activity that is not adequately captured by maxims of individual intention. Many who are complicit in collectively produced evils are not even well described as evil-doers.

Since 9/11, I have amplified my account of evil and modified it in three ways. Briefly, the modifications are (1) that evils are *inexcusable*, not just culpable, (2) that evils need not be extraordinary (probably most are not), and (3) that not all institutional evil implies individual culpability.[2] This chapter re-presents the atrocity theory with those revisions and defends them against certain natural objections. The revisions lead also to amplifications of the theory. First, they lead to an extended examination of collectively perpetrated evils (chapter 3). Second, they lead also to extended reflections on the question of to whom or to what evils can be done (chapter 4), with attention to evils suffered by groups. Chapters of Part II

---

[2] I share the views put forward in John Kekes's *Roots of Evil* that evils are inexcusable (Kekes, 2005, pp. 1–3) and that severe harm is an important element (Kekes 2005, p. 2), but not the view that an evil deed necessarily has a malevolent motive.

examine terrorism, torture, and genocide in light of the atrocity theory so revised and expanded. They address issues of recognition that arise because terrorism, torture, and genocide are seldom so called by perpetrators, and they address issues regarding temptations to use torture or measures that are terrorist or genocidal either in retaliation or as weapons of defense.

My first two modifications of the atrocity theory – that evils are inexcusably wrong and that they need not be extraordinary – appear initially and in opposite ways to jeopardize two objectives that animate my construction of a philosophical theory of evil. One of those objectives is to avoid demonizing most perpetrators. The other is to distinguish evils from lesser wrongs. Restricting evils to inexcusable wrongs narrows the scope of evils. The question arises whether doing so risks demonizing most perpetrators after all. At the same time, if evils need not be extraordinary, their scope is broadened. Does that broadening erode the distinction between evils and lesser wrongs? Does it lessen the gravity of judgments of evil? Sections 2 through 5 of this chapter defend the "inexcusability" and "ordinariness" modifications against these worries.

I begin in the next section with a quick review of the theory of the atrocity paradigm and of reasons to preserve the distinction between evils and lesser wrongs despite a continuing history of political abuse of the concept of evil. There follows a discussion of the influences of Hannah Arendt, Stanley Milgram, and Philip Zimbardo on my approach. Barely mentioned in *The Atrocity Paradigm*, these thinkers were nevertheless very much in the background. A new way to look at their work supports my revisions. Following that discussion is an overview of the revisions and then an extended examination of each. The chapter concludes with an illustrative look at implications regarding the US debate over the death penalty, introducing the topic of collectively perpetrated evils, which is the subject of chapter 3.

1. *The Atrocity Paradigm*

The Atrocity Paradigm (Card 2002) developed the theory that evils are reasonably foreseeable intolerable harms produced (maintained, supported, tolerated, and so on) by culpable wrongdoing. So understood, evils have two irreducibly distinct components: a harm component and an agency component. What distinguishes evils from lesser wrongs is the harm component. In contrast to lesser wrongs, evils do intolerable harm. Ordinarily these harms, rather than the motives of perpetrators, are what distinguish evils from other wrongs. Evil-doers need not be evil ("wicked") people. On a radio call-in show where I was interviewed just after publication of

The Atrocity Paradigm, callers asked if I thought Saddam Hussein was evil, or (then) President George W. Bush. Few asked whether I thought this or that deed or practice an evil. My focus is on deeds, institutions, practices – evils (plural). My motivating interest is not in putting labels on people (or empires or alliances).

The analysis of *The Atrocity Paradigm* does not yield a comprehensive theory of ethics. It presupposes that there are defensible norms of right and wrong. But it neither specifies a particular theory of those norms nor does it depend very much on what they are. The atrocity theory is compatible with many non-utilitarian theories of right and wrong, such as those of Immanuel Kant (1996a) and W. D. Ross (1980 [1930]). I did not expect the theory, abstractly stated, to be controversial. Everything interesting, I thought, would lie in the interpretations of culpable wrongdoing, intolerable harm, and reasonable foreseeability. Yet an aspect of the theory has been controversial in a way that I now find justified. As originally stated, it does not capture well the evils of social practices, institutions, and other social structures, including many paradigms of evil in my lists of atrocities. Those lists include the Holocaust, carpet-bombings in WW II, and the Tuskegee syphilis experiments, all collectively perpetrated (Card 2002, pp. 8–9).

I call my theory the atrocity paradigm (or atrocity theory) because atrocities are my paradigms of evil. Atrocities I define only ostensively; I list several. My lists include, besides the atrocities just mentioned, Stalin's gulags, the 1937 rape of Nanking, the 1995 Oklahoma City bombing, the 1964 murder of the three civil rights workers, James Cheney, Michael Goodman, and Andrew Schwerner, in Mississippi, and the dragging murder of James Byrd in Jasper, Texas, 1998. Natural catastrophies, such as hurricanes, tornados, floods, and earthquakes, can be as devastatingly harmful. They are not atrocities when they are not produced, aggravated, and so on by culpable wrongs. Also, not all evils are atrocities. Murder is an evil when there is no moral excuse for it. Yet not every murder is an atrocity. Atrocities are useful as paradigms not for their shock value or even the number of victims but because they are uncontroversially evils, if anything is. In atrocities the ingredients of evil are writ boldly.

Three tasks guide my inquiries. One is to clarify further the differences between evils and lesser wrongs. Marcus Singer writes that "evil," used precisely, "is the worst possible term of opprobrium imaginable" (Singer 2004, p. 185). What underlies that opprobrium? Through most of the history of ethical theory, moral philosophers have not, in fact, systematically distinguished evils from lesser wrongs. They have referred loosely to anything bad or wrong as an evil. Yet outside academic philosophy, "evil" carries the emotive load that Singer notices. "Evil" in this more specific sense tends to be reserved for the worst wrongs, those we think no one should have to suffer. Genocide is an evil. Premeditated murder is an evil. Petty theft and tax evasion are not.

Why distinguish evils from lesser wrongs? One reason is to help set priorities when resources are limited for preventing wrongs and repairing harms. Another is to set limits to excusable forms of defense against or retaliation for atrocities perpetrated or threatened by others. With regard to the first of these concerns, the temptation is often to address lesser wrongs first, deferring indefinitely attention to real evils. Lesser wrongs can be easier to repair. But evils are urgent. Life and basic quality of life are at stake. Many lesser wrongs do not necessarily add up to an evil. Nevertheless, deep and pervasive inequalities that may not be evils considered simply in themselves can set a stage for evils, generating resentments and fostering abuses of power, as Nannerl O. Keohane argues in discussing Rousseau's thoughts on evil (Grant 2006, pp. 75–99; Rousseau 1950, pp. 176–95). Collectively perpetrated evils can also be the cumulative result of wrongful deeds which, considered individually, are not evils. And so, there are good reasons not to go to the opposite extreme of neglecting lesser wrongs just because their victims' needs are not urgent. Still, the harm of evils is intolerable, often irreversible, frequently uncontainable. Progress in containing, terminating, preventing, and repairing what can be repaired is apt to be incremental. But even slow progress can save many lives.

In regard to the second concern, limiting excusable forms of defense or retaliation, it is important to rule out measures that are inhumane or degrading and incompatible with basic democratic values. Inhumane responses by a government not only jeopardize the possibility of post-conflict peaceful coexistence but also rightly undermine the confidence of a people in the government that so responds. Such responses are unworthy of a government that means to offer protection against evil. They tend to be sufficiently shocking that those in power are tempted to maintain secrecy around them. Secrecy jeopardizes accountability and procedural justice. It results in an improperly informed electorate. Confidence is weakened in an electorate that comes to know or strongly suspect that it is improperly informed. Even with an unaware electorate, the government's trust*worthiness* is weakened.

A second task guiding my inquiries is to rehabilitate the concept of evil in the face of widespread skepticism, especially among intellectuals, given the ongoing history of political abuses of the label "evil." Three myths facilitate such political abuses. One myth is that evil-doers are monstrous and cannot be reasoned with. A second and related myth is the Manichean fantasy that humanity can be divided into the good (most of us, or, on some religious views, an elect few of us) and the evil ("them"; the rest). A third myth is the idea that evil is a metaphysical power or force that possesses some individuals. Given the harm done by such myths, it is fair to ask again why evil is a concept worth retaining. My first response is that the myths themselves have been instrumental in the perpetration of much evil. To sustain that judgment, it is necessary to make sense of evil independently of the myths. And so my second response is that evil can be demythologized. A demythologized understanding of evil is useful for thinking about how to respond with as much honor as possible to the worst wrongs of which humanity is capable. It is helpful for setting priorities, constraining responses, and encouraging moral imagination. The dismal history of the concept of evil has been about labeling agents, not identifying evil deeds and practices. That history has also involved religious beliefs that are not part of my project.

Finally, a third task guiding my inquiries, which comes to prominence in chapters 6, 8, and 10 in Part II, is to facilitate the identification of evils, in the hope that once they are identified, people who currently support a number of evil practices might cease to do so. Carrying out this task is aided by clarification of the differences between evils and lesser wrongs and by the general demythologized appreciation that evils need not be extraordinary.

My secular approach to understanding evil mediates between Stoicism, which takes evil to reside solely in wrongful intentions, and Epicureanism, which takes it to reside solely in the experience of harm. Evils, on my view, have both a Stoic and an Epicurean component, neither reducible to the other. Intolerable harm (the Epicurean component) deprives victims of basics ordinarily needed to make a life (or a death) decent. "Intolerable," here, is a normative concept. It refers not to what individuals cannot in fact tolerate but to what a decent life cannot include. That is not an entirely subjective matter, even if what is worth tolerating is somewhat relative to time and place, available resources, available knowledge, and so on. Examples of intolerable harm include lack of access to non-toxic food, water, or air; lack of freedom from prolonged and severe pain, humiliation, or debilitating fear; prolonged inability to move one's limbs or to stand, sit, or lie down; lack of affective bonds with others; and the inability to make choices and act on at least some of them effectively. The degree of deprivation that is intolerable varies. Still, intolerable harm is not simply relative to what can be withstood. Freedom from such deprivations are basics that all humans, as members of a common species and regardless of cultural differences, need for our lives to be not just possible but decent, and for our deaths to be decent. Evils rob us of these things or jeopardize our access to them. Lesser wrongs do less serious harm. The *motives*, however, to both evils and lesser wrongs are often the same – greed or impatience, for example.

This analysis still seems to me a good beginning. But there are gaps to fill, qualifications to develop, disclaimers to make, and modifications to incorporate. Initially I intended to follow *The Atrocity Paradigm* with a book on responses to atrocities that preserve humanitarian values: apologies, truth commissions, reparations, memorials, education, and the like. Thinking about responses brought a shift in my focus from the harm component to the agency component of evils. Thinking from the agency perspective led to thinking about temptations to evil responses. A connecting thread between my initially imagined book and the current project is the moral challenge of avoiding evil responses to evil. Meeting that challenge, by the way, need not require forswearing revenge or retaliation – only evil forms of it. Revenge is not always evil. It need not do intolerable harm, or any harm at all. My revenge on those who did what they could to impede my professional endeavors is to exploit opportunities they inadvertently opened up for me to achieve what success I can in developing a theory of evil.

Thinking about how to avoid doing evil, I was led to a new view of the later work of Hannah Arendt and the famous experiments in social psychology of Stanley Milgram and Philip Zimbardo. The work of all three thinkers had initially confirmed me in the idea that evils differ from lesser wrongs only in the severity and nature of the harm they do, not in anything special about the agency of their perpetrators. I no longer find that view adequate. Nor do I think it quite the right conclusion to draw from their work. What is shocking about evils is not only that the harm is intolerable but also that the deed producing it is utterly without moral excuse. Although none of these thinkers comments on that fact, and perhaps they would not agree, I find it a common element of the disturbing choices they studied.[3]

---

[3] Arendt might have agreed. But my hypothesis throws a monkey wrench into the idea widely associated with social psychology that it is (if not *only*, then *mainly*) the situation that distinguishes evil-doers from others, not something about the agents.

2. DEMYTHOLOGIZING EVIL: ARENDT, MILGRAM, AND ZIMBARDO

The myths that evil-doers must be monsters and that the human race can be divided into the good (most of us) and the evil ("them") take a powerful hit in the later writings of Arendt and in the well-known experiments conducted by Milgram and Zimbardo. Milgram's obedience experiments and Zimbardo's Stanford Prison Experiment (SPE) are widely cited in support of Arendt's controversial observation regarding "the fearsome, word-and-thought-defying *banality of evil*," which concludes the last chapter of her book on the 1961 trial of Adolf Eichmann in Jerusalem for crimes against the Jewish people (Arendt 1965, p. 252). These three thinkers are often misunderstood as offering hypotheses about evil in general. They sometimes say things that encourage that misunderstanding. But their focus is actually more specific, namely, the monstrous deeds of people who are not (or not necessarily) monsters. None of these thinkers claims or implies that no one is monstrous. One might even disagree with Arendt's view that Eichmann was not monstrous (and cite the very banality of his motives as evidence that he was) without disagreeing with her view that much evil is a result of shallow thinking and culpable failures to think at all. The work of Arendt, Milgram, and Zimbardo need not be read as support for the view that there is an Eichmann in all of us (clearly, not Arendt's view). Their points are far more modest: that agents need not be deeply vicious or freaks of nature to do monstrous deeds.

Listening to Eichmann at his trial and reporting on his conversations and his last words, Arendt was taken aback by the superficiality of his character. His speech was trite. He utterly failed to consider the perspectives of his victims. Her diagnosis of what underlay his willingness to plan and coordinate trains to the death camps was that he never learned to think. He seemed unable to put two and two together morally for himself, although he was innovative in devising means to ends. This failure to take moral responsibility does not distinguish him from many bureaucrats who never become major criminals. In a morally less demanding political climate, as Arendt noted, he might have led an unremarkable life.

Regarding the Milgram and Zimbardo experiments, as well as the case of Eichmann, I was struck initially by a basic similarity in the motives from which people do evils and the motives from which they commit lesser wrongs. I concluded that since evils and lesser wrongs can be committed from the same motives (say, greed, impatience, or desires for approval), motives do not define the differences between them. Both evils and lesser wrongs are culpable. But only evils do intolerable harm. I still find truth in that view. But I also think it not the whole truth about the agency component of evils. What strikes me now in addition is a certain *contrast* between the agency exhibited by Eichmann, most of the subjects in Milgram's obedience experiments, and most of the "guards" in Zimbardo's SPE, on one hand, and the agency, on the other hand, of many less serious wrongs, such as lying to protect someone against undeserved harm. For such a lie there is at least a good reason, one that carries some moral weight, although perhaps not enough to justify the lie, all things considered. But subjects who thought they were inflicting severe shocks in Milgram's experiments (and SPE "guards" who badly abused "prisoners") had *no moral excuse* for their choices, no comparably good reason. It is still true that their motives are not what stand out. What stands out is that lack of any moral excuse, given what they knew or had reason to believe about the harm they were being asked (in Milgram's experiments) or permitted (in Zimbardo's SPE) to do. Their culpability is unmitigated by any diminished capacity for agency and by any even partly justifying reason. They had reasons, to be sure. But those reasons do not begin to justify their choices. To elucidate further, it is necessary to summarize those experiments and then clarify what I mean by "no moral excuse."

Milgram's 1960s obedience experiments were motivated by his desire to understand how so many citizens of the Third Reich, from unskilled workers and housewives to educators, lawyers, and doctors, became complicit in the Holocaust. Milgram asked people in advance of his experiments how many they thought would obey requests by an authority to do something they could foresee would inflict intolerable (even potentially fatal) harm. He and they were astonished to learn from the experiments that in fact the number was not the tiny fraction they had anticipated but roughly two-thirds of the subjects who were tested.

Milgram's *Obedience to Authority* (1974) describes experiments carried out from 1960 to 1963 while he was in the Department of Psychology at Yale. To review, Milgram asked subjects to push a switch that he said would deliver an electric shock to a subject in a neighboring room as punishment for giving a wrong answer in what was presented as a "learning experiment." With each wrong answer, Milgram asked the switch-pusher to deliver what he said was an increasingly severe shock. Subjects actually received conflicting information. Milgram said the shocks would do no permanent harm. Yet the highest level of shock was clearly marked "danger," and the responses and eventual lack of *any* response from the "learner" at the higher levels of shock sent a message incompatible with

Milgram's assurance. Hence, the experiment offered an interesting test of Arendt's hypothesis regarding thinking.

In reality, the "learner" was a collaborator, not receiving shocks. The point was to see how far ordinary people would go in obedience to authority. Critics take Milgram to task for using deception to induce subjects to do things they might find it hard to live with later, for disanalogies between his experiments and situations actually faced by atrocity perpetrators (many of whom were policy makers, not just followers), and for conclusions he and others have drawn about why subjects behaved as they did (Blass 2000; Fromm 1973; see also Berkowitz 1999). Yet, those experiments remain breathtaking for their incontrovertible demonstration that so many individuals who tested as psychologically ordinary were willing (often despite their own clear discomfort) to keep pushing the escalating switches in spite of yells, pleas to stop, and finally complete silence from the learner.

Philip Zimbardo, a high-school classmate of Milgram's (later, briefly, his colleague at Yale), designed an experiment, carried out in August 1971, which ended up testing whether it was even necessary to *tell* people to inflict harm once they occupied a role giving them authority and power to do so with impunity. His results also surprised everyone. Zimbardo's book *The Lucifer Effect* (2007) describes the SPE in a level of detail not published previously.[4] To recap briefly, in a simulated prison in the basement of a Stanford University building, some subjects (not all students) played "prisoners" and others "guards." They had no scripts. Guards were given only a role, no specific directions on what to say or do to prisoners, except not to use physical violence, an instruction not altogether respected. The guards were so hard on prisoners that the experiment, originally planned for two weeks, was terminated on day six. Two prisoners were so stressed they had to be released earlier, one on day two. A film based on the SPE has been viewed by military personnel concerned to eliminate the sorts of abuses at the US military prison at Abu Ghraib that were documented in the 2004 International Committee of the Red Cross (ICRC) Report on the treatment of prisoners of war (POWs) and others in Iraq (Zimbardo 2007, pp. 324–79).[5]

Milgram and Zimbardo are social psychologists. Their philosophical conclusions are not what interest me. One need not conclude, for

---

[4] For an earlier account, see Haney, Banks, and Zimbardo (1973).
[5] The documentary film *Taxi to the Dark Side* (2007) depicts abuses at Abu Ghraib; see Greenberg and Dratel (2005, pp. 383–404) for the 2004 ICRC Report on the treatment of POWs and others in Iraq, also available at: www.globalsecurity.org/military/library/report/2004/icrc_report_iraq_feb2004.htm.

example, that good people can become evil by being put under stress, confronted with the expectations of authorities, or assigned a role giving them authority and power to do as they will. The accounts of applicant screening offer no evidence that those selected were good people, only that they had no known histories of violence. Even in Plato's myth of the ring of Gyges, which makes its wearers invisible and so enables them to elude detection, the ring causes no character *change* but only brings out the character already there (*Republic* 11: 359c–62c; Plato 1961, pp. 607–09). Still, Milgram's and Zimbardo's experiments offer evidence that more people than many might have thought can easily be induced, without serious duress, to inflict intolerable harm on others without excuse, without any *morally defensible* reason – in short, to do evil.

It is the lack of a morally defensible reason in those who kept pushing the lever and those who kept abusing prisoners that stands out for me now as I review those experiments. In lesser wrongs, either there is no reasonably foreseeable intolerable harm, or the agent willing to inflict it has some good (morally defensible) reason. By a morally defensible reason, I mean some reason that counts morally in favor of the deed, even though, on balance, other considerations outweigh it. The choices of the abusive guards and of the lever-pushers who did not quit were morally inexcusable. That is what is shocking (pun unintended). It is not simply their willingness to inflict great harm or even the wrongness of what they did. What is shocking is that no good reasons mitigate their choices. That an experimenter says to do it is not a good reason to inflict, for the sake of science, what you have reason to believe is a potentially fatal shock. That you can do so with impunity is not a good reason to abuse defenseless others who are at your mercy. It is not that these reasons are insufficient. They do not count morally in favor of the deed. They carry no moral weight.

Lesser wrongs can also be inexcusable. If they do no reasonably foreseeable intolerable harm, they are not evils. I now find that it is not intolerable harm alone but, rather, that harm together with the lack of any moral excuse for it that distinguishes evils from lesser wrongs. Banal motives, such as ambition, can still be at work in both evils and lesser wrongs. Lack of excuse is not a motive. It is more apt to be a matter of lacking or failing to apply constraints on one's motives.

Some who are as persuaded as I am by Arendt, Milgram, and Zimbardo that a great many more people than one might initially have thought can easily become complicit in atrocities nevertheless part company with me over the judgment that the atrocities are evils. An alternative approach to atrocities denies that they are evils just because the perpetrators are not monsters. Many agree with Nietzsche that "evil" is a dangerous idea. It is used to demonize. It serves Manichean tendencies to bifurcate the world into "us" and "them." Wielded ideologically, it feeds hatreds that lead to atrocities. For such reasons, some refuse to describe even atrocities as evils (Cole 2006).[6] What can one say? All those concerns are valid.

Yet, my approach, in contrast, is to begin from the premiss that atrocities are paradigmatic evils. In calling them "paradigmatic" I mean they are among the least controversial instances. If they do not count as evils, I cannot imagine what would. Empirical claims regarding atrocities on my lists may be controversial. But if the facts are as I understand them, those events are paradigmatic evils. My hypothesis is that scrutiny of how they are perpetrated and what they do to victims can yield insight into what evils really are and thereby demythologize the concept.

Consider the following analogy with witchcraft during the Renaissance in Western Europe. One approach, the most common today, begins by accepting conceptions of witches (sorceresses) articulated by the mortal enemies of the women who for centuries were accused, tortured, tried, and turned over to secular authorities to be burnt. For example, the fifteenth-century *Malleus Maleficarum* (Institoris and Sprenger 2006), a tool of the Inquisition, defines witches as heretics who exercised strange powers by acting in cooperation with demons. The next step is to deny, on the ground that demons do not exist, that there ever were any witches. Witches, so understood, would have to perform real magic, defy laws of nature, copulate with demons, use demonic powers to kill fetuses in the womb, make men impotent, make pain disappear, and so on. On this view, the witch-burning episode was a colossal mistake, a product of scientific naiveté, like belief in unicorns only not so harmless. Witches are not just a myth but a dangerous myth. No one should believe that myth today. Witch-hunts are irrational.

An alternative approach espoused by radical feminist critics (Daly 1978; Ehrenreich and English 1978) is to demythologize witchcraft by inquiring into actual practices of women who were burnt as witches. Were they skilled in the use of anesthetic herbs? Did they perform abortions and prescribe contraceptives? Did they know how to promote healings that, of course, have scientific explanations? Did they engage in activities that are currently the prerogative of licensed physicians but that could well have appeared to observers then to be magical (especially when engaged in by illiterate practitioners)?

---

[6] For criticism of Nietzsche's rejection of judgments of evil, see Card (2002, pp. 27–49).

This approach begins from the premiss that many of the women who were burnt as witches are paradigms of what it is to be a witch.[7] To understand witchcraft, we do well to look at who they really were and what they really did and not to accept unquestioned the definitions put forward by their mortal enemies. On this approach, the witch-burnings raise moral questions that are buried by the other approach. Did the witches really do intolerable harm? If not, why were so many resources devoted to hunting them down, torturing them, trying them, and burning them? Was their independence from male control a problem? What kinds of social services did they perform? Was the witches' exercise of their craft stifled for any good moral reasons? Can we learn anything valuable from studying the activities of witchcraft? If it is impossible that anyone could engage in witchcraft, if witchcraft is pure mythology, these are not genuine questions. There is nothing to study but the delusions of the accusers and judges of pitiable women.

Demythologizing evil requires us to examine the activities of paradigmatic evils, as demythologizing witchcraft requires us to examine the activities of paradigmatic witches. To the previously mentioned items in my atrocity lists, I would add the massacre at Wounded Knee (and other atrocities against Native Americans), medical experiments of Japanese military unit 731, the My Lai massacre, and the Cambodian genocide. Whatever such atrocities really are, that is what evil really is. But if there are no evils, questions of how to avoid doing evil in response are as much pseudo-questions as are many questions about witchcraft for those who deny that witches ever existed.

If likelihood of the ideological abuse of a concept were sufficient reason to abandon the concept, we should probably abandon all normative concepts, certainly "right" and "wrong." That advice is, of course, self-defeating in its appeal to the normative concept of abuse, if not in its appeal to what we should do. What normative or value concept is invulnerable to abuse? The Third Reich demonstrated that concepts Nietzsche favored over moral ones – health, vitality, free spirits – are equally vulnerable. A better strategy is to expose the abuses.

To demythologize evil we must also acknowledge that "perpetrator" and "victim" are abstractions. Real people are often both. Victims easily become perpetrators. Some are targeted because of evils they were believed

---

[7] There is evidence that some were accused only in retaliation for their refusals of sexual favors for their accusers (Daly 1978, pp. 201–02). Paradigmatic witches were accused on the basis of activities that appeared to involve the exercise of strange powers.

by others to have perpetrated. Institutional evils make complicity difficult to avoid, even by victims.

Finally, the atrocity paradigm avoids reifying evil as any kind of metaphysical force or demon. Evil personified as a demon or reified as a force is not something to be reasoned with or understood. We need only destroy it if possible, or defeat it, however temporarily. Demons are monolithic, malevolent through and through, never ambivalent or changeable. They are literally inhuman. Evil on the atrocity paradigm wears a human face. Atrocities are perpetrated by agents who have epistemological limitations and emotional attachments. They are ambivalent, deluded, changeable, fickle. "No moral excuse" does not mean "no humanly understandable reasons."

This, in brief, is evil demythologized. Further rejection of Manichean tendencies is reserved for the examination of Kant's moral excluded middle in chapter 2. Evil is at least as understandable as goodness. If we acknowledge human freedom in a very robust sense, we have to grant that there are limits to what we can understand of both good and evil in human conduct.

3. OVERVIEW OF REVISIONS

As historian Alfred McCoy put it, Milgram's obedience experiments taught US intelligence agencies an interesting lesson about who can be trained to become a torturer (McCoy 2006, pp. 47–79). I have that lesson well in mind in modifying my account of evils.

My most basic modification substitutes "inexcusable wrongs" for "culpable wrongdoing" in the analysis of evils. The revised definition is "evils are reasonably foreseeable intolerable harms produced by *inexcusable* wrongs." This revision preserves and clarifies culpability in the evil deeds of individuals, and it allows an improved account of evil in institutions.

Evils lack excuses of two kinds. One kind pleads reduced responsibility or even no responsibility. Aristotle divided such excuses into those based on compulsion and those based on ignorance (Aristotle 1925, p. 48). These excuses apply not only to individuals but, to some extent, to organizations and corporations. For they, too, can act. These excuses do not apply to social practices, which are not agents and so cannot have diminished capacity to act. Compulsion and ignorance mitigate or remove culpability by diminishing or removing responsibility. Because this kind of excuse focuses on the ontology of agency (on whether moral agency even exists in a particular case), I call it a *metaphysical excuse*.

A second kind of excuse, one that I find more interesting for understanding evil, mitigates culpability *without* reducing responsibility. This kind of excuse does not plead diminished capacity. Rather, its argument is that there was a morally appropriate and defensible reason in favor of the deed or practice, a reason that carries moral weight even though not enough weight to justify the deed or the practice on the whole. What is justifiable on the whole needs no excuse. Evils lack this kind of excuse as well. In the case of utterly inexcusable deeds perpetrated by individuals or organizations, culpability is unmitigated. This kind of excuse applies to practices as well as to institutions and individuals. Practices can be indefensible because even though they are not agents, they are norma-tive, and so, they are appropriate objects of evaluation, criticism, and defense. Practices can even be culpable, in a way. They can be at fault (or faulty), whether or not anyone is to blame. To contrast this kind of excuse with metaphysical excuses, I call it a *moral excuse*. Its focus is the morality (more specifically, the moral defensibility) of a deed, practice, or institution.

For a moral excuse, it is not sufficient that the agent *thinks* there is a good reason. There must *be* one (and it must be the agent's reason), a rea-son defensible on reflection and in terms of moral values. A good goal is not sufficient to provide a good reason for just any means taken to achieve it. The means must be morally defensible also.

Besides enabling the atrocity theory to give a better account of evil in institutions and social practices, there is a further advantage of changing "culpable" to "inexcusable" in the analysis of evils. There are degrees of culpability. It can be grave, minor, or something between. Moral excuses mitigate culpability. When culpability is highly mitigated, "evil" can be too harsh a judgment, as it is for accidental harms regardless of the harm's severity. Inexcusable wrongs are the ones that remain unmitigated by any morally good reason.

My second modification in the atrocity theory, after changing "culp-able" to "inexcusable," is to cease contrasting evils with ordinary wrongs. Taking atrocities as paradigms makes that contrast natural. Many atro-cities truly are extraordinary. But to contrast evils with ordinary wrongs is to imply that evils are uncommon. I do not believe they are and have never really thought so, although my past tendency to contrast evils with ordinary wrongs implied that they are. And so I now say "lesser wrongs" instead of "ordinary wrongs." Appreciating the low-profile terrorism and torture that are routine under oppressive regimes, in racist environments, and in families devastated by domestic violence has made me cautious about equating "grave" with "extraordinary." When an evil is common, it is easy for many not to perceive it as an evil. I consider why in section 5

below. Chapters 6 and 8 discuss examples of ordinary evils that are often
not perceived as such.

My third modification of the atrocity theory is a more nuanced account
of evil in practices and institutions. On the new account, evil in institutions or practices does not imply culpability in participants. Participants
can be culpable. But that is a further matter. That an evil practice lacks
moral excuse means only that there are no good moral reasons in its favor.
It is morally indefensible. At least three kinds of things can be indefensible
in an institution or practice. First are the norms or rules (or some of them)
that define or structure it. Second are the ways those rules are administered. Third are the often unanticipated (even though reasonably foreseeable) ways that norms can work together to produce intolerable harms
(often a result of piecemeal change in a practice). An institution or practice
such as torture, slavery, or the death penalty can embody or give rise to
evils of all three kinds. Whether an institution is itself an evil depends on
whether its evils can, realistically, be eliminated without destroying it.

A major difference between evils done by individuals (such as domestic
battery) and institutional evils is the role of culpability. An individual whose
deed is metaphysically and morally inexcusable is culpable. But the indefensibility of a norm does not settle the question whether a responsible agent
who applies or benefits from that norm is culpable. Individual culpability
depends on such things as what options and what knowledge an individual
has and the costs, including moral costs, attached to those options.

It is necessary also to consider implications of the fact that a practice
that still embodies evils can be a morally significant improvement over
prior practice. It may be the best alternative realistically available at a
given time, the best that a community is likely to be persuaded to accept
at a given time. Lack of a better realistically available alternative does not
imply that the *evils* remaining in the improved practice have now become
morally acceptable. That would be incoherent. But some forms of *tolerating* or even *supporting* a practice despite the evils it contains may be, at
least for a time, morally defensible, if the practice represents, on the whole,
a step in the direction of justice. I return to this idea at the end of this
chapter in taking up the US debate over the death penalty.

4. MORAL EXCUSES

As I now define them, evils are reasonably foreseeable intolerable harms
produced by *inexcusable* wrongs. I want to focus next on what it means to
say of a wrong that it is morally inexcusable and to consider the question

of whether that idea makes monsters of evil-doers after all. Lack of a moral excuse has different implications when the wrong is an individual deed and when it is institutional. I begin with institutional wrongs.

Institutions and social practices are defined and structured by rules of varying degrees of formality, such as the rules in US criminal justice systems that permit and encourage plea bargaining for persons accused of crimes. A rule is morally inexcusable when it is not defensible, even partly, from a moral point of view. It is *evil* when it is further the case that implementation of that rule produces reasonably foreseeable intolerable harm. Such a rule becomes *an* evil when it is actually implemented. A rule can be evil even if no one deliberately chose to institute it (perhaps it evolved through common practice) and even if many are unaware that intolerable harms are traceable to it or to its conjunction with other rules. Such lack of awareness, if not culpable, provides individuals with a metaphysical excuse (Aristotle's ignorance excuse) for not trying to change or eliminate the rule.

Further, we can internalize rules without being aware that we are doing so. To use a distinction developed by the late British philosopher of law H. L. A. Hart between the internal and external aspects of rules, rules that we learn and apply without being aware of having done so still have an "internal aspect" when they *guide* our conduct, as opposed to simply describing regularities in our behavior. Mere regularities constitute their "external aspect," observable by others (Hart 1961, pp. 55–57). If it is not reasonable to expect the internalizers of evil rules to appreciate at a particular time that they have done so, there may be no individual culpability at that time. There may come a time, however, when that metaphysical excuse no longer applies.

Injustices do not always presuppose a culpable individual, a point that exercised Aristotle and led him to treat justice separately from other virtues (Aristotle 1925, pp. 125–28). We can be treated unjustly (dealt less than our fair share) even though no one is at fault. Likewise, we can suffer evils even though culpability in individual participants, beneficiaries, or others is non-existent. The analysis offered in *The Atrocity Paradigm* did not accommodate that point. Its insistence on culpability was meant to distinguish evils from natural catastrophes. But the indefensibility of rules also distinguishes the harms they do from natural catastrophes (to which the idea of defense does not apply). The revised analysis in terms of inexcusability accommodates the Aristotelian point in regard to evils. One can suffer intolerable harm as the result of a practice that is indefensible (even unjust), even though no one is culpable.

When a deed is inexcusable, morally and metaphysically, the doer's culpability is unmitigated. That is a kind of extreme: no excuse at all. The question naturally arises whether "inexcusability" makes monsters of perpetrators after all. I think not, for the following reason. That a fully responsible agent lacks a morally acceptable reason does not imply that the agent is weird, unintelligible, inhuman, or unamenable to rational persuasion. Not all of the ordinary reasons we have for what we do are moral reasons or reasons that are defensible in terms of moral values. Some humanly understandable explanations, such as laziness, apathy, or even self-interest or a desire for approval, do not begin to justify our choices morally or lower the bar of expectation. Self-interest or a desire for approval often suffice to justify deeds that require no moral defense. But those reasons tend to lack moral weight for deeds that do.

Whether the Milgram and Zimbardo experiments showed anything significant about evil, understood as inexcusable willingness to do intolerable harm, depends on whether participants had any morally defensible reasons for their choices. My own conclusion, from the accounts Milgram and Zimbardo provide, is that Milgram's subjects who kept pressing the lever and Zimbardo's abusive SPE guards had no morally defensible reasons.[8] They had reasons. But those reasons do not amount to even a partial justification. They explain without mitigating. That is why the results of the experiments are so appalling. In Milgram's subjects, we can suppose the reasons were, "he said to do it, and he said it wouldn't do any permanent harm." That might do from an adolescent. But adults are expected to evaluate what they are told and to appreciate the harm they might do, regardless what others say. In Zimbardo's abusive guards, we may suppose the reasons were, "I felt like it; it was fun; besides, it was only an experiment." Yet they could see firsthand, up-close and personal, the stress they were inflicting.[9] Given that fact, those reasons lack justificatory force. It is not just that they are not good enough. They are not good at all. In Arendt's sense, these subjects were not thinking, morally.

Here is an example from history (not an experiment): the desire for *Lebensraum* (living space) for the German people did not begin to justify the Third Reich's forcibly removing and concentrating, let alone

---

[8] Not all Milgram's subjects obeyed, and not all Zimbardo's "guards" behaved badly. But most of them did.

[9] If any of the guards had good reason to think the prisoners were faking distress, they had some excuse, at first, for not appreciating the harm they were doing. Yet, they knew about the prisoners who begged to be released and were released. And they should have known that the experiment provided no "safe words" for subjects who could not tolerate their treatment.

slaughtering, inhabitants of Poland and other countries who were not ethnic Germans. Desire for *Lebensraum* was a reason (an explanation). But it carried no moral weight. The policy was morally inexcusable. It remains a further question whether particular individuals who participated in carrying out the policy had any excuse for what they did, and the answers can be expected to vary with cases.

The kind of excuse that mitigates without reducing responsibility is not accommodated by a widely accepted philosophical understanding of excuses, that of British philosopher J. L. Austin (1961, pp. 123–52). Austin proposed that when I offer an excuse, I claim that, in a way, I did not do the deed: my agency is diminished if not obliterated. But I do not contest the judgment that the deed was bad. Austin's excuses are what I call metaphysical excuses. Thus, if I physically bump into you and apologize, "I'm so sorry; I was pushed by the crowd," I offer a (metaphysical) excuse. I do not claim there was anything good about my bumping into you. I suggest that it was really the crowd that did it, in a way, not I. In contrast, when I offer a *justification*, I take responsibility but deny that the deed was bad. Thus, if I am stopped for speeding and apologize to the officer, "I'm sorry but I'm a midwife on my way to deliver a baby," I take responsibility, offering both my regrets and a justification.

The modification of Austin's view that I would make is to allow that a partial justification, one that is not completely successful, becomes an *excuse* that mitigates culpability without claiming reduced responsibility. This is what I call a moral excuse. Thus, if the midwife's explanation is good as far as it goes but does not go far enough to justify her on the whole, it becomes her excuse for speeding (for which she takes responsibility). It is at least a morally good reason, unlike, say, that she enjoys the thrill of high-speed driving.

The contrast between excuse and justification even in law is less sharp than Austin makes it seem. Moral excuses, which assume responsibility rather than denying it, are recognized by legal scholars Jeremy Horder (2007, pp. 41–47) and Anthony Duff (2007, pp. 49–55). On their view, an excuse can explain one's agency, rather than explaining it away. When I offer such an excuse, I offer reasons that reflect favorably on me, cast me in a less negative light, even though they are insufficient to justify me, all things considered. Austin's contrast between excuse and justification overlooks moral excuses, like that of the midwife. Philosopher of law Marcia Baron gives another example: "my excuse for not staying for the discussion after your lecture was that I needed to confer with my child's teacher, not that I was bored with your lecture" (Baron 2007, pp. 21–39). I want credit for sensitivity to expectations and possible hurts. I do not claim that my choice was right (even if I really think so; I do not want to *say* that my conference was more important than your lecture), but I take responsibility and claim only that my reason was a good one. If it really is, my culpability (if any) is mitigated.

Horder writes in *Excusing Crime* (2004) that excusatory reasons in criminal law can be divided into "explanatory" and "adopted" reasons. Adopted reasons are reasons one chooses, on which one acts, as when one's (inadequate) reason for doing something that violated the law is that one's religious beliefs called for it. Explanatory reasons explain one's action or what happened without appealing to one's choice, even though there was still a "morally active dimension" to what one did, as when I fail to get a grip on myself and end up killing someone in fear, even though I was not in fear for my life or for the life of anyone else. In Horder's terms, religious belief is an adopted reason; the fear in this case, an explanatory reason. Terror here does not diminish my responsibility but can result in a mitigated sentence. Terror functions here the way a partial justification (moral excuse) would: it reduces culpability without reducing responsibility. But Horder (like Austin) seems not to recognize that an "adopted reason" can function also the way terror does in his example. Like the speeding midwife, I need not regard my adopted reason as sufficient to justify my deed on the whole; I can recognize that it does no more than cast me in a less unfavorable light.

On Horder's account, "adopted reasons" successful as excuses make the action seem to the agent at the time of acting to be justified on balance. This account appears not to recognize partial excuses. Perhaps that is because in law "excuse" functions as a technical term in an all-or-nothing way: no partial excuses. *Black's Law Dictionary* says that "mitigating circumstances" neither excuse nor justify, although they reduce culpability (Gardner 2004, p. 260). In extra-legal contexts, however, the idea of a partial excuse does some of the work apparently done in law by mitigating circumstances. Partial excuses of the "adopted reason" kind present the agent in a more favorable light even though they do not let the agent off the hook. Baron's lecture excuse is of this kind. Her adopted reason offers a relevantly good reason that may just be insufficient.

Inexcusable wrongs are frequently matters of succumbing to temptation, failing to think a thing through, failing to identify and examine assumptions critically, or caving in to peer pressure. These are weaknesses, not ordinarily malevolent. Temptations and pressures sometimes excuse, but not always. Temptation can exert an attraction (curiosity, for example) and pressure can exert an influence (threats of disapproval, for example) without providing a good reason. In failing to think a thing through, we fail to be influenced adequately by good reasons. When it is clear that others may be threatened with serious harm, failing to think is no excuse if we are in good health, free from other pressing demands on our attention, and have the time and opportunity. For normal adults, under circumstances that are not extreme, temptations of greed do not excuse. Neither does fear of losing the esteem of those whose esteem is based on indefensible values.

The objection might be raised that if all evils are inexcusable (completely unmitigated), then all individual evil-doers must be equally culpable and equally blameworthy, which is implausible.[10] A torturer who does it reluctantly for money, doing no more harm than necessary to get paid, is less reprehensible than a torturer who does it enthusiastically with no scruples about limits.[11] Yet, if the wrongs are equally unmitigated, does that not imply that both torturers are equally culpable, deserving equal blame?

Equally culpable, in one sense, yes. But not in a sense that justifies equal blame. "Equally culpable" is ambiguous between (1) "equally responsible and thereby equally *liable* to blame" and (2) "liable to equal *degrees* of blame." Only in the first sense are they "equally culpable." Evil-doers are equal in what they lack, namely, an excuse. They not are equal in what they have, namely, their reasons, objectives, circumstances, faults. Some who are equally liable to blame are more blameworthy in that they have worse reasons or do worse things. That one could have had an even worse reason than one had is not a mitigating condition. True, a less bad reason casts one in a less unfavorable light. But mitigation requires either some *good* reason or a condition or circumstance that reduces responsibility or lowers the bar of expectation. Another way to put the point is that absence of aggravating factors is not a mitigating factor.

Perhaps it goes too far to claim that to be an evil, a deed must be *utterly* without excuse, without *any* good reason. Some moral excuses may be too paltry, carry too little moral weight, to mitigate culpability enough to make judgments of evil unwarranted. And so, perhaps we should understand evils as having no *good* moral excuses. Allowing for that possible refinement, I will, for convenience's sake, continue to use the language of inexcusability in characterizing evils.

---

[10] John Tasioulas raised this concern in responding to a paper I presented at the symposium "Why Criminal Law?" at the British Academy, London, January 2007.

[11] The example is Tasioulas's.

5. ORDINARY EVILS

The idea may seem obvious, once stated, that inexcusable wrongs that produce reasonably foreseeable intolerable harm need not be extraordinary. Why, then, can it seem so natural to contrast evils with ordinary wrongs? One reason is a legitimate concern not to weaken the force of judgments of evil by casual use. Admission that evils need not be extraordinary may seem to open the door to casual use. Yet an equally legitimate concern pulls in the opposite direction. We need to be alert to the evils of our own time and appreciate the dangers of complicity in them.

What is extraordinary is not only noteworthy but unusual, rare. But the rarity of a kind of deed is relative to its context. What is common in one society can be rare in another. Under Joseph Stalin and Pol Pot, ideologically motivated murder was not rare. During the McCarthy era in the US, evils of public character assassination proliferated. Under the Third Reich, evil was the default. Even Plato did not protest slavery. In his dialogue *Euthyphro*, Plato has Socrates castigate Euthyphro for being impious in taking his father to court for having allowed a slave to be left to die in a ditch (Plato 1961, pp. 169–85). At no point in the ensuing reflections on piety is the morality (or even the piety) of slavery brought into question. Slavery was ubiquitous in Plato's time. What is extraordinary is not the *existence* of evils but their *recognition as evils* by contemporaries. The danger of complacency regarding the status quo exists as much for us as it did for Plato.

What makes a deed or practice evil is not its frequency but that it is inexcusable and intolerably harmful. That a deed or practice is morally serious in this way is compatible with its being widespread, as slavery and torture were for millennia. Aggravated rape and severe domestic violence are so common today that crisis workers in major cities across the US put in long hours, and shelters have insufficient beds.

I am optimistic enough to think that non-malevolent evils are probably commoner than malevolent ones. They need not be less serious. Non-malevolent evils can do great harm and be very difficult to prevent. Intoxication and text messaging while driving increase the likelihood of hitting and killing or irreversibly maiming a cyclist, pedestrian, passenger, or other driver. Yet irresponsible mobile phone usage, if not drunk driving, is widely tolerated.

There is some tendency to tolerate the intolerable just *because* it is common. Until the 1990s, rape in war was overlooked by those in power partly on the grounds that it was so common (Human Rights Watch

1996, pp. 27–31). There can be multiple reasons for such tolerance. One might think the intolerable must be shocking. But shock is partly a function of surprise, and what is common is no surprise. There is a danger of conflating "ordinary" with "normal" or "natural." In misogynous environments, many perceive rape as natural male behavior under stress and tolerate it because it is so widespread, whereas it becomes widespread because it is so tolerated. Efforts to suppress common behavior can be futile when enforcers include perpetrators, as was the case during the era of Prohibition in the US. But a deed's perceived frequency can also interfere with common recognition that it is evil. Here is how that may work.

First, it is easy to imagine ourselves in the shoes of those who do what is commonly done. This is how we are socialized. We model ourselves after many (significant) others. Second, perpetrators are liable to an erroneous perception, described by psychologist Roy F. Baumeister in his account of "the magnitude gap" (Baumeister 1997, pp. 18–19, 46). According to studies he cites, there is a gap between perpetrators' and victims' perceptions of the seriousness of a wrong. Perpetrators tend to minimize the gravity of the wrongs they do, whereas victims tend to exaggerate the gravity of the wrongs they suffer. Nietzsche notes in the first essay of his *Genealogy of Morals* that victims perceive perpetrators as monsters (Nietzsche 1969, pp. 31–52). Perpetrators often do not remember. Some do not even notice. It is harder for victims not to notice. Many never forget.

More specifically, it would make sense that we are liable to distort the element of an evil with which our acquaintance is less direct. Thus, perpetrators might tend especially to minimize the *harm* they do (which victims experience more directly). Victims might tend to exaggerate the *reprehensibility of perpetrators' motives* (to which perpetrators have more intimate access). Then, when what is commonly done is an evil, it becomes easy for observers who are not victims (even some who are) to underestimate the harm. They take the perpetrator's perspective.

The magnitude gap does not provide reason to modify the concept of evil. Neither does it provide an excuse. The magnitude gap describes tendencies to opposing illusions and delusions made familiar to us from an early age. From childhood, we are taught to attend to more than one side of a conflict. But some perspectives tend to lack representation in cultural traditions and the dominant media. A tendency to take up perspectives of perpetrators who are well represented in a community makes us vulnerable to the illusion (or delusion) that their wrongs are not so bad. Awareness of that tendency should serve as a caution. Philosophers trained as I was in the ordinary-language tradition of analytic philosophy should be cautious about relying on what "people" say is or is not evil. We should form the habit of asking, which people? Whose voices (if any) are dominating the conversation?

Everyone who is not a saint does inexcusable things, not always with harmful results. Many of us can easily recall having done inexcusable wrongs, or we can recall that members of our families have. Not all inexcusable wrongs are evils but only those that do reasonably foreseeable intolerable harm. Yet some of us are just lucky that serious harm did not result. My father, a traveling salesman, drove fifty years with no seatbelt, on increasingly congested highways. (There were no licenses when he began). Although he advised his children to wear seatbelts (there were no restrictions yet on children in front seats), he never wore one. He consumed formidable quantities of alcohol daily, stopping frequently at roadside taverns. To my knowledge, he did not kill or injure anyone. He was a skilled driver. And a lucky one. Even after I was adult enough to know better, I did nothing to try to dissuade him. He was my father. And while he lived, I had no driver's license. Those are at best explanations. Not excuses.

Social psychologist Leonard Berkowitz reports that in popular views, evils appear (to observers) to make no sense, and so, evil-doers are apt to appear to others to be non-rational (Berkowitz Unpublished, p. 7). Often when people judge a deed evil, they have a hard time imagining themselves capable of doing "such a thing." This reaction may indeed be part of what many think of when they think of evil. Some pride themselves on being unable to understand how anyone could do evil unless the doer were so deluded as to think the deed good. Such an inability to understand may in reality reflect a wish to keep evil at a distance and unwillingness to imagine oneself in the shoes of an evil-doer. But an observer's understanding or willingness to empathize is not what makes the difference between evils and lesser wrongs. What makes the difference is whether the doer could reasonably have foreseen intolerable harm and whether there was any excuse for its infliction.

An observer's difficulty in understanding how someone could do evil makes sense in terms of the magnitude gap. In judging some deeds, we take the perspective of victims, who tend to see perpetrators as monsters. Had we taken the perspective of the doer, we might have been less apt to judge the deed evil. But we may be reluctant to take perpetrators' points of view when we already appreciate that the harm they do is intolerable and that there is no moral excuse.

The tradition in American culture of rooting for the underdog may also feed into tendencies to embrace the perspectives of victims and disown points of view that we recognize as those of perpetrators. Yet there are good reasons to take up the perspectives of potential perpetrators in whom we can recognize ourselves. Any of us can face temptations to inexcusable wrongs that could produce intolerable harms that are reasonably foreseeable if only we look. If we think that impossible, we may be less likely to look, and we may then be unprepared. To see myself as someone who might become capable of a deed or to imagine myself doing it is not necessarily to judge the deed or myself leniently. Illusions of the magnitude gap are not inevitable. We may be most vulnerable to those illusions when we take up a point of view without realizing what we are doing. In that event, we may fail to judge at all.

A caveat. Some evils are so malevolent that most people truly could not imagine themselves as perpetrators, and there may be no good reason why they should. To be able to take the perspectives of potential evil-doers, it is not necessary (and probably not desirable, unless one is a therapist) that one be able to imagine oneself as a Jeffrey Dahmer or a Nero. But many evils, certainly such large-scale atrocities as genocides, are the shared responsibility of multiple agents, many of whom have ordinary motives, ambitions, and failings. Even torture has been carried out at the hands-on level by survivors who learned how from having been tortured and who have difficulty, for a variety of reasons, finding and keeping better jobs.[12]

I have been interpreting "extraordinary" as "out of the ordinary, unusual, rare, and worthy of note." If "extraordinary" meant simply "extreme," these objections to regarding evils as extraordinary would not apply. But what is common, in that sense ordinary, can be morally extreme and deserve not only the notice but the careful scrutiny that it is unlikely to receive.

6. INSTITUTIONAL EVIL: THE CASE OF THE DEATH PENALTY

Some evil practices, such as domestic battery, can be carried out by an individual. It is clear how to apply the atrocity paradigm there. Reasonably foreseeable intolerable harm can result over time from a policy, not a particular deed. The lone implementer of that policy who lacks a metaphysical or moral excuse is culpable. But many evil practices or institutions

---

[12] My source for this piece of information is survivor-activist Hector Aristizabel, who presented and discussed a street theater performance at a torture conference sponsored by the philosophy department at California State University in Fullerton in 2007.

are implemented collectively. Different agents play different roles. Not all have the same options or the same degree of knowledge. Genocides have been universally perpetrated collectively, even if conceivably an individual might attempt it with advanced technology.

In *The Atrocity Paradigm* I proposed that institutions are evils when (a) it is reasonably foreseeable that their normal or correct operation will result in intolerably harmful injustice and (b) individuals who have the power to abolish or alter those institutions culpably fail to do so (Card 2002, p. 140). The death penalty was one of my examples.

There is a serious problem with that analysis. We should be able to identify a practice as evil independently of knowing whether anyone has the power to change or abolish it at a given time. That a practice is evil is a reason to *seek* power to change or abolish it.

My modified definition of evils, invoking inexcusability rather than culpability, allows us to identify evils in the rules that define or structure a practice without presupposing that anyone yet has the power to change or abolish the practice. It also allows us to identify practices as not evils when they are somewhat morally defensible, even if no one has yet attempted the defense. A reason that offers a partial justification for a rule need not be a reason anyone actually has (although some might have it). A rule is justifiable in terms of reasons that could be given, whether anyone actually defends the practice that way or not. In this way, moral excuses for institutions or practices differ from moral excuses for individuals. To have a moral excuse, an individual must actually have a morally defensible reason. It does not suffice that the reason be conceivable. For an institution, it suffices that a morally good reason be conceivable.

Several issues remain. Harm reasonably foreseeable at one time may not have been foreseeable earlier. The implication seems to be that an institution that is evil at one time may not have been evil before, even though its rules did not change. Further, what is reasonably foreseeable by some may not be reasonably foreseeable by others. By whom must the intolerable harm of an evil institution be foreseeable? By participants? Those who oversee it, if anyone does? Those who created it, if anyone did? Those who can change it, if anyone can? Observers or critics, who may neither participate nor have the power to affect the practice but can evaluate it?

For an individual deed, the answer to "foreseeable by whom?" is "foreseeable from the perspective of the doer" where "reasonably foreseeable" means "would be foreseen if that agent were to exercise reasonable care." For a social practice, the answer is not obvious, as agents stand in many relationships to a practice. Perhaps it is not necessary to specify a position from which the harm is foreseeable. It may suffice to say that a morally indefensible rule or practice or institution is evil if *anyone* can reasonably foresee its intolerably harmful consequences. Those who cannot reasonably foresee the harm (and have insufficient reason to believe others who can) simply lack good reason to find the practice evil. Extending that idea over time, we could also make sense of saying that a practice was an evil even at times when no one *then* could foresee or appreciate the harm that it does, if others at later times can appreciate that it does intolerable harm for which there is no moral excuse.

I want now to return to the idea that temporary toleration of evils in a practice, or even of an evil practice, can be at least excusable, if not justifiable, as an improvement on prior practice and so as a move in the direction of justice. Tolerating does not mean overlooking or failing to evaluate. The very idea of toleration presupposes a negative evaluation of what is tolerated.[13] To tolerate is to refrain from intervening coercively (from punishing, for example). It is compatible with non-coercive intervention, such as rational persuasion that does not take unfair advantage of others' weaknesses or ignorance. Tolerating is not ordinarily morally equivalent to engaging in a practice, even though toleration can be among factors that enable a practice to continue. Whether coercive intervention is warranted or even required is a function of many factors besides the evil of the practice. Those factors include the position of potential interveners, their relationship to those with whose conduct they would intervene, the history of that relationship, available means of non-coercive intervention, the nature of the available coercive interventions, likely consequences, and so on. As John Stuart Mill notes in "On Liberty," even the harmfulness of a practice to others is insufficient to justify coercive intervention when the coercion is as harmful as, or more harmful than, the practice it would stop (Mill 2002, p. 13). It is possible at a given time that the only morally justifiable ways to promote certain social changes are non-coercive. Non-coercive intervention may also be the best hope for lasting change. Restricting interventions to those that are non-coercive is one way of tolerating.

In *A Theory of Justice* John Rawls suggests that slavery, although unjust, may have been tolerable as a lesser injustice at a time when enslaving a conquered people made possible the exchange of prisoners and so was an

---

[13] This negative evaluation underlies lesbian and gay activists' rejection of toleration of same-sex relationships as a social ideal.

improvement from everyone's point of view over the prior practice of kill-ing the conquered. But his discussion suggests something stronger than toleration. He imagines a case in which "city-states that previously have not taken prisoners of war but have always put captives to death agree by treaty to hold prisoners as slaves instead" (Rawls 1999a, p. 218). If city-states enter into such a treaty as a progressive step that would eliminate some of the worst evils of conquest, they would authorize slavery, not merely tolerate it. Slavery is still an evil. But even if the treaty is wrong, it is not a further *evil* if the (moral) excuse for it is the reasonable belief that it prevents a worse evil. Signatories are complicit in the practice. But it is misleading to call them participants, if they are not slave-holders. If sign-ing such a treaty is the only realistically available move toward more just social practice, perhaps that signing is not *excusable* but justifiable. Yet the practice (slavery) that the treaty authorizes remains an evil.

It was also Rawls's view that the evils of slavery gave rise to a responsi-bility at the same time to work for better (more just) institutions. He did not claim there was any *obligation* to support slavery, even temporarily. Thus, he seems to leave open that it might have been heroic for someone who objected to both practices to refuse such a treaty even as a progressive step. Whether to refuse on principle to be party to such a treaty is a ques-tion Rawls does not take up.

A similar dilemma arises regarding the death penalty in the US and the question whether one ought to support, as a progressive step, a move to long-term imprisonment as the most severe penalty allowable for the civil crime of murder. The question whether the death penalty is jus-tifiable in any form has troubled me since the early 1960s. France, at that time, employed the guillotine. England had hanging. Most death-penalty states in the US used the electric chair. And the US Supreme Court had not yet ruled that death sentences as then authorized were un-Constitutional.[14]

It is usually assumed without question that the death penalty is more severe than life in prison, with or without parole. The usual question is whether there is any moral excuse for the death penalty in a society wealthy enough to support prisons. There is a tendency to ignore the most serious harms suffered by prisoners, many as irreversible as death. Prisons in the US expose many inmates to rape or murder by other inmates and

---

[14] I wrote an undergraduate thesis on justifications of legal punishment (Card 1962) and a PhD the-sis (Card 1969) on retributive justice in legal punishment. In neither case did I get as far as my projected chapters on the death penalty, which motivated both undertakings.

to AIDS and other serious illnesses.[15] Some prisoners die for lack of health care. Even when prisons are relatively humane in those respects, imprisonment robs inmates of the power to shape the rest of their lives meaningfully. That concern led Mill (and in 1976 Gary Gilmore) to find life in prison a *worse* penalty than death, although Mill said he would support prison over death if there were much chance of convicting the innocent (Ezorsky 1972, pp. 271–78).[16] The main advantage of long-term imprisonment over the death penalty is that it is sometimes possible to make some reparation to the wrongfully imprisoned, whereas it never is to those wrongfully executed.

Abstractly, it seems difficult to deny the existence of moral arguments in favor of the death penalty. How can those who willfully take human life complain if made to forfeit their own? Yet absence of a basis for offender complaint does not imply presence of a justification for others to impose the penalty. Further, the retributive argument presupposes that those sentenced did commit murder. Inevitably, wrongful convictions result from innocent error. Non-culpable errors are not evils, although legislation that ignores them may be. But it appears pragmatically unavoidable that, in a huge society with a burgeoning criminal caseload, normal implementation of the rules of the criminal justice system will result frequently in wrongful convictions that are *not* errors but are based in corrupt judgment, inexcusably poor defenses, or abuse of prosecutory discretion. Those convictions are evils. It is not obvious that there is any moral excuse for the state to impose death sentences when it is reasonably foreseeable that there will be many such evils. What moral weight is carried by the argument that a murderer deserves to die, when the criminal justice system can impose that sentence as a result of inexcusable wrongs that undermine the trustworthiness of guilty verdicts?

---

[15] On 23 June, 2009, *The New York Times* reported that a National Prison Rape Elimination Committee says there were an estimated 60,500 sexual assaults in state and federal prisons in the US in 2007 (Moore 2009, p. A17). Judge Reggie B. Walton, chair of the commission, is reported to have said that despite a 2003 law meant to provide safeguards against sexual assaults "prison rapes were so common that they were almost a cliché in public discourse" (Moore 2009, p. A17).

[16] Gary Gilmore, who had previously spent many years in prison, was convicted of the murder of one of the two men he shot in Utah in 1976. He was given a death sentence. His death by firing squad (his choice) in 1977, after he battled several stays of execution, was the first execution in the US since the Supreme Court declared in 1972 that the death penalty as then administered was un-Constitutional. Norman Mailer's Pulitzer Prize-winning novel *The Executioner's Song* (1979) tells the story and was made into a film of the same title (1982) by Lawrence Schiller. For a non-fictionalized account, see the memoir by Gary's brother Mikal (Gilmore 1994), also made into an excellent film, *Shot in the Heart*, by Agnieszka Holland (2001).

The most popular argument against the death penalty is that the threat of long-term imprisonment should suffice for the legitimate aim of deterring murder.[17] Long-term imprisonment may be the only alternative in the US that has a realistic chance of gaining support. The deterrence debates are not merely empirical disputes about relative effectiveness. No penalty deters one hundred percent. "Should suffice" means "is sufficient for *an acceptable degree*" of deterrence. What makes a degree normatively acceptable depends on its moral costs relative to alternatives. A moral cost of any additional deterrence produced by the death penalty is the evil of irreparable injustice to those whose wrongful convictions are inexcusable. Moral costs of less deterrent penalties than death are the evils of other murders than might not otherwise have been committed (depending on what other steps the state takes to address crime).

Given the flaws in the retributive argument when bureaucratic evils are factored in, proponents of the death penalty might turn to the deterrence argument.[18] Suppose, for the sake of argument, we grant the empirically controversial claim that the death penalty is more deterrent than imprisonment, at least for premeditated murder and when execution is fairly certain and not greatly delayed. Delay is, of course, required to allow for appeals, which become especially important in a system in which corruption is not rare. Proponents of the death penalty should then consider restricting the death penalty to murder for hire or profit, to aim the threat of the penalty at the most deterrable potential murderers.

Neither the death penalty nor long-term imprisonment is free of irreversible and intolerably harmful consequences. Innocent people are killed, either way. But everyone does not run equal risks, and not all are equally equipped to defend themselves. The indigent, a largely involuntary minority, are more vulnerable to corruption in criminal justice and relatively invulnerable to murder-for-profit. The non-indigent, a larger and more voluntary group, are more vulnerable to murder-for-profit and less vulnerable to corruption in criminal justice. Implicit in the deterrent defense of the death penalty appears to be the judgment that protection against murder-for-profit is worth the moral cost of convicting the indigent innocent. That sounds like a quasi-utilitarian defense: more people would die evil deaths without the death penalty than under it. Like utilitarian

---

[17] For development of this and other arguments, see essays in Bedau and Cassell (2004).
[18] Amazingly, Kant is silent on the issue of corruption in the administration of criminal law in his evaluation of the death penalty for murder (Kant 1996a, pp. 472–77).

arguments, it aggregates bad consequences across individuals. Here the bad consequences are evils, not disutilities. Still, the result is better protection for the non-indigent, a morally irrelevant condition.

Aggregating evils is not sufficient to decide the issue and not only because of inequity in the distribution of protection. There is also the question whether support for either alternative would make the state complicit in the resulting evils. A state that backs a criminal justice system in which corruption inevitably sends innocent persons to death is complicit in those deaths insofar as it authorizes and continues to support the system. In contrast, a less deterrent penalty would not make the state complicit in murders committed by others that might not have been committed under the death penalty. Long-term imprisonment is not an authorization to kill. Substituting long-term imprisonment for the death penalty would, however, involve a choice to tolerate less protection from criminal justice against murder-for-profit or for hire.

The position of those who would substitute long-term imprisonment for the death penalty is in certain respects analogous to the position of those who would support enslavement over slaughter of the conquered. Because enslavement enables prisoner exchange, it is arguably less intolerably harmful than slaughter. Because imprisonment enables some rectification in the case of wrongful convictions, imprisonment is arguably less intolerably harmful than the death penalty. Still, there are evils in both practices. Knowing that, we have a social responsibility to seek better alternatives.

Were there a referendum on the death penalty versus life imprisonment, the heroic course might be to vote for neither.[19] Yet, one who was morally opposed to both might, with some justification, temporarily support long-term imprisonment as a move in the direction of greater justice, if it appeared that the substitution would make more likely the eventual abandonment of both practices. The heroic choice of refusing to support either could be defended if it appeared doubtful that substituting long-term imprisonment would have that effect or if there were even a good chance that it might make abandonment of long-term imprisonment *less* likely. Perhaps that sort of entrenchment did occur in regard to slavery. Writing enslavement into treaties may have made it harder to abolish. Many in the US seem to find it as inconceivable to abolish both the death penalty and long-term imprisonment as it was to the ancients to abandon both enslavement and slaughter. Yet the European Union has set an example worth

---

[19] I am grateful to my colleague Harry Brighouse for raising this point.

attending to, insofar as it has abolished not only the death penalty but also very long-term imprisonment for all but major human rights violations.[20]

To eliminate the evils of both penalties, the solution – people taken as they are and laws as they might be (Rousseau 1950, p. 3) – seems abstractly clear. There is probably no way to eliminate inexcusable wrongdoing from criminal process, short of eliminating criminal process, and there is probably no way to eliminate inexcusable criminal wrongdoing, short of eliminating criminal law. Assuming that abolishing neither would be viable or desirable, at least part of the solution, then, must lie with the upper limits of severity in criminal penalties. If no penalty imposed intolerable harm, a wrongful conviction, however inexcusable, would not be an evil.

Suppose the state were authorized to impose no criminal penalty more harmful than what anyone could reasonably be expected to endure in case of a wrongful conviction. There are many ways to achieve that result, ranging from shortening sentences to improving prisons and the conditions of imprisonment. A cost of shortening sentences might be a temporary increase in crimes for which more severe penalties are currently imposed. But the scruple of not fighting evil by using evil means is a scruple that requires forgoing certain kinds of defense against evils. By instituting a prohibition on cruel and unusual punishments, modern democracies choose to tolerate the risk of crimes by those deterrable only by penalties comparable in severity to drawing and quartering or boiling in oil. Abolishing both the death penalty and long-term imprisonment for most crimes would be in line with the humanitarianism of prohibiting cruel and unusual punishments. It would not make the state complicit in the crimes of those deterrable by nothing short of the threat of an inhumane penalty. But states do remain complicit in wrongful convictions that result from corruption in the administration of their criminal justice systems, just as Rawls's ancient treaty-signers remained complicit in the evils of slavery.

---

[20] Article 2 of the *Charter of Fundamental Rights of the European Union* (2000) states, "No one shall be condemned to the death penalty, or executed" (www.europarl.europa.eu/charter/pdf/text_En.pdf). A modern prison in Austria takes seriously Article 10, par. 1 of the 1976 *International Covenant on Civil and Political Rights* (www.umn.edu/humanrts/instree/b3ccpr.htm), signed and ratified by the US, which says, "All persons deprived of their liberty shall be treated with humanity and with respect for the inherent dignity of the human person." With balconies and glass walls this prison is flooded in daytime with sunshine. To visitors who say, "maybe I should move to Austria and rob a couple of banks," administrators respond, "No one, however down and out, wants to go to prison, however comfortable it may be" (J. Lewis 2009, pp. 48–53). According to John Grisham's only work of non-fiction (Grisham 2006), Oklahoma's death row is below ground and prisoners never see daylight, even when they exercise.

The treaty-signers are at least supposed to have had the excuse of no better way available at the time to eliminate the evils of slaughtering the conquered. It is more difficult to make the case that there is any moral excuse for supporting long-term imprisonment today for any but exceptional cases (such as serial killers), given the example of the European Union.

CHAPTER 2

Between good and evil

The question arises whether a middle ground may not at least be possible, namely that, as a species, the human being can neither be good nor evil or, at any rate, that he can be the one just as much as the other, partly good, partly evil. (Kant 1996b, p. 70)

In this passage Immanuel Kant says "as a species." But he goes on to discuss the individual human will and argues that for it there is no middle ground. I call this view Kant's "moral excluded middle." Kant's view on this point is shared by many who hold that only those who are good deserve heaven and those who are evil deserve either purgatory or hell. The idea that human beings can eventually be sorted into those who deserve to go to heaven (people of good will) and those who deserve purgatory or hell (people who lack good will) presupposes that of those who are capable of morality, any who are not good are evil and that of those who are evil, some may be redeemable, but others are not. Kant rejects the idea of diabolical evil as inapplicable to human beings. But he accepts the idea that a will that is not good is evil. In this chapter, I disagree with Kant's moral excluded middle. But I defend a distinction between diabolical evil and lesser evils.

A widely shared common-sense view is that good and evil, unlike right and wrong, are not contradictories. They are contraries. It is not possible to be both good and evil in the same respect at the same time. But it is at least logically possible to be neither. This chapter defends common sense on that point and suggests ways of being between good and evil that lay a groundwork for an extended look in chapter 3 at complicity in structural evils. Many more distinctions, besides that between good and evil, are needed to capture the complexities of moral psychology and the morality of human conduct. Elsewhere I have argued that an evil-*doer* is not necessarily an evil *person* (Card 2002, pp. 21–22). It is possible to act out of character. It is also possible to be drawn culpably into an evil activity without developing a disposition to evil choices. Now I go further and hold that people who are complicit in an evil practice need not even be evil-*doers*. Their particular contributions may not be evil, or not without qualification. Those who are complicitous in evil practices may be a mixture of good and evil or something in-between good and evil, not positively good but not downright evil, either.

Kant understood the idea of diabolical evil as evil for evil's sake. That, he insisted, goes beyond evil as we find it in human nature, which is always for the sake of something perceived to be good (a view widely held among philosophers). The last section of this chapter proposes an alternative interpretation of the diabolical, which makes sense of conduct that Kant's view does not capture well. There I draw on International Humanitarian Law (IHL) and folk paradigms. Common sense is right not only that although complicity in structural evils can be wrong, it need not be evil. I believe it is also right that some torturers and masterminds of evil structures are not just evil but diabolical, in accord with one or more paradigms presented later in this chapter.

I. KANT'S THESES ON RADICAL EVIL

Kant's account of "radical evil in human nature" in Book I of *Religion within the Boundaries of Mere Reason* (Kant 1996b, pp. 57–215; hereafter, *Religion*) is one of the most extended and well-developed philosophical accounts of evil. Despite its opening a work with the title *Religion*, Kant's account initiates a basically secular philosophical approach to evil. One need not share his theistic faith to share his understanding of an evil will. Yet, as a theory of evil, his account is seriously incomplete. It offers, more specifically, a conception of radical *culpability* and treats all culpability as evil to some degree. A fuller theory would include also a conception of radical *harm*. It would recognize that reasonably foreseeable intolerable harm is critical to distinguishing an evil will from less reprehensible ways of lacking good will. To be fair, Kant's objective is an account of evil in human nature, which makes his focus on culpability appropriate. Yet even his view of culpability needs to be deepened with a conception of harm that goes beyond failures merely to *respect* humanity. For culpability increases, other things equal, with the depth of harm that a wrongdoer willingly does. A deeper harm than disrespect of humanity is the *destruction* of humanity in those who still live, a harm that Kant may not have thought possible.

That destruction was Hannah Arendt's idea of radical evil in her early work on totalitarianism: destruction of humanity in those who still live, the production of "living corpses" (Arendt 2000, p. 132), "ghastly marionettes with human faces, which all behave like the dog in Pavlov's experiments" (Arendt 2000, p. 135). Influenced by Kant, she at first appropriated his term "radical evil" but then later abandoned it. She abandoned it partly for fear that "radical" made evil sound attractive or exciting. But she was also convinced at Adolf Eichmann's trial in Jerusalem that the psychology of Nazi bureaucrats was not deep but utterly superficial. She wrote in a letter of 24 July, 1963, responding to a letter from Gershom Scholem, that evil "can overgrow and lay waste the whole world precisely because it spreads like a fungus on the surface" (Arendt 2000, p. 396). She had earlier used the term "radical evil" not to mark deep culpability, however, but to mark the harm of being dehumanized. That harm is not superficial.

Destroying or undermining moral agency inflicts a harm that strikes at the capacity that Kant regards as giving human beings dignity. Kant regards dignity as a worth with no equivalent. The capacity for moral agency matures and can deteriorate, which implies that one can have or lack it to various degrees. It can be encouraged or undermined, often as a result of actions imputable to oneself or to others. Further, capacities for agency are enhanced when agents join together to do things none of them could have done alone. Capacities for collective action are also vulnerable to being undermined or destroyed, and they, too, can develop or mature. Such possibilities, explored in sections 4 and 6, are suggestive for quasi-Kantian ways to make sense of some of what lies between good and evil and even of the concept of diabolical evil. Although they are not Kant's own ideas, and he might well have disagreed with them, they reconcile much that is best in Kant with much that is sound in common sense.

In *Religion*, Kant does not consider collective action. His concern is with individual choices to act on maxims that can be evaluated in terms of the moral law. Six controversial theses emerge from Book I of *Religion*. They offer an overview of Kant's conception of evil. They seem naturally to be responses to the following questions. (1) Is there anything intermediate between a good will and an evil will? (2) Do human beings ever do evil for its own sake (just because it is evil)? (3) What is the worst principled form that evil takes in human beings? (4) Can we ever know, ultimately, why someone opts for good or for evil? (5) Are we responsible for our own good or evil will? (6) Can evil ever be purged from humanity?

Here in brief are Kant's answers, which I call his "theses." First is his moral excluded middle, the denial that there is anything intermediate between a good will and an evil one (Kant 1996b, pp. 70–73). He also denies that a will can be partly good and partly evil, good in some respects but evil in others. He does acknowledge grades of evil (Kant 1996b, pp. 77–78); but for Kant a will that is not good is thereby evil, in one grade or another.

Second, Kant denies that we ever embrace immorality as such (Kant 1996b, pp. 35–36, 81–83). We never will "evil *qua* evil" – that, he says, would be *diabolical* (Kant 1996b, pp. 82, 84), not human (Kant 1996b, p. 82). There is an asymmetry between Kant's conception of a good will and his conception of an evil will. A good will is committed to duty as such, but an evil will is not committed to immorality as such. Rather, its commitment to duty is qualified by a more basic commitment to self-love, in a fairly narrow, prudential, sense of self-love.

The third thesis is that self-love, understood as a principled and unqualified pursuit of self-interest, is the worst principled form of evil in human beings (Kant 1996b, pp. 83–84). Even an evil will, according to Kant, aims at goods, albeit prudential goods. In the *Metaphysical Principles of Virtue*, Kant distinguishes some vices as worse than others. He says lying is "the greatest violation of a human being's duty to himself" and that gratitude is "a *sacred* duty" (Kant 1996a, pp. 552, 573), suggesting that ingratitude is especially heinous. Yet, the principle underlying all vices is the same, a principle that prioritizes self-love over duty. Some manifestations of self-love are worse than others. Yet the worst evil still aims at some (perceived) good for its agent.

Fourth is Kant's "inscrutability thesis." Our ultimate reasons for acting are inscrutable, unknowable (Kant 1996b, pp. 71, 74, 88–90, 95). Why are some people good and others evil? Why is the same person sometimes good and at other times evil? Ultimately, we cannot know.

Fifth is his "imputability thesis" (Kant 1996b, pp. 70, 74, 77, 88, 90–92). My good or evil will is imputable to me. *I* determine what I will, and I can always change myself (Kant 1996b, p. 87). I am responsible not just for specific evil *deeds* but for my very *propensity to* them. In contrast, my predispositions to good are not imputable. They are given with human nature.

Last is Kant's "inextirpability thesis." The propensity to evil imputable to us, he says, is nonetheless inextirpable (Kant 1996b, pp. 83, 94). We cannot root it out, although we can overcome it. It would have been clearer had Kant said simply that we cannot be rid of human vulnerabilities to weakness and impurity, although they need not defeat us, which he believed. But he seems actually to say that the *propensity to evil*, which he asserts is a choice, is inextirpable.

"Choice" is ambiguous between an option one elects ("this is my choice") and the having of options ("have I any choices?"). The best sense I can make of Kant's inextirpability thesis is that we cannot alter the facts that we always have options regarding how to order our incentives and that we inevitably lean toward prioritizing self-love. We can choose in opposition to that leaning, or we can give in to it. Either choice is imputable to us. I cannot make sense of Kant's apparent assertion that this very leaning (propensity) that we must overcome is *also* an act imputable to us.[1] Given our nature, we can be good (have the right priorities). But we cannot be holy. That is not an option. A holy being has no temptations and so does not have to overcome any. Not being holy is not a choice imputable to us.

Kant does not number or label these theses as I have. But he asserts and elaborates them in more or less this order. Richard Bernstein offers a stimulating and provocative discussion of tensions between Kant's imputability and inextirpability theses, arguing that Kant is "at war with himself" in holding both (Bernstein 2002, pp. 11–45). Elsewhere (Card 2002, pp. 77–95), I have discussed Kant's self-love thesis, his inscrutability thesis, and, briefly, his denial of diabolical evil. The next four sections of this chapter argue with Kant's moral excluded middle.

2. KANT'S MORAL EXCLUDED MIDDLE

Kant says our "disposition as regards the moral law is never indifferent (never neither good nor bad)" and also that it is impossible for us to "be morally good in some parts, and at the same time evil in others" (Kant 1996b, p. 73). He argues thus: "if [a man] is good in one part, he has incorporated the moral law into his maxim," and "were he, therefore, to be evil in some other part, since the moral law of compliance with duty in general is a single one and universal, the maxim relating to it would be universal yet particular at the same time: which is contradictory" (Kant 1996b, p. 73). There appear to be two sorts of intermediacy that Kant denies. One is a judgment that someone's will is neither good nor evil but something in-between. The other is a judgment that someone's will is partly good and partly evil. Unlike Kant, common sense acknowledges the validity of both kinds of judgments.

Kant's point is not that our will must be consistent over time. We can always choose to accept or reject the moral law as our supreme practical

---

[1] Perhaps Kant was trying, in view of the censors, to accommodate the idea of original sin.

principle, whatever we have done in the past (Kant 1996b, p. 87). His point is that in prioritizing the moral law, we are committed to applying it to all of our (material) maxims, not just to some of them, and each maxim either passes the test or does not. If we have reservations about applying the moral law to all of our maxims, then our fundamental commitment is not to morality.

Kant offers a three-stage account of the will's descent into radical evil and then a two-stage account of the ever-present possibility of overcoming evil. The first stage of overcoming is a revolution in fundamental principle. The second stage consists of the slower and more difficult tasks of reform, purifying and strengthening the will to act in accord with its new fundamental commitment (Kant 1996b, pp. 91–92). Although he does not acknowledge any intermediacies between good and evil, Kant acknowledges gradations of evil by way of the three progressively worse stages of descent into radical evil: frailty, impurity, and corruption (Kant 1996b, p. 77).

A person with a frail will is committed to the moral law but nevertheless fails to live up to it on particular occasions. Kant distinguishes acts of two orders or levels of willing, two kinds of acts. One level (the higher-order act) is exemplified by becoming committed to the moral law (the act of adopting it as one's fundamental principle), which then governs other (lower-order) acts, such as making honest promises and keeping them. The act of prioritizing the moral law (the higher-order act), he says, is not performed in time, unlike such observable acts as promising (Kant 1996b, pp. 74, 79, 88). Observable acts do not reveal our underlying commitments. The same kind of observable act might conceivably flow from different, even incompatible, commitments.

Observable acts can also go *against* one's commitment, as when I act wrongly out of weakness. Kant writes, "'What I would, that I do not!' i.e. I incorporate the good (the law) into the maxim of my power of choice; but this good, which is an irresistible incentive objectively or ideally (*in thesi*), is subjectively (*in hypothesi*) the weaker (in comparison with inclination) whenever the maxim is to be followed" (Kant 1996b, p. 77). I do wrong, but I do not endorse the wrong. I lie but do not rationalize the lie, unlike a thoroughly wicked person or even a person with mixed incentives. My will just needs strengthening. The best we can hope to achieve by such strengthening is still only a good will. A being with a holy will has no frailties. But even the best of human beings is vulnerable, has a propensity to evil (Kant 1996b, p. 78).

The second stage or grade of the descent into evil is "impurity": mixed incentives. Here, duty is insufficient to move me, and so I rely partly on interest or inclination. "Although the maxim is good with respect to its object (the intended compliance with the law) and perhaps even powerful enough in practice," Kant writes, "it is not purely moral, i.e. it has not … adopted the law *alone* as its *sufficient* incentive but, on the contrary, often (and perhaps always) needs still other incentives besides it in order to determine the power of choice for what duty requires; in other words, actions conforming to duty are not done purely from duty" (Kant 1996b, pp. 77–78).

It is easy to foresee a slide from stage one to stage two, from frailty to impurity. For, instead of capitulating to temptation or strengthening one's moral commitment, a weak person might begin to rely on self-interest to buttress the motive of duty. Instead of cheating, I might remind myself not only that it is wrong but "besides, there is the danger of getting caught" and rely partly on prudence. Impure acts may still (even always) happen to be in accord with the moral law, whereas acts done from frailty violate that law. Yet Kant finds impurity worse than frailty. Impurity is worse because it begins a process of corruption in the will, a process of ever greater reliance upon self-love.

The end of the descent into evil is stage three, the third grade, which Kant describes variously as depravity, corruption, or perversity. The ordering of practical principles is now reversed from that of a good will. Instead of the moral law taking priority and limiting self-love, self-love takes priority and limits morality. We are willing to do our duty only as long as it does not conflict with self-love. At stage three, evil is finally rooted in the will as a fundamental commitment, thereby truly radical. Kant says a corrupt will "reverses the ethical order as regards the incentives of a free power of choice; and although with this reversal there can still be legally good (*legale*) actions, yet the mind's attitude is thereby *corrupted at its root* (so far as the moral disposition is concerned), and hence the human being is designated as evil" (Kant 1996b, p. 78; emphasis mine).

Because he says that "the mind's attitude is thereby corrupted at its root," and because he presents this rootedness as the deepest form of evil in the will, I read him as holding that radical evil is reached specifically in this third stage. This reading also makes good sense of the full title of Book I of *Religion*: "Concerning the Indwelling of the Evil Principle along with the Good, or of the Radical Evil in Human Nature" (1996b, p. 69). For only at this stage does evil become principled. The evil *principle* is the principle of prioritizing self-interest *over* duty, which goes beyond stages one and two.[2]

---

[2] Some commentators treat the whole three-stage sequence as Kant's conception of radical evil, apparently because it is evil in the will. But then, with what would "radical" be contrasted? What other kind of evil could there be for Kant?

Even at stage three, there can be *legally* good (outwardly right) actions, owing to fortuitous coincidences between duty and prudence. And so, Kant says, we tend to deceive ourselves. We rationalize. We endorse our choices. They are no longer made in weakness. In the first two stages, our guilt is unintentional (Kant 1996b, p. 84); in the third stage, "it is deliberate guilt (*dolus*), and is characterized by a certain *perfidy* on the part of the human heart (*dolus malus*) in deceiving itself as regards its own good or evil disposition, and, provided that its actions do not result in evil (which they could well do because of their maxims) in not troubling itself on account of its disposition but rather considering itself justified before the law" (Kant 1996b, p. 84). "This is how so many human beings derive their peace of mind" (Kant 1996b, p. 84).

Whether it makes sense to suppose that one's will can be partly good and partly evil depends on how the will is conceived and how evil is conceived. Kant's conception of the will, as we have seen, is complex: the will has a legislative aspect and a decision-making aspect. But these aspects do come apart and conflict with each other in the case of frailty, when I violate my own principle. The legislative will can evaluate my maxim and its incentive on a particular occasion but does not necessarily determine what I do in the observable world on that occasion.

In the opening paragraph of the first section of the *Groundwork of the Metaphysics of Morals*, Kant says of the will that is to make use of our talents that its "distinctive constitution is therefore called *character*," and he contrasts character with temperament (Kant 1996a, p. 39). Neither temperament nor character is defined simply by one's choice and its incentive on a particular occasion. Temperament is defined by dispositions, character by commitments, which can be strong or weak. In the more complex account of character in *Religion*, one's commitments impose an ordering on a given set of predispositions. But what is to prevent an agent from being ambivalent, of two minds, with regard to a particular ordering? An ambivalent person needs yet another layer, or aspect, of will that can take responsibility for achieving integrity at the level of what Kant calls self-legislation, that is, take responsibility for *producing* a *coherent* legislative will (a self with integrity). I return to this idea in section 4.

Kant's conception of evil also presents another kind of difficulty, distinct from the difficulties in his conception of the will. He does not have enough distinctions to be able to contrast grave wrongs (such as murder), ethically, from relatively trivial ones (such as petty theft). Kant (like so many other moral philosophers) does not distinguish evils from lesser wrongs. It is not that he takes "evil" simply to *mean* "wrong" (contrary to duty). For Kant, evil (like moral goodness) includes the incentive as well as the material maxim. In both impurity and corruption, evil in the will need not produce an actual violation of duty. One might do the right thing, but for a non-moral reason. But for Kant *every* wrong is evil, since it must have been done from weakness, with impure motives, or from a corrupt will. Kant's three grades of evil yield degrees of culpability. But, when the motivation is the same, he has no ethical (as distinct from juridical) way to judge that atrocities, such as torture or mass murder, are worse than such wrongs as petty theft or defacing public property.

Kant may have believed that there are no trivial wrongs. But suppose that a closeted lesbian were to lie about her sexuality to protect her privacy without causing anyone reasonably foreseeable suffering. On Kant's view, the lie is evil. Yet, the severity of that judgment can be disputed (as it is in section 3 below) without resorting to utilitarian ethics or any form of consequentialism and also without disputing the act's wrongness, the wrongdoer's culpability, or even Kant's view that should harm in fact result, it would be imputable to the wrongdoer.

In light of these issues, and against Kant's excluded middle thesis, I offer five kinds of intermediacy worth taking seriously. I sketch them briefly in the remainder of this section and take them up at greater length in the three sections immediately following. The first intermediacy requires but a simple modification in Kant's terminology. The second requires a substantive change in his ethics (although less drastic than he might have thought). The third and fourth require further complexity in Kant's moral psychology, building on a distinction he already acknowledges. The last challenges most ethical theories, not just Kant's.

In brief, here are the five kinds of intermediacy. First is what Kant calls frailty. Kant regards frailty as the first grade of evil. But "evil" is ordinarily too severe a judgment for choices made out of weakness, especially if they are made under duress. It is usually too severe a judgment even for giving in to temptation – depending somewhat on the nature of the temptation. Most frailty is better regarded as intermediate between good and evil – not good, but hardly evil. Exceptions are weaknesses that would be easy to overcome, if giving in to them foreseeably does intolerable harm when no comparable harm threatens the agent. Even so, a frail will is not evil without qualification. There remains something good about it: the moral commitment that it fails to live up to. Kant admits that a frail will is divided against itself: "'What I would, that I do not!' i.e. I incorporate the good (the law) into the maxim of my power of choice; but this good, which is an irresistible incentive objectively or ideally (*in thesi*), is subjectively (*in hypothesi*) the weaker (in comparison with inclination) whenever the maxim is to be followed" (Kant 1996b, p. 77).

There are at least two good reasons not to regard most frailty as evil. First, one's basic commitment is not yet corrupted. Second, the concept of evil is diluted when it is applied to even the best of us. Everyone has frailties. President William Jefferson Clinton's notorious frailties led to his impeachment by the United States House of Representatives in 1998.[3] Yet even his lies to cover his tracks, although wrong, were not *evil*. He fudged the labeling of his philandering (what counts as "having sex"?) but did not, in the end, endorse his conduct. He apologized. Publicly. In contrast, if Susan McDougall's memoir is accurate, US independent counsel, special prosecutor Kenneth Starr, did real evil by engineering her eighteen months' confinement in progressively worse prisons that harmed her health and jeopardized her life, all for her refusal to implicate the Clintons falsely in Whitewater wrongdoing (McDougall 2003). To my knowledge, Starr has admitted no wrongdoing.

The Clinton–Starr contrast takes us to my second intermediacy, which it also illustrates. This one consists in fully culpable wrongdoing that is not foreseeably harmful (or not very). Common sense distinguishes evils from relatively minor wrongs not just by the agent's motives or strength of commitment but by the depth of the harm that is wrongfully but willingly done. Other things equal, more harmful wrongs are more reprehensible, when the harm is reasonably foreseeable. But according to Kant's grades of an evil will, culpable wrongs that are similarly motivated are ethically (although not juridically) on a par, regardless of differences in foreseeable harm. More harmful offenses can make one deserving of more severe punishments. But they are not, for Kant, ethically worse.[4] Ethically, as an evil, petty theft is on a par with murder, for Kant, when the incentive of both is self-love. Both violate the Categorical Imperative in the same way: one cannot will that everyone act on the maxim in either case. Foreseeable harm is not only, on this view, not definitive but irrelevant to the ethical gravity of a wrong.

---

[3] On December 19, 1998, the House of Representatives approved two of the proposed articles of impeachment. Without confirmation by the Senate, no further action was taken.
[4] Kant's discussion of duties of virtue in the *Metaphysics of Morals* does imply that not all vices – failures to adopt certain ends – are equally grave, although he does not grade vices by the depth of the harm they do, and he offers no systematic way to determine relative gravity among vices. Some violate perfect duties and others violate imperfect duties. Yet, it is not altogether clear that Kant held the implausible view that all violations of imperfect duties are worse than any violation of a perfect duty.

A third intermediacy is ambivalence or indecisiveness at the level of principle. Kant assumes that we are never without a fundamental commitment regarding the moral law. Yet, appearances in everyday life and in ordinary moral development fly in the face of this view.

A fourth intermediacy is illustrated by persons who appear systematically to exercise good (even exemplary) moral judgment in certain contexts or on certain types of issues and, during the same time period, astonishingly poor moral judgment in others. They seem to have a good side and an evil side, which is what we commonly say.

Finally, a fifth intermediacy, which presents a challenge for most ethical theories, is found in what Primo Levi called a "gray zone" (Levi 1989, pp. 36–69). In a gray zone, victims of oppression who are under severe duress operate the very machinery of oppression. Theirs is no ordinary weakness. Some kinds of duress do not so much reveal frailties in human nature that a good person would strive to overcome as challenge one's very principles and the limits of human obligation. The meaning of "good will" here can become unclear. Some degree of moral choice remains as long as some options are clearly worse than others. Still, despite their best efforts in a situation with no good options, gray-zone survivors often feel morally compromised. That sounds intermediate, not in the sense of "partly good and partly evil," but in the sense of "neither clearly good nor clearly evil."

Of these five kinds of intermediacy, frailty is now sufficiently clear. So let us take a closer look at the remaining four.

3. EVILS VS. LESSER WRONGS

In most paradigms of evil, such as genocide or torture, what is most salient is the harm to victims. Evils do intolerable (radical) harm. Harm becomes radical when it gravely, irreversibly, or irreparably jeopardizes access to basics that are ordinarily needed to make a life (or a death) tolerable or decent, from the point of view of the person whose life (or death) it is. Such basics include non-toxic air, water, and food, sleep, freedom to move one's limbs, spheres in which one can exercise effective choice, and freedom from severe and prolonged pain, humiliation, debilitating fear, disabling or disfiguring diseases, and extreme, prolonged isolation.

Although (in her early work) Arendt used the term "radical evil" to describe practices that produce a very deep harm, whereas Kant had used that term to characterize deep culpability, in principle, the two can be combined: one can be radically culpable in inflicting radical harm. We might have expected Arendt to assert later that Eichmann exemplified that very combination. But she did not. What struck her about Eichmann was his shallowness. She refused to describe as radical the conduct of a man who struck her as totally superficial. But she went on to claim that he had no intent to do wrong, that he lost the ability to distinguish right from wrong, and that "nothing would have been further from his mind than to determine with Richard III 'to prove a villain'" (Arendt 1965, p. 287). Eichmann, she concluded, was guilty of sheer thoughtlessness.

One can take issue with Arendt's readiness to believe Eichmann's protestations that he was not anti-Semitic. By his own admission, he deliberately coordinated trains whose destinations he had seen and understood firsthand from his visits to the eastern front and to death camps. There is no reason to think he ever forgot what he saw. Because he did his work meticulously, knowing what he knew, "thoughtless" is apt to mislead anyone not attuned to Arendt's special understanding of "thinking," which implies a certain autonomy of reasoning and evaluation. Eichmann fits Kant's third degree of evil. He prioritized his own advancement (self-love) over the Categorical Imperative, which he quoted at his trial with reasonable accuracy, admitting that he had ceased to follow it (Arendt 1965, p. 136). But his subordination of morality to self-love is not the most salient thing. What he did was so much worse than what others have done when they prioritized self-love. More salient in Eichmann's conduct are the depth and extent of the harm that he knowingly and willingly furthered, the fate to which he sent trainloads of people, and the gross disproportion between that harm to others and what he stood to gain from it (career advancement). Yet neither mass death nor that gross disproportion were what Arendt had in mind by "radical evil," when she was still willing to use that term.

Radical evil, for Arendt, literally *dehumanizes* victims, producing "living corpses," those "ghastly marionettes with human faces" who behave like Pavlov's dogs (Arendt 2000, pp. 132, 135). Radical evil was suffered not by those killed immediately upon arrival at the death camps but by those who survived long enough to be deprived of human dignity. This thought is in the spirit of Kantian values, although Kant does not acknowledge that human dignity is something of which one can be deprived. Wrongful willingness to strip people of their human dignity aggravates the culpability of even Kant's third gradation of evil. But Arendt did not pursue that thought. Her (early) view was that radical evil dehumanizes perpetrators as well. When perpetrators also become living corpses, lacking spontaneity, interchangeable with each other, then responsibility and culpability have disappeared, a state of affairs more chilling than Kant's radical culpability

(Arendt 2000, pp. 119–45). Arendt abandoned that view of perpetrators after reporting on the trial of Eichmann in Jerusalem.

In contrast to wrongs that do extreme harm, wrongs that foreseeably do no harm (or little harm) do not warrant the gravity of the judgment "evil." Kant's disregard of differences in the harmfulness of offenses, from an ethical point of view, makes sense if he reasons that an individual who would commit petty theft from calculated self-interest is also prepared to commit murder should it become profitable since, barring fundamental character change, the underlying principle would be the same: prioritize self-love. But that last premiss may be false. The underlying principle may be more complex. A self-loving thief could have scruples against murder or torture, drawing the line not from fear of detection (self-love) but because of the depth of the harm to victims. Imagine a Robin Hood who would *steal* from the rich but would not *murder or torture* even the rich, not because he is squeamish but because of the seriousness of the wrong. The case is different if Robin Hood thinks he is morally right. My "Robin Hood" concedes the wrongness of his thefts but does them anyway, partly because he enjoys being the instrument of others' good fortune (self-love is one incentive) but also partly because he does not think the wrong very *serious*, since it does only harm that his victims can easily absorb. A scruple qualifies his self-love: inflict no intolerable harm, or none from which victims cannot readily recover. He would not murder or torture to become a still greater benefactor or even steal from the rich who have physical disabilities. This character's scruples are captured neither by Kant's moral law nor by simple self-love but by a principle of self-love that makes concessions to morality. "Evil" is too strong a condemnation. "Slippery," maybe, but not evil. Or, not yet.

Similarly, those who are willing to lie about their homosexuality in order to protect their privacy, despite the questionable morality of doing so, might not persist if they became convinced that the practice of living in a closet contributes to intolerable harm. Those who are willing to lie only on the assumption that the practice harms no one seriously might well change that policy if persuaded that, as Harvey Milk argued in the 1970s, such a policy enables the persistence of myths that lead to gay-bashings, including murder.[5]

To cast the point in Kantian language, the *contents of one's material maxims* might be used to distinguish evils from lesser wrongs. How to state

---

[5] See the Academy Award-winning film *Milk* (2008) for a good portrayal of Harvey Milk arguing this point.

the maxim of one's action (what one is willing to do) is a well-known difficulty for any non-utilitarian theory of ethics, such as Kant's. It is known as the problem of relevant act-descriptions, as any act can be described in a multitude of ways. Kant does little to clarify the content and structure of material maxims beyond noting that (unlike formal maxims) they do not abstract from ends (goals). He offers widely disparate examples. Maxims are subjective principles that state our intentions in general form. They state what we are willing to do, which can include more than just our aims. They include at least an act and a purpose, and sometimes also circumstances. When he gives examples, Kant states his material maxims in value-neutral terms; that, at any rate, seems his intent. In some of his best cases, such as the lying promise, harm may truly not be foreseeable in the individual instance. It may never occur without the similar conduct of others, and there may be no good reason to anticipate the similar conduct of enough others to produce serious harm. But in other cases, such as torture, murder, and rape, major harm is not only foreseeable but deliberately brought about. Maxims could reflect those differences. Perhaps the agent would not perform the (admittedly wrong) act if it were reasonably foreseeable that others would, or even might, do likewise and that if they did, serious harm would result.[6] Utilitarians might want to say that an agent with such a scruple does no wrong when no harm results or harm is unlikely. A moralist moved by Kantian values might want to say, rather, that the wrongs of such an agent are not evils.

If foreseeable radical harm were included in a material maxim to be subjected to Kant's universality test, the harm would still not determine whether the maxim was morally permissible. The universality test would determine that. But harm included in the statement of the material maxim would indicate in a morally relevant way what one is willing to do. The ethical significance of the presence in one's maxim of reasonably foreseeable harm would be that, should the maxim fail the universality test, and should the agent lack any moral excuse for acting on it, acting on that maxim would be not merely wrong but evil. That seems correct. Such an emendation would make Kant's ethics less stoic, insofar as the harm is not

---

[6] I add "or even might" because of white-collar crimes such as those of the Enron scandal in the US that led to bank failures and widespread mortgage foreclosures that left families and even renters homeless. In the beginning, those who cooked the books may not have been in a position to foresee the harm that eventually resulted. But as their schemes developed, they could understand the disasters that might result if others did likewise and if risks they took did not pan out. They were "smart" about money. See the documentary film *Enron: The Smartest Guys in the Room* (2005), based on the book *The Smartest Guys in the Room* (McLean and Elkin 2004).

simply a function of anyone's will. But it would not reduce judgments of evil to a calculus of utility. Harm would not determine duty. It would supply one of the conditions that distinguishes evils from lesser wrongs.

4. TWO WAYS TO LACK UNITY IN THE WILL

The intermediacy discussed in section 3 is a will that is neither good nor evil. What is willed is wrong, but not harmful enough to be evil. Even if it is harmful enough, there is the further question whether the agent had any moral excuse. In the two intermediacies taken up next, the agent wavers or fluctuates between good and evil, sometimes doing good and other times evil, but not out of weakness. Such an agent is commonly said to be good in some respects (or to have some virtues) but not in others, or to be good to some extent but also to have a bad side (or "a mean streak"). Rather than acting against a fundamental commitment as in the case of weakness of will, these agents waver with respect to making such a commitment. They waver at the level of the higher-order act of (in Kant's legalistic metaphor) legislating a fundamental principle for themselves.

Kant assumes a basic coherence or unity of the will. He implicitly rejects the common-sense views that some of us lack basic commitments and that some of us even have plural and incompatible commitments. Evidence of ambivalence and of the lack of a single underlying commitment lies in conflicting observable patterns of action, each with its own priorities. No pattern need clearly dominate, although when someone is said to have "a mean streak," the implication is that the meanness is somewhat unpredictable, not the usual thing.

Consider, first, a parent who is unpredictably irresponsible. He blows hot and cold. Some days he beats his children severely for "offenses" that do no real harm but irritate him (such as laughter at the wrong moment or spilling milk), although he knows they do not deserve it and that he can (and does) injure them. He does this not from weakness but because he wants them to know who is boss and he does not care, then, about the price of that lesson. It is what seems most important to him *then*. On those days, his children learn to walk on eggshells. On other days, however, he is patient with his children for the same "offenses" and is moved by parental obligation to make accommodations for their immaturity and attend for as long as it takes to their needs. He is patient and caring then because he feels it his obligation as a parent, and his children's needs are what seem most important to him *then*. This parent is ambivalent, not frail, not clearly committed even to self-love, but at a basic level uncommitted. Kant would have to say that his basic commitment changes frequently. The common-sense view is that he is immature, has not "got his act together," has not yet developed a fundamental commitment (and possibly never will). We also tend to hold that against him.

Kant might object that this parent does not exhibit a good will and a bad will at the *same* time. Strictly, that possibility might seem to be all that Kant denies. Kant also notes our fallibility in regard to our own motives. Appearances can mislead us about our own fundamental principle. But is he right to assume that at any given time we must have a fundamental principle, whether we know it or not? What counts as "a time"?[7] Must it be a moment? Can it be a *stretch*? For a basic commitment, a stretch seems right. Kant says our basic disposition is an act, a choice, "an intelligible deed, cognizable through reason alone apart from any temporal condition" (Kant 1996b, p. 79). Although he presents this choice as not temporal, the choice of a commitment needs a stretch of time for its realization. As Aristotle says of friendship, the wish for it arises quickly, but friendship does not (Aristotle 1925, p. 197). Friendship requires time and trials. Likewise, moral commitment; quickly chosen, it does not materialize overnight. In discussing the overcoming of impurity and frailty, Kant sees this. But he does not acknowledge that the time required to translate commitment into action opens a space for ambivalence or indecisiveness *in regard to particular commitments or even whether to become committed at all*, not just space for weakness in regard to a particular commitment. Kant's account of how we can overcome evil implies that one can exhibit a good will and a bad will at *different* times. He envisages scenarios in which a person's will deteriorates or improves over time. There is a different trajectory in each case. But with fundamental ambivalence, there is no clear trajectory.

When conflicting *patterns* of behavior appear in the same stretch of time and in the same contexts, they suggest a will that is fundamentally *un*decided, *un*committed. Such a person might be called a moral "flip-flopper." To insist that at any moment one's commitment is fundamentally either good or bad is to miss (or dismiss) the salient pattern in flip-flopper agency. What we ordinarily call *lack* of commitment is not revealed in a moment but only over time. Such ambivalence seems common among children, adolescents, adults with troubled pasts, and those who live under stressful conditions.

---

[7] I am grateful to Marilyn Frye for raising the question, "What counts as 'a time'?" long ago in a different context (Frye 1992, pp. 109–19).

The moral flip-flopper exhibits *unpredictably* different patterns in the *same* contexts, a fairly common case. A less common but by no means unusual case that also appears to exemplify lack of unity in the will is the person who exhibits *systematically* different and conflicting patterns in *different* contexts. Some people behave predictably well in some contexts and equally predictably poorly in others. That difference may not always be explainable by the agent's relative ignorance of empirical facts in the second context. To illustrate, some people have excellent judgment in positions of public responsibility but not at home in family life or in intimate relationships. This is not an unusual sort of case, although it can become extreme enough to seem bizarre and raise questions regarding the person's status as a responsible agent.

Consider this example from real life. I choose an extreme case because it illustrates so clearly the challenges for a Kantian interpretation. It is a case of someone who appears to have been in many respects not only normal but exemplary. Sue William Silverman, an incest survivor, writes the following about her father in her memoir (published after his death). He was Chief Counsel to the United States Secretary of the Interior from 1933 to 1953. He played key roles in establishing statehood for Alaska and Hawaii, in Philippine independence, in creating the Puerto Rican Commonwealth, in home rule for the Virgin Islands, Guam, and Samoa, and in the establishment of civilian rule of Japanese possessions after WW II. From 1954 to 1958 he was president of large banks. He was photographed with President Harry Truman, with Adlai Stevenson, and with other influential political figures. And he was a child molester. For many years, he assaulted his daughter sexually, severely, locking her bedroom door at night, beginning when she was less than five (Silverman 1996, p. xv).

Were those who placed this man in positions of public trust *totally* deceived about his character? Or did he have a good side and an evil side? Although establishing statehood for Alaska and so forth are not moral descriptions of what he did, it seems unlikely that he would have developed such a record of trust and responsibility if he had not impressed others as morally reliable. He appears at first to embody the contradiction that Kant thought impossible: being committed to both good and evil, prioritizing duty in some contexts but prioritizing his sexual inclinations in other contexts. If that is a correct description, he has more than one higher-order will. If he is responsible for both patterns, his character is not at its *most* basic level defined by either of them. At its most basic level, his "character" is defined by a failure to take responsibility for overcoming his evil side (the evil legislator within). People who find themselves with more coherent and more conventional inclinations are morally lucky that they do not have to confront such a task. The failure to develop integrity is not captured by a formal maxim that prioritizes self-love. This man appears not to have had a sufficiently coherent self that one could say what it would mean for him to love himself. His problem is not frailty. How much strength could it take not to rape one's five-year-old daughter behind a locked door, time and again, for years? There is a policy here, not a lapse.

Whether (and if so, when) an individual is responsible for failure to develop an integrated self is a matter on which not even psychiatrists agree. Silverman indicates in her memoir that her father was probably also subjected to sexual abuse during his own childhood. What, if anything, did he remember about that? She does not know, as she was not able to come to terms with her own history, let alone his, until after his death. There is probably no simple answer to questions of responsibility that would do for all such divided persons. If he is not responsible for this failure, then he is better described as neither good nor evil, no "moral personality" at all, a kind of moral limbo. For myself, I see no conceptual barrier to holding responsible a man who shouldered the morally complex political responsibilities that this man shouldered. He learned to perform admirably in contexts of collective action. Yet holding him responsible for failure to overcome his evil side presupposes that there can be complexities in the will that go beyond Kant's legislating and deciding aspects of the will.

A man who did achieve his own integration, who confronted conflicting ideals that battled within his soul, is the African American sociologist W. E. B. DuBois. In the first chapter of *The Souls of Black Folk*, DuBois reflects philosophically on his "double consciousness," "this sense of always looking at oneself through the eyes of others." He writes, "One feels ever his twoness – an American, a Negro; two souls, two thoughts, two unreconciled strivings; two warring ideals in one dark body, whose dogged strength alone keeps it from being torn asunder" (DuBois 1969, p. 45). DuBois refused to embrace or abandon either "soul" completely but faced up to the challenge of deciding what was worth keeping from each and what was worth integrating with what. Although the conflicts he faced were different from those of Silverman's father, DuBois's experience is instructive for developing a view of the will that builds on but goes beyond the distinctions that Kant recognizes. The capacity for rational agency might include still higher-order acts of will than those that Kant calls "legislative acts" (second-order acts). If acts of a second order (Kant's legislative acts) can adjudicate conflicts at the first-order level, perhaps acts of a third order can adjudicate conflicts at the level of legislation. To continue

Kant's legal metaphor, the capacity for moral agency might include the development of a moral "supreme court" within oneself.

If we read the character of Silverman's father as Kant apparently would have read it, we must take the father's treatment of his daughter to reveal the real man beneath the sham of his public face. We must then wonder what unexposed abuses he perpetrated in his public trust. Not likely that he could occupy such positions for so long without confronting moral conflicts, situations in which he could succeed in taking unjust advantage of others' weaknesses. He does not appear to have undergone deep character change. He continued the same Jekyll/Hyde pattern of behavior over many years. Possibly his "good" public behavior was motivated by the rewards of reputation and salary, and his public duties luckily coincided with what was prudent. Perhaps in the public sphere, he simply could not get away with taking gross advantage of others' weaknesses, as he could at home. Or perhaps he thought it was a good investment in his reputation to make whatever sacrifices morality might require in the public sphere. In that case, he was not morally good even in his public roles and the appearance to the contrary was merely a sham. That seems to be how Robert Louis Stevenson regards Mr. Hyde, who, finally, can no longer hide behind Dr. Jekyll.[8]

And yet, is it not also *possible* that Silverman's father made moral decisions conscientiously on the job (rejecting maxims that he could not will universally) because that was the right thing to do (not for reputation's sake), despite his failure to negotiate family life honorably? Could he not have been in truth a moral model in public and a moral monstrosity at home? To look at him moment by moment and ignore the patterns is to dismiss what is most striking, even morally sinister, in his agency: his failure to heal that deep and persistent split.

If appearances do *not* mislead, moral flip-floppers are neither fundamentally good nor fundamentally evil, because of the absence of an enduring fundamental disposition. Yet we often hold people responsible for such a lack of integrity. Failure to develop a stable basic commitment can be due to culpable negligence. To use Arendt's language, there may be a moral failure here to *think* (reflect on and appreciate) what one is doing. Culpable negligence is a well-known problem for Kant's ethics, as

---

[8] In Robert Louis Stevenson's novella *The Strange Case of Dr. Jekyll and Mr. Hyde*, there appear to be multiple plays on "Hyde," which suggest "hide" both as disguise and the thick skin of a hairy beast (Stevenson 1991, pp. 439–88).

the negligent agent may have no maxim of negligence (no intention) to subject to the universality test. There may be resources, however, within Kant's ethics for addressing such issues. Barbara Herman suggests taking Kant's valuing of rational agency to be a more fundamental aspect of his ethics than the Categorical Imperative test for the maxims of actions (Herman 1993, 2007). Herman's creative use of that approach to begin to address some of the issues presented by omissions is one of the inspirations for my proposal of a third level of action within the capacity for moral agency.

In contrast to moral flip-floppers, Jekyll/Hyde characters seem to have two enduring but opposed dispositions ("legislative wills") underlying their observable deeds. Failure to achieve moral integrity appears to be a moral failure insofar as the Jekyll side points toward a well-developed capacity for moral judgment and not merely, as Stevenson might have thought, a facade to mask Hyde. But such failures to achieve moral integrity are more troubling and more puzzling than ordinary immaturity or ordinary self-interestedness. For these are individuals who appear often to do what is right in the face of strong pressures to do otherwise. Analogous cases might include those of some slave-owners, such as President Thomas Jefferson, in the ante-bellum American South, and some of the Nazi doctors interviewed by Robert J. Lifton (Lifton 1986). If DuBois was able to get it together in the context of a deeply racist society, can we not expect many others, who live more privileged lives, to do so as well?

Kant admits that our best evidence of the nature of our will consists in patterns of choice that we observe over time in our conduct (Kant 1996b, pp. 77, 116–17). Some of these patterns seriously challenge his faith that underlying the appearances at any particular time is a single, coherent fundamental commitment. Although we can deceive ourselves about our own commitments, it is more plausible that particular acts might mislead us as to the true nature of our will than that large-scale patterns of behavior over long periods of time would do so. Kant does not explicitly consider lives in which more than one pattern appears repeatedly over the same period. His analysis has the virtue, however, of acknowledging layers in the will: the layer that legislates and the layer that carries out the legislation (or fails to). Positing a further layer that confronts ambiguity or divisions within the self at the level of legislation, or that refuses to confront them, or neglects to do so, builds on that Kantian insight of complexity in the will.

5. GRAY ZONES

In his reflections on Auschwitz and on the Nazi-created ghettos, Primo Levi identified a "gray zone" in which some victims of evil become perpetrators of the very evils they suffer.[9] They come to occupy such a position by accepting offices that give them power over others. In that capacity, they inflict harms on others in exchange for rewards that may be only a postponement of their own suffering or death. Levi cites prisoners in death camps who became *kapos* (captains), prisoners who served on ghetto councils charged with selecting other prisoners to be sent to their deaths, and prisoners who served as ghetto police and were charged with rounding up the selected prisoners and putting them onto the trains, as well as with enforcing ghetto rules that predictably resulted in deaths. Some prisoners refused such service. Most who refused did not survive. Knowing this, others were torn. Should we refuse on principle? Should we exploit opportunities that might enable us to save others, not necessarily ourselves?

The realities were that accepting such a position almost certainly made one complicit in evils. But did it make one's *will* evil? Or is it genuinely unclear how one ought to confront such a choice? And if genuinely unclear, does that mean only that reasonable people might disagree about what the right responses are? Or is it *sometimes* the case that there are no unambiguously right choices, that the ambiguities are in the nature of the case, not just its appearance? If the ambiguities can be in the nature of the case, there is room here also for a will that is neither unambiguously good nor unambiguously evil. Multiple ambiguities in Levi's gray zones offer substance to the idea of "gray areas" between good and evil, areas of neither indifference nor mere ambivalence.

I suspect that most of us, most of the time are somewhere between good and evil. The reasonably foreseeable harms and our common moral failings that contribute to them, including somewhat culpable complicity in structural evils, tend to fall short of either the intolerable or the inexcusable. But also, processes of moral maturation, like those of moral deterioration, involve ambiguities and uncertainties of principle, not just of judgment regarding particular cases. On our way to becoming good or evil, we may pass through more or different stages than the three levels of the Kantian descent into radical evil or Kant's two-stage recovery program. Kant's theory of evil provides a groundwork for further empirically, phenomenologically, and politically sensitive analysis.

[9] For a fuller exploration of Levi's and other gray zones, see Card (2002, pp. 211–34).

6. DIABOLICAL EVIL REVISITED

Kant understands "diabolical evil" as "evil for evil's sake." He explicitly rejects the idea that human beings ever do evil simply because it is evil: "The depravity [*Bösartigheit*] of human nature is therefore not to be named *malice* [*Bösheit*], if we take this word in the strict sense, namely as a disposition (a subjective *principle* of maxims) to incorporate evil *qua* evil for incentive into one's maxim (since this is *diabolical*), but should rather be named *perversity* of the heart" (Kant 1996b, p. 84; italics in the original translation; German words in brackets were supplied by the translator in footnotes). In *The Atrocity Paradigm* I argued that "evil for evil's sake" – interpreted as Kant apparently does – is not the most interesting way to understand the idea of diabolical evil (Card 2002, pp. 211–34). "Diabolical" signals a special low even among atrocities, suggesting the merciless practices or decrees of a Nero, Caligula, Hitler, Idi Amin, or Pol Pot. But there is no need to suppose any of these men thought of their deeds as evil, let alone that they acted on a principle of doing evil as such.

The creation of what Levi called gray zones is diabolically evil, if anything is. That example suggests a more plausible interpretation of "evil for evil's sake" than that of acting on a principle of doing evil as such (that is, evil just because it – the act one is doing – is evil). A more plausible interpretation is "doing one evil for the sake of another." The creation of gray zones, an evil itself, served an end that was also evil, namely, the Final Solution. Gray zones destroyed or undermined capacities for moral agency in many of their victims (a morally inexcusable intolerable harm) as a means toward the end of exterminating the Jewish people (another morally inexcusable intolerable harm). There is no need to suppose that those responsible regard either means or end as an evil or even that they care. "Evil for evil's sake" can be understood simply as doing (what is truly) evil for no better reason than to promote (what is truly) another evil.

Another factor tends to distinguish the worst among evils. Not all evils are naturally described as incomprehensible. The harm may be outrageous, but the motives and sensibilities of perpetrators are depressingly familiar: need, greed, selfishness, opportunism, negligence, and the like. What the doer hopes to gain is commonly something that, apart from the means used to obtain it, is good, at least not bad, considered simply in itself. But Jeffrey Dahmer's luring youngsters of color to his apartment to drug them for sex and then killing and dismembering them (and the rest) seems incomprehensible.[10] Likewise the invention and use of such a device as the brass bull designed by Perillos of Athens for Phalaris, tyrant of Akragas, Sicily (Abbott 2005, pp. 37–38). This instrument, used as a method of execution, was designed with flutes in the bull's mouth so that the screams of victims roasting inside emerged sounding like music, or like the bull's lowing, by some accounts (Abbott 2005, pp. 37–38). The bull (in which Phalaris is said to have died and in which he tortured its creator) was used to torture and kill Christian martyrs. One need not be squeamish to find such torture incomprehensibly cruel. Likewise hacking to death with a machete, from sunup to sundown, day after day, everyone – women, men, and children, including neighbors – identified with a particular ethnicity. Kant's "radical evil" offers no explanation why Dahmer's murderous activities, those uses of Phalaris's brass bull, or the Rwandan genocidal practices should be any less comprehensible, morally, than ordinary murder by gunshot for money or revenge. To say only that self-interest is getting priority over morality is to ignore the costs to others of satisfying the prioritized interests and the evils in those interests.

In a now classic essay, "Wickedness," Stanley Benn notes, as he puzzles over Kant's denial that human beings are ever diabolical, that if devils can do evil for evil's sake, there must be no logical contradiction in that idea (Benn 1985, p. 805). The incomprehensibility of the diabolical is not a matter of logical incoherence or contradiction. That observation led me to reflect on what people think devils do. What makes a *devil's* deeds "diabolical"?

Folk wisdom and IHL are rich sources of concepts and paradigms that are helpful for answering that question. To borrow the language of the 1984 UN Convention against Torture and Other Cruel, Inhuman or Degrading Treatment or Punishment (Burgers and Danelius 1988, pp. 177–90), diabolical evils are especially *cruel, inhuman, or degrading*. If we combine that idea with the interpretation of "evil for evil's sake" as "doing one evil as a means to another," the result is a conception of diabolical evil as extremely cruel, inhuman, or degrading treatment as means to an evil end. Ordinary evils are inexcusable. But all that means is that the agent's reasons do not begin to justify the deed. Those reasons do not have to be grounded in interests in promoting an evil end. In diabolical evils, the agent's reasons are so grounded.

Three folk conceptions of the diabolical highlight some common forms of extremely cruel, inhuman, and degrading treatment that fit that

---

[10] For more on Dahmer and other serial killers, see Tithecott (1997).

conception. I think of them as the Torture Paradigm, the Nero Paradigm, and the Serpent Paradigm.

The Torture Paradigm, symbolized by a devil with pitchforks torturing sinners in hell for eternity, is a paradigm of cruel and inhuman diabolical treatment. For the sake of what does the devil torture sinners? I always heard that the devil loves company, the company of evil-doers in suffering the wages of evil. But torturing others eternally for no better end than not to endure torment alone is doing evil for an evil end. Companionship here does not bring compassion. It does not lighten the devil's burden. Companionship here only multiplies torment.

The Nero Paradigm is marked by profound betrayal coupled with great callousness and lack of proportion. It is illustrated by the murders committed by serial rapists Jeffrey Dahmer and Ted Bundy. In order to be able to continue activities that temporarily gratified their sexual lusts, each lured vulnerable and trusting victims to their deaths. Again, this is evil conduct for an evil end: murder for the sake of being able to continue raping. Their grotesque betrayals and the bizarre disproportion between the harm they did and what they got out of it make their deeds sufficiently inhuman to warrant the judgment "diabolical." The sources of their lusts and the possibility that these killers lacked a capacity for empathy need not soften that judgment as long as the killers retained a capacity to recognize the disproportion between their temporary sexual highs and the price they extracted from others for them and as long as they had the ability to make a different choice based on that recognition. Lest this paradigm seem too identified with violent sex, one could argue that deeds of Wisconsin Senator Joseph McCarthy, his aide Roy Cohn, and former Federal Bureau of Investigation Director J. Edgar Hoover in their pursuit of crypto-communists in the 1950s fit the Nero Paradigm also in callousness, gross disproportion between the harm they did and what they hoped to achieve, and in the most apparent ends – entrenchment of their power to manipulate others – for which they brought down so many.

Degradation is salient in the Serpent Paradigm, which couples deception and manipulation with hostile envy. Here, there is a destruction of what is good in others. If the serpent cannot have it, others will not have it, either. The serpent corrupts others; bringing them down when doing so does not elevate the serpent but simply allows the serpent to feel that others are no better or even that they are worse. This paradigm is embodied in the Christian reading of the serpent in the Genesis story of Eve's temptation in the Garden of Eden as Satan in disguise (Genesis 3:1–24; Holy Bible,

Revised Standard Version 1952, pp. 3–4) and its identification of Satan as a devil who rules in hell.[11] On that reading, the story of the Garden of Eden is a tale of corruption and betrayal. Satan, in the guise of a serpent, lures Eve into first destroying her own innocence and then becoming complicit in the destruction of Adam's. Thus the serpent engineers the Fall of Eve and Adam from Eden to earth, to the level of a serpent, with the consequence that they will die although they can reproduce at the cost of great pain to Eve and her female descendants, and all can be supported at the cost of great labor to Adam and his descendants. The serpent was not raised up by the Fall of Adam and Eve. On the contrary. From the text, one can infer that the serpent lost its legs, since part of its punishment is to have to crawl henceforth on its belly. The serpent's only "profit" is to no longer have to feel that Eve and Adam were so much better off or so much more beloved of God. The result for Eve and Adam, on this reading of the story, is degradation. At any rate, they drop to a seriously degraded environment and condition. The text might suggest that the so-called Fall was actually the price of a certain upgrade, since after eating the apple, Eve and Adam are said to have become more like God through their knowledge of good and evil. By the same stroke, however, they become more like the serpent. Again, one evil (the serpent's inexcusable deception that results in death and pain) is done for the sake of another (to rob Adam and Eve of God's favor, although it is unclear from the text whether the serpent can be presumed to foresee the particular punishments forthcoming).

Levi wrote that conceiving and organizing the *Sonderkommando*, special squads of Jewish prisoners assigned to crematorium duty at Auschwitz, was "National Socialism's most demonic crime" (Levi 1989, p. 53). If we read "demonic" as "diabolical," Levi's judgment that this crime was demonic is triply right.

First, and most obviously, the creation of the *Sonderkommando* illustrates the Torture Paradigm, with extremes of both physical and mental torture. As Arendt observed, "the reality of concentration camps resembles nothing so much as Medieval pictures of Hell" (Arendt 2000, p. 127). Pitchforks and flames were the special province of the *Sonderkommando*.

---

[11] Entries for "Satan" and "Serpent" in Miller and Miller (1961, pp. 647–48, 665–66) indicate that Satan is often referred to in the New Testament as "the serpent." That may account for the Christian interpretation of the serpent who tempts Eve in the Garden as Satan in disguise. Satan in the Hebrew Bible and contemporary Judaism is not the name of an evil being; the Hebrew word translated as "satan" meant "adversary" and was used not to name a particular being but to refer to "any one of the angels sent by God for the specific purpose of blocking or obstructing human activity," and the Greek *diabolos*, which became "devil," literally means "one who throws something across one's path" (Pagels 1995, p. 39).

Second, conceiving and organizing the *Sonderkommando* illustrates the Nero Paradigm in its reliance on gross betrayal, callousness, and the infliction of harms wildly disproportionate to the gains produced or sought. A bizarre entertainment, reminiscent of Nero's coliseum games, was the playing of recreational games between teams composed of *Sonderkommando* members and teams composed of Nazi camp guards. *Sonderkommandos* were callously disposed of after a few weeks or months and replaced with a new squad.[12] It was the squads' job to systematically betray fellow Jews by complicity in the deceptions surrounding the gas chambers. What did those in power gain by having Jewish prisoners do this? They did not have to get their own hands dirty, and they could confirm their negative stereotypes of Jews by what the *Sonderkommandos* were willing to do – scant benefits for Nazis from a profoundly evil deed. Yet those benefits also facilitated implementation of the Final Solution. Again, one evil for the sake of another.

Finally, the creation of the *Sonderkommando* illustrates the Serpent Paradigm in the degradation of everyone involved. Squad members were made to operate the very machinery that would be used by other squad members to murder them as well. They were offered hideous options, enabling camp administrators to feel that however shameful their own conduct, Jewish prisoners were no better or even that they were worse. That was a structure that, like the serpent in the Garden of Eden, brought everyone down (but without making anyone more like God).

---

[12] Filip Müller was an exception. He survived to write about his three years in the *Sonderkommando* (Müller 1979) and is interviewed in Lanzmann's documentary film *Shoah* (1985).

CHAPTER 3

Complicity in structural evils

Structural injustice is a kind of moral wrong distinct from the wrongful action of an individual agent or the willfully repressive policies of a state. (Young 2007, p. 170)

I. COLLECTIVELY PERPETRATED EVILS

Many atrocities, including genocide and slavery, are collectively perpetrated. Many are collectively suffered. Many (including genocide and slavery) are both. Accordingly, two sets of questions present themselves, corresponding to the agency and the harm components of an evil. Agency questions include the following: What are the wrongs in collectively perpetrated atrocities? Who or what are the agents? How are they related to the harm? What does it mean to say of a collectively perpetrated deed that it was inexcusable? Where, if anywhere, is culpability located? Harm questions include the following: Who or what can suffer intolerable harm? What kinds of harms can be suffered collectively? Is harm to the group always and only harm to individuals considered as group members? What does it mean to say of harm to a group that it is intolerable? Agency questions are this chapter's main subject. Chapter 4 takes up harm to non-sentient beings, including some groups. Yet, both sets of questions are sufficiently interconnected that at certain points issues regarding harm to groups make an appearance in this chapter as well. This chapter and the next raise more questions than either is able to answer.

A social collectivity can be transformed from a mere aggregate into unified group in two fundamentally different ways, one internal and the other external. Both are discussed in Larry May's work on the morality of groups (May 1987, 1996). Internal unification is through structures or relationships of cohesiveness, such as those of a team. A team's internal cohesiveness enables it to *act* as a group. External unification is through relationships of individuals to services, materials, practices, or activities external to members of the group and their relationships with one another. Computer users are such a group, united not by their relationships to one another but through their uses of computers, which give them common interests, thereby making them vulnerable to special harms as a group. Computer users differ in this way from a mere aggregate, such as persons shopping on Michigan Avenue in Chicago on a particular day. That sort of commonality among shoppers does not ordinarily create common interests, although, as will become apparent, it can.

A group can be unified in both ways. But many are unified in one way or the other. Groups structured by internal relationships, social norms, processes, or other forms of internal cohesiveness ("solidarity") have received considerable attention in philosophical action theory (Bratman 1999; Gilbert 1989; Tuomela 1995). There is a tendency in action theory even to define "social group" in terms of the possibility of joint action. But a group that lacks the structure or cohesiveness necessary for action can still be vulnerable to harms as a result of its members' relationships to external materials, activities, and processes. Although this chapter is primarily concerned with agency and so with groups of the first kind, the other kind of group enters the picture, too, since group agents can *be* the externals that give rise to groups of the second kind.

A question left hanging in chapter 1 is how individual agents are related to the harm done by evil institutions. In the quotation heading this chapter, Iris Young finds the wrongs of structural injustice to be distinct from the wrongs of individual agents. Rules of social structures can be inexcusably faulty. Or they can join or collide in unforeseen ways with other rules to give rise to harms. But rules do not act. Human beings implement the rules, individually or collectively. We apply or misapply them, are guided by them, influenced by them, sometimes disobey or rebel against them, and so on. Participants in a faulty institution, and non-participants who are complicit, need not be culpable, although often they are. The nature and degree of their culpability varies with their individual positions and powers, options available to them, what they know or should know, and so on.

The conduct of many of us who are complicit in collectively perpetrated evils tends to fall into the areas between good and evil discussed in chapter 2. Our conduct is not positively good. Nor is it downright evil, even when activities in which we are complicit clearly are. We often act (or fail to act) from weakness or inertia. We may go along uncritically with practices we suspect are questionable, giving others the benefit of our doubts. We can be culpable when we do not investigate. We may not mean or foresee serious harm. But how well do we develop habits of reflection on what we are actually doing together, habits of inquiry into the history and consequences of institutions in which we participate or from which we benefit? We may come to see that an institution (such as a slaughterhouse) does intolerable harm (not only to animals but to uninsured immigrant workers).[1] Yet what we do as consumers, restaurant workers, reporters, or teachers often seems, and often is, remote from that harm.[2] Connections between our choices and the harm are mediated by the choices of many others. Furthermore, institutions can structure the options of participants and others in ways that offer no good choices. Individual culpability is often mitigated by circumstances that provide some excuse.

In principle (however unlikely), there can be institutional evils for which no individuals are culpable. A group can be faulted even when its members cannot. Joel Feinberg offers two examples to illustrate what he calls "collective but not distributive" contributory group fault, that is, fault that contributes to a harm (Feinberg 1970, pp. 248–49). One example is the Jesse James train robbery, which succeeded because none of the passengers rose up to fight back. The other is a philosophy department that had no one willing to supervise the dissertation of one of its graduate students after the death of the student's adviser and the departure for another university of the only other faculty member who would have been willing. No individual in either case was at fault. But the group, he suggests, might be faulted for lacking an appropriate contingency plan.

It would seem, then, that members of a group can be implicated in an evil simply through their (presumably voluntary) group membership, even though there is no way to distribute fault among them for the harm. It appears that the philosophy department had a responsibility that it was not meeting and that it might reasonably be held accountable for as a department, even though no individuals failed in their individual responsibilities. Individual members of the department may have tried to institute a contingency plan but failed to reach agreement, although no individual was culpable for the failure.

It is less clear that the train passengers can be faulted, even as a group. For they do not, presumably, have internal relationships with one another or any structures or other cohesiveness that could enable them to act as a group. It is more plausible that those in charge of passengers (if anyone was) were culpable for *their* lack of a contingency plan.

---

[1] For ugly details on slaughterhouses in the US, see Eisnitz (1997) and Schlosser (2001, pp. 169–92) or the film *Fast Food Nation* (2006).

[2] The film *Food, Inc.* (2009) makes many of the connections very explicit and offers a lucid account of certain structural evils that have developed in the food industries in the US since the 1950s.

In the case of the philosophy department, four factors make it seem intuitively correct to regard members of that group as complicit: (1) their choices causally contribute to the harm, (2) the harm could have been prevented if some members of the group had made different choices (even though their choices, under the circumstances, were not culpable), (3) they were all in a position to know these things, and (4) none of them (let us suppose) was under obligation not to make those different choices. Yet, making a causal contribution and being able to prevent something from occurring are not necessary conditions for complicity. One can be complicit not only through voluntary membership in a group but through what Christopher Kutz calls "ratification" of an evil, without making a causal contribution to harm and without being in any position to prevent it (Kutz 2007).

Further, evils can be collectively perpetrated by way of social norms, some of them racist and sexist, learned so early in life that those of us who internalize those norms are not aware of having done so. We do not think of ourselves as participants in a practice. If we think about it at all, we are apt to think of our behavior as spontaneous, normal, or self-interested, not as learned. Actions guided by norms that systematically exclude women or non-Caucasians from activities open to men or Caucasians may not do intolerable harm considered simply individually. Taken together, they can. One sense of the claim that structural injustice is a kind of moral wrong distinct from the wrongful action of an individual agent is that the structural wrong may not be capturable by way of the maxims of action of individuals who are complicit in the wrong. Joint action is often capturable by "we"-maxims that state what we are intending together, as opposed to "I"-maxims that state what an individual intends as an individual (Bratman 1999; Gilbert 1989; Tuomela 1995). But not all structural injustice is capturable even by "we"-maxims. Some of it is unintended by anyone.

Individuals can be culpably complicit, however, even when they are not participants in an evil institution. Their positions need not be defined by the institution. Their conduct need not be required by any institutional rule or consist in the exercise of institutionally defined powers. Yet they can knowingly offer support. Many who never joined the Ku Klux Klan (KKK) or the Nazi Party ratified the activities of those organizations informally and refused to aid victims. They contributed by what they taught their children and through what they were willing or unwilling to report, protest, or testify to.

From a moral point of view, complicity in collectively perpetrated evils is more elusive than complicity in a crime, such as murder, is from a legal point of view. "Complicity," according to *Black's Law Dictionary*, is "association or participation in a criminal act; the act or state of being an accomplice" (Garner 2004, p. 303). An accomplice is any of a plurality of perpetrators and can be either a principal or an accessory. Accessories before or after the fact need not be present at the crime. They can still aid the principal or help cover up the crime. But in such collectively perpetrated evils as long-term race or sex oppression, there are relatively few clear analogues of principals and accessories. Here there is not one crime but many that are interrelated. In addition, there are contributory deeds (informal verbal support) and omissions (failing to speak up) that are not and should not be criminal, even though many are wrong. One might begin to wonder at this point whether we are all complicit in all the evils of our time, since, ultimately, everything is connected. But not all connections promote, support, or in other ways aid in the perpetration of an evil or its cover-up, and not all connections come back ultimately to something voluntary that we have done or to some culpable omission.

To begin to illustrate the complexities of answering complicity questions, consider the following ordinary examples from my experience. They are familiar and relatively simple in contrast to the large-scale atrocities and structural evils that ultimately concern me. From the year I was born until the year I entered high school, my father was a traveling salesman for a large tobacco company. Throughout my childhood tobacco put food on my table and clothes on my back. The tobacco industries are deeply complicit in great numbers of premature and painful deaths annually (including those of both my parents). As a youthful beneficiary of those industries and for nineteen years an adult consumer of cigarettes, I bear an association with those industries and, through them, with many unnecessarily premature and painful deaths. It does not make me legally liable. It nevertheless gives rise to a sense of complicity that I think is not irrational or misplaced. A child's complicity is not culpable. But it can give rise to an appropriate adult sense of responsibility to challenge those practices and to use ill-gotten benefits to help others who might suffer from the practices. Adult consumers who support a lethal industry are culpable to the extent that they have options and the capacity for responsible choice, as well as access to relevant knowledge. Yet the evil-doers in this collectively perpetrated evil are corporations and their knowledgeable, wealthy adult owners, managers, marketers, attorneys, and so forth – not ordinary consumers who become addicted to the product in their teens as a result, in part, of corporate marketing practices and protections of those practices secured by corporate lawyers. A Kantian refusal to acknowledge anything morally in-between good and evil leads either to exonerating consumers or to painting their choices as evil. Neither does the consumer justice. Consumers' choices can be neither good nor evil (even if, ultimately, wrong).

Complicity in my father's drunk driving (introduced in chapter 1) is simpler than the tobacco case. I was in my early thirties when my father died in the aftermath of a massive heart attack, brought on by a life of heavy drinking, heavy smoking, indulgent eating, and no exercise (save an annual November hunting weekend and a day of golf in June, each leaving him barely able to move). In these respects he was fairly typical among men of his generation in our village. The complicity that concerns me is not in his lifestyle generally but his drunk driving specifically. Drunk driving is an evil. Yet I rode with him often enough (I had no driver's license then) and failed even to try to persuade him not to drive after drinking and not to stop for drinks at roadside taverns. Sometimes I drank with him. It is unclear what moral responsibilities that behavior leaves me today. Surely roadside taverns who serve men like my father are even more complicit than I was. Their relationship to the evils of drunk driving is more direct. My father, as noted earlier, was lucky in the risks he took; to my knowledge, he caused no injuries, fatalities, or even accidents. My complicity is not rooted in causal contributions to harm (at least, not harm of that sort). Yet decades later, I gesture toward assuming some responsibility in my choice of classroom examples in lectures on ethics at a campus infamous for binge drinking. Teaching with such examples seems one appropriate response, as my complicity took the form of wrongful condoning, even ratification.[3]

These familiar sorts of tobacco and alcohol examples are as complex as they are because of institutions and other social structures involved in the production, distribution, sale, and use of these products. Had I grown my own tobacco solely for my own moderate use, I would not have been complicit as an adult in the harms done by the tobacco industries.[4]

Collectively perpetrated institutional evils also include, besides evils in the rules or their administration, evils produced as a result of interconnections among institutions or practices – such as the way that the institution of imprisonment and the practice of plea bargaining can work together to

---

[3] I routinely tell students how long I smoked, how I quit and how hard that was, how my parents died, and that my parents and I got started as major consumers of tobacco and alcohol when we were students on the campus where I now teach.

[4] The closest I came to such initiatives was to roll my own cigarettes, briefly.

result in confinements based on false confessions. Some interconnections develop over time in ways that no one planned, foresaw, or was in a position to foresee. They are paradigms of what Young means by "structural injustice" (Young 2007, pp. 167–72) and "structural oppression" (Young 1990, pp. 40–42). And so I turn next to the concepts of a social institution or practice, and of social structure.

2. INSTITUTIONS AND SOCIAL STRUCTURE

Start with the idea that a social institution or practice is a form of activity structured and defined by rules.[5] Institutions are not always easily individuated or identified. And what counts as the same practice can be unclear. Rules defining slavery, for example, shift with time and place. In ancient Rome, some slaves were permitted to own others (Melzer 1993). Slaves in the United States were not permitted to own property, including property in human beings (although some former slaves became slave-owners). Wittgenstein's idea of "family resemblance" concepts is useful for concepts such as slavery, which have evolved historically with variations (Wittgenstein 1958, p. 32e).

Not concepts, however, but actual practices are evils. "Institution" is ambiguous between relatively generic concepts, such as slavery or genocide, and particulars, such as Stalin's gulags or his show trials, which can be regarded as instantiating more generic concepts. A wrongful intention to do intolerable harm remains an evil intention but is not an evil if it is unimplemented or unsuccessful. Likewise, an institution (generic) is evil but not *an* evil if, although it is indefensible and its successful implementation would do intolerable harm, it is never implemented. Strictly, only particular institutions, such as American slavery, are evils. Slavery is rightly said to be an evil only because of its actual embodiments. It is not just a concept (as some believe that hell is).

An institution, as John Rawls understands that idea, is "a public system of rules, which defines offices and positions with their rights and duties, powers and immunities, and the like." The rules "specify certain forms of action as permissible, others as forbidden, and they provide for certain penalties and defenses, and so on, when violations occur." As examples he lists "games and rituals, trials and parliaments, markets and systems of property" (Rawls 1999a, pp. 47–48). But when are the rules public? Must

---

[5] Hereafter, I treat social institutions and social practices together and do not always mention both explicitly.

everyone know them? All of them? Must everyone understand them the same way? Must the knowledge be self-conscious? The answer to the last two questions is clearly negative. One reason for courts (an institution) is that rules of other institutions need to be brought to the attention of, or clarified for, those they govern. Rules need to be fine-tuned and interpreted. Conflicting interpretations need to be adjudicated.

Some institutional evils express the will of a tyrant (Nero) or tyrannical organization (the KGB). But institutional evils are not always perpetrated, ordered, or overseen by tyrants. With regard to racist and sexist practices, such as routine use of racist or sexist language, jokes, myths, and stereotypes, no one plays the role of a Hitler or Stalin or even of the Nazi or Communist Party. Responsibility is distributed among many agents, many of whose acts are not individually harmful enough to be evils, although they contribute to real evils (in ways to be considered later), such as the practices of lynching and rape. If the term "structural evil" were reserved for social evils that lack a tyrant, we could contrast structural with tyrannical evils, as Young was inclined to contrast structural with tyrannical injustice, especially in her early work (Young 1990), but also in the quotation heading this chapter (Young 2007). And yet, tyrannical evils are also commonly perpetrated by way of social structures – Hitler's sterilization and "euthanasia" programs, for instance, or Nero's coliseum games.

In a broad sense of "structural," all institutional evils are structural.[6] Institutions and practices are structured by social norms. Institutions also give rise to larger structures in the ways that they come to be interconnected. Yet, an evil or an injustice is most apt to be explicitly called "structural" when the responsible structure is not self-consciously created or administered, when there is not a conspicuous tyrant or tyrannical group, or when the practice comes over time to be interconnected with other practices in ways not specifically intended and then, owing to those connections, has consequences not specifically intended. It has been a matter of scholarly debate between "functionalists" and "intentionalists" whether, and if so to what extent, the Nazi Final Solution was such a consequence. What Rawls calls "the basic structure of society" (Rawls 1999a, pp. 6–7) – "the way in which major social institutions distribute fundamental rights and duties, and determine the division of advantages from social cooperation" – is "structural" in that sense: some ways that major social institutions work together to define (or preclude) basic rights and

---

[6] On the concept of social structure, see, for example, essays in Blau (1975).

duties may not have been foreseen or intended. Yet, once in place, they can be evaluated as just or unjust, oppressive, and so on.

Structural evils so understood appear to fall out of an "invisible hand" opposite in character to that of Adam Smith. Adam Smith's invisible hand was benign (Smith 1937, p. 423). The fallout from the invisible hand of structural evils is malignant. Because of the apparent lack of intention to produce the harm, it is tempting to think no one culpable. Yet that does not follow. Individuals may be culpable in what they did intend, or in what they omitted, even if not for intending the particular harms that resulted. Individuals who routinely use racist language and stereotypes can be culpable for that and incur some responsibility for the fallout, even if they never, and never would have, intended a lynching.

As markets become global and their interrelations increasingly complex, and as information technology develops, structural evils become both more likely and more easily foreseeable. One response is to create higher-order institutions to monitor relations among lower-order institutions. Yet there may not be structural solutions to all of the problems of structural evil. Higher-order alertness, reflection, and moral imagination may also be necessary in individuals who would avoid complicity or meet the responsibilities to which their complicity gives rise. Hannah Arendt's observation that Eichmann did not *think* what he was doing (Arendt 1965, pp. 287–88) can be taken as an observation regarding his attitude – lack of moral attention, reflection, and imagination – toward the larger schemes in which he played so pivotal a role.

Speaking of Eichmann (although he was no *ordinary* bureaucrat), bureaucracies are especially worrisome. Bureaucracies are systems of administration staffed usually with non-elected officials who operate by adhering to complex and relatively inflexible rules. Larry May elaborates well the dangers of bureaucracy highlighted by Arendt in her work on totalitarianism. These dangers include compartmentalization with its diffusion of responsibility, anonymity and its tendency to make everyone feel (and be) replaceable, elevation of loyalty and efficiency into the highest virtues, identification of loyalty to the system with loyalty to family, and so on (May 1996, pp. 65–85). Bureaucracies discourage thinking. Eichmann was discouraged in all these ways from reflecting morally on his choices. That does not excuse him. But it suggests that bureaucracies, too, were instrumental in who he became. Responsibility is not a zero-sum game.

Thinking is also often absent in complicit individuals whose support and cooperation contribute systematically to bureaucratic and other institutional effectiveness, individuals who are not bureaucrats and do not have other institutionally defined roles. They, too, become participants in the social structure. To illustrate, consider what I have long called "rape as a terrorist institution" (Card 1996, pp. 97–117). Rape in civil [sic] society is a social practice governed by complex informal norms that are taught and learned early.[7] The norms define positions, privileges, and liabilities. They define what counts as tacit consent or provocation ("a woman alone is asking for it"). They define who can and cannot be raped ("a wife cannot be raped by her husband"; "a prostitute cannot be raped" – that is, nothing done to either counts as rape). As with slavery, the rules vary with time and place. The consequence for women in general (not just those raped) is patriarchal protectionism, under which women provide, for protection against assault, services that range from laundry and cooking to childcare and sex.

Participants and others complicit in a practice need not regard their behavior as norm-governed. Rapists, for example, may regard their own choices as spontaneous or simply self-indulgent. They may be unmoved to reflect on sources of their inclinations. They may never reflect on protectionist consequences for women, let alone intend them. Yet they are guided by norms that define the practice ("a woman alone is asking for it"). What may begin as tolerated habits take on the character of norms when they create patterns of expectation, failure to live up to which becomes an occasion for socially sanctioned criticism. People who criticize raped women for having been "alone" (without a male guardian) become complicit in the protection racket. They may or may not sit on judicial benches and juries. They may only be in position to aid or refuse aid to victims, to come forward or not to testify as witness to an assault, to teach their children, and so on. Through such contributions, non-rapists lend stability to the practice.

"Structural evil" is a metaphor that has a potentiality to mislead. For "structure" masks individual human agents who collectively bring about the evil. To probe some of the difficulties of identifying the individual agents of structural evil, I turn next to sex oppression, a paradigm of structural injustice.

3. OPPRESSION

Oppression is usually described by feminists from the point of view of the oppressed. To appreciate the significance of this fact, it is useful to recall (from chapter 1) what Roy F. Baumeister calls "the magnitude gap"

---

[7] The institution of rape as a form of terrorism is discussed in chapter 6.

(Baumeister 1997, p. 46). The magnitude gap is that discrepancy between the perceptions of perpetrators and the perceptions of victims regarding the same wrong. Baumeister reports that studies show that victims tend to exaggerate the wrongs they suffer, whereas perpetrators tend to downplay the wrongs they do. My refinement on his account is to relate each distortion to one of the elements of an evil. Victims tend to distort perpetrators' motives, to which they have less direct access; they are less likely to distort harm they experience directly. Perpetrators tend to ignore or minimize the harm they do, which they experience less directly; they are in a better position to know their own motives. What feminist analysis of oppression tends to offer is the perspective of those who suffer the harm. The focus is not on agents behind the harm. As perpetrators tend to underestimate the harm, they tend not to see their conduct as oppressive. Were we to begin, then, with perpetrators' perspectives, it would be easy to fail to discover any evil at all, especially when the evil in question is collectively perpetrated. So let us *begin*, as feminists generally do, with the perspectives of the oppressed and the experience of being trapped by social structures.

Consider, for example, Marilyn Frye's analysis of oppression (Frye 1983) and the further development offered by Young. Frye begins by reminding us that oppression is a specific concept that does not cover all harm or suffering (Frye 1983, pp. 1–16). Being hurt or injured (say, in a ski accident – her example) is not the same as being oppressed. Oppressive practices hinder, in deep and far-reaching ways, the development and exercise of basic human capacities.

Young notices that some unjust practices *exploit* (rather than stifle) basic capacities of the people they dominate (capacities for productive labor, for example). A practice can diminish another's autonomy without diminishing many of that other's capacities to act or grow. Building on Frye's analysis of oppression, Young defines a just society as one that is not characterized by the oppression or domination of any of its social groups (Young 1990, pp. 39–65). The values of self-development and self-determination, she observes, correspond to "two general conditions of injustice." The first of those two general conditions of injustice is oppression, which she defines as "institutional *constraint on self-development*." The second is domination, which she defines as "institutional *constraint on self-determination*" (Young 2000, p. 31; emphases mine). Young's focus is on agency. But it is the diminished agency of those who are oppressed or the controlled agency of those who are dominated, not the agencies, that lead to oppression or domination.

Applying her training in the philosophy of language, Frye notes that "oppress" contains the root "press," which suggests "mold," "immobilize," "reduce." Yet her focus remains on those who are molded, immobilized, and reduced, trapped like a bird in a cage (Frye 1983, pp. 1–16). The agencies responsible for the stunted or warped development of the oppressed remain hidden, glossed as structures, like cages.

Building on Frye's metaphorically suggestive account of oppression as structural, like a cage, Young presents exploitation, marginalization, powerlessness, cultural imperialism, and violence as five "faces" of oppression. She finds it an advantage that the structural approach does not presuppose an oppressor group corresponding to each oppressed group. Still, she acknowledges that for each oppressed group, another group is relatively privileged. One could add that a further advantage of a structural approach that emphasizes interaction, as Young does, is that it makes room for the recognition that oppressive conduct is found not only among the privileged but also among the oppressed. Women, for example, are heavily complicit in women's oppression. Yet the disadvantage remains that a structural approach tends to mask the individual agents whose choices produce domination and oppression. Young's *faces* of oppression are *masks*. What agency exists behind the masks?

Exploitation is the first mask. Young invokes Marx's account of exploitation as appropriation (Marx 1967, vol. I, pp. 177–311). Exploited workers are not just used – they are used *up*, drained, sucked dry. In losing products of their labor, they lose substance, not just control. But the substance they lose does not disappear. It is acquired (appropriated) by others whose agency and well-being are thereby enhanced. To use Frye's language, the substance of the oppressed is grafted onto others. Who or what does the grafting? Those who benefit (who think they have earned the benefits)? Social structures (norms) that sanction such a distribution of benefits? Everyone who acts in accord with those norms? Do workers graft their own substance onto others? Presumably, the rules determine who does it, rules that may or may not have been instituted knowingly or deliberately. And so, it would seem, power lies in the hands of whoever can change the rules, which can include the exploited if they can combine to act collectively.

If the exploited are disempowered too much or too rapidly, exploitation becomes self-defeating. Hence, the well-known tension between oppression and exploitation: to be exploitable, workers must remain useful, at least until they can be replaced. Exploitation, then, is not the worst oppression. Exploiters have reason to maintain in existence those they exploit.

There is a brief shift in perspective here to an exploiters' point of view. Superficially, it suggests aid rather than harm. But the "aid" is only for the purpose of enabling appropriation. Yet the enabling is action that is apt to be done self-consciously and deliberately, and not by workers themselves, at least, not so knowingly or calculatedly.

Young notes that in contrast to exploitation, marginalization may be the most dangerous face (mask) of oppression. Eventually, it is the face on which she comes to focus. As examples of the marginalized, Young cites the elderly, people with disabilities, single mothers and their children, the involuntarily unemployed, and American Indians, "especially those on reservations" (Young 1990, p. 53). So far, the account is in the passive voice. The marginalized are excluded from making useful social contributions. Others may then have no motive to keep them alive and functioning. Here, again, is a brief shift in perspective, suggesting that oppression also takes the form of omissions, in this case, failing to interact with people who are not exploitable, failing often even to perceive them.

One might object that people who have major disabilities are not necessarily marginalized. Franklin Delano Roosevelt presided over the US from a wheelchair (for more than three terms). Young's later work on exclusion and inclusion accommodates such facts. Individuals can belong to many social groups, some of them privileged. Membership in a privileged group can negate or diminish one's vulnerability to oppression. Who or what, then, is marginalized? The group? Unlucky members? The facts of disability?

Instead of answering this question asked in this way, Young revisits marginalization in *Inclusion and Democracy* (Young 2000) by way of its opposite, inclusion. The shift to "inclusion" may sound like a shift in perspective, from passive to active. But what Young proposes is a structural solution, in this case an institutional solution: practices of democratic representation. *Inclusion and Democracy* offers a layered analysis of marginalization (now called "exclusion") that invokes practices of democratic representation and the many possibilities of inclusion and exclusion that representation opens up. That a group is inadequately represented does not, because of multiple group membership, entail that individual members are expelled from social life or that they are materially deprived. Thus, marginalization becomes a matter of the degrees to which and ways in which individuals can be excluded from having a voice in democratic processes. One might be included (represented) as a person of color, yet be excluded (from representation) as lesbian or gay. Rules of democratic process do the including or excluding, insofar as those rules are followed.

Once again, the agency of individuals is masked, although much excluding easily results from the omissions of individual agents who together craft the rules of representation in democracies. Rules of representation in a democracy are crafted only by a subset of those whom they govern, not all with equal access to that subset.

Eventually, for Young, marginalization becomes basic to oppression. She treats disempowerment (one of the "five faces") as a form of marginalization: exclusion from positions from which one could exercise political power. She does the same with cultural imperialism (another face). Cultural imperialism is a form of domination that falsely universalizes as simply "human" the perspectives of a dominant group, thereby rendering invisible (excluding from view) other points of view.

Violence, Young's last mask, is the most conspicuous aspect of oppression, although not the most basic. Systematic vulnerability to violence is a consequence of marginalization (including disempowerment) and cultural imperialism, rather than an initiating source of oppression. Violence aggravates and reinforces oppression initiated elsewhere. What Young presents in violence as a face of oppression is yet another exclusion: exclusion from the protections routinely available to others against murder, assault, battery, robbery, and other violent crime. Oppressed groups are more vulnerable to violence as a fact of everyday life because everyone knows that the penalties for violence against the oppressed are less, and less likely, than for violence against the powerful. A look at how this vulnerability is maintained reveals widespread individual complicity. Perpetrators of assaults against those already marginalized are less likely to be held accountable when potential witnesses, law enforcement officers, reporters, and others look the other way or take the crime less seriously. Although Young's account of violence is initially from the point of view of those who suffer it, that account tacitly refers to two kinds of individual agency. Violent assailants are the conspicuous agents. Less visible are individuals who tolerate, encourage, or ratify the behavior of assailants. They may never assault anyone. Yet, without their tacit support, assailants are able to do far less harm.

Young held that the objects as well as beneficiaries of sex oppression and race oppression are social groups. Describing both groups as "structural," she distinguished them from aggregates, from deliberately constituted associations, and from cultural groups. By a structural group, she meant a group that is unified by the relationships of its members to external practices and materials rather than by relationships among members themselves. Not all structural groups are oppressed. Some are privileged. But structural groups differ from other social groups in that they cannot *act* as a group until they develop internal structures, processes, or other internal cohesiveness of their own. I turn next to a more extended look at the idea of a structural group.

4. STRUCTURAL GROUPS

Following Jean-Paul Sartre in the first volume of his very difficult late work, the *Critique of Dialectical Reason* (Sartre 1960, 1976), Young argues that some social collectivities are the result of oppressive social structures. Eventually she rejects the idea that social collectivities determine our identities. Her considered view is that we determine our own identities, although groups to which we belong (many of which we did not choose) "condition" us by delineating our options and the range of our possibilities (Young 1997, p. 31; 2000, p. 101). Groups into which we are born include much of what I call elsewhere luck in "the unnatural lottery" (Card 1996, p. 20). Rawls refers to the assets and liabilities with which one is born as one's luck in the *natural* lottery (Rawls 1999a, pp. 12–15). By the *un*natural lottery, I meant networks of unjust social institutions into the midst of which we are born, which, as parts of the basic structure of society, determine our starting points in life and consequently often our future prospects. Some of Young's paradigmatically oppressed groups (women in patriarchal society, for example) are heavily defined by a basic structure that includes the patriarchal family. Still, we make our own identities, she maintains, through our interactions and through the importance we attach to the groups to which we belong. For some of us, she notes, it is not group membership but significant events in our lives that become central to our identities.[8]

Young opened *Justice and the Politics of Difference* (Young 1990) with the question, "What are the implications for political philosophy of the claims of new group-based social movements associated with left politics – such movements as feminism, Black liberation, American Indian movements, and gay and lesbian liberation?" (Young 1990, p. 3). These political movements reveal the "differences" of that book's title: differences of gender or sex, race or ethnicity, sexuality. Yet groups based on these differences

---

[8] Support for the view that significant events, rather than groups, can become central to our identities, can be found in the work of novelist Kathryn Harrison, who says traumatized lives are often experienced as divided into a "before" and an "after" (see Harrison 2008, not fiction but true crime in the tradition of Truman Capote; see also her memoir, 1997).

form an odd list, as Young soon realized. Women, ethnic groups, and people identified by sexual orientation, as well as age groups and religious groups, which she adds a few pages later (Young 1990, pp. 42–43), are not all "groups" of the same order.

In the same treatise Young wrote, "A social group" is "a collective of persons differentiated from at least one other group by cultural forms, practices, or way of life," and she claimed that its members "have a specific affinity" with one another based on these things, which leads them to associate with each other either more than with those outside the group or in a different way (Young 1990, p. 43). Perhaps she was thinking of activist members of cultural groups, such as African American or American Indian groups, when she wrote that. But she soon came to draw distinctions among kinds of groups in light of such facts as that many women in patriarchal society appear to have no special affinity for women. Worse, a well-known result of oppression is horizontal hostility, that is, hostility between members of the same group. Yet, affinities are there, too, if only under the surface. As Adrienne Rich observed three decades ago:

"Women have always lied to each other."
"Women have always whispered the truth to each other."
Both of these axioms are true. (Rich 1979, p. 189)

A few years later, appreciating all this and more, Young borrowed Sartre's idea of "seriality" (Young 1994, 1997) from the first volume of his *Critique of Dialectical Reason* (Sartre 1976, pp. 256–341) and used it to illuminate social activities that produce groups. Such activities account for the truth in Simone de Beauvoir's famous observation that "One is not born, but rather becomes, a woman" (Beauvoir 1953, p. 273). Sartre distinguishes *series* from other social groups, illustrating series by the examples of people waiting in line for a bus and people listening to the radio. Bus riders and radio listeners are members of series that do not construct their members' identities. Nor do members share common characteristics or have a particular affinity for one another. Radio listeners may have no awareness of themselves as belonging to any social collectivity. Yet they are not a mere aggregate. The glue that binds them together is routine activity, habit, and materials that each engages for their own purposes. These things give rise to common interests and vulnerabilities. Young explores the idea that women, like radio listeners, are a series, or as she puts it, a serial collectivity. She identifies two basic "externalities" (her term) that unify women: a sexual division of labor and enforced, institutionalized heterosexuality (Young 1997, pp. 28–29).

Compulsory heterosexuality, together with a sexual division of labor that gives men considerable economic advantage, enables most men and some women to exploit women who play by the rules of heterosexuality. That is, it enables exploiters to appropriate the labor of many women, graft onto themselves the substance of many women, and so forth. To the extent that women play by these rules, they are complicit in the oppression, even when they lose by it. At the same time, the conjunction of these institutions (compulsory heterosexuality and a sexual division of labor) enables those who play by the rules to marginalize those who do not (lesbians, marriage resisters, and other unassimilable females). Resisters aim not to be complicit, although that is difficult when the social meanings of one's conduct are heavily determined by those whom one would resist. These externalities (compulsory heterosexuality and a sexual division of labor), in the ways they work together, are structures of the exploitation and oppression of women generally.

If Young is right that these institutions are key to the oppression of women, all who participate in them, lend them support, or endorse them are complicit. Not all who are complicit are culpable, and not all who are culpable are equally so. Yet even non-culpable complicity can give rise to an appropriate sense of responsibility to participate in efforts at repair. What Young called in her early work "faces" of oppression are, like masks, surfaces. Below the surface are institutions (compulsory heterosexuality, compulsory sexual divisions of labor) in which individuals participate or in which they are complicit, oppressive junctures of institutions that benefit individuals who willingly take advantage, and broader social structures that include individuals who may not participate directly in the institutions they endorse, ratify, and support.

At first, Young followed Sartre in reserving the term "social groups" for self-conscious unions that members of series ("serial collectivities") sometimes form deliberately. Series can be the background to the formation of new social groups. Members of a series sometimes unite deliberately in response to social structures in which they had previously participated unselfconsciously. One of Sartre's examples was bus riders who finally organize to protest fares or schedules. Before women's groups were consciously formed, "woman" was not an identity widely embraced by women (although "wife" was). We who are women tended to identify ourselves in terms of our relationships to significant others, mostly men. Men, in contrast, tended to identify themselves as butcher, baker, candlestick maker, and so on. We often signed our publications with initials and a patronym, even in countries where that custom does not prevail. We thought of ourselves as human beings. Not as women. We wanted to be perceived as human beings. Not as women. Men had no analogous problem, as everyone thought "man" was synonymous with "human." Yet even when "woman" became for some of us an important, even central, part of our identity, that was not because of a common female anatomy or psychology. It was because of the importance we placed on shared experiences of external structures – such as sexual divisions of labor and enforced heterosexuality – that gave us common interests (made us into a Sartrean serial collectivity).

Suppose those who benefit rather than lose from a practice have less motivation to notice the benefit until it is jeopardized. Suppose also that those who are harmed have more motivation to notice and eventually reflect on sources. It would not be surprising, then, if men were not motivated to identify themselves in terms of their sex or gender except when there was a danger of being perceived or treated as women. It would be easier for most men not to be aware of their conditioning by sexual divisions of labor and compulsory heterosexuality, which, of course, limit their options, too, but in ways that tend to benefit their development or autonomy. Not noticing, one takes the status quo to be natural, normal, and defends it against attack. Again, an omission becomes part of the agency of oppression: not noticing. Perhaps the agency here is not as passive as "omission" might suggest but takes the active form of ignoring. Noticing can be an act of rebellion that draws severe punishment.

In her later work, Young moves further from Sartre and develops her own vocabulary to mark differences in social groups. She distinguishes aggregates from associations and from social groups in a narrower sense of "social group." By an "association," she means what Sartre usually meant by a "social group," namely, a group formed deliberately, sometimes on the basis of a prior serial collectivity.[9] The American Philosophical Association, for example, is a deliberately formed group. Young then distinguishes associations from *social* groups, which are not founded or instituted by their members. Women, African Americans, and Caucasians are social groups, not deliberately founded. Finally, she divides social groups into structural ones and cultural ones. Ethnic groups are paradigmatic of cultural ones, whereas groups distinguished by gender, race, class, sexuality, or able-bodiedness are structural. It is less usual to join a social group (in

[9] Sartre is at first ambivalent about whether to call series groups. He does refer to them as groups ("groupe" and "groupement"; 1960, p. 310), but later reserves "group" for collectivities that can act.

this more specific sense) and more common to discover that one already belongs, even to several. Social groups are porous, not rigidly bounded. They overlap. They "emerge from the way people interact" (Young 1997, p. 90). "The attributes by which some individuals are classed together in the 'same' group appear as similar enough to do so only by the emergent comparison with others" (Young 1997, p. 90). Young cites as an example the Maori, who, prior to the British conquest of New Zealand, "saw themselves simply as belonging to dozens or hundreds of groups with different lineage and relation to natural resources" (Young 1997, p. 90). That example reminds me of a student in my "Feminism and Sexual Politics" class long ago who remarked, "I did not know I was Cuban until I came to the United States."

The example of the Maori suggests that cultural groups can also be at least partly structural. Instead of distinguishing cultural groups from structural groups, we might distinguish structural from cultural *aspects* of social groups, noting that the structural aspects consist of relationships created by externalities, whereas the cultural aspects are internal.

The ingenious idea that women are a highly structural group is an interesting way to make concrete Frye's proposal in her later work (Frye 1992, pp. 59–75) that what unify women into a non-arbitrary category are overlapping patterns rather than shared characteristics. Our relationships to externals form patterns, whereas "characteristics" would suggest that "it's something (internal) about the women." The patterns of interaction structured by the intersections of enforced sexual divisions of labor with enforced heterosexuality are excellent candidates to play the role of unifying women into a non-arbitrary category. No doubt there are other practices that contribute as well. Yet these two are likely keys to much else. Rape as a terrorist institution, for example, is one of the enforcers of heterosexuality.

Young's idea that compulsory heterosexuality and the sexual division of labor are the unifiers of the structural collectivity "women" implies that we are actually formed into women by oppressive practices, which, as women, we then help to maintain. The socially supported roles of women, embraced by most women much of the time, are critical parts of the structure of women's oppression. What it means to be a woman, on this view, is to be someone who interacts, or is supposed to interact, with men and with other women according to one or more of these roles, someone who does, or is supposed to do, certain kinds of work rather than others, who has, or is supposed to have, sexually intimate relationships with men (at least one), and so on. The etymology of "woman" ("wifman" in Anglo-Saxon) supports this view. Women were literally wives, eventually people who were supposed to be or were expected to become wives. Wives as a group were defined by the structures of compulsory heterosexuality and by sexual divisions of labor.

Who, then, or what, is oppressed? Who is molded, immobilized, reduced by these social structures? What would that being be like without oppression? Who can say? John Stuart Mill cautioned, in the first chapter of *The Subjection of Women*, that no one is in a position to say what would be an entirely natural development for human females (and, by implication, for human males as well) since none of us has been able to observe female development outside the contexts of oppressive social structures (Mill 2002, p. 144). Who, then, becomes a woman? Beauvoir: one does. "One is not born, but rather becomes, a woman" (Beauvoir 1953, p. 273; "On ne naît pas femme: on le devient," Beauvoir 1949, vol. I, p. 285). "Women are oppressed" is a tautology if there are no women apart from oppressive social structures, as there are no bus riders without buses and schedules and so forth. Women would disappear if those oppressive practices were abolished. We would not cease to exist. We would cease to be women. Who knows what we would become? If groups deliberately formed by women were to perpetuate the existence of "women" as descendants who inherit a certain past, "woman" would have changed its meaning. It would have evolved.

Would there be no lesbians if women did not exist? To whom are lesbians attracted? Mostly women, not just lesbians. Young's account of structural groups throws light on the radicalesbian feminist debate over whether lesbians are women. Insofar as lesbians cease to participate in the sexual division of labor and enforced heterosexuality, there are grounds for regarding lesbians as not women. Decades ago, Monique Wittig took that position, maintaining, in what was a maverick idea when she first espoused it, that a lesbian has to be a not-woman (Wittig 1992, pp. 9–20). And yet, whether lesbians have been conditioned by practices that form so many of us into women is not entirely a function of our choices. Molding begins long before we have developed our capacities for choice. Sexuality aside, many lesbians learn very early to "handle" men in stereotypically feminine ways. And so, except where such behavior is a deliberate act, one can also argue that many lesbians are also women, despite our choices. Most of us who identify as lesbian were raised to become women and are treated as women by most of the people we know, despite our resistance to marriage and sexual divisions of labor.

If the sexual division of labor and compulsory heterosexuality ceased to exist, there might indeed be no lesbians. All that means is that there might be no basis to classify parties to same-sex intimate relationships as members of a social group, any more than there is currently any basis for classifying left-handed people as members of a social group (as there might be if lefties' needs were systematically acknowledged in social practice).

Young begins to address responsibility for structural oppression in her last book, *Global Challenges*, taking a basically forward-looking approach (Young 2007, pp. 159–86). She supports including the oppressed in decisions that affect them. She suggests that one's responsibilities in regard to past oppression be determined simply by available resources and opportunities rather than by past activity. That suggestion runs counter to the responsibilities I feel to *create* resources and *make* opportunities for resistance and repair on the basis of my past and present as a beneficiary of and participant in structural evils. There is a need for further work here on distributing justly the burdens of social change. Young worries that concern with past activity leads to blaming and alienates those blamed, a disadvantage when their cooperation is needed for change. Yet, alienation cuts both ways. In distributing burdens of change, failure to distinguish beneficiaries from non-beneficiaries, culpable from non-culpable, and complicity from non-complicity can alienate non-beneficiaries, the non-culpable, and the non-complicit. Everyone's cooperation may be needed for social change.

My objective here is not to define a just distribution of the burdens of change but to make progress in clarifying some of the agency components in institutional and structural evils. And so, I turn next to a closer look at varieties of individual complicity in such evils.

5. COMPLICITY IN EVIL PRACTICES

Return to the point that not all complicity makes a causal contribution to harm. In his well-known essay on collective responsibility, Joel Feinberg notes that "in the standard case of responsibility for harm, there can be no liability without contributory fault." Vicarious liability and collective liability, on his view, are non-standard cases (Feinberg 1970, pp. 222–51). In vicarious responsibility, one becomes complicit through one's relationship to the person(s) who did the wrong. By "collective liability", Feinberg means "the vicarious liability of an organized group ... for the actions of its constituent members" (Feinberg 1970, p. 233). Feinberg distinguishes several forms of collective liability in terms of the presence or absence of fault, its distribution, and whether the fault contributes to a harm. A group can be liable, he notes, through the fault of some but not all members, through the *non-contributory* fault of each member, through the contributory fault of each member, or through the collective but *non-distributive* fault of the group itself (Feinberg 1970, p. 233). Each of these ways that a group can be liable suggests corresponding ways that an individual can be complicit in group activity.

To illustrate non-contributory fault, Feinberg mentions cases in which the absence of any causal linkage to the harm is only a lucky accident, "reflecting no credit on the person who is at fault" (Feinberg 1970, p. 241). For example, everyone who drank heavily at the party drove home, but only one hit a pedestrian – a case of moral luck, like that of Thomas Nagel's truck drivers who failed to have their brakes checked (Nagel 1979, p. 29). In Feinberg's case, it would not be inappropriate for other members of the party to consider themselves complicit, even though they did not contribute causally. Or did they, by omission (if omission can be a cause)? They might have had it in their power to prevent the accident. As a group, they failed to provide a safe way home for drinkers. Or they failed, as a group, to set moderate limits to consumption. A better example of non-contributory harm would be what Kutz calls ratification (Kutz 2007); in this kind of case, ratification of the problematic conduct, which might be exhibited in sentimental stories and jokes about drinking told uncritically after the party.

To illustrate collective but non-distributive fault, Feinberg mentions the Jesse James train robbery and the philosophy department case presented in section 1 above. He judges in the Jesse James case, first, that it would take a hero to fight back (and one cannot be faulted for not being a hero) and second, that a group might be faulted for not producing a hero or for not having a contingency plan (Feinberg 1970, p. 248).

Going beyond Feinberg's view, Kutz defends a complicity principle according to which complicity does not depend on the difference one's participation makes causally and does not presuppose even that one had the power to prevent the harm or the wrong. He cites cases that support the view that the extent of one's accountability need not be proportionate to one's causal contribution. Kutz's complicity principle states that "I am accountable for what others do when I intentionally participate in the wrong they do or the harm they cause" "independently of the actual difference I make" (Kutz 2000, p. 122). He explicitly rejects (1) the "individual difference principle," which says "I am accountable for a harm only if what I have done made a difference to that harm's occurrence" and "only for the difference my action alone makes to the resulting state of affairs", and (2) the "control principle," which maintains that "I am accountable for a harm's occurrence only if I could control its occurrence, by producing or preventing it" (Kutz 2000, pp. 116–17). Kutz's complicity principle does not imply that causal contributions and control are irrelevant, only that they are not necessary and that they cannot explain why in certain common cases we regard individuals as complicit.

Two kinds of complicity in evil have particularly engaged my attention. They are, first, victim complicity and, second, what might be called "legally innocent complicity," or, less cumbersomely, "lawful complicity." In both, complicity may or may not involve a causal contribution to harm. But the individual who does contribute is not ordinarily in a position to control whether harm occurs. Victim complicity is a sensitive topic, as it raises questions about the culpability of persons who have suffered a great deal or acted under great stress. I have written on that topic elsewhere (Card 2002, pp. 211–34). My focus here is lawful complicity, especially when it is morally culpable. Lawful complicity can overlap with victim complicity.

By lawful complicity, I have in mind conduct that tends to aggravate the harm of others' crimes but is not itself unlawful and apart from its aggravating function, would not be harmful, or not very. Most of it ought not to be criminalized. Examples are abundant in everyday racism and sexism, not only in speech but in exercising many preferences that people have a legal right to exercise.

Widespread everyday racist or misogynous conduct that is not unlawful creates an environment in which physical assaults against members of racial minorities and against women become far more harmful than they might have been. When perpetrators can count on a high probability of getting away with the crime (or a light sentence if caught) and so are frequently and in substantial numbers undeterred, their crimes can set a norm. Potential targets then live in a climate of fear and violence. Assaults in such a climate do more harm to both direct and indirect victims than otherwise similar assaults in an environment in which women's human rights are as respected as men's. This climate is the "violence" that is Young's fifth "face of oppression."

Yet much everyday racist and sexist behavior is not and should not be unlawful. Refusing to socialize with or live in the same neighborhoods as members of another race are examples of racism that are not unlawful (although in the US real estate agents and business proprietors are prohibited from taking certain steps to encourage those choices). Stereotyping that overtly insults and defames members of stigmatized groups is more serious. But in the US such stereotyping is not actionable if it does not target particular individuals. Misogyny that is not unlawful is illustrated by many verbal put-downs, name-calling, and sexist jokes. More serious is pornography that portrays violence against women as sexually exciting. Yet, in the US, none of these activities is unlawful. Mill's arguments in the second chapter of his essay "On Liberty" are often cited – rightly or wrongly – in support of the US position (Mill 2002, pp. 17–56).

Still, misogynous activities, institutions, and practices that are not unlawful aggravate the harm done by crimes against women. Consider the institution of violent pornography. Consumers enable the pornography industries and pornographic entertainment to continue publicly. Public support for violent pornography is part of a climate that gives potential assailants reason to believe they can harm women with relative impunity, that witnesses will probably not intervene or testify, prosecutors will have other priorities, judges will go easy, and so on. Enablers include men who are neither violent nor consumers but who knowingly associate with, even do business with, men who are, treating that fact as none of their concern.[10] The enabling support of friendships and business relationships need have no causal connection to particular violent crimes. But continued overtly friendly association with perpetrators sends a social message that "these guys are okay," which supports their morale and influences how others treat them. Most who continue such associations sound like what Kutz calls "ratifiers," accessories after the fact except that they do nothing unlawful and what they ratify is the appearance of respectability in men who deserve less, not directly the particular deeds in virtue of which those men deserve less. Enablers and ratifiers also include women who have internalized misogyny for survival and who judge *a priori* that a woman who is raped or battered was probably "asking for it."

Social scientists disagree about the causal effects of violent pornography. Some hold the "safety-valve theory" that imaginative enactments of violence create a safe outlet in fantasy for impulses that might otherwise be enacted in reality. Others hold that fantasies of violence increase the likelihood of real violence. Both could be wrong. In any case, that dispute focuses on the individual fantasizer: will a "safety-valve" fantasy work?

---

[10] Social workers, priests, therapists, and others who try to change the behavior and attitudes of violent men are not (ordinarily) enablers. They support the perpetrator without ignoring or intentionally supporting the violence. The final season of *The Sopranos* television serial questions, however, the extent to which they can succeed in not becoming enablers in the case of career criminals (Season 6, Part 2, 2007).

Or will the fantasizer cease to distinguish fantasy from reality? But the problem is not so individual. Common knowledge of the pervasive enjoyment of violent pornography effectively nullifies *external* inhibitors of whatever impulses there may be to violence against women. Public support for violent pornography is among factors that cumulatively send a social message to potential assailants that even though such assaults are technically criminal, they are not really regarded as socially beyond the pale, that assailants can expect impunity or a token punishment, that lots of women find it exciting, and so on. The failures here to separate fantasy from reality are collective failures, not (or not simply) individual psychoses.

The harm of such a climate is not only to women who are assaulted. All women are governed to some extent by the fear or knowledge that they might be, although the danger tends to be greater the more marginalized a woman is. Worse is a woman's fear or knowledge that she can probably do little about it and that probably no one else can or will, either. Again, this factor tends to be more severe the more marginalized a woman is. Not only is female mobility circumscribed but more serious damage is done in the morale-destroying realization that one's basic human rights can be so ignored without effective recourse. Some do not appreciate the direness of their predicament until they are assaulted or a friend is. Yet the dangers are real.

Had assailants no good reason to think they could get away with it, there would no doubt still be rapists and batterers, just as there may always be robbers and murderers. Not everyone puts a high value on prudence. But the inevitable assailants would be in no position to set a violent norm. Vulnerability to their violence would not become a face of oppression. Assault victims are less destroyed morale-wise in a society that vindicates their human rights.

In a misogynous climate, assailants acquire the power to shatter victims' lives. The misogyny of others is sufficient to give them that power. Ironically, perpetrators of violent crime against women need not be misogynous themselves, just as those who assault the elderly, children, or people in wheelchairs need not have anything against old or young people or people with disabilities. They need only have an eye for an easy victim. Misogynous environments give assailants good reason to believe they can get away with it, whatever their motives. Thus public support for violent pornography can be a factor in women's vulnerability to assault even by men who are not consumers of pornography. The same climate renders women vulnerable to many sorts of victimization (financial, for example), not just sexual.

Culpable complicity is a sensitive issue in the case of women whose internalized misogyny helps them survive. At the same time that it works for some women for survival, it aggravates and re-entrenches sexist practices. It thereby contributes to harms to all women, including those it helps to survive. Misogynous women are legally innocent complicit victims. Since they already suffer from the harm they do, perhaps they should also be less answerable morally to others. To some extent, they "answer" for it already.

Although I have referred to the *contributions* of the complicitous behavior described above, it may not be clear whether those contributions are rightly regarded as causal. Do complicit enablers contribute causally to the violence they enable? Whether they do depends on what counts as causal. Enablers certainly do not determine assailants to rape or batter women. Assailants make that decision themselves. But the reasoning of potential assailants is apt to be influenced by enablers whose behavior sends the message that they can probably get away with it, should they be so inclined.

CHAPTER 4

To whom (or to what) can evils be done?

> The atrocity paradigm can make sense of ecological evils the victims
> of which include trees and even ecosystems. (Card 2002, p. 16)

Much of this chapter is devoted to clarifying what it means for non-
sentient entities, including plants, species, and ecosystems, as well as
human groups, to *suffer harm* (as distinct from being wronged) and what
it means for that harm to be intolerable. More of this chapter is taken
up with plant life, species, and ecosystems than with human groups.
But chapters 9 and 10 revisit at greater length issues of harm to human
groups. Environmental atrocities are not represented in Part II of this
book, although torture of laboratory animals is considered in chapter 8.
Yet, in responding to atrocities, it is important to avoid not only evils to
other people but environmental atrocities as well. It is part of the agenda
of this chapter to give sense to environmental atrocities as not entirely
human-centered or even pain-centered. Thinking about harm to human
groups, insofar as they are not sentient entities, benefits from thinking
about harm to non-sentient entities in the natural environment. And so,
most of the focus in this chapter on harm to human groups is reserved to
the penultimate section.

I. CONTEXTS AND PROBLEMATIC CASES

In *The Atrocity Paradigm*, I baldly asserted that evils are done to trees and
ecosystems and then deferred indefinitely the task of explaining how or
what that would mean. Some may find, in the end, only one clear (and, at
that, hypothetical) sense in which trees and ecosystems can be victims of
evils. If they can suffer intolerable harms, they can sometimes suffer those
harms as a result of inexcusable wrongs to sentient beings. But can evils be
done to trees and ecosystems as a result of inexcusable wrongs that do *not*
do intolerable harm to sentient life? Can harm to trees or ecosystems be
part of what makes a deed evil, independently of interests that people or

other animals have in the harmed entities?[1] Can non-sentient life ever be wronged?

And what about human groups? Corporations and nations, for example, are non-sentient entities. They are defined by principles, values, relationships, and rules that govern their sentient members. These connectors and governors enable corporations and nations to survive complete turnovers of their memberships. Corporate bodies have interests. They act, thrive, and suffer setbacks. But do they suffer evils? Do only their (sentient) members suffer evils? What about groups that lack an internal structure enabling them to act as a unit but that nevertheless transcend their current members temporally in both directions – peoples, ethnic groups, for example? Are evils to such groups reducible to the wrongs and harms suffered only by living members?

My pre-philosophical sense is that many of the worst harms inexcusably inflicted by human agents have been to the natural environment, including species, ecosystems, and animals, and to human groups, not just individuals but families, communities, racial and ethnic groups, and nations. How much of that sense can survive philosophical scrutiny? Under what interpretation does it survive, if so? This chapter takes on such questions. In doing so, it problematizes my previous claims (heading this chapter) about trees and ecosystems, and raises more questions than it can answer in a fully satisfying way. There is no easy way to summarize my conclusions more specifically.

Because the atrocity theory analyzes evils into a harm component and a wrongdoing component, the question to whom evils can be done naturally breaks down into two questions of scope: (1) who or what can suffer intolerable *harm*, and (2) who, or what, can be inexcusably *wronged*? I set aside questions of scope regarding who or what can *do* evil. I would not dismiss as unworthy of consideration, however, the idea that higher primates, elephants, dolphins, perhaps even wolves and bears, might be capable of a rudimentary morality, including the rudiments of evil-doing.[2] But the only doers with which this book is concerned are human beings and groups that are capable of agency. Were there a justifiable moral presumption against doing intolerable harm to just any entity that is capable

---

[1] Hereafter, "animals" means "non-human animals."

[2] The idea that some mammals other than humans are capable of a degree of moral agency is taken seriously by Frans de Waal in his work on primates (de Waal 1989, 1996) and by Arne Naess (1979) in an essay on a community that included bears, sheep, and wolves, as well as humans. Some birds may deserve such consideration as well, given Irene M. Pepperberg's research on gray parrots (Pepperberg 2002, 2008).

of suffering it, violating that presumption sans excuse or justification would be an evil. There would then be no conceptual difficulty with the idea of evils to the natural environment and to some human groups. Yet we will shortly encounter good reason to reject as unjustifiable a general presumption against doing intolerable harm to just any entity capable of suffering it.

Some harms to certain kinds of human groups are best understood as harms to individuals that depend, for their explanation, on the group membership of the individuals. Daniel Hausman and Larry May find this true of groups that lack an internal structure enabling them to act (Hausman 2008, pp. 159–60; May 1987, pp. 135–55). Here, they find, harm to the group distributes to its members. Mostly, but not entirely, that is how I treat genocide in chapters 9 and 10. Ethnic groups that lack sufficient structure to enable them to act tend also to transcend their living members, although living members are the only ones who can be harmed as members. Ethnic groups, like internally structured groups that can act, such as states and baseball teams, survive generational replacements of their members. They have a history of members who no longer exist and so can no longer be harmed but whose (past) lives still contribute to the vitality and meaning of the group and its potentialities. A group's history can be lost or irreparably distorted. Ethnic groups transcend their living members toward an open future of potential descendants. That future can be closed by genocide. But potential members cannot yet be harmed. Is harm to the group, then, only harm to living members of current generations?

Is there a harm also to humanity when a people is destroyed, degraded, or lost, as W. E. B. DuBois argued in his early essay on the conservation of races (DuBois 1970, pp. 76–85)? That harm to an ethnic group can be more than what is suffered by currently living members of the group is suggested by Hannah Arendt's claim, in the summation of her report on Adolf Eichmann, that genocide is "first of all, a crime against mankind" that violates "an altogether different order and an altogether different community" than is violated by the crime of murder (Arendt 1965, p. 272). But then, what is "mankind" or "humanity"? Is it also a group? Is harm to humanity simply harm to currently living human beings considered as members of humanity? Is it harm to something larger that includes potentialities that outstrip those of currently existing individuals, and histories that may or may not matter to current members? Chapters 9 and 10, which take up genocide, and section 7 of this chapter return to these and other questions about ethnic groups.

The question of whether evils can be done to individual animals has not usually been about their vulnerability to *harm*. Apart from René Descartes and a few contemporary die-hard Cartesians who seriously doubt that animals are conscious, the philosophical question has usually been whether animals can be *wronged* and if so, how.[3] The common-sense view is that cruelty to animals is at least presumptively wrong and can be inexcusable, and that such cruelty is wrong not merely, as Immanuel Kant thought, because it makes us cruel to human beings, but that it is wrong on the basis of *the animals'* suffering, not ours (Kant 1930, pp. 239–41). But the idea that animals actually have *rights* and so are vulnerable to injustices remains a minority view, albeit one that merits more attention than it usually receives.[4] Still, it is clear that some animals *deserve* better treatment than they frequently receive from human beings. Like human servants, animals that perform services for human beings deserve to be cared for when they can no longer serve. An animal that can bond with human beings and enter into relationships of trust is vulnerable to not only pain but betrayal. If an animal can be inexcusably betrayed or made to suffer intolerable gratuitous or unwarranted suffering, evils can be done to it directly. Disagreements tend to be about what is gratuitous or unwarranted and whether a dependent animal is capable of trust, rather than about those general ideas. Philosophically more interesting are the cases of plants, species, and ecosystems.

Plants, species, and ecosystems are not vulnerable to cruelty, because they are non-sentient. Nor does the concept of trust apply literally to them. Yet there are rudiments of trust: plants, species, and ecosystems can become dependent on us as a result of our interventions. When that happens, they may cease to evolve self-protective capacities. They then can become much more easily vulnerable to destruction and degradation. Gratuitous or unwarranted destruction or degradation of forests and aquatic ecosystems not only harms the animals whose habitats they provide but reveals a lack of respect for nature more generally. If not obviously a moral failing, that lack of respect is not a merely aesthetic failing, either. It is a failure

---

[3] For Descartes's views, see selections in Regan and Singer (1976, pp. 60–66) from Descartes's *Discourse on Method* Part v and from two letters he wrote to contemporaries. Oddly, although Descartes refers to animals as automata and calls the body a machine, he also attributes to animals (in one of the letters) the emotions of fear, hope, and joy (Regan and Singer 1976, p. 64). For a contemporary Cartesian view of animals, see Carruthers (1992, pp. 170–96).

[4] The classic defense of moral rights for animals (at least, mammals over the age of two) and the most thorough critique of the Cartesian view is Regan (1983). A further developed proposal regarding interspecific justice is VanDeVeer (1979).

to value the natural environment other than for its utility, entertainment value, or aesthetic value for us.[5] That attitude is arrogant, and arrogance is an ethical, if not moral, failing.[6] Although some Christian traditions include the idea of a (human) stewardship of nature, European Americans have, on the whole, lacked norms of respect for nature, unlike the ethics of some Native American peoples. If non-sentient life is vulnerable to intolerable harm, the view that there is at least a presumption against inflicting such harm gains in plausibility, although more needs to be said to make the case. That vulnerability to intolerable harm is insufficient to make the case is shown by the case of evil organizations.

Systems and species, like organizations, can sometimes be destroyed or abolished without killing. Some can be destroyed without any harm to members, certainly without harming all of them. An organization oppressive to its members or others can be forcibly disbanded. Species can be systematically "crossed" with other species. Ecosystems can be dismantled and their components transported and re-established elsewhere. If the result is healthy and well integrated in the case of plant species and ecosystems, it is difficult to find any harm done. The case can be otherwise with an organization that is forcibly disbanded or whose members are transplanted to another environment. Those changes in an organization can be good for outsiders but irreparably harmful to the organization and its members. The organization, an entity capable of thriving and suffering setbacks, can take an irreversible hit with such intervention, putting an end to its functioning. Its heavily invested members can suffer irreversible setbacks. Yet, if the organization is evil, not only is destroying it justifiable "all things considered" but there is no general moral presumption to overcome against doing so. Destroying an evil organization needs, as an end, no justification, although the means used require justification, as the rights of individuals impose constraints.

The organization that came to be known around 1940 as "Murder, Inc." or "the Mob," and a decade later as "the Syndicate," was a "fantastic ring of killers and extortionists" that constituted organized crime in the US (Turkus and Feder 1951, p. xi; see, also, the film *Murder, Inc.*, 1960). Its members included Lucky Luciano, Frank Costello, Dutch Schultz, and Bugsy Siegel. Burton B. Turkus and Sid Feder report that in a ten-year

---

[5] The most well-developed and nuanced philosophical defense of the idea that lack of respect for nature is truly a moral failing is Taylor (1986).

[6] Etymologically, ethics (Greek for "habit") pertains to individual character, morals (from the Latin *mores*) to social norms. Moral philosophers, like the general public, often do not make that distinction. In this context, the distinction may be apt.

period Murder, Inc. was responsible for one thousand murders "from New England to California, Minnesota to New Orleans and Miami" (Turkus and Feder 1951, pp. 1–2). The Syndicate used murder to maintain "every known form of rackets and extortion," and "there was no method of murder their fiendish ingenuity overlooked" (Turkus and Feder 1951, pp. 1–2). Such an organization not only does not deserve to survive but has no claim, even initially, to moral respect.

Hereafter, I refer to the issue of atrocious organizations as "the Murder, Inc. problem." It is a problem for any theory that holds that if an entity is capable of thriving or doing well and is thereby vulnerable to harm, it has at least a prima facie claim to respect. Were there such a claim, there would be, correspondingly, a justifiable moral presumption against harming that entity. Murder, Inc. is a counter-example to that thesis. It is not that the claim of Murder, Inc. to respect is overridden. There is no such claim to override. Whether an organization has any moral claim to respect, independently of respect due the humanity of its members, depends on the nature, purpose, or unifying principles of the organization and whether it contains effective procedures for self-correction and moral improvement. If an organization's defining purpose, principles, and procedures are incompatible with fundamental moral values, there is no moral presumption of respect for it. The Southern Poverty Law Center (SLPC), as a matter of policy, bankrupts white supremacist organizations through lawsuits, making it impossible for those groups to function. That SLPC policy needs to overcome no defensible moral presumption of respect for the organizations it disables but only to make sure it disables them with due respect for the humanity of individuals, which it does by taking them to court rather than retaliating with vigilantism.

The Murder, Inc. case shows that harm is not always a wrong-making characteristic. Although harm and wrong are distinct elements of an evil, neither reducible to the other, they are not always entirely independent of each other, either. Reasonably foreseeable intolerable harm is often a huge part of why a deed is inexcusably wrong. A deed for which there might be some excuse were it not intolerably harmful can become inexcusably wrong when it foreseeably does intolerable harm. But in the case of organizations such as Murder, Inc., intolerable harm to the organization does not contribute to any wrong or count against the justifiability of the deed that inflicts it. Morally speaking, the organization cannot be wronged, although its members can be, and those who would destroy it can be morally constrained by other factors.

Does the Murder, Inc. problem arise only for a deliberately created organization whose purpose, defining rules, and structure are incompatible with basic moral values? What about animals and non-sentient living beings that are not immoral but just plain dangerous to the health and well-being of humans and many other animals? Rodents and lice transmit fatal diseases and are often exterminated for that reason. Do such exterminations require justification? Some plants are poisonous or in other ways hinder human health and are likewise killed for that reason. Does that practice require justification? Or, is danger a context in which *respect* for the organism perceived to be its source becomes *important*? Clearly, disease carriers and noxious plants can be intolerably harmed, and disease-causing organisms can be destroyed. Can they be wronged? Does danger function here the way evil functions in Murder, Inc. to exempt certain living beings from any presumption of respect? Is danger more fundamental than evil even in Murder, Inc.?

A reason to think that danger is not more fundamental is that many human groups can be dangerous to one another, and yet that does not make them unworthy of respect when they are not committed to evils, their basic principles and values are good, and they have means of self-correction and moral improvement. But are there analogous mechanisms of self-correction in animals that can become gratuitously dangerous to others? Perhaps so, at the level of the species. It is individual lice or rodents that become dangerous to humans and other animals, not the species. Perhaps the species deserves respect even when some specimens do not. At present, I do not try to justify a presumption of respect for even such species. Rather, I shift the burden of justification: why *not* presume worthiness of respect for the species even of lice and rodents? In the case of Murder, Inc., the answer is clear. It is not just dangerous. It is an evil. In the cases of species of rodents and lice, there is no comparably satisfying answer to "why not?"

It may not be necessary to answer comprehensively the question who or what can be wronged in order to answer the question to whom or to what evils can be done. Strictly speaking, the definition of evils as reasonably foreseeable intolerable harms produced by inexcusable wrongdoing (or wrongs) does not specify whether the entity harmed must also be the entity wronged. Many inexcusable wrongs to human beings also do intolerable harm to animals, plant life, and human groups. If a deed that inexcusably wrongs one person but does reasonably foreseeable intolerable harm only to another can be an evil, then perhaps a deed that inexcusably wrongs a sentient being but does intolerable harm only to non-sentient entities could also be an evil. There would be a disconnect in such evils between the elements of harm and wrongdoing: the party harmed would not be identical with the party wronged. Thus, if the US was inexcusably wrong to go to war in Vietnam, the massive deforestation accomplished there by the use of Agent Orange might have been an evil not simply in virtue of the resulting harm to Vietnamese people but also in virtue of foreseeable intolerable harm to the natural environment. Likewise, a major oil spill that results from inexcusable negligence might be an evil not simply in depriving fishing communities of livelihoods and aquatic animals of habitats but in its intolerable harm to entire oceanic ecosystems. If, however, non-sentient life is not only vulnerable to harm but also worthy of respect, there remains no conceptual barrier to the idea of evils to non-sentient life or any need for disconnect between the wrong and the harm. The final section of this chapter returns to these issues to raise questions about the disconnect idea and whether it is even needed, in the event that it proves impossible to sustain the judgment that non-sentient entities can be wronged.

Social philosophers, especially philosophers of law and philosophers who work in genocide studies, have analyzed harms to human groups. At the same time, environmental philosophers have done substantial work on the idea of harms to the natural environment, including species and ecosystems. Yet, there has not been a lot of exchange between philosophers working in these different areas regarding issues of harm to non-sentient entities, even though both groups of philosophers encounter such issues. The remainder of this chapter draws on and brings together ideas from both of these areas.

2. HARM AND WELL-BEING

Writing as a philosopher of law, Joel Feinberg maintains that harms are *setbacks to interests* (1984, pp. 31–36) and that other uses of the term "harm" are derivative. He understands "interests" as presupposing desires, wants, or caring, at least the having of an objective or goal. This understanding of harm applies not just to individuals but also to human groups that have purposes and an internal organization designed to further those purposes. Philosophical work on group activity has made excellent sense of group intention and group planning (Bratman 1999; Gilbert 1989; Tuomela 2002). But an understanding of harm that presupposes the existence of desires, wants, or aims dismisses too quickly as "merely derivative" the possibility of harms to the natural environment, to ecosystems, and to plants.

Feinberg dismisses as "derivative or extended" the sense of harm according to which "by smashing windows, vandals are said to harm property; neglect can harm one's garden; frost does harm to crops" (1984, p. 32). Like Immanuel Kant, he lumps together plants (at least domesticated ones) with inanimate artifacts as having only use value or aesthetic value. Such entities have no interests, on his understanding of "interest."

A deeper notion, however, that underlies the importance of interests is the idea of well-being, having a good of one's own, being capable of doing well or doing poorly, thriving or not, of a being's existence *going* well or not (Parfit 1984, pp. 493–502). The satisfaction of interests gets value from what it contributes to well-being (not necessarily the well-being of the party whose interests are satisfied). Accordingly, a deeper conception of harm would regard it as a setback to the well-being of an entity that has a good of its own, is capable of doing well or poorly, thriving or not, of having its existence go well or not. Those ideas do not presuppose desires or caring. Even a tree can thrive or fail to. Setbacks to well-being tend to be more fundamental than setbacks to interests. Interests based on desires or aims may or may not be compatible with their owner's well-being (or the well-being of others).

It is also true that some interests are more important than setbacks to the well-being of the individual whose interests they are. Interests in Feinberg's sense, what we care about, can transcend the well-being of an individual, even that of many individuals – an interest in the pursuit of justice, for example, or in the thriving of one's nation (or one's Alma Mater). Such transcendent interests appear to rest on the idea of *some parties'* well-being. But when there is a setback to such an interest, it is not necessarily the interest-holder who is harmed. When there is a setback to justice, it is not primarily those who care about justice who are harmed but, rather, the victims of the injustice and the community within which the setback occurs. It is tempting to regard such transcendent interests as elements of the interest-holder's well-being, as Bishop Joseph Butler seems to do in his famous sermon on human nature (Butler 1983, pp. 46–57). Although there is some justification for doing so, still, a setback to such an interest does not ordinarily injure the party whose interest it is. Harm to one's Alma Mater is not an injury to oneself, however disappointed one may be. In law, it is not regarded as the sort of interest that gives the "interested" party standing to complain.

This point was pivotal in the famous Supreme Court case of *Sierra Club* v. *Morton* (1972), which provoked Christopher Stone to write his (now classic) essay, "Should Trees Have Standing?" (Stone 1974). The Sierra

Club lacked standing to bring suit for an injunction against Walt Disney Enterprises, which wanted to build a ski resort in Mineral King Valley in the Sequoia National Forest. The club certainly had a healthy interest in the conservation and sound maintenance of national parks and forests. Without disputing that point, the court deemed that harm to the national forest did not constitute an injury to the club or to its members.

A pre-publication copy of Stone's essay influenced Supreme Court Justice Douglas's dissenting opinion (also included in Stone 1974, pp. 73–84). What was needed, Douglas argued (following Stone's essay), for the desired injunction against Disney Enterprises was standing for the forest itself, the sort of status that would allow its interests to be represented by a guardian who could then sue on its behalf, as a guardian might sue on behalf of a child or a severely impaired adult. The forest is what would have been harmed, had Disney gone ahead with the resort. In the cases of plants, species, and ecosystems, the concept of an interest either is not useful or is just a way of referring to what contributes to the well-being of the entity in question. To be vulnerable to harm, it is not necessary to be capable of *taking* an interest. All that is necessary is that the being in question has a good of its own, a welfare, that it is capable of doing well, thriving, having its existence go well and so is, conversely, vulnerable to setbacks.

In a well-known essay in environmental philosophy, "On Being Morally Considerable" (1978), Kenneth Goodpaster put forward the view, fairly radical then, that *all living beings* deserve, on the basis of their having a good, or a well-being, to be taken into consideration for their own sakes by moral agents. This view is now known as ethical biocentrism. Distinguishing "moral considerability" (a matter of scope) from "moral significance" (a matter of weight), Goodpaster sets aside the question of what weight to attach to the good of non-human lives and thereby sets aside also questions of how to resolve conflicts between beings who have different kinds of lives. He comes out neither in favor of nor against biocentric *egalitarianism*, which requires equal weighting. Quoting Kenneth Sayre on living beings as having the "typifying mark" of a "persistent state of low entropy, sustained by metabolic processes for accumulating energy, and maintained in equilibrium with its environment by homeostatic feedback processes" (Sayre 1976, p. 91), Goodpaster proposes that "the core of moral concern lies in respect for self-sustaining organization and integration in the face of pressures toward high entropy" (Goodpaster 1978, p. 323). Thus, even non-sentient living beings (macro or micro) can constrain us morally if they have *interests* that define or give rise to a good, a well-being, that can be harmed.

For our purposes, Goodpaster's essay is interesting for its contributions to a theory of well-being. Interests, as he understands them, do not presuppose desires or the capacity to care. What is in an organism's interests is what that organism needs in order to survive, to do well, even flourish. What contributes to its good or well-being makes its life go well. Because he is concerned only with living beings, Goodpaster does not take up the case of collectivities, such as organizations. The case of human groups would have forced him, because of the Murder, Inc. problem, either to deny that an organization necessarily has a *good* of its own or to acknowledge that having a good of its own is insufficient to generate moral constraints.

Paul Taylor's book *Respect for Nature* (1986) develops a biocentric theory of the bases of moral respect. "Moral respect" for Taylor is comparable to what Goodpaster calls "moral considerability." Taylor understands living beings as "teleological centers of life," a concept that also seems to capture Sayre's "typifying mark" (that persistent state of low entropy, sustained by metabolic processes and maintained in a state of equilibrium with its environment, and so on). Being a teleological center of life, he holds, gives an entity an inherent worth that warrants respect. Unlike Goodpaster, Taylor does explicitly consider ecosystems and species. He rejects the idea that ecosystems and species have goods of their own, as distinct from the separate goods of their members, on the ground that they (unlike their members) are not teleological centers of life. Taylor acknowledges only a statistical sense in which a species might be said to be doing well or poorly. He does not consider the case of human groups.

It is unclear that Taylor *should* be committed to excluding ecosystems and species from having intrinsic worth. I defer to section 6 of this chapter the question whether there is a meaningful sense in which such entities might be regarded as alive (and so as teleological centers of life, after all). Regarding ecosystems, what Taylor explicitly rejects are holistic environmental theories that systematically subordinate the worth of individuals to that of their ecosystems. Yet an environmental theory holistic enough to recognize that ecosystems are not mere aggregates but have goods of their own could allow that both individuals *and* systems have intrinsic worth, bases for moral respect, without holding that in cases of conflict, the system necessarily takes precedence. Likewise, acknowledging that a species can do poorly or well in an other-than-statistical sense need not commit one to prioritizing the good of a species over that of a specimen.

A theory of well-being that goes beyond the beginnings sketched by Goodpaster and Taylor is that of Richard Kraut in *What Is Good and Why: The Ethics of Well-Being* (2007). Inspired by Aristotle, Kraut offers what he calls a "developmental" conception of well-being as flourishing. This conception does not presuppose capacities for rationality, sentience, or desire and hence is not limited to human and other animal life. Kraut's view is narrower in scope than that of Goodpaster, if there are living beings that lack the complexity presupposed by the idea of development (perhaps viruses, if they can truly be said to be alive). But Kraut's view also seems potentially wider in scope than Taylor's, if Kraut's developmental conception can apply to species and ecosystems and to certain kinds of human groups.[7] In working out an application to groups (which he has not yet done), Kraut would encounter the Murder, Inc. problem. The problem, recall, is not that Murder, Inc. cannot have a good of its own. The problem is that the fact that it can develop and even thrive (if not "flourish") and so is vulnerable to harm creates not even a presumption against harming it.

What does it mean, on Kraut's view, for an entity to have a good of its own? Kraut points out that is not sufficient that some things be good for the entity and others bad for it. For that is certainly true of a piano or a bicycle, which does not have a welfare. It does not do well or poorly. When a piano's "capacities" are in good working order, it can be played by those who know how. (Were it automated, one could program it or flip a switch to make it play.) But it does not play itself. Its capacities are realized only in the performances of others or, ultimately, through their control. A being that has a welfare performs – "does" – well or poorly *itself*, although it may require a supportive environment. As Aristotle put it, the being is self-moving, capable of bringing about change or alteration from within itself.[8]

On Kraut's view, the concept of harm applies meaningfully to non-sentient natural beings, such as plants, which have capacities for

---

[7] That groups can also flourish is an important idea in Cuomo (1998).

[8] This idea is not unproblematic. Actually, Aristotle claims that the general capacity for self-movement characterizes all natural objects, as distinct from artifacts: "Of things that exist, some exist by nature, some from other causes. 'By nature' the animals and their parts exist, and the plants and the simple bodies (earth, fire, air, water) ... All the things mentioned present a feature in which they differ from things which are *not* constituted by nature. Each of them has *within itself* a principle of motion and of stationariness (in respect of place, or of growth and decrease, or by way of alteration). On the other hand, a bed and a coat ... have no innate impulse to change," *Physics* II:1:192b 8–19 (Aristotle, 1947, p. 236). For Aristotle, specific capacities of various natural beings, rather than the general capacity for self-movement, distinguish living from non-living beings. Plants have specific capacities for nutrition, growth, and reproduction; animals have in addition capacities for locomotion, perception, and so on. If Aristotle was wrong to think earth, fire, air, and water capable of self-movement, his view of natural objects, insofar as it applies to living beings, might be regarded as a crude anticipation of Sayre's view of living systems as sustained by metabolic processes and homeostatic feedback systems, although Aristotle's view is less ecological than Sayre's.

nourishment, reproduction, and growth. The flourishing metaphor comes from plant life, not animal life. But can harm be *intolerable* for a being that lacks sentience, awareness, and will? Or, should we seek alternatives or supplements to the concept "intolerable" to capture the gravity of harm to non-sentient entities? The next two sections develop affirmative answers to both of those questions. Section 3 offers an objective normative sense of "intolerable" that does not presuppose sentience, awareness, or will. Section 4 invokes the concepts of decency and degradation to elucidate harms to non-sentient entities.

3. WHAT MAKES HARM INTOLERABLE?

Kathryn Norlock takes up the challenge to make sense of environmental evils within the terms of my atrocity theory of evil. She offers a nuanced interpretation that makes harms to non-sentient entities, such as species, plants, and ecosystems, evils only in virtue of the connections those entities have with sentient beings that suffer intolerable harm. Evils can be done to non-sentient beings only insofar as they stand in certain relationships to sentient beings as part of an ecosystem in which all members are what they are, in part, because of their relationships to other members of the system (Norlock 2004, pp. 90–91). The point, however, does not seem to be that an evil is done to a tree simply when it or a sentient organism to which it is connected *ceases to be what it was*. Sentience, not identity, seems to be what Norlock finds critical to the existence of an evil. And the harm component, not the wrongdoing component, is what troubles her in regard to non-sentient organisms. Based on the idea that even non-sentient life has inherent worth, she finds no difficulty in acknowledging that such entities can be mistreated (Norlock 2004, p. 88). Rather, she takes issue with the idea that wrongs to non-sentient life, considered simply in themselves, could ever rise to the level of evil because of the requirement that evils inflict intolerable harm. An ecosystem that did not include sentient organisms might be damaged or destroyed. But how could such harm be intolerable?

Three assumptions could make sense of this reluctance to acknowledge intolerable harm to non-sentient natural entities. The first is an interpretation of "intolerable suffering or harm" as felt experience. Second is an interpretation also of "intolerable" as involving the will and of "tolerating" as willing. Third is a fairly literal reading of "standpoint" in the idea that the harm of an evil must be intolerable "from the standpoint" of those who suffer it (Card 2002, p. 16). Lacking will, sentience, and perception, how can non-sentient entities *suffer* harm that is *intolerable* from their own *standpoints?* They cannot refuse to tolerate it. They cannot feel and so cannot experience severe suffering or distress. They cannot perceive and so cannot take a point of view or have a standpoint.

With respect to the first assumption, that intolerable suffering requires sentience, on Kraut's theory of well-being, there is no such requirement for harm to be grave. On Kraut's developmental theory of well-being, even very grave harm need not be felt. It need only be undergone, in that sense, suffered. The concept of suffering is ambiguous between "feeling pain" and "undergoing harm." To make sense of harm to non-sentient beings, it is necessary always to interpret suffering in the second sense, as harm undergone, and sufficient to interpret harm in the developmental sense, as a setback to well-being or development. One need not experience pain to suffer (undergo) severe setbacks. Setbacks are intolerable when they are irreversible, incompensable, and cannot be survived at a decent level of well-being. Harms are often painful, but they need not be, even in sentient beings.

Nor is painful harm necessarily worse than harm that is not felt. Painless harms can be equally great or greater when they disrupt or destroy capacities central to the meaning or value of a life. If Frances Farmer's biographer is correct in his surmise about the transorbital lobotomy performed on her in the 1940s without her informed consent, that surgery is an example of disruptive harm far worse than the substantial pain that she also endured in her stay at the hospital where the surgery was performed (Arnold 1979).[9] Likewise, the main harm she suffered from repeated insulin injections was probably brain damage, whether she knew it or not (her autobiography betrays no awareness), a worse harm than any discomfort she might have experienced from the injections.[10]

Although she may have been unaware of the worst harms done to her, Farmer remained capable of sentience and awareness. Some might wish to understand harms of which she was unaware as genuinely harms only

---

[9] Farmer (1914–70), a talented, beautiful, and feisty movie star with Communist friends, was involuntarily committed twice by her mother to the mental hospital at Steilacoom in Washington State in the 1940s (Farmer 1972). Her biographer believes Farmer was a victim of Walter Freeman's "transorbital lobotomy" (entry under the eyelid), after repeated applications of drugs, insulin shock, and electroshock failed to break her will (Arnold 1979, pp. 7–9, 158–61). Freeman's biographer (El-Hai 2005, pp. 241–42) seems unconvinced that Farmer was one of Freeman's lobotomy patients. In her autobiography (1972), Farmer recalls very little of her final stay at Steilacoom, although her account of her first stay there is vivid and detailed. Her best films include *Rhythm on the Range* (1936), *Come and Get It* (1936), *Toast of New York* (1937), and *Son of Fury* (1942).

[10] This autobiography (Farmer 1972) appears to have been heavily co-written by her close friend, Jean Ratcliffe, who was with Farmer during her last years. It is difficult to gauge from it what Farmer knew about what was done to her at Steilacoom.

because of what she *would* have experienced had she been aware. Yet such hypothetical conditionals are inadequate to capture the harm of a lobotomy (and perhaps that of the repeated insulin injections as well). For the operation affects what one *could* experience. If we understand the harm as a setback to her well-being, rather than as her felt experience of it (or even what she would have felt had she been aware), these examples suggest that beings with lives defined by capacities other than for sentience can also suffer major harm, independently of their connections to sentient beings, when those capacities are damaged. A tree, for example, might incur damage to its capacity for photosynthesis. That could be a fatal setback to the tree's well-being, independently of the tree's relationships to sentient organisms.

With respect to the second assumption, that the idea of intolerable harm presupposes that the harmed entity has the capacity to will, it is necessary also to distinguish different senses of "intolerable." In one sense, "intolerable" is the normative idea of what ought not to be tolerated, what no one ought to put up with. That idea does treat tolerating as an act of will. In a second sense, "intolerable" simply means unendurable. Endurance does not presuppose willing. All endurance need mean is survival.

Although the second sense comes closer than the first, neither captures the meaning of "intolerable" in the definition of evils as "reasonably foreseeable intolerable harm produced by inexcusable wrongs." First, "what ought not to be tolerated" refers to something that it would be wrong to do. But, in the definition of an evil, "intolerable harm" is not another way of saying what is wrong. "Produced by inexcusable wrongdoing" is not redundant in "intolerable harm produced by inexcusable wrongdoing." "Intolerable" qualifies the harm, not the wrong. The intended reading is normative. But it is a different normative reading from "what ought not to be tolerated." Rather, harm is intolerable when it prevents the party harmed from doing minimally well, from enduring at a certain threshold of well-being. Bare survival is not enough. Toleration here does not presuppose willing, although if the party harmed does have a will, it cannot willingly put up with intolerable harm and still do minimally well.

With respect to the third assumption, that intolerable harm can only be from the standpoint of the party harmed if that party is capable of taking a stand or point of view, it is possible to rephrase the intended point without relying on the idea of a standpoint. To make clear that "intolerable" applies to what the party harmed can tolerate, not to what others might be able to tolerate, it is natural to contrast intolerable "from the standpoint of the entity harmed" with intolerable "from the standpoint of others." As Norlock correctly notes, trees lack standpoints, literally; they have no points of view. The intent, however, behind "from their own standpoint" is a contrast with *disutility* (or disvalue) to others. That contrast can be expressed alternatively using the concept of "a good of its own," obviating any need to refer to standpoints. If a tree can have a good of its own, intolerable harm to a tree can be explicated as a grave setback to the tree's own good, as contrasted with major setbacks to the tree's usefulness.

An underlying concern may be the worry that it weakens the concept of evils to grant that harms to non-sentient entities can be evils, independently of their connections with sentient life. Weakening the concept of evils would undermine the contrast between evils and lesser wrongs. This might be Norlock's concern when she observes, "The atrocity paradigm encourages us to see evils as producing great suffering, not just for direct victims but even indirect victims, into whole generations, and it is this strong sense of suffering that gets lost in talking about evils against systems and such individual entities as trees" (Norlock 2004, p. 89). To recognize as evils the culpable infliction of intolerable harm to such entities as the forests in Vietnam (a whole generation of forests) also suggests that evils are more widespread than one might have thought.

Yet, as argued in chapter 1, the fact that an evil is widespread does not lessen its gravity. If anything, it intensifies the gravity. All that may be lessened is the likelihood that the harm will be *recognized* as an evil by contemporaries. The important issue is whether even great harms to non-sentient entities are grave enough to sustain a significant contrast with the harms of lesser wrongs to sentient beings. The next two sections of this chapter offer reasons to think that harms to non-sentient entities can be grave enough to sustain that contrast.

4. DEGRADATION AND THE CAPACITY APPROACH TO HARM

Kraut's idea of well-being as developmental has the potential to allay concerns about lessening the gravity of judgments of evil. His developmental view of the capacities that define different forms of life opens spaces for degrees of intolerable harm, a relational understanding of the beings that develop, and differential contributions by relational beings to potentially thriving communities. Grounded in an Aristotelian understanding of life, Kraut's account is largely (although not entirely) a capacity approach to well-being, as contrasted with the sentience approach that interprets well-being primarily as absence of pain or distress.[11] In comparison with the capacity approach, the sentience approach is relatively static and nearly one-dimensional. The capacities that ultimately matter to it are vulnerabilities to pain and distress (if vulnerabilities can be rightly called capacities). Pain and distress have many forms. But what matter to well-being are their intensity, duration, and probability, regardless of whether they are past, present, or future and regardless of whether the pain or distress is helpful or useless in any way except as a cause of, or means of averting, further pain or distress.

In contrast, on the capacity approach, doing well consists in a normal development over time with relatively unimpeded exercise of the capacities that make the organism the kind of being that it is and enable it to function in relationships with others and in environments supportive of its flourishing. Whether a level of functioning indicates a harm depends on the organism's level of development relative to what is normal for organisms of that kind, given its age and the kinds of capacities that define organisms of that kind. It may not be possible to determine whether an organism has been harmed without information regarding its past development and a prognosis for its future development. Harm consists in such things as retarding or preventing a normal development, setting it back or in other ways interfering with it, damaging the organism's basic capacities (including the capacity to develop new capacities), preventing the organism from exercising its developed capacities, or seriously hindering such exercise. *Intolerable* harm consists in gravely diminishing or destroying capacities central to the meaning or value of the organism's life.[12] Severe and prolonged pain impedes functioning. But ordinarily, pain is a warning that something (other than pain) is wrong and needs attention. It would be disastrous to lose the capacity to feel pain, or even the capacity to mind it. Insofar as pain is a warning, it is a good thing (even though we dislike it), although when it interferes with functioning and its warning is redundant, it can become a harm.[13]

---

[11] Kraut's view is complex. Absence of pain and distress is also important to his view of well-being. The capacity approach to well-being is well developed in economic theory and global justice theory. See Nussbaum and Sen (1993, pp. 30–53) and Nussbaum and Glover (1995, pp. 61–104).

[12] Such a view is also developed in the environmental philosophy of Attfield (1982, esp. pp. 48–51). Cf. Kraut (2007, p. 5), "For most living things, to flourish is simply to be healthy, to be unimpeded in its growth and normal functioning."

[13] For a fuller and more nuanced discussion of the value of pain and of minding it, see Kraut (2007, pp. 150–53). The disvalue of pain is not reducible to its ability to incapacitate.

According to the atrocity theory, intolerable harms are major deprivations of basics that make a life possible and tolerable or decent, or that make a death decent. Such deprivations can be accompanied by severe pain or other felt suffering. But those basics are what we need in order to function (develop and exercise our capacities) at a tolerable level; absence of pain is not sufficient, and it is not always necessary. Basics for human beings include access to non-toxic air, water, and food, sleep, freedom from severe and prolonged pain or humiliation and from debilitating fear, having affective ties with others, having the ability to make choices and act on them, and having a sense of one's worth (Card 2002, pp. 16–17). They include what environmental philosopher Donald VanDeVeer, in his essay on interspecific justice, calls "basic interests" (VanDeVeer 1979, pp. 55–70). VanDeVeer contrasts basic interests with interests that are serious although not basic and with peripheral interests, which are neither. The best way to understand this ranking – "basic," "serious," "peripheral" – is not in terms of felt intensities of desire but as degrees of importance of the contributions to welfare made by satisfying the interests. If what VanDeVeer calls basic interests are only what is strictly *necessary for survival*, then my basics include more, as mere survival does not suffice for a decent life. My basics would then include some of what VanDeVeer's essay considers (merely) serious. Failure to satisfy serious interests can significantly diminish a life's quality and may push it below a decent level.

Human beings do not tolerate well serious deprivations of such basics as non-toxic water, although how much is serious varies, within a range, depending on the amount and nature of the toxin, the health of the drinker, and so forth. By not tolerating it well, I do not mean that the sufferer necessarily *minds*. As a generalization, for human beings (regardless how they feel) it is intolerable to be seriously deprived of access to non-toxic air, water, and food, and so on. When deprivation exceeds a certain range, we do not function at all. Even pain tolerance is measurable partly by how seriously the sufferer's functioning is impaired (whether, for example, its immune system is seriously compromised by the stress). Likewise, we measure such harms as those of second-hand smoke more by how well the sufferer is able to function (for example, to resist upper respiratory illness) than by the extent to which those exposed mind it. Thus, basics can be understood as what is necessary for an organism to function at a decent level. A decent life (even a decent death) is not possible without some (not precisely specifiable) provision for such basics.

But what, one may ask, is "decent"? By "decent" I do not mean "morally decent." Nor do I mean "modest" as that adjective has been used to praise feminine decorum. I mean simply meeting minimal standards of quality. "Decent" is not a high term of appraisal. A decent life is just not bad. It will do, is acceptable, passes muster for the kind of thing it is. A decent death is not unnecessarily painful, disfiguring, lonely, humiliating, frightening, degrading, and so on.

The concept of degradation is helpful for elucidating decency without appeal to such concepts as will, sentience, or perception. Trees cannot, of course, be humiliated or frightened. But they can be disfigured and in other ways degraded. So can communities. To degrade, in its general sense, is to reduce in rank or diminish in capacity or value. Degradation is not a specifically moral concept, although there is moral degradation. Ecosystems can be degraded, and, through harmful mutations triggered by toxic wastes, so can a species. A democracy can be degraded. A tree cannot be lonely but it can be harmfully isolated. Removed from its natural habitat, a species may deteriorate or die out. Degradation can take the form of disabling or diminishing. It has degrees. Serious degradation pushes a being below the level of a decent life, severely impairing capacities central to the meaning or value of that life. Understanding intolerable harm as major degradation is promising with respect to the aim of preserving the moral gravity of evils and retaining the contrast with lesser wrongs.

5. TREES AS VICTIMS

If an individual tree is not the victim of an atrocity, that is not because the tree is a single organism. What distinguish evils from other inexcusable wrongs, and atrocities from other evils, are the depth and significance of the harm, the importance of what is lost, diminished, or destroyed, and so on. Evils are not necessarily distinguished from lesser wrongs by the magnitude of the class of victims, although multiplicity of victims can contribute, especially when interrelationships construct the meanings of their lives.

Because evils deserve priority of attention from responders, if trees can suffer evils, then some wrongs to trees should take priority with responders over lesser wrongs to human beings. How plausible is that? The question is ambiguous. Does it ask about individual trees? A species? A forest? Is the comparison with harms to individual human beings? Or to human groups? If the first harm is to a forest or species and the second harm is to individual human beings, an affirmative answer to the priority question would not be surprising. Destroying a forest or species can plausibly be graver (independently of its utility to people) than a human being's suffering a non-fatal, temporarily and mildly disabling disease (say, the common cold). But one might wonder whether an affirmative answer to the priority question in regard to *individual* trees, as compared with individual human beings, presupposes an unacceptably radical species egalitarianism, according to which inexcusably killing a tree would be murder, on a par with inexcusably killing a human being.

The view that even trees can suffer evils does not imply such egalitarianism. The possibility that individual trees can suffer intolerable harm, worse than many harms to human beings, does not imply biocentric egalitarianism. Biocentrist Paul W. Taylor does, however, take that egalitarian position and regards it as sheer human chauvinism to think otherwise. He finds no differences of inherent worth in members of different species but regards as inherently equal all beings that have a good of their own (Taylor 1986, pp. 71–98).[14] It follows that inexcusably killing a tree is morally on a par with murdering a human being. What could lead anyone to take such a startling and, on the face of it, implausible view?

For Taylor, being a "teleological center of life" gives an organism inherent worth and grounds respect for it (Taylor 1986, pp. 119–29). Taylor writes, "To say it is a teleological center of life is to say that its internal functioning as well as its external activities are all goal-oriented, having the constant tendency to maintain the organism's existence through time and to enable it successfully to perform those biological operations whereby it reproduces its kind and continually adapts to changing environmental events and conditions" (1986, pp. 121–22). This idea of a teleological center of life sounds like a possible rendering of Aristotle's notion of the capacity for self-movement in living beings. But Aristotle distinguished increasingly complex forms of "self-movement" characterizing different forms of life and attached greater value to beings of greater complexity. In contrast, for Taylor, being such a *center* is what counts, not the range or complexity of the capacities. Taylor rejects the idea that human lives are more important than simpler lives. His argument is that a ranking, such as Aristotle's, "overlooks what it is about all living things that serves as the ground of their inherent worth … It is not their capacities taken by themselves. Rather, it is the fact that those capacities are organized in a certain way.

---

[14] For a helpful discussion of interpretations of "species equality," and a careful argument that at least one form of species equality is compatible with the view that members of some species embody more value than members of others, see Anderson (1993). Anderson's conclusions appear compatible with the idea that non-sentient beings can suffer intolerable harm, although his concern is with axiology in general, rather than with evils in particular.

They are interrelated functionally so that the organism as a whole can be said to have a good of its own, which it is seeking to realize" (1986, p. 148).

Yet the general idea that what grounds respect for an organism is the *organization* of its capacities to achieve a good of its own, rather than the range or sheer existence of its capacities, is compatible with the existence of greater inherent worth in an organization that embodies greater complexities that enable the organism to realize a greater good. Such a realization captures both the organization Taylor cites and further kinds besides. The goals Taylor incorporates into his concept of a teleological center of life (basically, goals of self-maintenance and reproduction) are goals Aristotle finds sufficient to define plant life. Why restrict the worth of animal and human life to the worth of what animals have in common with plants?

Underlying Taylor's biocentrism are concerns to reject human arrogance, to recognize the dependency of humanity on the non-human environment, and to acknowledge the value of the contributions of even very simple forms of life. I wonder if a factor might also be the sense that evils are more important than other harms, whether victims are sentient, rational, or non-sentient and non-rational, and that we ought to take evils seriously, regardless of victims' species. Those ideas can be granted without granting that evils to all living beings are *equally* serious.

In the *Nicomachean Ethics* Aristotle presents the "souls" of plants as defined by their capacities for nutrition and growth and for reproduction (Aristotle 1925, p. 25; 1947, p. 561). A tree, like a human, might still have a decent life if its capacity for reproduction were impaired or destroyed, although not if its capacity for nutrition were seriously impaired. Fine-tuning Aristotle's account, we might distinguish more specific capacities, such as – for a deciduous tree – the capacities to survive the dormancy of winter, for photosynthesis, to resist diseases, to heal from loss of branches, and so on. To avoid difficulties of a possibly infinite specification of capacities, we might note, with Anderson, that not every capacity is of value and that some might have or contribute toward the same value (Anderson 1993, pp. 359–60).

Picking up on Norlock's discussion of relationships between sentient and non-sentient life, we might add to Aristotle's capacities, as essential to an organism's identity, its capacities to enter into sustainable relationships not only with others of its kind (Aristotle recognizes in the case of human good the need for family and friends) but also with soils and waters in the locale or locales in which it lives. Not just normal development but sustainable development is needed, ultimately, for the well-being of organisms and communities. It becomes part of an organism's well-being to be able to develop and function sustainably as a member of a community in Aldo Leopold's sense of environmental "communities."

For Leopold, the land is a community whose members include "soils, waters, plants, and animals, or collectively: the land" (Leopold 1966, p. 239). "Community" here refers not to humanly instituted norms that guide participation in practices but to structures of causal interdependency. Some reject the community metaphor as inapt for that reason. Yet, the community metaphor conveys a judgment that these interdependencies can command respect, perhaps because of the development they enable. For non-sentient organisms whose identities include capacities to form relationships with others, part of their vulnerability to intolerable harm is due to the "communal" relationships that Norlock finds essential. The importance of such relationships to an organism's well-being implies that it is not only a good "of its own" that matters to thriving but also doing well in relationships that are part of a larger whole.

Taylor reserves the term "worth" for values the existence of which is independent of the valuing activity of valuers. He uses the term "value" for the result of valuing activity. Thus he speaks of the inherent worth of an organism as what grounds respect. He contrasts this worth with the intrinsic value that a valuer might place on the organism, in valuing it for its own sake rather than for its utility. My own usage tends not to mark that distinction with the terms "worth" and "value." I often refer to what Taylor calls "inherent worth" as "inherent value," meaning the same thing as he means by "inherent worth." But to the extent that capacities for communal or ecosystemic relationships are partly definitive of the good of an organism, "inherent" is inapt as a modifier. "Inherent" abstracts the individual from relations. To obtain the desired contrast with results of valuing activities, the value or worth realized by such an organism's capacities is better described as objective or realist than as inherent.

Severe damage to a tree's capacities to interact in an ecological community might become intolerable harm in the functional sense. It might so degrade the tree as to prevent its having, or continuing to have, a decent life. Yet what motivates concern for trees is typically not danger to a particular tree, unless the tree is sacred, unusual, or ancient (and, so, irreplaceable, or nearly so), such as the ancient giant redwood in California that eventually died from the tunnel for automobiles carved into its trunk. Even concern for that giant redwood was motivated basically by human interests. What usually motivate concern for trees on grounds of their objective or realist value are threats to species or forests. So, what about ecosystems and species?

6. THE "LIVES" OF ECOSYSTEMS, SPECIES, AND GAIA

A definition of intolerable harm that omits reference to life and death in favor of references to decent levels of sustainable functioning and to degradation can make good sense of intolerable harm to species, ecosystems, and some human groups. Yet, one may wonder whether there is a relevantly meaningful, non-metaphorical sense in which species and ecosystems, if not also some human groups, are alive.

One approach to that question, suggested by a straightforward application of the developmental capacity interpretation of well-being, is to argue that ecosystems and species are themselves organisms with capacities similar to, or analogous to, those of the organisms that are their members. Suppose we understand species not as universals of which individual organisms are instances but as giant particulars spread out in time and space, in that way like ecosystems. Both species and ecosystems might be thought of as (particular, historical) embodied processes. On some traditional understandings of universals, universals cannot be endangered. Species can be. Following Lawrence Johnson, suppose we understand a species as "an ongoing genetic lineage sequentially embodied in different organisms" (Johnson 1991, p. 156). Following Aldo Leopold, suppose we understand an ecosystem as referring to a biotic pyramid. A biotic pyramid is a tangle of "food chains" through which energy flows up from the bottom, in the case of land systems, through gradually less populated layers of soils, grasses, insects, and (depending on how well developed the system is) herbivores, omnivores, and carnivores. Specimens of each layer feed on those of lower layers. The energy then eventually returns through decay to contribute new soil (Leopold 1966, pp. 251–58). As Johnson sums it up, an ecosystem is "an ongoing process taking place through a complex system of interrelationships between organisms, and between organisms and their non-living environment" (1991, p. 216). Do species or ecosystems, understood as ongoing processes that develop over time, have lives of their own?

According to the "Gaia" hypothesis of James Lovelock, the planet earth – that is, the biosphere (atmospheres, oceans, lands) – is alive, a giant living system (Lovelock 1979). He had an interesting reason to think so. He argued that the earth shares with beings that clearly are organisms the capacity of being able, from within itself, to resist attacks and regain equilibrium, thereby preserving conditions requisite for the lives of plants and animals on earth. If that were true, the biosphere would appear to maintain itself in existence, fulfilling an important element of Taylor's teleological centers of life. Biologists tend to be skeptical of Lovelock's idea, however, on the grounds that the biosphere's apparent "capacities" seem to lack an evolutionary basis.[15]

Yet if the planet earth is not alive, perhaps its ecosystems are. Ecosystems appear to evolve. Like organisms, they have something like a life cycle. They grow and develop, endure for a span of time during which they have ups and downs, and then die out, although neither their beginnings nor their endings are as well defined, regular, or predictable as those of such paradigm organisms as individual plants or animals. Ecosystems can function poorly or well, deteriorate or thrive. Species play roles in ecosystems, with consequences to the vitality of both.

But have ecosystems or species (or even the biosphere of a planet) natural life spans? Do they reproduce? Like a cell, an ecosystem may divide, although it need not. Species evolve, branch off, and continue indefinitely. Principles of individuation for ecosystems and species are not so clear as for individual plants and animals. More to the point, ecosystems and species do not possess nearly the degree of functional interdependence of parts as do individual plants and animals.[16] Such empirical considerations may lead us to conclude that ecosystems and species are not *organisms*. But perhaps they are *living systems*, in Sayre's sense. Recall that according to Sayre, "The typifying mark of a living system ... appears to be its persistent state of low entropy, sustained by metabolic processes for accumulating energy, and maintained in equilibrium with its environment by homeostatic feedback processes" (Sayre 1976, p. 91). One might amplify this definition, as Johnson does, by specifying that the system also possess a certain internal unity and integrity. Still, Sayre's formulation seems compatible with the idea of "a life process that takes place through" individual organisms (Johnson 1991, p. 156).

What is the *ethical* significance of such a "living system"? Could intolerable harm to it, cutting short its potential for further development, be part of what makes a deed an evil? Can a living system be an appropriate object of attitudes of respect or gratitude? Peoples indigenous to North America have regarded species, ecosystems, and even earth itself as objects of respect and gratitude.[17] Those attitudes typically carry assumptions of ethical responsibility to the land: to use it wisely and well, repair or replace

---

[15] Elliott Sober, in personal correspondence. On Sober's own view, for Gaia to have adaptations the function of which is to preserve the entire earthly biosphere, these adaptations must have evolved by a process of interplanetary natural selection, a history that, he says, no one believes in.

[16] I am grateful to Sober, again, for attention to this point.

[17] See, for example, Paula Gunn Allen (1986); Hughes (1983); and Neihardt (1932).

what one can when one inflicts damage, make compensation, and so on. These are understood not simply as responsibilities to other human beings. Peter Wenz argues persuasively that the idea of restitution to environmental entities for damage usually makes sense only in relation to ecosystems or species, not individual specimens (Wenz 1988, pp. 287–92).

My point is not to vindicate these attitudes on the whole. It is, rather, to suggest respectfully their mature intelligibility, in view of apparent analogies between organisms and living systems and between relationships of mutual dependency that plants and animals have with each other and those they have with living systems. In contrast to the condescension of regarding respect for and gratitude to the natural environment as childishly anthropomorphic, the idea here is as much that we are like the rest of nature as that it is like us. It may be intelligible to regard species, ecosystems, and earth itself as alive, even if that belief is unsustainable.

Restorative and preventative responsiveness to being impinged upon or threatened with destruction are responses that suggest the agency of life. An intriguing account of such apparent agency in non-sentient beings is presented by Jon Moline in his discussion of the role of species in Leopold's land ethic (Moline 1986, pp. 99–120). Reflecting on the prickly pear, which appears to ensure its own survival as a species by producing an abortifacient that holds down, in alternate years, the population of antelope who graze on it, he argues that most of the living "citizens" of Leopold's land community (apart from humans) should be understood as species rather than as individual organisms. A species's thriving is distinct from that of a specimen. Prickly pears containing the abortifacient are not defended (although, of course, future specimens are). Is such biotic agency sufficiently autonomous to indicate that the species is alive? The question seems to involve empirical issues, not just philosophical ones.

Even if biotic systems are not living entities, perhaps they are sufficiently analogous to human organizations, such as corporations, that they might be accorded legal protections and even powers. Corporations are legal agents, with powers and liabilities. Why could biotic systems not also have legal powers and liabilities, with guardians to oversee them? Christopher Stone argued, in that essay cited by Supreme Court Justice Douglas in *Sierra Club* v. *Morton* (1972), that rivers and lakes, like corporations, could be granted legal standing to sue for damages. Stone even proposed, intriguingly and somewhat as an aside, that rivers might be held liable for damages they cause people – for example, in destroying crops (Stone 1974, p. 34). His idea was to establish a fund overseen by a guardian, with damages paid in by people who harm the river, which then could be drawn on to pay out damages to people for harm the river does them when it floods. If Stone were right about rivers (a kind of ecosystem), perhaps species could also be legal persons.

Cities are not thought to be literally alive although they are commonly described as thriving or decadent. The "life" or "vitality" of such bodies refers to the quality of relationships among residents (and with other cities) – their strength, solidity, integrity, endurance, intensity, and so on. Considered as belonging to individuals, this vitality is no metaphor. Social interaction is an important aspect of the vitality of individuals. But is the vitality of a city anything over and above that of its residents? Do species or ecosystems have something more that would justify attributing to them vitality that is not just the vitality of their members?

The capacity to recover from damage and return to a state of equilibrium suggests that perhaps they do. Cities and corporate bodies, such as banks, sometimes exhibit a capacity for recovery. But those capacities depend on deliberate efforts of individuals or on institutional structures deliberately created by individuals. There is no analogous explanation of recovery for species or ecosystems that recover without outside intervention.

Suppose the "life" of an ecosystem or species, like that of a city, refers to the vitality or vigor of a process or set of related processes embodied in organisms. A major oil spill or massive deforestation does major, perhaps irreparable, damage to these processes. Many organisms die. Yet some survive the death of parent ecosystems and become successfully integrated into other ecosystems, just as people who lose homes sometimes find new (even better) ones elsewhere. When relationships die (terminate), the parties to those relationships need not die but sometimes become free to form new relationships. There is a loss of vitality insofar as certain activities and interactions are no longer possible, even if there is no loss of *a* life or even of vital capacities.

Because ecosystem damage removes or degrades the context within which individual lives have their special significance and value, the value of an organism's survival can become questionable. A seabird covered in oil symbolizes major degradation of the context that gave meaning to its life and to the lives of flora and fauna with which it interacted.[18] Extinction of birds by pesticide poisoning harms not only individual birds but their ecosystems and thereby members of many species, such as trees that become disfigured or are killed by insects the birds would have consumed.[19]

[18] I am grateful to Chris Cuomo for this image.
[19] See Carson (1962) for many such stories.

Without a home in which to exercise whatever natural capacities remain, what is left to give meaning or value to survivors' lives (or, for that matter, their deaths)?

Intolerable harm to ecosystems and communities threatens to rob of meaning the lives of the organisms or people who are their members. This idea is important to elucidating the harm of genocide discussed in chapter 9.

7. HARM TO HUMAN GROUPS

What it means for a group to be harmed, and consequently what it means for it to be harmed intolerably, depends on the kind of group in question. Recall the kinds of human groups distinguished in chapter 3: aggregates (everyone who happens to be on Telegraph Avenue at noon on a particular date), organizations (the KKK, the Red Cross), social groups (religious or ethnic, such as Catholics or German Americans), and what Iris Young calls "structural groups" (Sartre's "series," such as bus riders, radio listeners, as well as – if Young is right – women and persons with disabilities). Setting aside mere aggregates, we can classify the other groups by reference to the two useful models introduced in chapter 3: (1) groups that are internally structured and so can act, and (2) groups that are structured only by their members relationships to certain externals (Sartre's bus rider and radio listener series; Young's "structural groups") but are not, or not yet, able to act as groups because they lack internal structure. In groups of the second kind, only individual members function, not the group as such, although the members' relationships to externals give rise to interests that unite them and distinguish them from mere aggregates. Many real groups, as Sartre saw, are hybrids of these two basic types.

Organizations, including corporations, such as General Motors, have an internal structure that enables them to act. Harm to the organization interferes with its functioning. Intolerable harm threatens its ability to function at a tolerable level. Whether that is a good or bad thing from a moral point of view is a further question that depends (because of the Murder, Inc. problem) on the nature of the organization, its history, and whether its basic values, principles, and processes are compatible with moral values.

With organized groups, there is a distinction to be drawn between harm to the group and harm to its members. Members of a team or political party are not necessarily harmed when the team or the party is harmed. Whether they are depends on such factors as how important it is to them to be members, how strongly they identify with the group, what membership in the group contributes to their basic needs, and so on. And conversely, harm to a member need not harm the organization. If the organization is a bureaucracy, like the Department of Motor Vehicles, individual members tend to be replaceable without changing the organization. Members can even be murdered without harming the organization, as appears to have been the case for quite a long time in Stalinist Russia and the Nazi Party.

Harms to women as women (a structural group, in Young's sense), in contrast to harms to members of an organization, do not depend on individual women identifying strongly or even at all as women. Women as a group are not organized. There are many women's groups. But women do not function as *a* group or *a* community. For structural groups that do not become organized, it is only the functioning of individuals that suffers when the group is harmed. There is no functioning of the group. Still, there is a distinction between what is good on the whole for the group – say, for women or bus riders – and what is good on the whole for those who happen to be its members. For its members are not only bus riders but also students, parents, workers, and so on. But even what is good on the whole for the group is good only for its members.

Aggregates cannot be harmed. They have no good of their own. Like structural groups, they do not function. Nor have they interests. Their members are not harmed *as* members of an aggregate. Referring to the aggregate contributes nothing to explaining harm to its members. When it appears that an aggregate is harmed – everyone who happened to be in the Twin Towers on the morning of September 11, 2001, for example – what *had been* a mere aggregate is transformed into a Sartrean series by the members' relationships to significant externals, in this case, the planes that struck the Towers. As soon as those planes endangered the Towers, occupants of the Towers were unified by the common interest of escaping the danger of death, or of burning to death. Yet they did not become a community. There was no time to establish internal structures that would have enabled them to act as a unit. (Still, subsets of them did act together, if only briefly, as when people traveling down stairways cooperated in aiding disabled persons and in retrieving dropped items.)

Social groups, such as religious or cultural groups, if they are very large, tend to become clusters of subgroups that are related to each other like the members of an extended family. Organizations within social groups have internal structures that enable them to act. But Christians, for example, or Muslims, as general groups, have no such structure. Conflicts between subgroups are common. Social groups are united more by recognition of common traditions than by structures that enable them to act jointly. Even the "common" traditions need not be valued or observed in the same way or to the same extent. Some who are born into a cultural or religious group choose not to identify with it. Yet outsiders may insist on so identifying them. Social groups can then take on structural features, coming to resemble Young's structural groups (women, bus riders) in that their relationships to outsiders can give them new common interests. When others behave oppressively toward (perceived) members of a cultural or religious group, excluding them from basic rights, for example, (perceived) members of the group acquire interests in being protected from those harms, independently of how they value their membership in the group. Lesbians, who previously thought of themselves only as women who happened to fall in love with other women, may begin to think of themselves as lesbians, on the basis of common interests to which exclusion gives rise.

In his first book on the morality of groups, Larry May argues that in the case of unorganized groups (such as women), harm distributes to individuals (each is harmed), whereas in organized groups, harm to the group does not necessarily harm each member (May 1987, pp. 135–55). When women are harmed as a group, individual women are vulnerable to harm only because they are (at least perceived as) women, not because of how they identify themselves. May's illustration of how this works is stereotyping on the basis of (perceived) characteristics of group members. To say that pornography harms women as a group is to say that all women suffer in virtue of their being (at least perceived as) women.

If, however, by "harm," one means a significant interference with or setback to functioning, thriving, or flourishing, then it is not obvious that all women really are harmed by either stereotyping or pornography. The claim that women as a group are oppressed seems to mean neither that women's functioning as a group is hindered (since women do not function as a group) nor that each woman's functioning is impaired by practices and attitudes that are oppressive to women. What, then, does it mean? The same question arises for the claim that anti-Semitism harms everyone who is (perceived as) Jewish, that anti-Black racism harms all Blacks, and so on.

What it means is that without special protection, luck, or privileges (which some have), members of the (structural) group are harmed. All are vulnerable in the sense that they have needs for special protection, luck, or privileges, if they are not, as individuals, to suffer the harms of oppression. Special protection or privilege comes typically through multiple group memberships, for many, through wealth or social class. Recall President Franklin D. Roosevelt, who was never marginalized, despite a very severe disability in a society that routinely marginalized the disabled. (Nevertheless, he refused ordinarily to be photographed in his wheelchair and stood whenever possible to deliver a public address, so that when you saw him, you did not see "a disabled person.") Some women have natural features, skills, or talents that shield them, for a time, from misogyny. Even if not totally protected, privileged members of an oppressed group may be able to offset or mitigate the harms they confront as members of an oppressed group.

Although harm to an organization need not distribute to its members, one of the ways in which organizations are harmed is by discrimination against anyone suspected of being a member. In that case, members of the organized group stand in the same relationship to harm as members of a structural group (such as women or people with disabilities): without special protection, luck, or privileges, they are vulnerable as individuals in virtue of how they are perceived by others. During the McCarthy era of the 1950s in the US, it was not only the Communist Party that took a hit but individuals who were suspected of Communist Party membership or even communist leanings.

8. CONCLUDING QUESTIONS

Two kinds of cases raise opposite sorts of problems for the possibility of evils to non-sentient entities. One case is the destruction of an evil group (such as Murder, Inc.) by means of an inexcusable wrong either to its members or to someone else. The other case is the destruction of an ecosystem as the reasonably foreseeable result of an inexcusable wrong to one or more human beings who are not themselves harmed, or not harmed seriously by that wrong. I take them up in that order. For there is an interesting relationship between them.

Suppose that an organization like Murder, Inc. is destroyed by means of manufactured evidence that sends a critical number of its leaders to their deaths by capital punishment. To make clear that this wrong is inexcusable, let us suppose that genuine evidence could have been obtained, although it would have taken a bit longer. It was easier to manufacture or plant evidence. My question is not whether the judicial murders of those leaders was an evil. It is, although perhaps not one that many non-lawyers outside the organization would regret. My question is whether intolerable harm *to the criminal organization*, brought about by the judicial murders of its leaders, is an evil in virtue of the fact that it resulted from inexcusable wrongdoing. Recall that on my atrocity theory of evil, an evil has two components: inexcusable wrongdoing and intolerable harm. So, to put the matter another way, my question is whether the deed is an evil even partly in virtue of the intolerable harm it does to an organization that deserves no respect. I have argued that it cannot be an evil to destroy an evil organization, which has no claim to respect. And yet, that unwelcome possibility seems to be opened up by an interpretation of the atrocity theory that allows a disconnect between the parties wronged and the parties harmed. For I have not argued that an evil organization cannot be harmed.

To preclude that possibility, such a disconnect might be ruled out in interpreting the theory. Or, more specifically, what might be ruled out is any interpretation that allows intolerable harm to an evil entity to count as even part of an evil. Both proposals seem a bit ad hoc. But the second exclusion seems entirely reasonable. I am less sure about the first.

If the party harmed by an evil must be the same as the party wronged, intolerable harm to species and ecosystems could not be evils in the extended sense suggested at the beginning of this chapter. That is, they could not be evils simply on the ground that they resulted from inexcusable wrongs to human or other sentient beings. Yet, that may not be an unwelcome implication. For, consider the following case.

Suppose someone obtains "undeveloped" land through a swindle and clears it to build an unneeded shopping mall, destroying a stand of trees in their prime. The swindled prior owner is wealthy, not really harmed (in the functional sense). There is nonetheless no moral excuse for the swindle. Unlike Agent Orange in Vietnam and massive oil spills in the ocean, in the swindle case no intolerable harm (let us suppose) is done to sentient beings. Birds and other small animals found new homes when clearing began. Yet the nearly wanton destruction of the trees seems more pertinent than the swindle to the question of whether any evil is done. Would the case significantly differ if the purchase had been honest? But, if not the swindle, then what is the relevant wrong? With no wrong, there is no evil. But is there truly no atrocity here?

Perhaps the relevant wrong consists in the practice of treating the land as property. That practice may be already an evil, as it is now recognized that treating human beings as property is an evil. The analogous position regarding animals is taken seriously by attorney and law professor Gary L. Francione. Francione argues that ownership of animals lies at the root of the evils they suffer (Francione 1995 and 1996; cf. Spiegel 1996), such as those to be discussed in chapter 8 on ordinary torture. The question of evil to the land seems to presuppose the intelligibility of Leopold's idea that the land can be wronged, not just harmed, as we now believe Odysseus's slave girls were wronged, not just harmed, when they were hanged after Odysseus's return (Leopold 1966, p. 237).

Yet, perhaps not. If a wrong need not wrong any*one* or any*thing* in particular, then intolerable harm to the land could still be an evil, provided that such harm to the land can be utterly indefensible, morally, independently of what it does to human or other sentient beings. There would be no need, then, to appeal to any disconnect between the party harmed and the party wronged, for there would be no need for a *party* to be wronged, only a party that is harmed. All that would be needed for the wrongdoing component of the evil is an inexcusable wrong (but not *to* anyone or anything) that is productive of intolerable harm to the land. If the practices of treating the land, living beings, and living systems as property are morally indefensible, they would be, like other inexcusable practices, utterly without justification. Just as indefensible practice need not be anyone's fault, perhaps an indefensible practice need not wrong anyone in particular, either.

PART II
Terrorism, torture, genocide

le of equal liberty, he argued that even though his Proviso would

CHAPTER 5

Counterterrorism

> Finally, one may ask whether the concept of justice implies that a
> religious sect which rejects the principle of equal liberty should itself
> be tolerated, that is, given the constitutional liberty which it would
> deny, had it the means, to others. (Rawls 1999b, p. 92)

"Counterterrorism" in the United States today has come to be regarded
as a military concept.[1] Yet it is unclear to what extent a military model
is really the model that has been used by the US for fighting terrorism since the attacks of September 11, 2001 (hereafter, 9/11; Luban 2002,
pp. 9–14). Military policies are governed by International Humanitarian
Law (IHL), which rules out most terrorism. Counterterrorist measures
need not be terrorist. But the temptation for responders to use terrorist means is there. This chapter explores that temptation and takes up
the question of whether there can be a moral justification, or at least a
moral excuse, for a government-sponsored program to fight terrorism
with terrorism.

John Rawls had a lifelong concern with issues of religious freedom and
intolerance. In his social and political philosophy course at Harvard and
in his writings he addressed the question of whether principles of justice
impose any obligation to tolerate even those who are intolerant (Rawls
1999b, pp. 92–94). By the intolerant, he had in mind religious sects (although the same issue arises for political sects) that do not accept the principle of equal liberty. He argued that even though the intolerant would
have no right to complain if they were not tolerated, others might have a
right to complain. Appealing to empirical data that indicate that intolerant
sects are not necessarily dangerous to others, he argued that in fact there
is an obligation to tolerate the intolerant, but also that this obligation has

---

[1] In defiance of my word processing program, but in accord with the practice of *The New York
Times*, I do not hyphenate "counterterrorism" but treat it as one word.

limits. The tolerant would have a right to curb the liberty of an intolerant sect when the tolerant "sincerely and with reason believe it necessary for their own security" (Rawls 1999b, p. 93).

An analogous question arises for violating the rules of war. Terrorism – on most plausible understandings of that concept – tends to violate requirements of IHL that are designed to protect human rights and curb the cruelties of war. Those requirements establish, at least for signatories, not only a political but a *prima facie* moral obligation to stay within the limits of the rules of war defined in the treaties and conventions that constitute IHL. But to what extent are states, their military forces, and their leaders morally bound, not just *prima facie* but *all things considered*, to observe those rules in responding to aggressors who flagrantly violate them? Might the extent of that obligation depend on the responses of other states or international groups to the aggression? Could a state that "sincerely and with reason" believed it necessary for its own security be morally justified in, or at least have a moral excuse for, violating IHL?

The 1984 United Nations Convention against Torture explicitly rules out exceptions to its ban on torture: "No exceptional circumstances whatsoever, whether a state of war or a threat of war, internal political instability or any other public emergency, may be invoked as a justification of torture" (Part 1, Article 2, section 2; Burgers and Danelius 1988, p.178).[2] There is to date no UN convention on terrorism comparable to its conventions on torture and genocide. There is less consensus on how to define terrorism. That concept is vaguer and more abstract than either the concept of torture or that of genocide. Yet, terrorist measures of counterterrorism need not include torture or genocide. If some terrorist measures that do not include torture or genocide can be morally justifiable, or at least excusable, then terrorism is not necessarily an evil. That is the conclusion, highly qualified, that this chapter defends.

This chapter has three main objectives. The first is to identify concerns that make terrorism morally problematic (to steal a phrase from Bat-Ami Bar On; Card 1991b, pp. 107–25). The second is to compare terrorism with war in regard to those concerns. The third is to explore an analogy between state-sponsored programs of counterterrorism on an international scale and counterterrorist defenses that have been improvised by individuals

---

[2] The UN Convention against Torture and Other Cruel, Inhuman or Degrading Treatment or Punishment (1984) can also be found at: http://velvetrevolution.us/torture_lawyers/docs/UN_Convention_on_Torture.pdf.

who face more private forms of terrorism.[3] The conclusions of this chapter
(1) leave open the possibility of a justifiable, or at least excusable, terrorist response to terrorism, but also (2) urge international accountability for
such decisions, and (3) suggest that states' collective assumption of international responsibilities should remove any excuse for the use of terrorist
means in a state-sponsored program of counterterrorism.

I. HOBBESIAN AND KANTIAN APPROACHES

What makes terrorism so very morally problematic? Consider the 9/11 suicide bombings of the World Trade Center and the Pentagon. Intentional
mass killing of unarmed civilians, aggravated by absence of warning and
absence of an existing military context, is a clear violation of IHL and
clearly an evil. What, if anything, does it add to one's moral understanding of those events if the bombings are interpreted as terrorist? Does terrorism make them worse?

If the bombings were terrorist, they were certainly worse than if they
had resulted from accidents (which many assumed briefly on witness-
ing the first impact), even accidents caused by inexcusable negligence or
drunkenness of the pilots. Accidents are not intentional, not murders. Are
the attacks worse than they would have been had they been the idiosyn-
cratic deeds of sadistic pyromaniacs? Worse than if they had been carried
out as revenge against (then) President George W. Bush by relatives of
persons who believed their kin were wrongfully convicted and executed
for murder in Texas during Bush's tenure there as governor? In neither of
these scenarios would the US have faced the difficult response issues that
the 9/11 bombings raised.

Unlike the pyromaniac and revenge scenarios, a terrorist interpretation
raises the spectre of more and worse to come – continued unpredictable
lethal attacks on masses of unarmed civilians, in this case by agents resi-
dent in the midst of the those they intend to kill, turning against them
their own technology, educational institutions, and trust. The terrorist
interpretation removes whatever metaphysical excuse might have been supplied by out-of-control passions. As terrorist, the attacks were controlled,
carefully calculated, probably over a long period of time with many opportunities for a change of mind or heart and with generous opportunity to
gauge the results. They were coordinated by many agents working together

---

[3] These individuals are discussed in section 4 of this chapter. That what they faced is truly terrorism
in their private lives is defended in chapter 6. Their counterterrorist defenses are not forms of terrorism. But what they did raises some of the same issues as terrorist counterterrorism.

and coolly implemented by many agents with distinct tasks. On a terrorist interpretation, there need be no sadism, no aim to cause prolonged
suffering to those who die. But there is an intention to create a heavy loss
of civilian life in densely populated areas and to produce massive chaos
with long-term impact. It is foreseeable that many more will suffer for at
least a generation and that recovery, to the extent that it is possible, will
be slow and expensive. On a terrorist interpretation, there is also, importantly, the intent to create tremendous long-lasting fear, not only in the US
but among allies, and to send a message to other potential targets. To the
extent that these elements of a terrorist interpretation aggravate the evil of
the bombings, the idea of a terrorist program of counterterrorism should
accordingly give responders deep pause. The legacy of terrorism is jeop-
ardy to the possibility of post-conflict peaceful coexistence.

Terrorism has become a much-contested concept. Like slavery, it
is a concept that has evolved historically and so a likely candidate for a
Wittgensteinian "family resemblance" approach to its meaning, an idea
pursued more fully in chapter 6. Some critics find the concept of terrorism
no longer useful, except as a term of vilification. But let us attempt to draw
out what it is in popular images of terrorism that is so morally problematic
that many regard terrorism as a paradigm of evil. What makes "terrorist"
a natural term of vilification? I defer to chapter 6 the project of examining the scope of the concept of terrorism. It may seem counterintuitive
to some readers not to begin with a definition. But philosophers tend to
feel lucky if they can conclude with a definition. Here my concern is with
what is morally problematic about phenomena widely and publicly perceived as terrorist, the high-profile cases, such as the 1995 Oklahoma City
bombing, the 1993 attack on the World Trade Center, and the 9/11 attacks.
Identifying what is morally problematic is a good place to begin, as moral
concerns are what evoke the accusation "terrorist!"

The high-profile cases just noted can mislead in an important respect.
Each focuses our attention on a spectacular event that occurred on a particular day. People in the US tend to remember what they were doing on
9/11 when the news broke. In trying to understand terrorism and the ways
that it is morally problematic, we should be wary of focusing too much
on the spectacle. The spectacular deed is part of a wider policy. Terrorism
is a theme that shapes hostile campaigns. It refers to a kind of program
carried out, or intended to be carried out, over time. "Terrorist" describes
practices in something like Rawls's sense of a practice as "any form of activity specified by a system of rules which defines offices, roles, moves,
penalties, defenses, and so on, and which give the activity its structure"

(Rawls 1999b, p. 20). That account may sound more formal than terrorism need be. But terrorism shares with Rawls's account of a practice the idea of an activity spread out over time with a normative structure that sometimes can allow it to endure despite major changeovers of personnel. Most importantly, practices give meanings to particular deeds and to the policies they realize. That is why the terrorist interpretation of the 9/11 bombings is so much more frightening than other imaginable scenarios of comparably spectacular events. Since terrorism describes policies, practices, or campaigns of hostilities, not simply spectacular deeds, a terrorist interpretation of the 9/11 attacks might naturally place them into a global pattern that includes such things as the bombings of US embassies and ships. The evil of the attacks is then magnified beyond what it would be if there was no such pattern (as there is not in the pyromaniac and revenge scenarios).

Some of the factors that aggravate the evil on a terrorist interpretation pertain to the agency of terrorism. Others pertain to the nature and extent of the harm done. Accordingly, two approaches to the question of what is morally problematic about terrorism focus respectively on its agency and its harms. I call them the Kantian approach and the Hobbesian approach. They give rise to two families of paradigms to be explored further in chapter 6. These approaches should not be regarded as incompatible alternatives. Rather, they indicate a focus of attention: the agency of terrorism, or the harm it does. The two approaches should supplement each other, although they can give rise to very different ideas about what terrorism is. I begin with the Hobbesian approach, as the harms are what are most salient in the public image of terrorism. The spectacle is symbolic of harms that outrun the spectacle.

Violence, or the threat of violence, against innocent civilians is the most obviously problematic feature generally associated with terrorism. Violence otherwise comparable in its severity or nature would not be described as terrorist if it were directed by authorized military forces solely against combatants. "Innocent" in this context usually means "defenseless," as the contrast with military combatants reveals. Political terrorists may not regard the adults they target as innocent in any other sense.

Violent attacks and threats against the defenseless are ordinarily cruel. They can also be perceived as cowardly, unless the life or safety of the assailant is risked in the attack. Because political terrorists often do risk their lives, cowardice is not ordinarily part of what is ethically problematic in the public image of political terrorism. The 9/11 suicide bombers, for example, do not come across as cowardly, as Susan Sontag pointed out in an article in *The New Yorker* in late September 2001, to the dismay of readers who thought she was praising the bombers for their courage (Sontag 2007, pp. 105–08). What does come across is extraordinary cruelty. It is difficult to gauge the depth of the cruelty behind the 9/11 bombings. Planners were apparently surprised that the Twin Towers collapsed. Yet additional bombings were apparently also planned that did not come off. And so it is not clear that planners had intended ultimately less destruction or loss of life. If the depth of cruelty is unclear, the fact of cruelty is not.

Bat-Ami Bar On identifies *cruelty* as the primary factor that makes terrorism morally problematic. In doing so, she puts into perspective and supplements the widespread more usual focus on the *injustices* of terrorism. Bar On was raised in Israel, where she completed two years mandatory military service before taking a master's degree in sociology at Tel Aviv University. She came to the US for her PhD in philosophy at the Ohio State University, where she was active in a group called Women Against Rape (WAR).[4] She has taught martial arts. Her work in WAR began a lifelong project of philosophical theorizing about violence.[5] In her essay on why terrorism is morally problematic, Bar On reflects on the long-term impact on the sensibilities and character of people who grow up, as she did, surrounded by terrorism. What emerges in her reflections as morally salient about terrorism is that it tends to produce cruel people (Card 1991b, pp. 107–25). Its ultimate cruelty is that impact on the character and sensibilities of people who live with its long-term threats and insecurities.

Samuel Scheffler's view of what is morally distinctive about terrorism is basically compatible with that view (Scheffler 2006), although his focus is more on the sources of that impact of terrorism. Scheffler cites Hobbes's *Leviathan* on what it is like to live in a condition of general insecurity for an extended period: "*continual fear, and danger of violent death.* And the life of man, solitary, poor, nasty, brutish, and short" (Scheffler's emphasis, Scheffler 2006, p. 4; Hobbes 1950, p. 104). Terrorists, he argues, "take these Hobbesian insights to heart," engaging in "violence against some people in order to induce fear or terror in others, with the aim of destabilizing or degrading (or threatening to destabilize or degrade) an existing social order" (Scheffler 2006, pp. 4–5). Prolonged conditions of fear and insecurity are cruel. Insofar as people who live under such conditions become "brutish" (as "brutish" tends to be understood, however unjust to animals), cruelty is an important aspect of the character they develop

---

[4] An autobiographical essay by Bar On is included in Yancy (2002, pp. 269–78).
[5] See Bar On (2002) for a fuller treatment of the subject of violence.

as they emulate significant others (including opponents) and learn how to survive.

Scheffler argues that this Hobbesian understanding does not restrict the idea of terrorism to attacks by non-state agents but also allows for the possibility of terrorism by state agents who use terror against other states. He prefers, however, to distinguish as "state terror" (rather than "terror*ism*") tyrannical regimes that many regard as terror*ist*. His reason is that tyrannical regimes use terror to maintain power and preserve an established order, not to produce or approximate a Hobbesian social chaos. Yet Scheffler acknowledges that even when the objective is to preserve, rather than destabilize, an established order, a state's reliance on terror to do the job deeply undermines social life. It degrades the quality of social life, even if it does not degrade the existence of order. Contrary to Scheffler's view, that fact can be sufficient warrant for regarding the use of terror to maintain power as another form of terrorism, even on a basically Hobbesian approach to terrorism. Such a reliance on terror undermines the social life that makes a stable society valuable. It has a largely comparable effect on its members, although it achieves that effect by different means. For life under oppressive regimes is also characterized by continual fear and the ever-present danger of violent death. Life is apt to be nasty, brutish, and poor if not solitary or quite as short.

Michael Walzer, in the classic chapter on terrorism in his treatise on just and unjust wars, proposes that *randomness* in the murder of innocent people is "a crucial feature of terrorist activity" (Walzer 1977, p. 177). The importance of randomness for terrorists is that it increases the likelihood that victims will be defenseless. It thereby contributes to an atmosphere of fear. Yet when victims are already defenseless, randomness may be unnecessary to produce the requisite atmosphere of fear. Randomness in the murder of defenseless or innocent victims is not a salient feature of the 9/11 bombings. On a macro level, the selection of 9/11 targets appears not to have been random at all. The World Trade Center and the Pentagon are symbols of global power used in the service of projects long perceived by some Islamic radicals to be hostile to Muslim peoples. Insofar as occupants of the Towers and the Pentagon were workers whose jobs required their presence in those buildings on that day, they do not appear to have been randomly selected as individuals, either. Anonymous, for the most part. But not random. On a less macro level, there may have been nothing random in the selection of which part of the Pentagon to bomb. The only truly random victims in the Towers were those whose presence then and there was not required and could not reasonably have been predicted – some, for example, who just happened that morning to be in the restaurant at the top of the first Tower that was struck. That level of randomness does not make the deed significantly worse than it would have been without the restaurant deaths. Insofar as randomness contributes to defenselessness, it aggravates the cruelty of an assault. But victims in the Towers and the Pentagon were already defenseless.

If the Hobbesian approach to terrorism emphasizes the impact on victims, a Kantian approach emphasizes terrorist intentions. An example of the Kantian approach is an early paper by Carl Wellman that presents terrorism as "the use or attempted use of terror as a means of coercion" (Wellman 1979, p. 250). He adds that the terror is produced by a threat of great harm to the target if demands are not met (Wellman 1979, p. 253). He also notes that actual violence is not essential (threats often suffice) and claims that in fact most acts of terrorism are not violent (Wellman 1979, p. 251). To clarify this point, Wellman finds it helpful to distinguish between two targets of terrorism. One direct but secondary target (the conspicuous target in a terrorist spectacle) is the victim of threatened harm. The other target, the victim of coercion, is indirect but primary (Wellman 1979, p. 254).[6] Terrorism sends a message to the indirect primary target by way of violence or the threat of violence to a secondary target. Thus, Patricia Hearst was the direct but secondary target when she was kidnapped in 1974 by the Symbionese Liberation Army (SLA). Her grandfather William Randolph Hearst was the primary target, from whom the SLA hoped to extort $6 million in a food giveaway program for the poor of California.[7] In some instances, Wellman notes, the direct and indirect targets are the same, as in an armed holdup (Wellman 1979, pp. 252, 254). There, the party coerced is the same as the party threatened with harm. Ordinarily, harm aimed at the direct target (say, a building and its occupants) sends a message to a *different* primary target (say, a government), threatening further harm unless demands are met (say, demands to release prisoners).

In contrast to Walzer's view, on Wellman's view, those who are targeted directly need not be any more randomly selected than the indirect targets, which are not randomly selected at all. On Wellman's model, direct targets, if they are to serve as a coercive threat to the primary target, have

---

[6] There is no uniformity among writers on terrorism regarding this usage of "primary" and "secondary." Scheffler designates as primary what Wellman calls the secondary target, but only because it is apt to be the (chronologically) *first* target. Wellman's usage is preferable, as it designates as primary the target that is first in *importance* to the terrorist, regardless of chronology.

[7] A riveting autobiographical account of this kidnapping and its aftermath is Hearst (1988).

to be selected for their relationship to the primary target. On the view of terrorism as coercion, terror is only a means, not an end. Terrorists might actually have other aims besides coercion, such as revenge. The use of terror as a means is what becomes morally salient on Wellman's view.

An implication of understanding terrorism as basically coercive is that terrorism is not always wrong, let alone evil. Wellman's own illustrations, which include the threat of punishing student late papers with a lowered grade, bear this out. The moral status of terrorist deeds then becomes a function of the more specific means used, the end sought, and whether those whose terror is used as means could rationally consent to their treatment – in short, whether they are used *merely* as means. In a later essay on terrorism, Wellman examines at length the idea that terrorism is always wrong because it violates victims' rights (Howie 1987, pp. 128–52). He concludes that "whether terrorism is ever morally justifiable remains an open question" (Howie 1987, p. 52).

On Wellman's approach, at least in the 1979 essay, what is wrong with terrorism when it *is* wrong appears not to be its cruelty (it need not be cruel). The coercion idea suggests that it is something else about the way terrorism treats its targets, such as that it treats them merely as means to ends they do not and could not rationally share, or in ways to which they could not rationally consent. This would be a Kantian approach, applying Immanuel Kant's second formulation of his Categorical Imperative as "*So act that you use humanity, whether in your own person or in the person of any other, always at the same time as an end, never merely as a means*" (Kant 1996a, p. 80; emphasis in the original). A Kantian approach centers disrespect for humanity. Terrorist disrespect for the humanity of victims consists in either disregarding (in the case of direct targets) or abusing (in the case of indirect targets) their capacities for rational choice. A Kantian approach makes it natural to see the point of the 9/11 attacks as to manipulate the US and its allies into paying more heed to the demands of Islamic radicals. On that view, Twin Towers workers directly targeted as they began their day – the "throwaway victims" – were used merely as a means to issue such (implied) demands.

The 9/11 bombers issued no explicit demands and left no explicit message stating their purpose. Still, tapes of Osama bin Laden – who has become a Western icon of evil (ironically, in some photos, resembling European images of Jesus) – reveal that the attacks were planned. The reporters, writers, and editors of the German magazine *Der Spiegel* include in their 2001 volume on the 9/11 attacks a collaborative translation, provided by the US government, of such a tape that is believed to have been made in mid-November apparently in Kandahar. It includes the following speech, attributed to Bin Laden:

we calculated in advance the number of casualties from the enemy, who would be killed based on the position of the tower. We calculated that the floors that would be hit would be three or four floors. I was the most optimistic of them all [... inaudible ...] due to my experience in this field. I was thinking that the fire from the gas in the plane would melt the iron structure of the building and collapse the area where the plane hit and all the floors above it only. This is all that we had hoped for. (*Der Spiegel* magazine reporters *et al.* 2001, p. 317; all ellipses and brackets are in the original)[8]

Other tapes indicate that an underlying motivation was the perception of the US and its allies as engaged in activities that threaten Muslim peoples.

If the bombings' intent was simply punitive, or if the bombings were simply meant to show the world that the US is not invulnerable, either they were not terrorist in Wellman's very specific sense (because they were not coercive in that they did not intend a message with demands), or else terrorism can have other messages than coercive ones and need not come with demands. A Kantian approach can accommodate such variations on Wellman's view. If not coercive, the attacks could still have used direct targets merely as means to convey a message. If the intent was simply to show the world that it could be done – that although the US had not experienced war on its soil since the attack on Pearl Harbor of 1941, it is not invulnerable – then there was a message and an ulterior motive, not to coerce the US but perhaps to encourage other potential attackers. The intent could have been to do both, or it may not have been precisely defined.

One may wonder whether both the Hobbesian and Kantian approaches to what is morally problematic about terrorism are too specific. Of the two, the Hobbesian approach seems less likely to be too specific, if it is understood to include what Scheffler regards as state terror. The Kantian approach, however, is less obviously applicable to many contemporary paradigms of terrorism. Consider suicide bombings in Israel. As portrayed in the film *Paradise Now* (2005), Palestinian suicide bombing appears to have become a rule-governed, even ritualized, practice. Yet, like the 9/11 bombers, Palestinian bombers in Israel typically leave no explicit message

---

[8] The reporters caution the reader that "Due to the quality of the original tape, it is NOT a verbatim transcript of every word spoken during the meeting, but does convey the messages and information flow" (*Der Spiegel* magazine reporters *et al.* 2001, p. 314).

or demand. If the Palestinian suicide bombings in Israel are nevertheless valid paradigms of terrorism, should we conclude that "terrorism" is now just a pejorative term for guerilla warfare?

Richard Hare observed long ago that terrorism is often the resort of people who lack the resources to wage conventional warfare, such as those who fought in the French Resistance during WW II (Hare 1979, p. 244) or, one might add, some of the Bielski Partisans in the forests of Poland, who were both rescuers and resisters (Tec 1993).[9] Mary Kaldor, of the London School of Economics and Political Science, presents overwhelming evidence that distinctions between war and other violence are eroding. The "new wars" of the 1980s and 90s began to blur distinctions among war, organized crime, and large-scale violations of human rights, and "the term 'low-intensity conflict'," she writes, "was coined during the Cold War period by the US military to describe guerilla warfare or terrorism" – suggesting that guerilla warfare and terrorism are more or less the same (Kaldor 2001, p. 2).

The worry on such grounds that the Kantian take on terrorism, unlike the Hobbesian view, is too specific can be largely met with a distinction. When terrorist acts are backed by organizations, we should distinguish the intentions of individuals who carry out the violence from the intentions of sponsoring organizations or groups that provide encouragement, support, and a context that gives meaning to their acts. An individual suicide bomber might be motivated by personal concerns that have nothing to do with coercing or sending a message. But if that individual is used by a terrorist organization, intentions of the organization can supply a context that gives the attack a coercive or other meaning that transcends the intentions of the individual agent. If "terrorist" describes, in the first instance, a campaign, policy, or practice that gives meaning to individual deeds, then we should not expect each such deed to carry its own individualized message. Nor should we expect that the message sent by the deed corresponds in any way with the intentions of the immediate individual agent of violence, any more than the intentions of prison guards, who may regard their jobs simply as a way to earn a living, determine the meaning of punishment.

"Terrorism" is not simply a pejorative term for guerilla warfare. Guerilla warfare can include terrorist campaigns but does not necessarily do so. What makes warfare "guerilla" are such things as the absence of uniforms

---

[9] See also the feature film *Defiance* (2008), which appears to be based on Tec's 1993 book of the same title.

and the use of indirect, clandestine, and unorthodox methods. Guerilla feminism in the 1970s consisted largely of such measures as trashing pornography shops and defacing billboards under cover of night, anonymous graffiti in restrooms naming rapists and other perpetrators of violence against women, and the like. It was intended to expose the violence of others and prevent them from continuing to get away with it or profit from it. Even in the midst of what is more generally recognized as civil or international war, guerilla attacks can take clearly non-terrorist forms, such as destruction of paperwork or computerized records, that does not aim at killing, kidnapping, or bodily harm to persons and does not even appeal to fear to manipulate others psychologically. Guerilla objectives can be more to win hearts in a local population and to disable enemies than to coerce anyone into complying with demands.

Hare reminds us that "to some extent terrorism is a substitute for conventional war," as is guerilla warfare (Hare 1979, p. 244). But terrorism is also employed, in flagrant violation of IHL, by the wagers of wars that are widely regarded as conventional. Prolonged campaigns of saturation bombing by the British in Europe and the Americans in Japan during WW II – not only the well-known bombings of Hamburg, Dresden, Tokyo, Hiroshima, and Nagasaki but carpet firebombings of a great many lesser-known cities – were expressly terrorist. They were explicitly intended to demoralize civilian populations to get them to stop supporting their nations' war efforts.[10] Civilian inhabitants of these burned cities were as much throwaways as the occupants of the Twin Towers. Most of them were women, children, the elderly, the ill, and the disabled; people who could not fight in military forces, were unarmed, and lacked escape routes.

Yet, if more campaigns are terrorist than some might have thought, not all hostile campaigns that terrorize civilians (even randomly) are terrorist. Consider the Columbine High School shootings, or sniper shootings by a tower gunman who aims to kill as many as possible before committing suicide.[11] Those killings are not means to further ends. In the case of assailants who turn the gun on themselves and whose slaughters are used or backed by no organizations, these are one-off hostile

---

[10] An awesome philosophical history of these campaigns is Grayling (2006, pp. 15–176).
[11] According to plans revealed in their notebooks and videotapes, the intentions of Columbine shooters Eric Harris and Dylan Klebold were to bomb much of the school during the first lunch period on 29 April, 1999 (Cullen 2009). Had their bombs detonated as planned, they would have killed at least hundreds (out of more than 2,000 students and faculty). Chapter 9 revisits this case to consider whether that project was something like a genocide.

campaigns. They express pent-up rage. No groups behind the scenes coordinate those assaults or facilitate them. And yet, as high school and college shootings gain publicity and are copied by others, as patterns begin to appear and the shootings begin to acquire the trappings of ritual, they might evolve into a social structure that bears at least a family resemblance to structures of terrorism. Hobbesian fear and insecurity might then begin to spread. Perhaps there is also a message, if we would but learn to read it.[12]

Likewise, although kidnappings like that of Patricia Hearst can be terrorist, other kidnappers, such as bride-seekers and sexual predators who prey on children, need have no terrorist intent. Contrary to the terrorist intent to send a message, their fervent hope may be that their deeds will receive no attention. Sexual predators may wish the kidnapped child would just be given up as lost. Bride-seekers may hope the bride and her family will accept her fate. Such kidnappings ordinarily serve no organization that has a terrorist intent. Nor need they be part of a policy, campaign, or practice that uses terror to manipulate or coerce others as means to further ends. Even when children and adult women are kidnapped by prostitution rings (as portrayed in the film *Taken*, 2008), terrifying as that practice is, there need be no intent to undermine or degrade the social order (kidnappers apparently hope to profit from aspects of the social order) or to treat victims as hostages and use them to manipulate others. If sexual predator kidnappings became too prevalent, Hobbesian fear and insecurity might spread, defeating the kidnappers' entrepreneurial aims.

Much of what makes terrorism so very morally disturbing is that it *is* a matter of policy. Whether it occurs in the context of a more conventional war or without that context, terrorism violates the human dignity of its victims routinely and makes a practice of cruelty. To a great extent, the same is true of war. Cruelty and disrespect need not be among the aims, but they are inevitably (if only in a pragmatic sense) among the means. That makes even wars fought for good causes morally problematic. International rules of war express attempts to respect the human dignity of war's victims and to restrain its cruelties. Yet, as Kaldor's research demonstrates, the rules of war no longer succeed very well in those endeavors, if they ever did (Kaldor 2001).

---

[12] Cullen (2009) is not persuaded by the view that Harris and Klebold were sending a message about bullying at Columbine. But Brooks Brown (Brown and Merritt 2002) presents a background of bullying that he and his friend Klebold experienced for many years at more than one school, including Columbine.

2. INTERNATIONAL RULES OF WAR VS. SUBJECTIVE IMPROVISATIONS OF TERRORISM

Merriam-Webster's Collegiate Dictionary says that "war" is "a state of open and declared armed hostile conflict between states or nations" (10th edn., 1993). As Kaldor's work shows, the idea of war has been extended to include non-state agents. But with that extension comes great unclarity regarding how the rules of war are to be interpreted and applied.

Carl von Clausewitz defined "war" generally as "an act of violence intended to compel our opponent to fulfill our will" (Clausewitz 1982, p. 101). That definition sounds like Wellman's view of terrorism. Clausewitz meant that each side aims to make the other capitulate. The main moral difference, as forms of armed conflict, between what is commonly called war and what is commonly called terrorism is that war has a long and continuous global history of regulation by international conventions, whereas terrorism does not. Terrorism has a long enough global history, but not a long and continuous history of regulation by international conventions.[13] Despite widespread grave breaches, the treaties and conventions that IHL includes represent good-faith efforts to limit the cruelties of war in the interests of future peace. In contrast, terrorism appears – at least, to victims – to be an explicitly "no holds barred" approach to hostile conflict. Individual terrorists and some terrorist organizations have in fact had a variety of scruples. Walzer notes that revolutionary honor codes governed nineteenth-century Western European "terrorists" who targeted powerful individuals (Walzer 1977, 198 ff.). He also notes that honor codes no longer appear to govern terrorism. There is, in any case, no uniformity in the scruples of different terrorist organizations, no continuous history of terrorist scruples, and ordinarily no way for victims to know what scruples, if any, particular terrorists may have.

Rules of war are codified in many international treaties and conventions that constitute a large part of IHL. These documents include the Hague Conventions of 1899 and 1907, the Nuremberg Charter of 1945, and the Geneva Conventions of 1949, as well as the Protocols of 1977 additional to the Geneva Conventions. They govern such matters as the treatment of prisoners of war (POWs), civilians, and medical personnel. They concretize the very abstract philosophical principles of just war theory. Just war theory evolved in Christian scholastic tradition to justify and

---

[13] For two very different historical overviews of terrorism, see Burleigh (2009) and Laqueur (2001).

limit wartime exceptions to the biblical commandment against killing. These principles have received extensive contemporary discussion (Lackey 1989; O'Brien 1981), especially in relation to the use of weapons of mass destruction (WMDs) and the threat of nuclear war.[14] An enormous body of interpretation has grown up around the key concepts and components. Comparable ethical constraints exist in the traditions of Judaism, Buddhism, Confucianism, Hinduism, and Islam (Hashmi and Lee 2004, pp. 213–401).

Briefly, the *jus ad bellum* (justice in going to war) part of Christian just war theory requires that the cause for which a war is fought be just and proportionate to the costs of and losses imposed by the war and that peaceful means of conflict resolution be exhausted first. There is also, traditionally, a requirement that a war be declared by appropriate authorities. That requirement is often no longer observed (for example, the US never officially declared war on Vietnam).

The *jus in bello* (justice in the conduct of war) part of just war theory consists basically of two principles. One is a principle of proportion to be applied to intermediate military goals (not just to the cause for which the war is being fought). The other – the focus of most contemporary controversy – is a principle of discrimination that requires that non-combatants and non-military targets not be intentionally directly attacked.

Terrorism is commonly understood by victims and potential victims by reference to the rules of war, or the principles of just war theory, that it violates. On Walzer's view, for example, terrorists disregard the principle of discrimination, targeting indiscriminately ("randomly") those who are completely innocent and defenseless as well as those who are perceived to be threats. Lacking a long and continuous history of conventions governing armed conflicts between parties that include at least one non-state agent, non-state terrorists are thrown back on their own subjective improvisations regarding who is and who is not "legitimately" targetable.

Within conventional wars fought by men in uniform, such as WW II, violations of the discrimination principle have often been clear, although also often not penalized even when the violations are gross (Grayling 2006). On Walzer's understanding of terrorism, carpet-bombing carried out to demoralize a civilian population and motivate it to stop supporting its nation's war efforts should certainly count as terrorism. International conventions govern who counts as a combatant, for purposes of conventional warfare. Medical personnel, for example, do not count as

---

[14] A useful overview of the evolution of rules of war is provided by Taylor (1992, pp. 3–42).

combatants, nor do farmers, although munitions manufacturers do. A problem for the ethics of terrorism and other armed conflicts with or between non-state agents is the lack of any comparably clear and widely accepted understanding regarding who should count as a combatant. Problems generated by that issue run throughout attempts to apply the rules of war to combat with or between non-state agents. As David Luban has noted, such difficulties pose a dilemma for counterterrorism. In a war between nations or states, terrorists can be treated straightforwardly as war criminals and held accountable for violating IHL. But outside the context of a war between states, should terrorists even be regarded as military opponents? Should they be dealt with through civilian criminal law? Each approach has advantages and disadvantages. Luban finds that the war on terrorism since 9/11 has improvised a combination of military and criminal law models, in an attempt to have the advantages without the restrictions of each (Luban 2002).

3. THE MILITARY MODEL OF COUNTERTERRORISM

Not only is terrorism not a state agent. It is not an agent. Of any kind. And so some find the idea of war on terrorism metaphorical, like "war on cancer" or "war on poverty." Yet, the choice of a non-agent as the target in the slogan "war on terrorism" is no doubt a public policy move. It is easier to enlist cooperation in hostilities against an abstract target like "terrorism" that cannot suffer pain or have its dignity abused, a target with which many are not apt to identify, than to enlist cooperation in hostilities explicitly against human beings who are as vulnerable as oneself. But the military force invoked in a war on terrorism (but absent in "wars" on cancer and poverty) is no metaphor. "War on terrorism" means, literally, that military weapons, prisons, interrogators, and so forth will be used against terrorists and their supporters.

Insofar as it relies on military weapons, prisons, interrogators, and so forth, a war on terrorism directly invokes a military approach to counterterrorism. A war on terrorism is a war on terrorist organizations and their allies, who are agents. Difficulties that lead such organizations to improvise their own rules of engagement are difficulties also for nations or states who would try to engage them militarily. Rules of war tend to make the idea of such engagement incoherent. The upshot is that "war on terrorism" is morally problematic in many of the same ways as terrorism. It tends to destabilize what fragile order exists internationally. For it becomes very unpredictable who will and who will not be treated as a legitimate military target or detainee. That unpredictability produces an international atmosphere of fear and uncertainty. If terrorists are thrown back on their own subjective improvisations, so are opponents who treat them as warriors. It is as unclear to the opponents of terrorism as to terrorists themselves, whom they cannot target directly and intentionally. Rules of war no longer help. How are terrorists to be identified? Who can legitimately be taken prisoner? How are prisoners to be treated – as POWs? As war *criminals*? These unclarities should worry other nations and non-state groups. When it is unclear what rules of war *require* in a such a conflict, how can it be determined that terrorists or suspected terrorists have *violated* them? The temptation is to use straightforwardly terrorist means but simply call them military actions. In holding without trial for an indefinite period, perhaps for the duration (whatever that may be), detainees who may have been arbitrarily rounded up and treated as though they were enemies, a war on terrorism fails to act toward victims on the basis of principles to which they could rationally consent. It treats them merely as means insofar as it uses them to threaten others.[15] "War on terrorism" thus appears to be a euphemism for terrorist counterterrorism.

Terrorist organizations are groups with enough internal structure that they can act. But they are not like state agents. They need not be organized in a way that authorizes anyone to conclude a peace in their name. Who, on the side of the terrorist organization, would be bound by agreements entered into by that organization? If a terrorist leader were killed, is there an established office that the next leader would occupy? Not only does al Qaeda not speak for all Islamic terrorists, it is unclear who speaks for al Qaeda, even that anyone can. Al Qaeda cells appear not to be a hierarchy but related more like knots in a net. Destroy a ladder's base, and the top collapses. Destroy a hierarchy's top, and the base lacks direction. Destroy cells in a network, and the rest may simply fill in to mend the net. With no one to negotiate a peace, how can a war against terrorists end? What is to prevent a war of extermination? Luban concludes that since new terrorists will always arise, such a war never can be concluded but only abandoned (Luban 2002, p. 13).

But would peace with a terrorist organization make any sense as an objective, even if it were possible? Or, is a terrorist organization, like Murder, Inc. (which included terrorism in its repertoire), a group that

---

[15] See, for example, the memoir by Moazzam Begg (2006), a British-born Muslim raised in Birmingham, who was seized from a family home in Pakistan in 2002 and held for three years in prisons at Guantánamo, Bagram, and Kandahar, where he reports that he was interrogated hundreds of times and that he witnessed the killings of two detainees.

deserves no respect? It is important to be careful, here, about what is meant by "a terrorist organization." A body (such as a state) might engage in some terrorism in contravention of its own principles or in very limited forms of terrorism. Organizations that resort to terrorism are not necessarily defined by terrorism. The idea of a terrorist organization sounds like the idea of a group the values and principles of which are compatible with and endorse terrorism, if not a group that exists primarily to engage in terrorist means of protesting, resisting, or implementing other values. If terrorism is basically a means, even a terrorist organization is not defined simply by values and principles that endorse terrorism.

Rules of war are designed to facilitate the achievement of a lasting peace by precluding the kinds of conduct during war that are certain to leave defeated parties thirsting for revenge. The object of war between states is ordinarily to subdue, not obliterate, the opponent. When one nation aims to destroy the other completely, its intentions are genocidal. Yet even the ideal object of a war on terrorism is not to conclude a lasting peace with terrorist organizations, any more than the ideal object of a war on drugs or on crime is to conclude a lasting peace with drug dealers or a lasting peace with criminal organizations, such as Murder, Inc. There is no presumption, moral or political, that drug cartels or organized crime have a right to exist or that opponents owe them respect. States ordinarily deserve a certain respect, despite evil administrations, on the basis of their underlying values and potentialities for self-correction and moral improvement. A terrorist organization that lacks redeeming values and procedures for self-correction or moral improvement would lack such bases for respect. But it is important to beware of labeling an organization "terrorist" in a way that begs that question. If any organization that has relied on terrorism to achieve any of its important ends is thereby a terrorist organization, then the superpowers of the world are all terrorist organizations.

Some of these issues are not unique to war on terrorism (or on drugs or on crime). Analogous issues can arise for civil wars, muddying the application of rules of war. By tradition, a just war is declared by appropriate authorities, commonly taken to be states, who also have the authority to negotiate for peace. But who has authority to declare war on a state from within or to negotiate a peace to conclude such a war? Who speaks for "the people" against its government? If no one has that authority, then, by the traditions of just war theory, no civil war could be just, which is implausible (although it appears to have been Kant's view; Kant 1996a, pp. 461–66). Basic rules for internal conflicts are contained in Protocol II of 1977 additional to the Geneva Conventions, although those rules do not provide for criminal liability. Perhaps future conventions will devise rules for other non-state agents, perhaps even some that today are called terrorist.

Not all the problems of the post-9/11 war on terrorism stem from the unclarities of armed conflicts with or between non-state agents. WMD pose a general problem that affects wars between states as well. WMD make it nearly impossible to target combatants without killing even more non-combatants. The attacks of 9/11 turned aircraft into WMD. Kaldor notes that a hundred years ago "the ratio of military to civilian casualties in wars was 8:1" but that by the end of the twentieth century that ratio "has been almost exactly reversed: in the wars of the 1990s, the ratio of military to civilian casualties is 1:8" (Kaldor 2001, p. 8). She concludes, "Behaviour that was proscribed according to the classical rules of warfare and codified in the laws of war in the late nineteenth century and early twentieth century ... now constitutes an essential component of the strategies of the new mode of warfare" (Kaldor 2001, p. 8). Some think that such facts about modern warfare make the *jus in bello* discrimination principle obsolete. One could as well draw an opposing conclusion: that since wars conducted with WMD cannot be just, *war* should be obsolete.

Yet there are ways and ways of killing civilians. The discrimination principle of just war theory is not yet vacuous. It makes clear that some kinds of *reasons* cannot justify targeting non-combatants: revenge, demoralizing a civilian population, or sport, for example. Nevertheless, the overwhelming difficulties at present of defining restraints on combat in a war on terrorism point toward the conclusion that a war so conceived cannot be fought justly. To the extent that the same problem infects modern warfare generally, the same conclusion looms there. Whether it can be morally *excusable* to wage or engage in such a war may depend partly on what other agents, who are not direct parties to the conflicts, have done or omitted to do. A look at some desperate responses by private individuals to terrorisms they have faced alone is suggestive.

4. AN ANALOGY WITH PRIVATE COUNTERTERRORISMS

The reigning stereotype of the terrorist is someone who carries out destructive acts against public institutions, such as governments, or in public places, seeking attention for clearly political causes. This kind of terrorism produces a spectacle. It has been pointed out by Jonathan Glover (Frey and Morris 1991, pp. 256–75), and long before by Emma Goldman (Goldman 1969, pp. 79–108), that the stereotype of spectacular terrorism ignores state terrorism, including what Scheffler calls "state terror," such as that of Nero, Hitler, Stalin, Idi Amin, and Pol Pot against citizens of their own states. States' reliance on terror (with the same patterns of direct and indirect targets) is often clandestine, sometimes masked by public show trials. It is relatively low profile rather than spectacular, so low that many do not see it as terrorism at all. Chapter 6 argues that the popular stereotype also ignores the even lower-profile terrorisms of violence in the home and ordinary civilian rape.[16] When high-profile terrorism is not being effectively restrained by international organizations or cooperation from other nations, responder nations might profit from reflecting on some analogous situations of private citizens who have responded to private terrorisms that the civilian criminal law could not be counted on to restrain.

On Walzer's view of terrorism, it is difficult to perceive either the practice of rape or systematic violence in the home as terrorist. Victims are usually not selected randomly by rapists and almost never by batterers. On Scheffler's view, the systematic use of terror in the home appears more analogous to what he calls "state terror," in that terror is used to maintain a certain order and a monopoly of power, rather than to destabilize or degrade a social order. Still, there are ways in which both the Hobbesian and Kantian approaches to terrorism do apply to the cases of rape and domestic violence. Cruelty is there not only in the injuries inflicted by assailants but also in the timing of their attacks and in the effects on children raised in terrorist environments. The unpredictability of attacks hampers self-defense, a predicament that leads to desperate measures by victims and potential victims. If a social order is not destabilized by unchecked rape and domestic violence, it is certainly degraded in that the quality of life for women within the social order is low and fear reigns, with most of the disastrous consequences of a lack of order: lives that are nasty, brutish, and poor, sometimes also shortened.

The disrespect salient in the Kantian approach is also present in the practice of rape and in violence in the home in the uses of coercion to maintain relationships that subordinate women.[17] As with punishment, threats do most of the intimidating. The intimidated include women who are not raped as well as women who are. Violence in the home need not occur daily to have a daily impact. Rape as a social institution and

---

[16] Chapter 6 takes up these kinds of clandestine terrorism and defends more fully the view that violence in the home and rape (both in the home and outside) are terrorist practices.

[17] Men, too, are victims of domestic violence, some from women, some from teenaged children. But that violence is not part of a more general social pattern that subordinates men to women.

systematic violence in the home often include "throwaway" direct targets used to send a message. Victims who are killed by rapists are used by others to send a message to women generally. Animal companions are killed by domestic abusers as a warning and demonstration of intent.

For anyone who is inclined to support the idea of a war on terrorism, it should be an interesting question whether the military approach would also provide an appropriate model of counterterrorism for women who have to defend themselves against rape terrorism and terrorism in the home. Should the more permissive standards of war, as opposed to the less permissive standards of civilian criminal law, govern women's responses to rape and domestic violence? Should survivors regard themselves as in a state of nature with respect to rapists and batterers, as though civil governments, criminal laws, and courts did not exist? In the US (and not only in the US), the law's record of response to these crimes is poor. Let us consider the cases of two women who stepped outside the law to protect themselves, as have so many others like them whose cases have not received comparable publicity or had nearly as satisfying outcomes for the women. Both were held accountable and both eventually exonerated, although in different ways.

The first case is the famous "burning bed." One night in 1977, Francine Hughes poured gasoline on her former husband, who was asleep, heavily intoxicated, in her home. She ignited it and then fled with her children. For years, he had been extremely physically abusive, inflicting injuries that sent her to the hospital. She divorced him. But she could not keep him out of her home. She called the cops. She appealed repeatedly to law enforcement to protect her and her children but with little success (McNulty 1980). Tried for murder, she was eventually acquitted on an insanity defense. But if it is justifiable in self-defense to step outside the law to deal with a terrorist whom the law appears unable or unwilling to restrain, should she even have been charged?

The second case is that of Inez García, who in 1974 shot at the two men who had raped her just minutes before, killing one of them. One of the men had held her down and assaulted her while his 300-pound accomplice stood guard. When they finished, García was physically free to walk or run away. After a phone call from one of them threatening her with murder if she did not leave the area, she instead pursued and shot at them, killing the accomplice. She regretted only that she did not succeed in killing the other man as well. He was never charged with any crime (Salter 1976; Wood 1976). Tried for murder in California, García was convicted and sentenced: five years to life. On appeal, she was exonerated. Attorney

Susan B. Jordan successfully argued self-defense. Should García not have been charged?

Hughes and García lacked legal authority to execute their assailants. Yet why does that matter, if not as part of a broader understanding of rules defining conditions of fair combat? Those rules are significantly breached already when men can rape and batter women with impunity. Is the real objection that war is not an appropriate female response? Or is there, perhaps, a legitimate concern that others' disregard for rules that define fair combat may not suffice to justify victims in disregarding those rules as well, as Rawls believed that others' intolerance may not suffice to justify our refusing to tolerate them?

Recall that Rawls's view was that the belief, with reason, that one's security is endangered by others' intolerance can justify refusing to tolerate them. At any rate, he believed that *justice* cannot require us to tolerate the intolerant when they endanger our own security. The justifying, or perhaps excusing, consideration is not simply the fact that others are intolerant but that their intolerance is reasonably believed to endanger our security.

Rawls was thinking of the justice of laws, not of individual responses to particular assaults. But a similar rationale can be invoked to justify, or perhaps excuse, individual refusals to tolerate the intolerant. In a context in which the state is charged with protecting our security, its history of failure to do so can provide at least a moral excuse for individuals to take measures to protect themselves that would not otherwise have been justifiable or excusable.[18] In the cases of Hughes and García, the justifying, or perhaps excusing, consideration was not simply the fact that the men they killed had violated their rights in ways that put them in mortal danger. Rather, the women believed, with reason, that the behavior that endangered them was not being restrained, nor was it going to be restrained, by anyone else. Similarly, a nation that believes, with reason, that its security is endangered and that the parties endangering it are not being restrained, nor are they going to be restrained, by anyone else might at least have a moral excuse for violating some of the requirements of IHL, if necessary, to defend itself. A history of failure to protect also gives the parties who have failed, when they are in a position to judge the case, special reason to excuse those who take the law into their own hands.

---

[18] It does not provide an excuse or justification for "whatever is necessary," as there are limits to what one can do, morally, even in self-defense or defense of others. This issue returns in chapter 7 on torture.

There is something outrageous, of course, in comparing the US to raped and battered women.[19] Women are relatively powerless, compared to their assailants, whereas the US is the most powerful nation in the world. The US can hardly claim to have suffered anything analogous to rape from its assailants. Yet the analogy is not that the moral history or even the power position of the US is comparable to that of García or Hughes. Rather, as targets of terrorism that was apparently unrestrained by any law or enforcement agencies, their dilemmas are intriguingly similar. Anyone can be vulnerable to terrorism, as 9/11 demonstrates, regardless of their power or moral position. The relevant similarity is that, like Hughes and García, the US in declaring a war on terrorism stepped outside of existing law (IHL, in this case) to defend itself against assailants who also had stepped outside the law *and who were not being restrained or held accountable by anyone else or by any law.*[20] If a counterterrorist war on terrorism is morally justifiable or excusable on the grounds that no one else is going to restrain terrorists who are endangering national security, then, under those circumstances, it is not the evil that it would be without such a history and context. Yet it is important to recognize the features that such a "war" shares with paradigms of terrorism. A war on terrorism, even if justifiable or excusable, remains at least as morally problematic as the actions taken by Hughes and García.

5. JUSTICE FOR THE UNJUST

How much justice should be shown those who disregard justice themselves? Criminals often flagrantly disregard justice and fairness in how they treat their victims.[21] Yet modern democratic states offer them a trial and legal representation. This practice is not a matter of turning the other cheek. Fair trials give the wrongly accused an opportunity to rebut charges. Striking back without trial ignores the likelihood of errors in identifying assailants and in understanding what they did and why, or the conditions under which they acted. The point applies also to international terrorism. Without fair trials for suspected terrorists, what assurance have civilians around the world that they will not be wrongly identified as terrorists and

---

[19] I encountered vigorous resistance to this analogy when I ran the idea by audiences at two feminist conferences.

[20] There may, of course, also be relevant differences in the realistic alternatives that each had and the alternatives, if any, that they had exhausted before making the choices they made.

[21] Not always, of course. Sometimes it is obedience to the law that is unjust.

summarily imprisoned or dispatched? They have no such assurance, as the history of detention centers in the war on terrorism demonstrates.

Further, a fair trial sends the message that those who are imprisoned or executed because they were found guilty did something wrong, not just that they were defeated by an enemy. That kind of issue was raised in defense of the creation of the International Military Tribunal (IMT) at Nuremberg in 1945. The realistic alternative to such a tribunal, following tradition, would have been to shoot Axis leaders from a select list decided on ("pricked") by the Allies. In defense of the Nuremberg trials and against that alternative, Chief Prosecutor Telford Taylor noted that "too many people believed that they had been *wrongfully* hurt by the leaders of the Third Reich and wanted a *judgment* to that effect," and "furthermore ... the spectacle of Joseph Stalin, who had sent uncounted thousands of his own countrymen to their deaths by his 'political decisions,' sitting as one of a triumvirate to 'prick' a list of Germans, would have made their decisions a target of mockery as long as memory endured" (Taylor 1992, p. 33). Even that solution was less than ideal, given the past deeds of Stalin, whose regime was represented in the judgments against German leaders. As perpetrators of saturation bombing during WW II, the US and Britain, like Stalin at Nuremberg, also had less than perfect credibility as judges of war criminals. All the more reason to insist on fair trials and to support an international court.

If Hughes and García had good reasons for their killings, given their circumstances and the existing law, the states of Michigan and California also had good reasons to charge them with the crime of murder and make them stand trial. It is true that the *moral* authority of those states to try the women for those crimes was compromised by the states' prior failures to take seriously enough the crimes of rape and domestic violence.[22] But trials can publicize and document those very facts. Trials and hearings determine formally whether a deed was defensible, thereby offering some assurance to others that they cannot be killed with impunity by just anyone who is afraid of them or apprehensive of what they might do. Unless the incineration of Hughes's batterer was torture (a matter to which I return in chapter 7), it could have been *morally* permissible to acquit her *without*

---

[22] Elsewhere (Card 1995, pp. 109–17) I have argued that the law should expand its understanding of battering to take account of patterns in relationship violence, as, in making stalking a crime in the 1990s, the laws of most states in the US took into account oppressive patterns of acts that were not individually illegal. Legal understandings of battering have tended to be modeled on the paradigm of a barroom brawl, an isolated episode. That paradigm fails to capture the terrorism of battering in the home, which is a campaign, a policy, not an isolated episode.

an insanity defense, had it been legally possible to do so, given her history of having exhausted less desperate responses. What was *legally* problematic was not that she used fire but that the man she killed was asleep, unforewarned, not attacking her at that moment. Her deed did not fit the legal understanding of permissible self-defense, and so the only way to acquit her in the state of Michigan at that time was to use the insanity defense, even though she may never have been saner up to that point.

Hughes and García engaged in pre-emptive strikes. Although he was asleep when she incinerated him, the batterer of Hughes was a continuing threat, as were the rapists of García. If pre-emptive strikes can in principle be justified or at least excused internationally, why not in the home or on the street?[23] I want to leave open the possibility that they can be. But process matters, too. For it is not only the immediate victim and perpetrator who have an interest in how the case is handled.

A nation that makes war on terrorism takes international law into its own hands, as Hughes and García did with the state criminal law. It steps outside the bounds and processes of law instead of working within them. Like all analogies, this one is imperfect. García did not make war on the institution of rape, nor did Hughes make war on the general practice of violence in the home. (Yet if other women followed their example, those practices would take a serious hit.) Still, both women acted as though they were in a state of nature, which is what terrorists appear to do; they work from outside the system, rather than using it from within. Their pre-emptive killings lacked the coercive aspect of terrorism, in that neither woman had an ulterior motive or used terror to send a message or to control or manipulate. There was nevertheless potential for the Hobbesian effect of destabilizing a social order in the precedent that would have been set, had there been no accountability. And it is unclear that any of these killings were compatible with principles to which rational parties could reasonably consent.

If Michigan was justified in trying Hughes and if California was justified in trying García for the sake of upholding the rule of law, would it not be justifiable on the same ground for international tribunals to charge and try as terrorists national leaders who respond to terrorism with terrorism? The alternatives (like the historic alternative to the kind of trial held at Nuremberg) could be more unjust on the whole, provided that in the event of a trial, neither a guilty verdict nor the failure of all appeals is a

---

[23] I am grateful to Mohammed Abed for formulating the question so aptly.

foregone conclusion. International trials for war crimes of the leaders of a state that wages a terroristic war against terrorists who were unrestrained by other states could be morally defensible for the message it would send to other nations and civilians around the world.

Yet it is surely still more just and more sensible to try suspected rapists and batterers than to leave women to defend themselves by whatever means they can improvise and then try *them* for violating the law. Likewise, it would be more sensible for nations collectively, or international organizations, to capture and try in international courts members or allies of organizations suspected of international terrorism than to leave targeted states to take matters into their own hands in an improvised "war" and then have them tried later in an international court for violations of IHL. If this is correct, nations have serious collective work to do on issues of intervention where terrorism looms. My conclusion is neither to recommend a terrorist response to terrorism nor to hold that such a response to terrorism is morally inexcusable (and thereby an evil), although I believe that some *kinds* of terrorist response are inexcusable (and thereby evils).[24] Rather, no nation should be left to confront international terrorism on its own. Nations should take responsibility together for preserving the rule of law, as was attempted at Nuremberg. That requires all nations, at least those most powerful, to support an international criminal court.

It is at least partly an empirical question in any particular case whether a nation targeted by terrorists was in fact abandoned by other nations or international organizations, as so many women have been abandoned by law enforcement to face rapists and batterers with nothing but their own resources and ingenuity. And it is at least partly an empirical question what alternative responses were available and had been tried.

---

[24] Chapter 7 argues that the use of torture is inexcusable. Genocide is also inexcusable.

CHAPTER 6

Low-profile terrorism

> Most of the preventable suffering and death in the world is
> not caused by terrorism. It is caused by malnutrition, and lack
> of education, and all the ills connected to poverty. (Martha
> Nussbaum, in Sterba 2003, p. 248)

Most evils are not dramatic attention-getters. Martha Nussbaum's contrast of terrorism with poverty may be true. But how would we know? The ability to make that observation seems to presuppose a high-profile paradigm of terrorism, at least that terrorism is as visible as poverty. Yet terrorism is far commoner than its high-profile paradigms suggest. Most of it is not very public and is not identified or documented as terrorism. Under oppressive regimes, in racist environments, in organized crime, in inner cities policed by gangs, and in the everyday lives of women, children, and elders everywhere who suffer routine violence in their own homes, systematic uses of terror degrade the environments of ordinary people without capturing any more public attention than most poverty does.

High-profile paradigms include the French Resistance, British carpet-bombings during WW II, activities of the Weather Underground in the United States and the Baader-Meinhof group in Germany during the 1970s, and even ongoing anti-abortion terrorism in the US.[1] But most terrorism is very low profile, unspectacular, except to those who suffer it. It is mostly executed with no pretense to justification or moral excuse. The previous chapter focused on international terrorism, which is relatively high profile. The focus shifts in this chapter to low-profile, everyday terrorism, most

---

[1] On the Baader-Meinhof group, see Aust (2009). On 1970s terrorism in the US, see the documentary films *The Weather Underground* (2003) and *The War at Home* (1979), both nominated for Academy Awards. In her contribution to *The Oxford Handbook of Crime and Public Policy*, Laura Dugan cites statistics indicating that between 1976 and 1994 anti-abortion groups were responsible for more claimed (that is, owned) acts of terrorism than any other group in the US (Tonry 2009, p. 439). In 1994, the federal government passed the Freedom of Access to Abortion Clinic Entrances Act (the FACE act), imposing civil and criminal penalties. During the ten years following the FACE act, there were significantly fewer instances of claimed anti-abortion terrorism (Tonry 2009, p. 444).

of it domestic, and much of that domestic in more than one sense. The objectives in this chapter are to justify an expanded range of paradigms that is not limited to high-profile practices, to use that expanded range of paradigms to gain further clarity about how terrorism works, to expose everyday terrorisms, and to do all of this without diminishing the moral gravity embedded in the concept of terrorism.

To recognize as terrorism the systematic uses of terror in the everyday lives of people who may never make headlines, and at the same time to deepen our appreciation of terrorism in more high-profile instances, it is helpful to experience imaginatively the positions of potential terrorists as well as those of potential targets. In his early essay on method, "Outline of a Decision Procedure for Ethics," John Rawls included in his definition of a "competent moral judge" a "sympathetic knowledge of those human interests which, by conflicting in particular cases, give rise to the need to make a moral decision" (Rawls 1999b, p. 3). Some of this knowledge we get by our own direct experience. But that is not enough. We must also be able to experience imaginatively the interests of others whose values and priorities may differ from our own. The same point applies more generally than just to understanding interests. Understanding how people think in crisis situations that we may be lucky enough not to experience directly also requires that we be able to experience those situations imaginatively, from the perspectives of parties who do experience them directly. By experiencing a situation imaginatively from another's point of view, I do not mean (nor did Rawls) endorsing their judgments or even being favorably disposed toward them. I mean entering imaginatively into their situations and taking up their points of view to gain a livelier and more nuanced appreciation of their feelings, options, reasonings, and motives. The two models of terrorism introduced in the next section set a stage for the thought experiment of the last section, which attempts this imaginative experiencing, first with terrorist victims and then with terrorists, in an effort to clarify how terrorism works.

Unlike torture and genocide, terrorism has not been defined in conventions of the UN. The historical evolution of what is today called terrorism invites a Wittgensteinian family resemblance approach to the meaning of that concept (Wittgenstein 1958, pp. 31–33), which I attempt here, supplementing it with my own variation on a Nietzschean perspectivism. In his *Philosophical Investigations*, Ludwig Wittgenstein observed of concepts that have a history and so have evolved, such as the concept of a game, that there need be no characteristic common to all instances of the concept. Instances are recognizable by resemblances they bear to other instances, as members of a family can be recognizable as such even when there is no feature, such as shape of the nose, that they all have in common (Wittgenstein 1958, p. 32e). Friedrich Nietzsche's perspectivism suggests also that the meaning of an event or a concept can vary tremendously according to the different points of view (often from different power positions) of those who experience the event or use the concept. He illustrates the idea with aristocratic and slave modes of valuation, which invite readers to take up the vastly different points of view of slaves and aristocrats on the interactions between them, yielding two very different meanings of "good" (Nietzsche 1969, pp. 24–26). Nietzsche's perspectivism suggests one way in which family resemblances can develop without a common or essential characteristic.

Accordingly, instead of searching for necessary and sufficient conditions of terrorism, I begin with two models of terrorism that fit high-profile paradigms, which I call the "the coercion model" and the "group target model." These models correspond roughly (but only roughly) to what I called in chapter 5 the Kantian and Hobbesian approaches to terrorism. We need not think of the coercion and group target models as the only models of terrorism. But they will do for present purposes if many forms of terrorism are recognizable by the strong resemblances they bear to one or the other. Each model has philosophical appeal. Each emerges from important histories. Even if, ultimately, one model might absorb the other, both remain useful for their encouragement of identifications with different parties. The coercion model encourages one to take up the perspective of a potential terrorist; the group target model, that of a potential victim.

I. TWO MODELS OF TERRORISM

One test of a satisfactory conception of terrorism is whether it makes sense of a wide range of paradigm instances. A paradigm is a real instance that appears to relevantly informed and clear-headed thinkers to be non-controversially an instance.[2] In calling such instances paradigms, I intend no judgment about their morality but only a judgment that these are clear instances of the phenomenon. Further, there need be no consensus on what *makes* something an instance, only on whether it is. Like Rawls's "considered moral judgments," these non-controversial judgments are firm

---

[2] Again, I borrow from Rawls, this time patterning my idea of a paradigm after his idea of a "considered moral judgment" (Rawls 1999b, pp. 5–7), which is a real judgment, not a hypothetical or imaginary one. Reitan (2001) employs this sense of "paradigm" in an insightful essay on rape as an essentially contested concept.

but also revisable (Rawls 1999b, pp. 5–7). Our paradigms are cases about which we are most confident now, based on what we think we know now.

Another test of a satisfactory conception is whether it enables us to recognize instances we had failed to appreciate before and to understand why we should have. Something like Rawls's idea of "reflective equilibrium" (Rawls 1999a, pp. 18–19), which he applies to moral theory, can apply to more specific moral and political concepts, such as terrorism. Thus, to arrive at a satisfactory conception of terrorism, we may go back and forth between an abstract conception and paradigm cases, now revising the conception, now rejecting old paradigms, perceiving them differently, or admitting new ones. A satisfactory conception will make sense of a significant body of uncontroversial cases, help us to appreciate instances that are not so widely recognized, and provide bases for arguing about controversial and borderline cases.

Think of a model as a blueprint for a definition or conception, an abstraction that highlights particular elements or relationships in what it models. Different models suggest different ways to conceive of terrorism by encouraging us to approach it from different angles and by highlighting different elements or relationships. The coercion model highlights elements that suggest the projects of terrorists, who may not appreciate fully the impact on victims. The group target model, in contrast, highlights elements that suggest the perceptions of victims, who may not appreciate terrorists' intentions. Each model is limited. Yet each points beyond its limits.

The coercion model is developed in Carl Wellman's 1979 essay on terrorism. It focuses on the logic of terrorism, how the terrorist thinks, what the terrorist hopes to achieve. Ultimately, it encourages inquiry into why such drastic means would be chosen to achieve those objectives. Recall from chapter 5 that as Wellman sees it, terrorism typically has two targets: the target of harm and the target of coercion. The target of harm is direct but secondary in importance and may be a person or persons or even property. The indirect target is primary in that it is the intended recipient of a message containing the terrorist's demands, sent to the indirect target by way of violence or a threat of violence to the direct target. Indirect targets must be human beings, not property, as only human beings can be coerced. Direct targets can be either. A classic example of terrorist activity that fits this model is bombing a public building (direct but secondary target) to pressure a government (indirect but primary target) to release prisoners or alter policies. The 1970 bombing of the Army/Math Research Center in Sterling Hall on my campus (the University of Wisconsin, Madison) by students known thereafter as "the Sterling Hall Four" fits this model if we read that bombing as carrying an implicit demand to the US government to get out of Vietnam or at least stop using napalm.[3] This deed was intended to destroy only property, although in fact it killed physicist Robert Fassnacht, who was working in the basement. The message of a terrorist bombing, often implicit, is "accede to our demands, or there will be further bombings." The building and its occupants may be treated as "throwaways." Their survival may not matter to achievement of the terrorist's objective, whereas survival of the primary target is usually essential to the terrorists' ends.

Other examples captured by the coercion model include systematic policies of hostage-taking, kidnap for ransom, some forms of witness intimidation, some forms of extortion practiced in organized crime, such as the Godfather's "offers one cannot refuse" (Puzo 1978), the practice of drive-by shooting by gangs, and cross-burnings by the Ku Klux Klan (KKK). On Samuel Scheffler's view of terrorism, these activities are not terrorist because they do not aim to destabilize a society (Scheffler 2006, pp. 11–13). They appear to do something like the opposite: stabilize an oppressive relationship. Yet because these systematic uses of terror create an atmosphere of terror that severely degrades the quality of living environments, which can be at least as grave a harm as destabilizing their order, they capture much of the spirit of the Hobbesian approach underlying Scheffler's view. Scheffler's point that not all uses of fear or terror are terrorist is nevertheless well taken. Appeals to fear that are ultimately benign, such as classroom threats of penalties for late papers (Wellman 1979), and more limited hostile uses of terror, such as muggings (at least, when not pervasive in a locale), do not deserve to be regarded as terrorist, as their negative impact on the whole environment is less grave. But even if the ambitions of KKK groups, drive-by shooters, and hostage-takers are more limited than those of terrorists who aim to destabilize a government, they are serious enough in scope and cruelty to warrant distinguishing them from ultimately benign appeals to fear and from criminal activity that impacts social environments far less. Like poverty, low-profile but systematic uses of terror for ultimately hostile ends may ruin more lives than are ruined or destroyed by terrorists who aim to take down a government, if only because the more ambitious terrorists are less likely to succeed.

---

[3] Bates (1992) is an excellent investigative journalistic account of this event and its aftermath. On October 18, 1967, students had protested the presence of Dow Chemical Company, as makers of napalm, on the University of Wisconsin–Madison campus to interview seniors. That event triggered "the war at home." (See note 1 above.)

Yet one might wonder whether the coercion model captures even such relatively high-profile uses of terror as those of partisan resisters in WW II who bombed trains headed for the death camps in Poland. These deeds are paradigm candidates for justified terrorism (Hare 1979, p. 247). They might not appear to fit the coercion model in that they do not present the primary target with a demand or offer a choice. Yet they send messages: to the Allies, "pay attention to these trains" and to Nazis, "we will not just stand by but will do all in our power to stop you," an urgent message in the context of widespread European acquiescence to Nazi policies. There is nevertheless a resemblance to the coercion model in that the pattern of a direct and indirect target and a message remains, even if coercion drops out. Coercion is not an option for those with little power. But the relatively impotent may still be able to use terrorist means to send a message.

Coercive terrorism is limited to those who have the power to coerce. Also, it carries certain risks for the terrorist. As with interrogational torture, it is possible for terrorists to go too far and defeat their purposes. The primary (indirect) target may be too devastated by harm to the direct target to care about the message or may be unable to comply with demands. The message may not get across, or not as intended. When communication fails, there may appear to be no message. But that conjecture gets ahead of this story, anticipating how targets perceive matters.

In presenting the coercion model, Wellman did not defend terrorism. Yet it seems no accident that he found that model apt in the 1970s. Popular paradigms of terrorism in the US then included an array of morally and politically motivated non-lethal violent crimes, mainly property destruction, carried out by citizens from well-off and highly respected families.[4] These crimes ranged from bombings by the Weather Underground to "monkeywrenching" by environmental activists, such as tree-spiking and sabotage of off-road vehicles used in projects destructive of natural habitats.[5] Environmental activists sent clear demands to stop specific practices. Their objectives, if not their methods, evoked sympathy from social critics on the left.

If the coercion model invites a focus on terrorist reasoning, the *group target model*, in contrast, invites a focus on target predicaments. The group

---

[4] Braudy's memoir (2003) details her career and background as a member of the Weather Underground. She eventually served twenty-two-and-a-half years in prison for complicity in a bank holdup. See, also, the documentary film, *The Weather Underground* (2003).

[5] The term "monkeywrenching" is taken from Abbey's novel, *The Monkey Wrench Gang* (1975). Tree-spiking is an example of throwing a monkey wrench into a project perceived to be environmentally destructive. For more examples, see Foreman and Haywood (1993).

target model appears to be at work in Michael Walzer's widely cited chapter on terrorism (Walzer 1977, pp. 197–206).[6] Although Walzer describes terrorist violence as targeting victims randomly ("its method is the random murder of innocent people"), what he has in mind is randomness *within a group*, as he also characterizes terrorism as "the systematic terrorizing of whole populations" in order "to destroy the morale of a nation or a class" (Walzer 1977, p. 197). Again, there is a primary target, often less obvious than the immediate (direct) targets. The primary target on this model is a group, a "class," which might be racial, ethnic, or religious, not just national. Immediate targets appear (at least, to members of the target group) to be randomly chosen in that they are selected not for their individual deeds (they are in that sense "innocent") but simply on account of their identity as members of the group. Immediate targets could also be persons or property of presumed value to the group, targeted for that reason. The apparent objective is to hurt the group (to demoralize them, for example); harm to immediate targets is either part of or a means to that end. There need be no further aim, such as to coerce.

The group target model makes terrorist sense of some ethnic, racist, and religious harassment that lacks a clear and specific coercive intent. An example is the routine physical beatings of Jewish students on their way to school by groups of Christian students on examination days, as recounted by Simon Wiesenthal in his memoir *The Sunflower* (Wiesenthal 1997, pp. 18–20). The immediate aim was to hinder Jewish students from passing exams, to exclude them from qualifying for the professions. Yet there was no evident demand, satisfaction of which would have ended the harassment of Jewish students. Were it not exams and the professions, it would likely have been something else. Other examples that fit the group target model are indiscriminate vigilante activities by race-supremacist organizations, such as KKK groups, and vendettas that sanction indiscriminate targeting of members of offending families.

The coercion model might be made compatible with the group target model by the supposition that there is at least an implicit coercive demand for the entire group to leave. But that demand is unrealistic when there is no place for the group to go. A more realistic goal is marginalization, exclusion from ordinary desirable positions in society. Terrorism so used becomes an instrument of oppression.

---

[6] A version of what I am calling the group target model is sketched by Reitan in a paper (unpublished) presented at the Pacific Division Convention of the American Philosophical Society, March 2005; cited with permission.

A shortcoming of the group target model is that it does not encourage inquiry into why assailants wish to harm the group. Perhaps the assumption is that it does not matter: people should not be harmed on the basis of their identity as members of such groups, whatever the reason. But without a rationale, we can be misled about who the primary target is. When we discover animating objectives, we sometimes identify the primary target differently, often more (or less) specifically, as I will argue in section 3 of this chapter with respect to rape terrorism.

Even if neither model entirely absorbs the other, many terrorist deeds fit both. On both models, individuals can be deliberately harmed (or threatened) without regard to anything they have done as individuals. Yet a lack of scruple regarding who is harmed is not central to the coercion model. On both models, targets may be coerced into acceding to terrorists' demands. Yet coercion appears not to be central to the group target model: terrorism may continue even though demands are met, and there may be no end to demands. The two models also incorporate some of the same features. On both, there is no procedural justice in target selection. On both, there is, if not major harm or an attempt at it, at least a credible threat of harm.

Yet there are also important differences. On the group target model, terrorism appears to lie on a continuum of hate crime, the extreme of which is genocide. The coercion model does not put terrorism on that continuum. On the contrary, the coercion model suggests grounds for relative optimism regarding terrorists' amenability to dialogue and argument. Coercive terrorists may hope to succeed by relying on threats and avoid ever having to carry them out.

It is the group target model, however, that captures much popular thinking in the US today about terrorism. Popular thinking about terrorism today would have US citizens identify not only *with* but *as* potential direct targets who have done nothing to provoke attack. It is no accident that this model enjoys popularity following the 1993 bombing of the World Trade Center and the massively lethal bombing in 1995 in Oklahoma City and those of September 11, 2001 (9/11) in New York City and Washington DC. Objectives behind these bombings have not been made specific and explicit. They evoke no widespread sympathy in the US on either left or right, although the 9/11 bombings have elicited many questions.[7] These deeds, along

---

[7] For a list of forty disturbing questions regarding 9/11, see Griffin (2004, pp. 197–201). Further materials (books, videos, websites) that raise and pursue questions about what occurred that day and in the aftermath are listed in *Global Outlook* (2005, no. 10), a periodical handed to me by an

with bombings of embassies and ships, are paradigms that underlay and informed the war on terrorism of the administration of former President George W. Bush. Interpreted through the group target model, they do not encourage inquiry into the motivations or reasonings of perpetrators.

2. WAR ON TERRORISM AND THE GROUP TARGET MODEL

The war on terrorism of the G. W. Bush administration appeared not only to invoke the group target model for the 9/11 attacks but also to exemplify that model in the way it routinely treated civilians who are, or who might appear to be, Arabs. The conduct of American soldiers in Iraq in rounding up detainees indiscriminately as "insurgents" illustrates routine military terrorism that targeted individuals randomly within a group. The Report of the International Committee of the Red Cross (ICRC) on the Treatment by the Coalition Forces (CF) of Prisoners of War and Other Protected Persons by the Geneva Conventions in Iraq during Arrest, Internment and Interrogation (2004) says:

Arresting authorities entered houses usually after dark, breaking down doors, waking up residents roughly, yelling orders, forcing family members into one room under military guard while searching the rest of the house and further breaking doors, cabinets, and other property. They arrested suspects, tying their hands in the back with flexi-cuffs, hooding them, and taking them away. Sometimes they arrested all adult males present in a house, including elderly, handicapped or sick people. Treatment often included pushing people around, insulting, taking aim with rifles, punching and kicking and striking with rifles. (Greenberg and Dratel 2005, p. 388)

The report goes on:

In almost all instances documented by the ICRC, arresting authorities provided no information about who they were, where their base was located, nor did they explain the cause of arrest. Similarly, they rarely informed the arrestee or his family where he was being taken and for how long, resulting in the de facto "disappearance" of the arrestee ... In the absence of a system to notify the families, many were left without news for months, often fearing that their relatives were dead. (Greenberg and Dratel 2005, pp. 388–89)

The report also notes that "certain CF military intelligence officers told the ICRC that in their estimate between *70 percent and 90 percent of the persons*

anonymous member of the audience at the University of Victoria, where I tried out some of the ideas in this chapter. The documentary film *Loose Change Final Cut* (2007) raises further questions.

deprived of their liberty in Iraq had been arrested by mistake" (emphasis added; Greenberg and Dratel 2005, p. 388).

"Mistakes" that occur 90 percent of the time are not mistakes. Nor is this the work of "a few bad apples." The group target model appears to fit. The *ostensible* purpose was to coerce information from detainees. But people were selected for round-up on the basis of their (perceived) identity, not on the basis of prior evidence that they had information. Terrorism was an expedient and a weapon. It may not be clear whether the message-to-others aspect of the coercion model also fits. There could be an implied message to others in the disappearances, if those disappearances are interpreted as hostage-taking: anyone else who knows anything had better come forward, or their families will be subjected to similar treatment. Even without any such message, this activity fits the group target model.

The post-9/11 war on terrorism was not a war on terrorism *in general*. Active opposition even to international terrorism *in general* would express a rejection of saturation bombings as practiced, for example, in WW II and would oppose the tactics described in the ICRC report. Opposition to all forms of terrorism would, in addition, publicly expose and aggressively oppose *as terrorist* many kinds of domestic criminal violence: disappearances of civilians engineered by oppressive regimes, systematic witness intimidation, practices of drive-by shooting, stalking, and rape, as well as ongoing intimate relationship violence. I select from this list for special attention, in sections 3 and 4 of this chapter, the cases of oppressive regimes and the doubly domestic crimes of rape and intimate relationship violence, all relatively low profile. A genuine war on terrorism might well begin at home.

It might be objected that because domestic violence and rapes are small scale compared with mass killings in the bombing of buildings or even ships, calling them "terrorist" alters the meaning and diminishes the gravity of the concept of terrorism. Widespread aggravated and forcible rape and poorly checked domestic violence are atrocities. But are they terrorism?

The appearance of a small scale comes from looking only at individual episodes or at episodes with a single victim or a few victims. Victims of rape and of domestic violence are more spread out in time and space than are the victims in bombed buildings. Collectively, rape and domestic violence victims are not less numerous. Individually, there are equally grave harms and fatalities. The environments degraded by such activities may be individually smaller. Collectively, they are vast. Those who suffer rape or violence in the home need not be prominent people or closely related to prominent people, and so, their traumas are less apt to be considered newsworthy. Such terrorism is better described as "low-profile" than as "small-scale."

The group target model is not apt for making the case that stalking and intimate relationship violence can take on terrorist dimensions. Because stalkers and domestic batterers target specific individuals who are not randomly chosen, it is not clear that they select their targets on the basis of a target's (perceived) group membership. The coercion model does not fit without tampering, either. For the coercion model to fit stalking or intimate relationship violence, the two targets must be collapsed into one. The party who is in danger of being harmed directly is also the party to whom a message, if any, is sent. Neither model as it stands is a good fit for the uses of terror in stalking and in intimate relationship violence. Nevertheless, these uses of terror bear strong resemblances to rape terrorism, which is a good fit for *both* models.

3. RAPE TERRORISM

Mass rape of civilians by soldiers and militias during the 1990s wars in the former Yugoslavia and in Rwanda has been publicly exposed as a weapon that was used in a deliberate and calculated manner.[8] It is now widely acknowledged that military rape is not simply a matter of "a few bad apples" but has been policy, that it can be torture, terrorism, and even a strategy of genocide.[9] That civilian practices of rape can also be terrorist may be less widely recognized except by feminist activists, who have been arguing the case since the 1970s.

War rape directly targets women and girls of all ages, even pregnant women, menstruating women, disabled women, injured women, sick women, even infants. The most salient feature of these targets is their gender, and so the crime initially appears misogynous and in that way to fit the group target model. Were the primary target simply females, however, its relation to war would appear to be only that war offers a context in which it is easy to commit the crime with impunity. That would not make rape, any more than looting, a weapon. When rape is a weapon, it is not simply a gigantic hate crime against women that happens to be

---

[8] The film *Hotel Rwanda* (2004), excellent in most respects, showed the machetes but failed to convey that mass rape was also a major weapon. For an account of the mass rape in Rwanda, including interviews with survivors, see Human Rights Watch (1996).

[9] How rape can be genocidal is the subject of chapter 10.

perpetrated by soldiers. A military objective of tolerating and encouraging war rape in the former Yugoslavia was to get Muslim *families* to leave the territory.[10] That means that rape and the threat of rape (direct targets of which were mainly female) were used as coercive weapons against a group (indirect target) that was not defined by gender. This crime, compatible with and no doubt expressive of misogyny, need not be motivated in the first instance and as a policy by misogyny.

As military policy, war rape fits both the coercion and group target models of terrorism. On the coercion model, the *primary* target is not women and girls. They are *direct* targets. The primary target is a people. A coercive threat (message) is aimed at those who resist or might resist leaving, slightly more specific than the people as a whole. Insofar as the objective is not simply to harm the group but to expel it, harm may appear secondary (although expulsion is itself harmful), which makes the coercion model seem right. The basis for selecting direct victims is that, because they are members of the group, public and publicized abuse of them can intimidate others into leaving.

It is less widely appreciated that much civilian rape is no more a matter of rotten apples than rape in war but is part of a widespread coercive practice. This practice also fits both the coercion and group target models. Feminist scholars have long argued that women and girls are targeted for rape for the most part not because they are pretty, flirtatious, or teasing but because they are vulnerable, female, and "do not know their place."[11] The group target model makes sense of that claim and of the idea that rape harms all women and girls, not just those raped. But the group target model also leaves us *mystified*, as it once did Susan Griffin. She opens her classic essay "Rape: The All-American Crime" with the observation:

I have never been free of the fear of rape. From a very early age I, like most women, have thought of rape as part of my natural environment – something to be feared and prayed against like fire or lightning. I never asked why men raped; I simply thought it one of the many mysteries of human nature. (Vetterling-Braggin, Elliston, and English 1977, p. 313)

---

[10] These events and their meanings are discussed further in chapter 10.

[11] "Second Wave" feminist scholarship on rape begins with the short essay on rape terrorism by Mehrof and Kearon in Koedt, Levine, and Rapone (1973, pp. 228–33); the self-defense manual by Medea and Thompson (1974); and the treatise by Brownmiller (1975). There are four ground-breaking philosophical essays on rape by Susan Griffin, Carolyn M. Shafer and Marilyn Frye, Pamela Foa, and Susan Rae Peterson in Vetterling-Braggin, Elliston, and English (1977, pp. 313–71), and a groundbreaking philosophical treatise by Clark and Lewis (1977). Angela Davis's essay on the myth of the black male rapist (Davis 1981, pp. 172–201) has become a classic. Also influential are sociologist Menachem Amir's Philadelphia studies on rape (Amir 1971).

A few pages later, Griffin invokes the coercion model to dispel the mystery. As in the case of war rape, the coercion model suggests a new identification of the primary target and a new view of the harm that rape does even to females who are not raped:

In the system of chivalry, men protect women against men. This is not unlike the protection relationship which [organized crime] established with small businesses in the early part of this [twentieth] century. Indeed, chivalry is an age-old protection racket which depends for its existence on rape. (Vetterling-Braggin, Elliston, and English 1977, p. 320)

As a *racket,* chivalry creates and maintains the danger against which it claims to protect women. The ubiquitous danger of rape is an artifact (to some extent, mythological) created and maintained by "protectors." Most men, even those who profess to abhor rape but nevertheless trade "protection" for domestic service (including sexual service), have an interest in the continued existence of (at least belief in) the dangers (to women) of rape, hence in not having rapists prosecuted too zealously. As argued in chapter 3, men who do not rape can be complicit through their willingness to look the other way and to take advantage of this artificially produced willingness of women to serve them. It is the intentions of men and women who are in positions to judge and respond, rather than the intentions of individual rapists, that determine and reveal the rules that define rape as a coercive practice. One reason rapists assault women is that they can. (Usually it is only in prisons that they can do it to men.) They usually get away with it, thanks to others' complacency and readiness to presume women responsible.

Griffin's analogy with organized crime invokes the practice of terrorist extortion. Insofar as the message is "good girls don't get raped (they get put on pedestals)," the message appears to be directed to females who may be insufficiently attached to, deferential to, or supportive of male "protectors." Individual rapists, however, often target particular individuals, not just "a woman" (not to deny that for some – or for many, under some conditions – any woman will do). Although rape as a practice is more about violence than about sex, the individual rapist engages in a sexual performance and may be able to do that only to certain women. Further, rapists tend to experiment with what rape crisis centers and women's self-defense classes call "little rapes" (invasions of a woman's space and uninvited touching) to see who is likely to resist. They pursue those who pretend not to notice. Hence, from a rapist's perspective, the selection of victims need not appear random. Yet an untutored victim may be unable to predict the selection, which makes it seem random to her. Nor need a rapist care about terrorizing women into heterosexual relationships. For such reasons, one might resist the idea that civilian rape is terrorist.

The individual rapist's intentions, however, are no more determinative than are the individual suicide bomber's intentions. What is determinative is how the deed is used, the practice in which it is embedded. The coerciveness of individual rapes is not sufficient to make them terrorist. It is only at the level of rules of social practice that mandate female attachment to male protectors that it becomes possible to see rape as a terrorist practice. The practice creates an all-pervasive atmosphere of terror for women who would, or might, violate the rules. The few rapists caught and punished are scapegoats.[12] Trials of men falsely accused and convicted (for example, because of what Angela Davis calls "the myth of the black male rapist") serve a function reminiscent of Stalin's show trials, enabling the terrorism to continue unrecognized (Davis 1981, pp. 172–201).

On the coercion model, civilian rape terrorism makes extremely ineligible certain options for females: independence, assertiveness, or a lifestyle in which a woman's most intimate and enduring primary attachments are to other women. Who, then, *is* the primary target? The message now appears directed to lesbians.[13] Perhaps the primary target really is females in general, conceived as potential lesbians or potential marriage resisters and other potential troublemakers for patriarchal politics.

It is a largely empirical question whether a rape protection racket exists in a particular locale, just as it is a largely empirical question whether rape is used as a weapon in a particular war.

4. BEYOND THE TWO MODELS

Restricting our understanding of terrorism to political violence aimed at groups seems as arbitrary as restricting it to political violence with a coercive aim. Emma Goldman and Michael Walzer have discussed political violence, including assassinations, that was not aimed at groups (Walzer 1977, pp. 197–206; Goldman 1969, pp. 79–108).[14] Many nineteenth- and

---

[12] Even a scapegoat need not be innocent. A scapegoat who is guilty can be made to carry also the burden of the guilt of others.

[13] For further development of the idea that heterosexuality is made compulsory by social practices, see Rich (1980).

[14] See, also, Goldman's highly readable autobiography (1931). Goldman was vilified as a terrorist on the basis of her alleged connections with the assassination of President McKinley and her association with the attempted assassination by Alexander Berkman of Henry Clay Frick.

early twentieth-century political activists aimed their violence at specific individuals who occupied positions of public trust and could affect public policy. Walzer notes that some assassins who killed in public apparently had scruples against allowing children to be killed, even as "collateral damage." The targeted nature of their killings (the absence of randomness) leads Walzer to distinguish such political violence from terrorism.

And yet, some assassinations committed in public places when people are out and about may belong on a continuum with less-focused terrorism. Predictably, bystanders are caught in the crossfire. Further, because the killings are preceded by no fair and public trials to justify the selection of one target rather than another (or any target at all), there may be nothing to restrain even assassins protective of children from continually moving on to new targets. It may also be impossible to prevent copycats from using the assassination as a cover for their own less-principled killings. Thus, in practice, assassination is apt to be less focused in its impact and more arbitrary in the harm it does than the term "targeted killings" suggests.

Like assassins (and like many rapists), stalkers and domestic partner abusers target specific individuals. These individuals are not selected randomly. To the extent that one is struck, as Walzer was, by the phenomenon of random selection within a group, it may appear that the group target model does not fit the terrorism of stalking or that of systematic violence in the home. Yet the group target model may actually fit. Most victims of stalking and domestic partner violence, and most of those seriously injured, are female.[15] Individual women are selected not on the basis of anything they have done (other than failing to protest the "little rapes") but because *as female*, they are presumed to be relatively vulnerable, they are easily accessible, and the penalties (if any) for abusing them are not likely to be high.

With an adjustment, the coercion model also fits. First, the direct and indirect targets of stalking (and of violence in the home) are characteristically the same person. In intimate relationships, as in punishment by the state, the message "do this or else" is sent to the same person who will suffer the "or else" if the demand is not met. Second, what is coercive is the whole relationship, not just particular demands. Even particular demands are often implicit and vague or general rather than explicit and clear or specific. There are coercive episodes; violence escalates when a partner attempts to leave, get a restraining order, or report violence to friends, doctors, or police. But not every threat, act of violence, or other deed that

---

[15] For statistics and further details on domestic abuse, see chapter 8 and see Card (2002, pp. 139–46).

contributes to a coercive pattern need come with its own demand. Some episodes are primarily dominance displays. They show who is boss or demonstrate the futility of resistance, rather than manipulate particular choices.[16] Yet they are part of a pattern that manipulates a partner's attitudes toward the batterer and toward resistance. Episodes that pretend to be punishments (coercive) often make better sense if they are construed as dominance displays, since the "offense" that ostensibly provoked them could not reasonably have been predicted to be an offense and will not necessarily provoke "punishment" next time. Abused partners must use imagination and ingenuity to anticipate what will displease or provoke, please or pacify.

Consider next the case of oppressive regimes. If assassinations, stalkings, and relationship violence have primary targets more focused than groups, terrorist *regimes* can cast a wider net and be even less discriminating than the group target model suggests. In oppressive regimes, harm is aimed by a ruling body against its own people, or against a subset that defies prior definition. Oppressive regimes are notorious for cannibalizing themselves. The French Revolution and the ensuing Terror of 1793–94, which bequeathed us the concept of terrorism, illustrate that point. The Terror ostensibly targeted the privileged – royalty, nobility, and clergy who supported royalty and nobles. But in practice, it targeted *anyone who was perceived as insufficiently supportive of the revolution (or of those aiming to gain more power or to stay in power)*. That group included former leaders of the revolution.[17] Likewise, Stalin and Pol Pot (and closer to home, for me, former Wisconsin Senator Joseph McCarthy, as well as former Director of the Federal Bureau of Investigation J. Edgar Hoover) were apt to target anyone who incurred their disfavor or whose potential power they feared.

For terrorist regimes, such as that of Stalin or the Third Reich, the group target model is unhelpful and misleading. The regime's alleged principles of target selection do not really explain why particular individuals are targeted. They do not even yield a group the members of which could have been identified in advance. It may appear that certain groups are primary targets – homosexuals, Bolsheviks, Capitalists. In practice, however, those groups are like the targets of the French Terror: anyone who incurs political disfavor or whose potential power is feared. Victims may come to be

---

[16] An excellent discussion that makes this point, using Amnesty International's Chart of Coercion, is Jones (1994, pp. 81–105, especially the charts on pp. 90–91).

[17] For accounts of the French Revolution and the Terror of 1793–94, I rely on Durant and Durant (1975, pp. 13–87) and Carlyle (1937, vol. III). An interesting film that dramatizes this aspect of the Terror is *Danton* (1982).

branded "queer," "Bolsheviks," or "Capitalists" *after* the fact (after they are targeted). People who never identified themselves as members of such groups may be so identified by others, for any number of reasons, and treated accordingly. Hence, the terror.

The French Terror approach can also be taken by terrorists who are not in a position to be agents of oppressive regimes. Twin Towers workers were citizens of many nations, members of many racial, ethnic, and religious groups. The Towers may have been targeted in part because of this very diversity. The message may not have been specifically "Americans, take note!" but more generally, "anyone who benefits from, supports, or condones those who kill Muslims or endanger Islamic communities, take note!" – a "group" apt to be constituted more like the targets of Stalin or the French Terror than like the targets of racist or homophobic hate crimes. There is no need to understand such terrorism in a manner that puts it on a continuum with genocide.

The message not to do anything that would bring one into political disfavor is unhelpful to potential targets, as there is no reliable way to predict what would stave off political disfavor. Regime violence is often better understood as a dominance display and as coercive in many of the same ways as intimate relationship violence. The social environments of those who live under oppressive regimes, like the environments of those in oppressive intimate relationships, keep victims walking on eggshells. Some demands, such as "do not even attempt to leave," are specific and explicit. Citizens who tried to escape Soviet domination by going over the Berlin Wall were shot, as are many battered women trying to leave a partner. But not all demands are specific or explicit. What targets are coerced into is, basically, maintaining a relationship, as are abused intimate partners.

If neither the group target model nor the coercion model is an entirely satisfactory fit for oppressive regimes and intimate relationship violence, the terrorism of such regimes and relationships bears a strong resemblance to rape terrorism, which fits both models. Targets in all three cases are systematically intimidated into maintaining dependent relationships. In all three cases dominance is displayed through cruelty and threats of further cruelty for non-compliance. The coercion and group target models are thus best treated not as offering analyses of terrorism in terms of necessary and sufficient conditions but as invitations to understand the concept of terrorism better by identifying with different parties to a relationship that at least one party perceives as terrorist. That thought experiment is the subject of the next section concluding this chapter.

Following the lead of the coercion model, which takes us inside the terrorist's head, suppose we consider what circumstances and objectives might drive one to use terrorist methods. What could make them appear attractive or tempting? What advantage might terrorist methods offer, as compared with alternatives? Similarly, following the lead of the group target model, which invites us to identify with a potential target, suppose we consider what, if anything, is distinctive about what potential targets have reason to fear. Under what circumstances does one become liable to such fears? What can the fears do to those who have them? What is so terrifying?

As the term "terrorism" suggests first of all the perspective of those who experience terror, let us begin with the perspective of targets or potential targets. Terrorism does not always succeed in arousing terror. But it creates an *atmosphere of grave uncertainty and insecurity* in the face of what could be imminent danger. Uncertainty and insecurity can make fears *reasonable*. Grave uncertainty, the likelihood of imminent danger, and one's own defenselessness against it make terror a natural response. But what is critical is not whether actual terror is experienced. What is critical is defenselessness in the face of uncertainty and danger. People who belong to an ethnic group, members of which have been targeted because of their group identity, *have reason* to fear for their own safety (whether they actually fear or not). For all they know, they could be next. And next could be any time. There may be nothing effective they can do to shield themselves or reduce the danger.

Knowing that one is a member of a deliberately targeted group is not the only basis for grave uncertainty. Terrorists' willingness to do "collateral damage" also creates reason for many who are not members of a targeted group to fear being next to be caught in the crossfire. We have reason to fear being next when we cannot predict what instruments are apt to be used as weapons, when we cannot detect instruments or carriers of danger (an issue with chemical and biological weapons), when we cannot predict *where* the danger may be located (what streets, cities, or airlines to avoid), and if we do not know *when* or for *how long* to be alert. For there then appears to be nothing we can do to escape, shield ourselves, or even get braced for the assault. Our sense of helplessness is aggravated by the thought that these uncertainties are deliberately created by malevolent parties who are monitoring us while we are unable to monitor them, that they are in control and we are not.

Grave uncertainty about whether one might be next is prominent in the group target model. On that model, what keeps uncertainty alive is the hope by members of the group that not all will become direct targets. Without that hope, resignation might take over, which could work to defeat the terrorists' ends. The term "terrorism" suggests targets who are not resigned but still vulnerable to fear and capable of hope.

The coercion model relies on different reasoning in targets from that of the group target model to keep uncertainty alive, to stave off resignation and keep fear manageable. On the coercion model, if demands are met, the threat of harm may be withdrawn, or so terrorists would have targets believe. In reality, as targets should know, demands may escalate with success.[18] Hence, uncertainty and the instability of a fear that is in danger of passing over into resignation present a challenge for the terrorist. Again, such challenges for terrorists get ahead of the story. The point to note here is that there appears to be something that a potential direct target of coercive terrorism can do, namely, pressure a primary target to accede to demands. That task keeps hope, and likewise uncertainty, alive. It does not enable the target to change the options.

The kinds of uncertainty vary with the kinds of terrorism. Unlike most members of hated groups, many targets of stalkers and violent partners know specifically that they are direct targets. They do not have to wonder *who* will be next. But often they cannot predict *when* an assault will be triggered, *what* will trigger it, what *places*, topics of conversation, or potentially offending behaviors to avoid, and so on. If they can predict timing and triggers, they may remain uncertain what instruments will become weapons or what torture the next assault will bring.

"Reason to *fear*" understates the predicament of a terrorist target. Fear need not overwhelm. Fear can be advantageous for mobilizing self-protection. Terror is an extreme. It tends to be incapacitating, makes us less able to resist, focuses our energies non-productively, interferes with the ability to think and plan. In these ways it undermines competence. Terror is a panic response. Uncertainty in confronting imminent danger when we are defenseless need not produce panic. But it makes us vulnerable to panic, irrationality, imprudence. Former US President Franklin Delano Roosevelt's famous pronouncement, "The only thing we have to fear is fear itself" was a warning about panic.[19] Those who survived the economic crash of 1929 learned to fear panic.

The crash of 1929 can take us back to the contrast of poverty with terrorism that opens this chapter. Like terrorism, poverty gives rise to grave

---

[18] Dershowitz (2002) argues persuasively that terrorism continues because it succeeds.

[19] Roosevelt's famous pronouncement is from his first inaugural address, which was in 1932. The text of that speech can be found at www.bartleby.com/124/pres49.html.

dangers and uncertainties. When harmful (as it commonly is when it is not voluntarily chosen), it can be as physically ravaging as terrorism. Those who neglect or bring about others' poverty can be as morally reprehensible as terrorists. Sudden impoverishment can even produce panic and become fatal, as it did for many in the US who committed suicide when their banks failed in 1929.

But the onset of most poverty is not sudden. People are oftener born to it. Many of its dangers are not imminent, anticipated, or even perceived. When they are anticipated or perceived, poverty gives more play to fortune, encouraging hope. People have time to think, plan, experiment, take chances. Often they feel less helpless than they are. More importantly, although some can be deeply culpably responsible for others' unchosen poverty, the deeds of those responsible need not be intended to produce or to use anyone's vulnerability to panic. If they were, one might make a case for regarding those deeds as terrorist. Had someone deliberately engineered the crash of 1929 as part of a policy to harm investors as a group (as the Unabomber chose systematically to harm proponents of high technology in the US), or to create widespread poverty as a warning to the US to change its economic policies, the crash would have been terrorist.[20]

Just as evils are most apt to be called evils by victims and seldom by perpetrators, terrorism is apt to be called something else by those whom others identify as terrorists: "freedom fighting," "enforcing discipline," "romantic pursuit," "eliminating traitors," "war," even "war on terrorism." Public perception tends to be controlled more by regimes and by dominant partners in intimate relationships than by the oppressed or dominated, a likely factor in why the oppressive policies of regimes, of men who rape, and of dominant intimate partners are less widely recognized as terrorist than are deeds that target states or prominent men.

But those who think they are targets are not always right about that. Victims of deliberate and unpredictable property violence may perceive as terrorist deeds that are basically intended as rescues, such as break-ins by the Animal Liberation Front (ALF) to save animals from being used in painful, disabling, and often fatal laboratory experiments (Newkirk 1992), or deeds of "monkeywrenching," such as tree-spiking, by those who, like Dave Foreman, describe themselves as eco-warriors (Foreman 1991). Because they act with the scruple of not injuring living

---

[20] For the philosophy of Theodore J. Kaczynski, now serving a life sentence in prison, see Kaczynski (1995).

beings (warning workers in advance of the presence of spikes in trees, for example), animal liberators and eco-warriors tend not to apply the term "terrorist" to themselves. They compare themselves not to the Resistance in WW II but to the Underground Railroad in pre-Emancipation nineteenth-century US, most members of which did not have terrorist ambitions (the exception of John Brown duly noted). Conductors on the Underground Railroad were primarily interested in effecting escapes from slavery, certainly less interested in causing harm to slave-owners than in helping to effect successful escapes.[21] Yet some methods of rescue put people at risk. They can create grave uncertainties, just as terrorists do whose intentions are less benign. Insofar as rescuers are willing, in order to achieve their ends, to break laws to which they do not object (unlike those who were trained by Martin Luther King in civil disobedience), it is unclear to others what their scruples are. It may be unclear to rescuers themselves. Law-breaking can escalate in unforeseen ways in efforts to evade capture. Further, as with the scrupulous assassin, environmental activists may unwittingly (although predictably) encourage or provide a cover for others to engage in far less scrupulous deeds. Justifiable or not, eco-sabotage may be borderline as terrorism. But we begin to see what there is to argue about.

Now let us consider more fully the position of the terrorist. Like interrogational torture, terrorism can be an expedient. But torture assaults a victim who has already been rendered defenseless (tied up naked on a table or rack, for example). Terrorists, in contrast, often attack targets who are anything but defenseless in terms of their power positions and the resources to which they have access. Terrorism offers the advantage over more conventional modes of attack that it is able to make strategic use of the element of *sudden surprise*, or, more basically, *unpredictability*, to make up for either or both of two serious sources of disadvantage in a struggle. One source of disadvantage is being on the short end of a gross *power disparity*, the usual case with individual citizens in relation to their government. The other source of disadvantage is being unable to *justify* one's demands to those of whom they are made, typically the case with an intimate abuser and with oppressive governments. A terrorist can be at both disadvantages simultaneously. But often it is one or the other. If

---

[21] Although John Brown is remembered for his terrorism, he was also a conductor on the Underground Railroad and helped many slaves to escape. For discussion of those activities as well as of Brown's differences with many abolitionists over the use of violence, see the magnificent biography by Reynolds (2005).

terrorism is ever justifiable or excusable, it is most likely in the case of those who use it to overcome a severe power disadvantage in relation to an oppressive state or an oppressive partner who has demonstrated unwillingness to listen to reason. Terrorism is least likely to be justifiable in the case of those who use it because they are unable to justify their demands so as to elicit voluntary compliance.

For terrorists who are poor in resources or politically disempowered, the element of sudden surprise (or unpredictability) has the advantage of giving victims no chance to mobilize their greater resources for protection and defense. The reason it may not matter to the terrorist whether targets actually feel terror or even whether they are actually surprised is that what is important is that the target is placed in a situation of grave uncertainty and lack of control. Panic increases defenselessness. Unfortunately for the terrorist, it also risks making a target less prudent and, thereby, less manipulable.

The sudden surprise of terrorism is created many ways. One way, captured by the group target model, is arbitrary selection of members of an ethnic, racial, national, or religious group. Sudden surprise in rape terrorism is also often a result of arbitrariness: one is not surprised to learn that a woman was raped, but one is often surprised to learn who it was. Often, a victim is also surprised at who did it. Women who survive nighttime excursions unharmed without a protector in many downtown urban environments of the US consider themselves "just lucky." They seem, if anything, surprised to escape, suggesting that they would not have been surprised if assaulted. Yet, constant alertness to a danger is compatible with sudden surprise when it becomes a reality, for the timing and the perpetrators are often unpredictable.

Other ways of creating surprise, which produce a sense of betrayal, include such measures as turning against people instruments they have come to depend on in daily life and regard as benign (box cutters) or attacking when it is least expected or in circumstances under which people are likely to have let down their guard (in the middle of the night when they are sleeping, which is when terrorist regimes arrest people, when US soldiers in Iraq arrested detainees, and when Chicago police raided the apartment of Fred Hampton).[22] Surprise in the terrorism of rape also can include unexpected betrayal, as in marital rape and war rape by neighbors.

---

[22] On FBI involvement in the Chicago police raid of Hampton's apartment, fatal to Hampton, who died in his bed, see Gentry (1992, pp. 620–22).

Sudden surprise is not in itself problematic. Contestants in sports and games aim to surprise opponents, take them off guard, in order to win. Opponents expect surprise to be used strategically against them. What, then, is distinctive about its use in terrorism?

One answer is that terrorists strike (or threaten to strike) not just to win but in such a manner that their targets, who are involuntary and not playing games but in real danger, cannot mount a defense. Lives tend to be at stake. "Winning" is not exactly the right concept. "Beating" is closer. Terrorism is not so much a mode of fighting as a set of practices that reduce the necessity of fighting, which explains why it is a resort of those who lack the resources to fight or are incapable of justifying their aims. A general presumption exists, not only in sports and games but also in politics and intimate relationships, that individuals should be granted a decent opportunity to defend themselves, especially when stakes are high. Contestants who violate that presumption are unsporting. Political opponents and other oppressors who do it are terrorists.

Traditions of just war theory and requirements of IHL define distinctions between acceptable and unacceptable ways to take advantage of an enemy's vulnerabilities. They rule out, as "hitting below the belt," the kinds of surprise on which terrorists rely to gain advantage over adversaries. It should be as difficult to justify or excuse terrorism as to justify or excuse hitting below the belt. Modern warfare is unclear about where the belt lies. As noted in chapter 5, the *jus in bello* discrimination principle is less helpful than it used to be before modern WMD. Nevertheless it is widely agreed that biological and chemical weapons strike below the belt. In civil society, criminal offenses become terrorist when a violent perpetrator systematically takes unthinkable advantage of others' vulnerabilities, as did the Washington DC snipers Lee Boyd Malvo and John Allen Muhammad in 2002 when they shot thirteen apparently randomly selected consumers and pedestrians who were going about such ordinary activities in broad daylight as waiting for a bus, mowing grass, or filling their automobile tanks with gasoline.[23]

The 9/11 bombers exploited the element of sudden surprise, attacking literally out of the blue, using box cutters, we are told, to subdue passengers and pilots so as to gain control of civilian transport planes and turn them into WMD. The planners of these attacks turned against the US its own resources and technology. If the identification of perpetrators in *The 9/11 Commission Report* is accurate, they also turned against the US its

[23] On the Washington DC snipers, see Horwitz and Ruane (2003).

history of trust and good will toward legally admitted immigrants who come to pursue an education or occupational training.[24] Suicide bombers in many parts of the world disguise themselves as ordinary pedestrians, customers, clients, or passengers, exploiting the trust of everyday life that constitutes so much of the glue that holds a society together. What make their deeds terrorist are as much these betrayals as their principles of target selection or the use of some targets to coerce others. All contribute to creating atmospheres of grave uncertainty, the inability of targets to shield themselves, and consequent vulnerability to panic.

For terrorists who occupy positions of political power, and for dominant partners in abusive relationships, sudden surprise violence has special advantages. It intimidates potential questioners and keeps them occupied with urgencies. Like terrorist governments, intimate terrorists use unpredictability to keep targets constantly attentive and deferential. Terrorists in intimate relationships can be as creative as the 9/11 bombers in the use of betrayal and surprise to create atmospheres of grave uncertainty, taking advantage of special vulnerabilities.[25] They, too, strike below the belt, not just figuratively. Suddenness and surprise are advantages also for terrorist governments that would deceive a public, as victims have no opportunity to tell others when or where they are taken.

Even if it is true, after all, that most preventable suffering and death are caused not by terrorism but "by malnutrition, and lack of education, and all the ills connected to poverty," an enormous amount of preventable major suffering and death within nations, families, and neighborhoods is caused by terrorism against ordinary people whose voices are seldom heard. Credible campaigns against terrorism might begin by exposing the limits of high-profile paradigms and learning to recognize terrorism closer to home.

---

[24] For sketches of some of those named as agents, see National Commission on Terrorist Attacks upon the United States (2004, pp. 145–73).

[25] For examples of intimate terrorist creativity, see the film *What Ever Happened to Baby Jane?* (1962). The film *Sleeping with the Enemy* (1991) portrays the use of surprise but fails to capture the inventiveness of abusers in creating it.

CHAPTER 7

Conscientious torture?

I mean to inquire if, in the civil order, there can be any sure and legitimate rule of administration, men being taken as they are and laws as they might be. (Jean-Jacques Rousseau 1950, p. 3)

April may or may not be the cruelest month. But in 2009, it was a month of revelations of cruelty and of responses to cruelty. In consecutive issues of *The New York Review of Books* Mark Danner published a two-part essay on the International Committee of the Red Cross (ICRC) Report on the Treatment of Fourteen "High Value Detainees" in CIA Custody (Danner 2009a, pp. 69–77; 2009b, pp. 48–56). The ICRC report, submitted as a confidential document in 2007, became available in April 2009 on the Internet.[1] Danner poses the moral question whether torture is ever justified. He also presses the factual question whether the use of torture "really did produce information that, in the words of the former vice-president [former United States Vice-President Richard Cheney] was 'absolutely crucial to getting us through the last seven-plus years without a major-casualty attack in the US'" (Danner 2009b, p. 55). Even if critical information was obtained, the question remains, as pointed out by US President Barack Obama in a nationally televised news conference (29 April, 2009), whether enough information could have been obtained by other methods. President Obama also went on record regarding waterboarding at that conference, stating without qualification that waterboarding is torture.

That same month, *The New York Times* in the space of a week published front-page articles reporting that the Central Intelligence Agency (CIA) is closing the secret overseas prisons "where it subjected Al Qaeda prisoners to brutal interrogation methods" (Shane 2009b, p. A1) and summarizing as well as excerpting CIA memos detailing those methods (Mazzetti 2009, p. A7; Mazzetti and Shane 2009a, pp. A1, A10). To my ears, the closing of

---

[1] www.nybooks.com/icrc-report.pdf.

those prisons (the "dark sites") and public exposure of the memos are welcome pieces of news. Yet philosophical issues of meaning and justification that surround the use of harsh interrogation are not resolved by decisions of the CIA, the election of a new president, or answers to the factual question pressed by Danner. Ultimately for President Obama, as Commander-in-Chief, the political question is whether using torture makes the US safer. His view is that it does not, that torture is fuel for US enemies, making it easier for them to recruit soldiers. Ultimately, the main *philosophical* question is whether the moral cost of intelligence so gained is too high, even if that intelligence were to purchase greater security than intelligence obtainable by other means. This chapter argues that, at least in a democracy, the moral cost is too high. Further, if torture is not only unjustified but inexcusable, it is not just wrong but an evil and should never be an option in a program of counterterrorism. The concluding section of this chapter argues that there is no moral excuse for torture.

The "conscientious torture" of this chapter's title refers to two ways in which torture has been defended on moral grounds. One way is as a lawful policy of interrogational torture, to be reserved for extreme cases, as an element in a program of counterterrorism. The other way is as a violation, again in extreme cases, of a (justifiable) lawful ban on torture. Those who defend torture in either way tend to grant that moral presumptions against torture are so strong that torture should never be used casually. Its use in crisis situations is defended as the lesser of evils. Yet, if torture is truly an evil, other options should be sought – or created. Other options will be discussed, briefly, in this chapter and some of their advantages over torture cited, with illustrations from recent interrogations carried out successfully without harsh methods.

Chapter 5 left open the possibility that some forms of terrorism might, under some circumstances, be justifiable, or at least excusable. This chapter argues that policies of torture never are. Chapters 9 and 10 take for granted the wrongness of genocide and proceed to other issues. But the wrongness of genocide, unlike that of torture, needs no argument. For genocide is the murder of a people, and murder is by definition unjustifiable. No *a priori* argument analogous to that one is available for torture. Torture is not wrong by definition. And so, I proceed by attending to the moral costs of torture as it has been and is likely to be implemented, human beings "taken as they are and laws as they might be" (Rousseau 1950, p. 3). Empirical issues are woven throughout, as torture does not occur under ideal conditions of knowledge and control.

For two centuries, democratic societies have been reluctant to openly endorse harsh coercive interrogation procedures. This does not mean they have been reluctant to use those procedures. Historian Darius Rejali (2007) documents, in his comprehensive survey and critique of "clean torture" in the twentieth century, that tortures that leave no marks were pioneered, developed, and exported by modern democratic nations: the US, Britain, and France. Rejali's central hypothesis is that "Public monitoring leads institutions that favor painful coercion to use clean torture to evade detection, and, to the extent that public monitoring of human rights is a core value in modern democracies, it is the case that where we find democracies torturing today, we also find stealthy torture" (Rejali 2007, p. xviii). In the US after 9/11, there was less reliance on stealth and less reluctance to endorse harsh interrogation openly, although much reluctance to call it "torture."

Two kinds of philosophical challenges share the stage in contemporary torture debates. They are challenges based on definitions and challenges regarding alleged justifications. In the US political arena, the challenges have been mainly those of definition. What does "torture" mean? What sorts of treatment should count as torture? Are certain harsh techniques of interrogation, such as waterboarding, stress positions, death threats and threats to family members, really torture?[2] For academics, the questions are oftener those of justification: is torture ever morally right? Could it be morally required? Could a conscientious agent ever endorse it? Is it sometimes at least excusable? If so, under what circumstances, for what purposes, and by what authorization?

Both sets of questions need to be answered by anyone concerned to avoid evil-doing in a program of counterterrorism. As popularly understood, torture inflicts intolerable *pain* and is intended to do so. It is less widely understood that torture also inflicts intolerable *harm*. The harm can be more important than the pain. Failure to note that distinction gives rise to some of the disputes regarding the moral status of methods of harsh interrogation (taken up in chapter 8). Even if a procedure was to do intolerable harm, if the procedure was morally justifiable (or at least

---

[2] The term "waterboarding" has been applied both to full body ducking of prisoners strapped to a board and to pouring icy water over a cloth placed over the face of a prisoner who is strapped down. The aim is to simulate the experience of drowning. Abu Zubaydah, in his interview with the Red Cross, describes his waterboarding as follows: "A black cloth was then placed over my face and the interrogators used a mineral water bottle to pour water on the cloth so that I could not breathe. After a few minutes the cloth was removed and the bed was rotated into an upright position ... I vomited. The bed was then again lowered to horizontal position and the same torture carried out again ... On this occasion, my head was in a more backward, downward position and the water was poured on for a longer time. I struggled against the straps, trying to breathe, but it was hopeless. I thought I was going to die. I lost control of my urine. Since then I still lose control of my urine when under stress" (Danner 2009a, pp. 73–74).

excusable), it would not be an evil, even if it was torture. Thus, questions of the definition of torture and questions regarding its moral status track the two main elements of an evil (intolerable harm and inexcusable wrong), asking whether or how these elements apply to the procedure in question. Questions of definition ask about whether the procedure does intolerable harm. Questions of justification consider whether use of the procedure is morally wrong and if so, whether there is any excuse for it.

The administration of US President G. W. Bush sidestepped issues of justification to focus on definition. Its argument was that although certain forms of coercive interrogation may be cruel, inhuman, or degrading, they fall short of torture, and so the question of justifying torture does not arise.[3] Chapter 8 takes up issues of definition. The rest of the present chapter addresses issues of justification.

As in the case of terrorism, it may seem to some readers counterintuitive not to address questions of definition first. Again, the response is that philosophical investigations tend, for good reason, not to begin with a definition. Such beginnings make it too easy to beg important questions of justification. The hope is, rather, to *conclude* with, if not a definition, then perhaps an analysis, or some account of the meaning of the concept at issue that does justice to controversies over what is justifiable or excusable.

I. THE REVIVED TORTURE DEBATES

Although torture as a standard part of criminal process was phased out in Europe toward the end of the eighteenth century, Cesare Beccaría found it necessary even in 1764 to publish his critique of the practice anonymously as a chapter in his essay "On Crimes and Punishments" (Beccaría 1963, pp. 30–36). Beccaría argued against the routine use of torture to elicit confessions to capital crimes. For centuries, European criminal process required either a confession or the testimony of two witnesses for conviction of a capital crime.[4] Two witnesses can be difficult to produce for murder. And so, resort to the torture option to extort a confession was not uncommon. The case of Beatrice Cenci is an example. A victim of incestuous rape by her father, she was executed for parricide in 1599 in Rome after suffering *la corda*, in which "the victim's arms were tied behind the back and then twisted by mechanical process to force the shoulders out of joint, causing

---

[3] For memos by US government officials regarding what should count as torture, and discussions of these memos, see Danner (2004); Greenberg and Dratel (2005); and Greenberg (2006).
[4] Classics on the history of torture include Langbein (1977); Peters (1985); and Ruthven (1978).

such agonizing pain that most victims gave in and accepted the allegations made against them" (Jack 2005, p. 15).

When contemporary scholars mention torture as a lawful practice, it has usually been to congratulate European states for having abolished such procedures and requirements.[5] Almost a century ago, James Williams wrote in the torture entry of the *Encyclopedia Britannica* (Williams 1911, vol. XXVII, p. 72), that this "whole subject is one of only historical interest as far as Europe is concerned." I thought the same was true as far as the US was concerned in the early 1960s when, researching the death penalty for my dissertation, I encountered Beccaría's critique. I skimmed over that chapter quickly, never expecting to see the debate revived. Yet here we are.

The subject of contemporary political debates, such as that of Beccaría's critique, is torture for purposes of interrogation. But the procedures at issue today are not for use in criminal proceedings – criminal procedure in contemporary democracies bars evidence extracted under torture – and their use is alleged by governments not to be routine. Most who support torture on ethical grounds today defend it only as an emergency measure, a last resort in extreme situations. Jeremy Bentham and Alan Dershowitz offer qualified philosophical defenses of the view that torture as a legally approved tool of interrogation can be justifiable in such situations (Twining and Twining 1973; Dershowitz 2002). That position is rejected by philosophers Henry Shue in an early essay (Shue 1978) and Seumas Miller in his "torture" entry for the online *Stanford Encyclopedia of Philosophy* (Miller 2008). Shue and Miller reject torture as a lawful practice, even if the practice were restricted as Bentham and Dershowitz would have it. But both Shue and Miller have at certain points defended torture as a possible form of *conscientious disobedience* by an *individual* facing extreme circumstances. In 2005 Shue, however, reversed the position he took in 1978 on that issue and now finds no justification for torture, even as a form of conscientious disobedience (Shue 2005). I do not know whether Miller has changed his views on that point.

Dershowitz's torture warrant proposal, outlined in a chapter of his provocative and engaging book *Why Terrorism Works* (Dershowitz 2002, pp. 131–63), has shocked and puzzled many readers. It is widely believed, as Beccaría argued, that interrogational torture is useless for learning the truth because the weak will say whatever they think will end the torture, and the strong will die rather than give in. Yet, today's methods are

---

[5] Peters's history defines "torture" as a legal or at least public procedure (1985, pp. 2–3).

more sophisticated than those of earlier centuries, thanks to psychological research and thanks to what the US learned about methods employed by communist interrogators on US POWs during the Korean War.[6] Dershowitz insists that sometimes interrogational torture works, meaning not just that it gets the tortured to talk but that it elicits life-saving information, which is why it continues. Evidence that torture works does not, however, show the moral costs or whether alternatives could work well enough.

Sophisticated methods of torture, designed to meet Beccaría's objections, are discussed in detail in two powerful contemporary critiques of belief in the efficacy of torture. One is an essay published two years after Dershowitz's book on terrorism by Jean Maria Arrigo (2004) of the International Intelligence Ethics Association (IIEA).[7] The other is a chapter in Darius Rejali's *Torture and Democracy* (2007), published three years after Arrigo's essay. Both challenge Dershowitz on empirical grounds, citing psychological, sociological, and historical research.

A utilitarian justification argues either that the good outweighs the harm done by a course of action or that no alternative course of action would produce a lesser balance of harm.[8] Either way, a utilitarian defense of interrogational torture rests on belief in torture's efficacy. Dershowitz's own defense of his proposal for highly regulated torture warrants is not directly utilitarian. Rather, it is based heavily on the beliefs that most people would be persuaded by a utilitarian defense of interrogational torture in a national crisis and so, in national crises, there will be torture,

---

[6] Shane and Mazzetti (2009, pp. A1, A14) describe the history of the methods critiqued by the ICRC as having originated in the Survival, Evasion, Resistance, and Escape (SERE) program of the US military, created "to give American pilots and soldiers a sample of the torture methods used by Communists in the Korean War, methods that have wrung false confessions from Americans." McCoy (2006, pp. 21–59) describes in detail government-sponsored research that led to the new methods in which SERE trained pilots and soldiers.

[7] According to its homepage (http://intelligence-ethics.org/), IIEA was formed in 2005 and incorporated in Virginia in 2006. It publishes the *International Journal of Intelligence Ethics*. Its mission is to "Develop a theory of ethics for application to the problems and dilemmas that confront intelligence practitioners ... Develop intelligence ethics as a field of research ... Become a resource ... Work with like-minded academic and professional institutions ... Increase the academic and professional resources for intelligence ethics available to the intelligence community ... [and] Encourage international and cross-cultural dialogue on the subject of intelligence ethics."

[8] A less plausible but more popular interpretation of utilitarian ethics is that a course of action is right only if it produces more good on the whole than any alternative, or, more precisely, that it is wrong if some alternative would produce a greater balance of good on the whole. Hence, the (profoundly ambiguous) slogan: "the greatest good of the greatest number" (widely attributed to Jeremy Bentham, although the closest approximation I have found is in Beccaria (1963, p.8): "the greatest happiness shared by the greatest number") or, in the preferred language of John Stuart Mill, "the Greatest Happiness Principle" (Mill 2002, p. 239).

lawful or not. The challenge, as he sees it, is to limit the inevitable, in the interests of protecting civil rights and democratic values.

In assessing just how well torture really works, Rejali addresses the specific questions of whether it can be scientific, whether it can be restrained, whether it can be professional, whether it works better than alternatives, how well interrogators spot the truth, and how well interrogees remember (Rejali 2007, pp. 446–79). The findings he sets out by those who have gathered empirical data should unsettle popular assumptions about torture's efficacy.

Arrigo distinguishes three causal models of torture and highlights substantial unintended negative consequences of torture on each model (Arrigo 2004, summarized in her chart on p. 4). These models also illuminate how torture can continue to be used as a tool of interrogation after Beccaría's critique.

The first and oldest model, which Arrigo calls the "animal instinct model of truth telling," is the one that Beccaría criticized. This is the model most people have in mind when they think of torture. On this model, torture is designed to gain compliance as a result of the subject's fear of pain or death. Beccaría identified two of its weaknesses from the standpoint of utility: (1) the strong will die before giving in and (2) the weak will say whatever they think will stop the torture. To these, Arrigo adds (3) the danger that bodily injury will impair the interrogee's ability to convey the truth and (4) the danger of causing "premature" death (a matter discussed in detail by Rejali). To safeguard against these last two dangers, torturers enlist the help of health care professionals who "determine the types of torture a person can endure, monitor the person for endurance under torture, resuscitate the person, treat the person to prepare for further torture, and administer non-therapeutic drugs" (Arrigo 2004, p. 5). To cover up torture, physicians also "falsify health certificates, autopsy reports, and death certificates" (Arrigo 2004, p. 5). Thus begins a process of enlisting professionals and others in activities that violate many codes of professional ethics. Finally, and most importantly, Arrigo clarifies what "fanatics, martyrs, and heroes" do that enables them to resist: they *interpret* their pain in ways the torturer cannot control (Arrigo 2004, pp. 6–7). "Anthropologists identify the 'punitive pain' envisioned by the torturer as only one of several competing interpretations. In addition to the value of 'military pain' … we recognize the 'medical pain' of surgery, the 'athletic pain' of the marathon,; and the 'sacrificial pain' of martyrs" (Arrigo 2004, p. 8).

The second model, which Arrigo calls the "cognitive failure model of truth telling," is designed to address the problem on the first model of being unable to control the tortured subject's interpretation of the pain. The new model is designed to undermine the ability of "fanatics, martyrs, and heroes" to resist. On the new model, physiological and psychological stress (sensory deprivation, sleep deprivation, unremitting observation, solitary confinement, and the like), developed through biomedical research, are applied to make it impossible for subjects to engage in deception and maintain their own interpretations. These measures create "a state of disorientation in which the subject is unable to maintain a position of self-interest and becomes suggestible or compliant under interrogation" (Arrigo 2004, p. 8).

A utilitarian weakness of torture on the second model is that these procedures take much longer, which can greatly diminish the value of information obtained. Another weakness, which might well apply to all three methods (although Arrigo discusses it specifically in relation to the second model), is that it is very hard on the persons who must be extensively trained to administer the procedures. Arrigo notes, "The utilitarian argument for torture, therefore, must justify the additional sacrifice of the torturers – made vulnerable to 'perpetration-induced traumatic stress' and severe social stigma – or develop some hitherto-unknown ... regimen for training and after-care of torturers," which should "include support staff and families, where secrecy, stress, and stigmatization take their toll over decades" (Arrigo 2004, pp. 11–12). Arrigo cites the research on torturers of criminologist Ronald Crelinsten and Alistair Horne, historian of the Battle of Algiers, who concluded that torture "tends to demoralize the inflictor even more than his victim" (Arrigo 2004, p. 11). Finally, it is difficult on this model for interrogators to distinguish true from incorrect statements by the subject, a matter discussed in more detail by Rejali (2007, pp. 463–66)

The third model, which Arrigo calls "the data processing model of knowledge acquisition," is intended to address some of the weaknesses of the second model. On the third model, "ordinary subjects" – which appears to mean subjects who are not necessarily suspected of being guilty of anything – are provoked to yield data that are then analyzed comprehensively across subjects. This sounds like the process described by survivor Hector Aristizabal, who was tortured as a suspected communist when he was a student in Colombia. Currently an activist who does "Theater of the Oppressed," Aristizabal explained at a 2007 conference on torture at California State University at Fullerton that his interrogators employed what he called "the jigsaw puzzle method": a little piece of information from this interrogee, a little piece from that one, and so on, like the pieces of a jigsaw puzzle, until many pieces can be assembled to form a picture larger than any one interrogee could have supplied. Interrogees do not even know when or what they are contributing to the big picture. They may think what they say is innocent or trivial (where they had dinner last Tuesday, what they were wearing, and so forth). Since they have no way to know what contribution to the big picture might be made by anything they say, they cannot determine when or how to lie or figure out what to say to stop the torture. It can be necessary for interrogators to torture a great many interrogees in order to get a coherent picture. That, says Aristizabal, is what they do.

Aristizabal at least thought he was a suspect. As described by Lawrence Wilkerson, a retired US Army colonel who served as chief of staff to Secretary of State Colin Powell, there was not even a pretense of suspected guilty knowledge in the rounding up of interrogees in Afghanistan. Danner quotes Wilkerson:

Simply stated, this philosophy held that it did not matter if a detainee were innocent. Indeed, because he lived in Afghanistan and was captured on or near the battle area, he must know something of importance ... All that was necessary was to extract everything possible from him and others like him, assemble it all in a computer program, and then look for cross-connections and serendipitous incidentals – in short, to have sufficient information about a village, a region, or a group of individuals, that dots could be connected and terrorists or their plots could be identified. (Danner 2009b, p. 54)

A utilitarian disadvantage of this model, Arrigo points out, is that the data overwhelm analysts. This, of course, can produce the time-delay problem noted in regard to the second model, resulting in diminished value of information obtained. Further and more importantly, implementation of this model requires coordination of torture agencies with not just health care personnel but also police, the judiciary, the military, and the government. Historically, she notes, this collaboration has led to unintended social corruption on a vast scale, an example of what Iris Marion Young called structural injustice. "How," Arrigo asks, "will the counterterrorist program uphold a monopoly on the use of torture? Investigators of many other crimes will consider their own pursuits compelling, some at the level of national security" (Arrigo 2004, p. 15). With regard to biomedical research for torture programs, Arrigo notes, one unintended consequence is "the opportunity for secret, illegal research on human subjects for other purposes ... by their own biomedical scientists, who have negotiating power over these very valuable resources" (Arrigo 2004, p. 10). Her powerful accounts of the potential for large-scale social corruption have convinced many philosophers who have read her essay that the disadvantages of torture as a legally authorized practice far outweigh its advantages, even from the standpoint of utility. Although the "jigsaw puzzle method" does not fall prey to the classic objections of Beccaría, it creates the spectre of a torture culture worse than that of Beccaría's day.

And so, contemporary philosophical debates, granting that a torture culture would be a political disaster, have come to focus more on the exceptional case. Of course, the tortures that arouse citizens' concern in contemporary democratic societies have not been confined to "ticking-bomb" exceptions but have become routine. Yet even routine torture can have conscientious beginnings. Arrigo quotes a vignette reported in the *Atlantic Monthly* in 2002 (the year in which Dershowitz's proposal appeared) that demonstrates the continuing utilitarian appeal of torture on the first model: an officer confronting three suspected terrorists took out his pistol, pointed it at the forehead of one of them, and shot him dead. "The other two ... talked immediately; the bomb, which had been placed in a crowded railway station and set to explode during the evening rush hour, was found and defused, and countless lives were saved" (Arrigo 2004, p. 5; Hoffman 2002, p. 52). I do not know whether the story is true. The point is, it could be.

My own conclusions, in a nutshell, are as follows. First, torture is like slavery (and unlike genocide or murder) in that there is no self-contradiction in the *abstract* idea of morally justifiable torture, or morally excusable torture, or even morally *required* torture. But the academic search for morally justified cases remains deeply disturbing. As others have pointed out (Luban 2005; Shue 2005), assumptions made about such cases tend to be unrealistic in philosophically interesting ways. What is unrealistic is not the supposition that individuals might make those assumptions. Nor are the circumstances that might tempt even a conscientious agent to use torture unrealistic. They are common enough. Unrealistic are assumptions about what a potential torturer *knows* and what a potential torturer can *control*. It is unrealistic to think that it is predictable when torture *would* elicit information that *would* actually prevent a disaster. (We will probably never read about officers who shot one of three suspects only to find that the other two knew nothing or that there was no bomb, or that it would never have detonated, thanks to its maker's incompetence.) This is true of all three models. It is unrealistic to think it determinable when torture would be containable, when it would not proliferate into a horrifying practice. It is unrealistic to suppose that inexperienced torturers will know how far they can go without killing or horribly mutilating (and sobering to ponder how the requisite experience might be gained).[9] It is unwarranted to assume there are no humane methods that are equally if not more effective. It is disastrous to reduce motivations (and funds) to seek and develop those alternatives. Given torture's extremity, it is unacceptable to be satisfied in a "ticking-bomb" case with the level of evidence ordinarily available to interrogators regarding a suspect's identity or knowledge of critical detail, ability to recall that critical detail, or reasons for not providing it. Finally, but most importantly, the moral costs of even successful interrogational torture seriously jeopardize or negate the gains sought, at least in democratic societies. Of course, the costs of forgoing torture, like the costs of forgoing any evil option, can be heavy. And not everyone is a democrat.

2. THE MISNAMED "ONE-OFF" CASE

A popular philosophical approach to the ethics of torture is to distinguish between torture as a practice regulated by law and torture in a particular case, a crisis. This strategy has become commonplace since the appearance of Dershowitz's chapter "Should the Ticking Bomb Terrorist Be Tortured?" (Dershowitz 2002, pp. 131–63), in which he makes that distinction and opts to support a highly regulated practice but not unregulated instances of torture. Miller's *Stanford Encyclopedia of Philosophy* entry on torture (Miller 2008) also has been influential in making this distinction pivotal. But whereas Dershowitz favors a highly regulated practice, Miller argues that objections fatal to justifying torture as a practice (for reasons detailed by Arrigo) are not convincing in a one-off case. Miller's conclusion is that in a single instance, torture might be justifiable, although torture as a legitimate practice would not. From the standpoint of utility, that conclusion should not be surprising: a legitimated practice is bound to have more and different consequences than a particular case.

But "single case" vs. "lawful policy" does not exhaust the alternatives and is misleading. What we are really being asked to entertain, under the rubric "one-off case," is an unlawful policy, whether on the part of governmental officials, law enforcement officers, or private individuals. The distinction between torture as a lawful act and torture as a criminal act committed out of moral conscientiousness is clear enough. But the distinction between torture as a practice and torture as a one-off deed is,

---

[9] Arrigo's essay introduces the subject of training torturers, and Jessica Wolfendale (2006, pp. 269–87) develops in detail just what that means.

practically and morally, a distinction without a difference. The problem is not just the empirical likelihood of moral drift, although that is a serious issue. Consider the logic of the conscientious "one-off" torturer's reasoning. Arguments that appear to sustain the judgment that torture would be right in the single case are presented as leaving no apparent morally permissible alternative. Were there such an alternative, a conscientious agent would take it. That means that torture is being presented *not just as permissible but as apparently required*. If it were the *only* permissible option, it *would* be required. And it would be required for the same reasons in relevantly similar circumstances whenever they recur. A conscientious torturer who believed that torture was required in a certain kind of circumstance would be committed to doing it again and again, whenever those circumstances, or ones that appeared to be close enough, were present.

Even if torture appeared to be only permissible but not required, "one-off" is a misleading characterization. Conscientious decisions to defy a torture ban in extraordinary circumstances imply an intention (in Kantian terms, a maxim) to do a certain kind of thing in a certain kind of circumstance. Why assume that the circumstance would present itself only once? Extreme situations are not uncommon, especially in politics. Michael Walzer noted long ago regarding "the dilemma of dirty hands" that dilemmas that confront political figures with sets of options all of which are "morally distasteful" in one way or another are "a central feature of political life" that arise "not merely as an occasional crisis in the career of this or that unlucky politician but systematically and frequently" (Walzer 1973, p. 162).

In the allegedly "one-off" crisis scenarios most discussed, the torturer (whoever is responsible for the decision to use torture) is a person in authority who has the public trust, and yet the decision to torture is made secretly, in defiance of existing law. If torture is done conscientiously, then, by the reasoning just given, those in authority who are responsible for it are committed in principle to a policy; not just a single crime but a criminal policy. With, by hypothesis, no regulation of such defiance, what check is there on judgments about the extraordinariness of circumstances? What check is there on judgments about the likelihood of torture's effectiveness? Problems analogous to those that John Rawls identified more than half a century ago with a practice that permitted "telishing" burden the misnamed "one-off" torture idea as well (Rawls 1999b, pp. 20–46).

Rawls anticipated philosophically in regard to the practice of punishment the kinds of social horrors that Arrigo documents historically in regard to the practice of interrogational torture. Rawls invented the word

"telishment" (from "telos" and "punishment") to get around an objection
to a critique of utilitarian defenses of punishment. The critique asks us
to imagine a practice that would authorize the secret deliberate framing
and punishment of an innocent person during a crime wave when the
real criminals eluded detection, in order to deter potential copycats and
end the crime wave. To the objection, "but that would not be *punishment!*" Rawls's response was, simply, then call it *telishment*; the question is
whether it is justifiable, whatever you call it. Similarly, the question arises
whether it would be justifiable for government officials to employ torture
secretly in emergency situations to prevent a disaster. Walzer thinks many
of us would want them to do that, at least some of the time (Walzer 1973,
p. 162). But Rawls offers very good reasons to worry about authorizing discretion for such serious acts to be carried out secretly by public officials.

Rawls understood "telishment" as an imaginary *legal* institution, not as
systematic *disobedience* to a legal institution. Yet it is the idea of a practice,
not whether it is legal, that is important here. The problems Rawls identified for the practice of "telishment" arise as well for an informal policy
of conscientious disobedience engaged in secretly. "What check," Rawls
asked, "is there on officials?" How are the risks of systematic deception
(including self-deception) to be limited? What is to prevent the potential
torturer's assuming complete discretion to torture anyone?

It is far from obvious that a morally conscientious thinker would endorse a policy that so jeopardized democratic accountability. And so, one
variation on the "one-off" torture case has the responsible (authorizing)
official resign afterward, confess, stand trial, and accept punishment for
violating the law. I return in section 4 of this chapter to the matter of what
a court would be justified in doing with such a case. The question here
is whether one could justify a policy of defying a torture ban in extreme
circumstances, incorporating subsequent resignation and so forth into the
policy. If Walzer is right about the nature of politics, such a policy would
involve a lot of resignation and consequent instability in government and
law enforcement.

The resignation-and-standing-trial variation on the "one-off" torture
case invokes something like the idea discussed at the end of chapter 5
regarding counterterrorist measures that violate domestic or international
law, as in the cases of Francine Hughes, Inez García, and a state-sponsored
war on terrorism. In none of those cases was the violation committed with
intent to stand trial afterward. Nevertheless, the argument there was that
courts could be justified both in trying the violators and in mitigating their
penalties, pardoning them, or finding them not guilty, on the grounds

either that the violations were morally justified, or at least, that the perpetrators had a moral excuse, given the past failures of potential enforcers to intervene in ways they should have to prevent the dangers against which the law-breakers were defending themselves. The case is otherwise with torture. That kind of excuse – a history of the past failures of others – does not provide a good reason for torture.

Terrorism, recall, is a much more abstract concept than torture. Terrorism can include torture. And so, my conclusions regarding the possible moral justifiability or even moral excusability of terrorism have to be qualified, if I am right about the inexcusability of torture, to exclude torture. If Hughes's incineration of her sleeping, heavily intoxicated former husband was torture, and if torture is morally inexcusable, her only possible excuse would be the metaphysical kind: reduced capacity for rational agency (which is what the court decided) or nonculpable ignorance. If her husband died in his sleep without suffering intolerable pain, it is another story. There may be no way to determine whether he did.

3. DERSHOWITZ, THE TICKING BOMB, AND TORTURE WARRANTS

Initially, the ticking-bomb question sounds simple and straightforward: to avert a mass slaughter, could it not be justifiable to torture an uncooperative suspect who is credibly believed to know the densely populated urban location of a ticking bomb? The danger is imminent, the potential disaster great, potential victims innocent, helpless, and numerous, and the suspect uncooperative. Alan Dershowitz unearthed a version of the "ticking-bomb" scenario sketched by Jeremy Bentham in the nineteenth century but only published (and buried) in an Irish law journal in 1973 (Twining and Twining 1973). For that amazing piece of research, I am grateful.[10] Bentham's version, which applies the principle of utility to a particular act, features an urban arsonist, rather than bomber, whose accomplice has escaped.[11] A version that actually features a ticking bomb was popularized in a snappy two-page *Newsweek* article by philosopher Michael Levin, who imagined an atomic bomb set to detonate in Manhattan on July 4 (Levin 1972, pp. 434–35; Schulz 2007, pp. 227–29).

---

[10] Bentham's discussion is now available also in Schulz (2007, pp. 221–26).
[11] Twining and Twining (1973) reproduce writings from Bentham Mss. Box 46, 56–62 and 62–70. Dershowitz (2002, pp. 142–43) quotes Bentham's version of the "ticking-bomb" defense.

Bentham confessed to having reversed his initial opposition to torture, and he went on to offer a list of fourteen rules to govern its use (Twining and Twining 1973, pp. 306–56). Following Bentham's idea of regulation, Dershowitz proposes bringing back legal warrants to torture, but only for emergencies comparable to the ticking bomb (Dershowitz 2002, pp. 132–63). His intention is to institute accountability, to reduce the incidence of what now occurs "below the radar" (as he puts it), with the participation of governments that officially disavow it.

Dershowitz's proposal is more sophisticated than Levin's or Bentham's. Not only does Dershowitz envisage a legally authorized practice, as opposed to a particular deed, he envisages as part of that practice a guarantee to the interrogee of immunity from prosecution, to avoid the dangers of self-incrimination, and that the interrogee would first be interrogated by conventional methods. Only after such methods failed would a warrant to torture be applied for and only in extreme situations would it be issued. A major advantage of his proposal, he notes, is that the decision to torture would require the judgment of more than one person and would never be left to low-level enforcement officers. He anticipates that this kind of check on judgment (which is responsive to one of Rawls's concerns about "telishment") would reduce the incidence of torture.

Dershowitz's proposal has provoked loud criticism, much of it justified and yet, also, more than it deserves from critics who opt for the alternative of conscientious disobedience. That alternative is precisely what worries Dershowitz. As a civil liberties attorney, he appreciates the importance to democracy of accountability, the rule of law, and civil rights, even if he overestimates the effectiveness of warrants in reducing the incidence of torture and underestimates the likelihood of corruption in enforcement. Believing on the basis of polls (including his own polls of audiences) that most people in the US since 9/11 would endorse the use of torture in ticking-bomb situations, Dershowitz considers how to regulate such use.[12] Although he does not cite Rawls, he seems concerned to address the kinds of problems of trust and instability that Rawls identified with the idea of *telishing*. Dershowitz does not take up the further complexities discussed later by Arrigo regarding the trauma to and stigmatization of torturers or the involvement of health care personnel, biomedical research, the police, the judiciary, and the like.

---

[12] Polls in the US and other countries on the subject of ticking-bomb torture fluctuate in their results. Since the exposure in 2003 of maltreatment at Abu Ghraib, many appear to have reconsidered the opinion they formed right after 9/11.

Replying to Dershowitz's chapter, Elaine Scarry notes that it is thanks to the radar screens of non-governmental organizations (NGOs), such as Amnesty International (AI), that we actually do know that clandestine torture is widespread (Levinson 2004, pp. 281–90). The problem, she argues, is not ignorance of torture "below the radar." The problem is states' unwillingness to enforce torture bans and willingness to exploit other states' readiness to violate them. The misnamed "one-off" case seems in recent decades to have become the rule.

Yet, the radar screen that worries Dershowitz is a screen of accountability, not visibility. The problem is not just ignorance. AI can detect and publicize human rights violations. But it lacks power to hold violators accountable.

The warrants that Dershowitz proposes would certainly violate both Article 3 of the United Nation's 1975 Declaration against Torture and Other Cruel, Degrading or Inhumane Treatment or Punishment, which says "Exceptional circumstances such as a state of war or a threat of war, internal political instability or any other public emergency may not be invoked as a justification of torture or other cruel, inhuman or degrading treatment or punishment" and the provision of Part 1, Article 2 of the 1984 UN Convention against Torture and Other Cruel, Inhuman or Degrading Treatment or Punishment, that reaffirms that position, using the same language (Burgers and Danelius 1988, pp. 178, 192).[13] Further, in an essay responding to critics of his ticking-bomb chapter, Dershowitz states unequivocally, "I am opposed to torture as a normative matter" (Levinson 2004, p. 257). Why, then, does he support instituting warrants for it? His position is that if regulation reduced its incidence and made torturers accountable, then legally regulated torture would be a lesser evil than a ban agreed to by nations that then violate that ban covertly and with no accountability (Levinson 2004, pp. 257–80). It sounds rather like the position of abortion opponents who prefer state regulation to clandestine practice with no accountability, if only because regulation would prevent needless deaths.

Yet, although avoiding needless deaths is one concern, Dershowitz is not the utilitarian many readers seem to think he is. That misperception is probably based on his lively presentation of the utilitarian case for torture and of the likelihood revealed by post-9/11 polls that ticking-bomb

---

[13] The full texts of the 1975 UN Declaration and the 1984 Convention can be found in Burgers and Danelius (1988, pp. 177–93) and the text of the 1984 Convention is available at www.hrweb.org/legal/genocide.html.

torture would receive much popular support on straightforward utilitarian grounds. Dershowitz's own hopes are that instituting warrants would better secure civil rights, the rule of law, and accountability as well as reduce the incidence of torture. Are those hopes well founded?

Dershowitz is right to be concerned about jeopardizing such core democratic values as civil rights, the rule of law, and accountability. Yet, procedural justice is a core element of the rule of law, and torture to obtain information, like torture to obtain confessions, is procedurally a moral disaster, even if regulated, as torture for confessions was in Beccaría's day. On all three models that Arrigo describes, "uncooperative" suspects or detainees who in fact know nothing have no convincing way to demonstrate that fact to a torturer (which Shue also noted in his 1978 essay) and so are driven to false confessions. A real danger is that the ignorant will be tortured to death by enthusiastic interrogators, although that problem might be addressed to some extent by setting enforceable limits in advance. The main procedural problem highlighted by the predicament of the ignorant is that although torture is more extreme than most punishments legally permitted in democratic states, interrogees who have immunity from prosecution have not been determined by tolerable and checkable standards of evidence to be guilty of anything, not even guilty of withholding vital information. Torture *is* the *procedure* (the "trial") – like the ordeals of earlier eras – by which it is sometimes learned for sure that an interrogee knows or remembers something vital, although often that may never be learned at all.

Dershowitz suggests that interrogational torture is a natural extension of the practice of incarcerating witnesses who refuse to testify or to answer certain questions or answer them as fully as a judge would like, to pressure them to do so. This is the practice that led to the incarceration of Susan McDougall (see chapter 2) for what she describes as refusing to incriminate the Clintons falsely in Whitewater wrongdoing (McDougall 2003). If witnesses can be cited for contempt and incarcerated simply because a judge is dissatisfied with their testimony or disbelieves it, that practice has a problem of procedural justice analogous to that of torture: how is it determined that a witness is holding back in defiance of an order by the court, rather than simply answering as honestly or as honorably as he or she knows how? The answer may be that it is only determined by seeing whether incarceration produces further testimony.

An individual might be persuaded of a suspect's guilty knowledge (as law enforcement officers have been) by evidence that does not meet legal standards, is legally inadmissible, has not been subjected to the tests of a hearing or trial, or is simply not publicly demonstrable. But if that individual is an officer of the law or government, what he or she is justified in believing is not all that counts. It is important to maintain public trust and credibility. On what basis are others to be satisfied with officers' judgments? How are they to be confident that officers were not biased or just lucky? What assurance have citizens that they will not also become suspects? If the price of torture is to undermine the credibility of government or its officers, then what is protected?[14]

To deal with credibility issues, it becomes tempting to destroy evidence that torture was used (regardless of success), which has meant, historically, murdering torture survivors. Whether or not useful information is extracted, victims of clandestine torture have been, historically, vulnerable to being "pumped and dumped," as they were under the CIA's Phoenix project in Vietnam, "pumping suspects for information by torture and then dumping the bodies, more than twenty thousand of them between 1968 and 1971" (McCoy 2006, p. 119). The "information" may simply be pieces of a jigsaw puzzle, or possible jigsaw puzzle. Because of the lack of procedural justice, even more specific and directly useful information obtained by torture cannot be used in modern democracies to obtain legal convictions. Yet torture survivors may appear too dangerous, especially to torturers, to release – dangerous not only (or even necessarily) to others but dangerous to torturers themselves and to those who authorize torture. Just as rape victims are vulnerable to being murdered to eliminate the only witness, torture victims have been eliminated to prevent them from testifying against torturers. Dershowitz's intention may be to terminate that practice by regulating torture. But why think states that violate international bans covertly would stay within the limits of a warrant requirement? If the practice includes the secret authorizing of torture, what reason is there to think that even the authorizers would stay within legally instituted requirements? Would they not be dependent for their beliefs about the extraordinariness of the circumstances and about the vitality of information possessed by a particular suspect on information supplied to them by those applying for the warrant? Where, then, is the check on judgment? What is to keep authorizers from authorizing "pump and dump"?

Three sources contribute to popular mythology regarding the effectiveness of the torture that Dershowitz's proposal is intended to regulate. One

---

[14] This kind of issue is not peculiar to torture and incarcerating reluctant witnesses. Entrusting snipers to kill hostage-takers also raises problems of checks on judgment and accountability. Even allowing police officers to carry and use guns in law enforcement raises those issues.

source is fictional portrayals in television serials (notably, the Fox network show *24*) of instantly effective brief torture sessions (the "animal instinct model") by professionals, whose training is not portrayed. Second, there are a few widely publicized cases in which torture is credited with preventing a disaster. One is the plot to blow up eleven trans-Pacific aircraft in 1995 (cited by Dershowitz 2002, p. 137), allegedly foiled by torture. In another case, a police officer from New South Wales successfully tortured a suspect to find a kidnapped toddler (cited by Miller 2008, pp. 10–11).[15] Third, there is the assertion of former Vice-President Cheney that harsh interrogations of prisoners during the administration of President G. W. Bush yielded information that enabled the prevention of more terror attacks like those of 9/11, although corroborating details are, as of this writing, classified and so cannot be released to the public and therefore cannot be publicly checked.

What the television serials do not portray (besides the training of torturers) is the practice of torturing someone for weeks, months, or even years, which is not fiction. With respect to the plot to blow up Pacific aircraft, historian Alfred McCoy, whose research specialization is the Philippines, cites a *Washington Post* report that Manila police obtained all the important information "in the first few minutes" when they seized Abdul Hakim Murad's laptop and that "most of the supposed details gained from the *sixty-seven days* [emphasis mine] of torture that followed were, as one Filipino officer testified in New York, police fabrications that Murad mimed to end the pain" (McCoy 2006, pp. 110–12). If that is correct, torture was not necessary to prevent the attacks and should not be credited with foiling that plot. Regarding the kidnapped toddler, the concluding statement in the account Miller presents is that although the toddler was alive, no long-term prognosis regarding brain damage was available (Miller 2008). Thus it is unclear that torture saved the toddler's quality of life. Miller's source does not say how the torture victim fared.

A question not addressed in popular mythology is how torturers learn to do it effectively and without mishaps (such as premature death or unnecessary or counterproductive injuries). Consider the police officer from

---

[15] Another widely publicized case is the Daschner case in Germany from 2002. Frankfurt Deputy Police Chief Wolfgang Daschner *threatened* to torture Magnus Gaefgen if he did not reveal the location of a kidnapped eleven-year-old boy. Gaefgen admitted at once that the boy was dead. Gaefgen was sentenced to prison for murder. Daschner was charged with coercion, a misdemeanor, rather than with having extorted statements, a felony. See article of December 13, 2004 by Justus Leicht at the World Socialist Web Site: www.wsws.org/articles/2004/dec2004/tort-d13. shtml.

New South Wales. Are we to suppose this was the first time he did it? But if it appeared justifiable then, why not likewise in relevantly similar situations? Are dangerous kidnappings so unusual? Gaining skills for torturing poses still greater issues for Dershowitz's proposal, which would require systematic training of torturers in schools designed for the purpose. Such schools exist. As Jessica Wolfendale notes in a thoughtful article on training torturers (Wolfendale 2006), training is a major expense for an activity that is not supposed to occur very often. Dershowitz, sensitive to torture's history of proliferation, quotes Abraham Maslow, "to a man with a hammer, everything looks like a nail," but then argues that if torturers must get judicial approval, they will use their hammers more carefully. Yet, either jobs will be found in order to justify the expensive training of torturers, in which case the incidence of torture is not likely to shrink, or the rarely permitted instances will be done by torturers who lack training and experience; not a pretty scenario, either.

Instead of torture training schools and torture warrants, is it not preferable to invest in training interrogators in the arts of persuasion, rhetoric, and confidence-gaining, and would it not be preferable to issue warrants to use those formidable skills in interrogation of terror suspects? Even many of the most successful criminals do not rely on violence but, rather, on deception and manipulation, confidence games. McCoy reports that FBI members claim that far more effective than torture in getting interrogees to open up are persuasion and gaining the trust and confidence of interrogees (McCoy 2006, p. 203). Military interrogators have also taken that view (Mackey and Miller 2004).[16] Military interrogator Matthew Alexander gives a detailed account in his memoir *How to Break a Terrorist* (Alexander 2008) of how he obtained information that enabled the military in Iraq to find and kill Abu Musab al Zarqawi, who was more sought after than Osama bin Laden.[17] Alexander reports that he did it by gaining the respect and trust of a key interrogee without using torture or harsh physical or psychological procedures that rely on stress to break the interrogee's will.

---

[16] "Chris Mackey" ("for security reasons" a pseudonym) submitted his manuscript, as required of a member of the Military Intelligence Corps, for a security review and reports that the Army did not censor his account of events, although some material was removed, details were obscured, and he was not allowed to use certain names (Mackey and Miller 2004, p. xxvii).

[17] "Matthew Alexander" is also a pseudonym. Mark Bowden, author of *Blackhawk Down* (1999), wrote the introduction to Alexander's book. Alexander's book was submitted to the Department of Defense (DOD), which blacked out many sentences. "Break" refers not to breaking the interrogee's will but to getting the interrogee to start offering information, as in getting a "break" in the case.

Methods Alexander uses include conveying a knowledge of and respect for the interrogee's religious traditions and cultural history, which are important to gaining respect, trust, and confidence. Yet it would be misleading to describe his methods as non-coercive or morally unproblematic. For, although they do not appeal to fear of imminent physical pain or death or use severe psychological or physical stress to break down resistance, they do include Prisoner's Dilemma (PD) tactics, lies, and manipulation that exploits weaknesses of the interrogee that emerge in "friendly" interrogation.[18] Some methods have nicknames like "Fear Down," "You're Totally Screwed," and "Boss Introduction." They deserve the scrutiny from moral philosophers that torture has received. I had a mixed reaction to some of the cases that Alexander recounts. Yet, although there is room for moral improvement, it is also the case that insofar as a level of mutual respect is maintained, these methods appear vastly preferable to torture. I return to the issues of the relative merits of persuasion *vis-à-vis* torture at the end of this chapter.

4. THE FAILURES OF EXCUSES FOR CONSCIENTIOUS TORTURE

If attempts to justify conscientious torture are not totally successful, is there nevertheless sometimes a moral *excuse* for torture? By excuse, in this context, I mean a partial moral justification, one that would mitigate the culpability of a conscientious torturer. The existence of a moral excuse would mean that conscientious torture to prevent a real evil, however wrong, would at any rate not be a further *evil*. There can always, of course, be excuses of the kind that reduce the *responsibility* of the agent who tortures. In taking the position that torture is morally inexcusable, I do not mean to deny the possibility that a torturer's responsible agency was diminished. Rather, the excuse that concerns me here is the kind that reduces the culpability of an agent whose responsibility is not in question. An excuse in this sense is a reason that counts morally in favor of the deed, although it is not enough to justify the deed, all things considered. Whether a reason is even a moral excuse is not determinable by considering the reason by itself in abstraction from the act it is alleged to excuse and the circumstances in which it is invoked. Whether a reason morally

---

[18] For an account of PD in game theory, see Luce and Raiffa (1957, pp. 94–97). It basically involves questioning suspected collaborators separately, telling each that there is a deal for the one who talks first and a serious penalty for the other one. A disadvantage is that PD can provide each an incentive to confess to a crime when they are innocent but cannot prove it.

excuses depends very much on the act in question and its circumstances. A reason that might excuse some acts in some circumstances might carry no weight at all for other acts or in other circumstances.

Cognizant of difficulties for proposals such as that of Dershowitz, both Miller and Shue (in his 1978 essay although not in his 2005 essay) have suggested that courts might nevertheless justifiably go easy on torturers whose conscientious disobedience met certain moral criteria: sentence them as the law requires but bar them from office and commute most of the sentence. Miller suggests that for such torturers, the penalty might be appropriately commuted to "one day in prison" (Miller 2008, p. 24). Such leniency comes close to what Kutz calls "ratification" (Kutz 2007, pp. 289–305). It would be ratification were it not for the legal finding of guilt. Although in the case Miller imagines, the torturer is thought to have been morally *justified* on the whole, a similar proposal might be made for someone who had a strong moral *excuse*.

A court might respond this way in a case in which, like that of the officer who shot one suspect to make the other two talk, many lives were saved, especially if among the lives saved were those who were sitting in judgment. Would there not be a pull of gratitude? How could they punish someone to whom they were so beholden? (Miller does not comment on what the court might do to an equally conscientious torturer who saved no lives.) Such stories appeal to the probability that many, upon learning that their lives were saved by information gained through torture after humane interrogation failed, would be relieved, perhaps even grateful. At least, they would probably not prefer to have died. Many might even, in advance, want torture to be applied in some situations. Such feelings and wants are natural enough. But they are not reliable as indicators of right and wrong. What is in question is not whether we generally prefer to live or die but the moral status of the means used to protect us. Even if a court would reduce penalties for torturers who saved lives, the question is whether it should. Did the torturers have any moral excuse for the means they used?

To support the view that torture is inexcusable is a philosophical challenge, because it requires one to argue for the *non-existence* of something (an excuse). The strongest argument would expose a self-contradiction in the idea of an excuse for torture and conclude that such an excuse *could not* exist, that it is inconceivable. I have not been able to produce a plausible argument of that kind. The remaining strategy is to argue case by case with regard to alleged excuses that their plausibility dissolves under scrutiny. The arguer is in something like the position of Rawls when he wished to defend his principles of justice over alternatives but could not be sure he had thought of all the alternatives (Rawls 1999a, pp. 105–09). The best he could do was to consider, one by one, the most plausible alternatives, given the history of political thought. There may be no better method here than to consider the most plausible candidates for a moral excuse for torture, given the history of its discussion and its uses.

Let us first get out of the way something that might appear to be an excuse but actually rests on confused thinking. One might think that the very fact that torture was done conscientiously means that the torturers had a morally good reason for doing it. But all that fact really means is that the torturers *thought* they had morally good reasons. Yet one might persist: when you think you have a good reason, does the fact that you think so not become a good reason *for you*? Does it not show a certain integrity to act in accord with what you take to be a good reason, even if you are mistaken in thinking so? Should one act *against* one's conscience?

It may indeed show a certain integrity to act in accord with what one takes to be good reasons. But that integrity does not turn bad reasons into good ones. The fact that a torturer is conscientious does not mean that the deed is not evil. Enormous evils have been done by persons whose conscientiousness is not in doubt. Dostoevsky's legend "The Grand Inquisitor," although presented as fictional, is a classic portrayal (Dostoevsky 1950, pp. 292–314). Presenting the alternatives simply as acting in accord with or contrary to what one takes to be good reasons masks the fact that we are responsible for our judgment about which reasons are good. If there is no time to think, we may have a metaphysical excuse. But there is no need to wait until we are in a crisis before we begin to think.

If torture is morally inexcusable, there are no reasonably plausible moral arguments in its favor. Yet this is not to say that none are *tempting*. The ticking-bomb scenario suggests four tempting excuses: (1) urgency – humane methods would take too long; (2) relative mercifulness – torture would be actually less than an uncooperative suspect deserves for being willing to let a bomb kill masses of innocent people (or being willing to leave a baby to suffocate); (3) last resort – kinder methods of getting the suspect to provide the needed information have been tried, and they have all failed; and (4) self-defense or defense of the innocent – the objective is eminently worthy: saving innocent lives. These seem to me the most initially plausible candidates for a moral excuse in a ticking-bomb scenario. What I wish to argue is not that these reasons are outweighed by opposing considerations. I wish to argue, rather, that when the question is whether to use torture as a means to gaining critical information, these are not even good reasons. Each might be a good reason for other deeds in other circumstances. But for interrogational torture in a crisis, whatever weight they might initially appear to carry dissipates under scrutiny. Here are some thoughts on each.

(1) **Urgency**: the bomb is ticking (or the toddler is abandoned in an overheated car on a super-hot day). The question is whether shortness of time counts in favor of torture as a tool of interrogation in such a crisis.

Consider, first, the ticking bomb. We are told the time that the bomb is set to go off. We may be unable to verify that. But we may have good evidence that the suspect was involved in previous bombings and so rightly regard the threat as too credible to ignore. If we have multiple suspects, it might be effective to shoot one to motivate the others to talk. (Again, it might not: a gamble.) Yet summary execution (as opposed to threatening it) is not what philosophical defenders of ticking-bomb torture have wanted to defend. Nor have they wanted to defend torturing the suspect's innocent children (as opposed to threatening to do so). So let us consider a multiple-suspects case but modify it to entertain torturing one in front of the others to motivate the others to talk. Immediately, the urgency excuse becomes less plausible. And for the same reasons, it is no more plausible when the person tortured is a lone interrogee. Why?

If there is no time for humane methods, there is no time for wild-goose chases. On the first of Arrigo's models, interrogees who thought they knew the bomb's location and the time remaining would send interrogators on fruitless hunts.[19] Shortness of time would help them endure. Torturers can be expected to know also that when time is short, the interrogee's best strategy is to delay, regardless of the method of interrogation, at least as long as there is a good chance of survival with (more or less) bodily and psychic integrity. Further, if torturers have an urgent need for good information, interrogees can have an equally urgent need to withhold it. If they survive, they may be vulnerable to worse treatment later by their collaborators for whatever they reveal now. And, as Arrigo points out, they can interpret their pain under torture not as punishment for non-cooperation but as the price of their commitments.

If there is no time for humane methods on the first model, there is certainly no time for torture on the second and third models that Arrigo

---

[19] The film *Public Enemies* (2009), based on a novel about John Dillinger, has a scene in which Dillinger's woman friend is tortured by police interrogators for information about his whereabouts. She uses this strategy (successfully).

discusses. Both take far too long for urgent needs. But the appeal to urgency even on the first model of torture (which appeals to the subject's fear of pain or death) presupposes that torture is a quick solution. Recall, however, that real torture often does not work quickly. It can take as long to be effective as more humane methods. Jennifer Harbury writes about the long-term torture of victims like her husband, whose death was announced falsely while he was tortured over a period of months (Harbury 2005). For individuals who tolerate pain by interpreting it in their own way, it may be fear, not pain, that is effective, if anything is. Pain can be inflicted quickly. But the time required to produce an effective level of fear may not be short.

Further, for the appeal to urgency to count, morally, as a reason, it is not enough to argue that the information is *necessary* to prevent a disaster and that the interrogee might have it. When the means are as drastic as torture, there must be good reason to believe that with that information, there is a decent chance that a disaster can be prevented and there must be good reason to believe that the interrogee does (or interrogees together do) have that information. A 1 percent doctrine, or even a 50 or 60 percent doctrine, does not wash.[20] The harsher the treatment, the higher should be the standard of evidence for conclusions that make a person vulnerable to that treatment. A well-known trade-off in criminal law opts for higher standards of evidence than in civil law to reduce the likelihood of victimizing the innocent, even though higher standards increase the likelihood that some who are guilty will escape. I defer, briefly, the reason why that risk of escape should be tolerated here. As the standard of evidence rises, it begins to look almost as though torture would be justifiable only if it were unnecessary.

In the ticking-bomb scenario there is little or no time for evidence gathering; evidence regarding what interrogees know and whether the person to be interrogated has been identified correctly would have to be obtained in advance. The same is true regarding evidence for the belief that with information the interrogee can supply, there is a decent chance that an explosion can be prevented. But if there was time beforehand to obtain all that information, why was there not time to intercept or thwart plotters before they planted a bomb? Torture may deflect attention from the prior failures of those who would authorize it. In any case, if there was not time

---

[20] See Ron Suskind (2006, p. 62) for the quotation from former Vice-President Cheney, "If there is a one percent chance that Pakistani scientists are helping al Qaeda build or develop a nuclear weapon, we have to treat it as a certainty in terms of our response."

beforehand to obtain all that information, there is surely no time to obtain it now.

Consider, next, the toddler abandoned in an overheated car by the thief in New South Wales. In the case that Miller presents, a woman at a filling station left her toddler and her car keys in the car on a very hot day while she went to pay for gasoline (Miller 2008). She returned moments later to find the car (and child) gone. Video cameras recorded the thief, who appeared to be "a heavy set Pacific Islander with a blonde-streaked Afro" (Miller 2008, pp. 10–11). Apprehended after he had apparently ditched the car upon discovering the child in the backseat, he kept insisting "it wasn't me" when officers asked where he left the car. They appealed to his self-interest, asking if he would not rather be charged with "take and use" than with manslaughter. He contemptuously insisted "it wasn't me," until a severe beating broke him. He confessed only when he realized that the beating was not going to stop until he talked. The child was found dehydrated but alive.

The officer had the right man (as the officer who shot one to make two talk had the right suspects). But did he have a moral excuse to torture? Many questions are inadequately answered. Did the officer have enough experience beating suspects to gauge the likelihood that this suspect would break? If so, much more is at issue than the torture of one suspect. The appeal to urgency begins to sound like an excuse for not facing the issues of a police culture of torture. Was the officer warranted in believing he had the right man, or was he just lucky? A "heavy set Pacific Islander with a blonde-streaked Afro" in a continent colonized by the British? We are not told the officer's race. Do Pacific Islanders look as much alike to Australians of European descent as African Americans have looked to Americans of European descent? Have Pacific Islanders as much reason to be contemptuous of Australian police as many African Americans have had to be contemptuous of American police? When racial tensions have undermined trust for decades or longer, it may not be possible for officers (of whatever race) to gain the confidence of suspects who belong to an oppressed racial minority, especially when time is short. Torture is then especially likely to seem expedient. It may be expedient. Nothing quite analogous to a bomb plot can motivate this interrogee to hold out, although a suspect who is stubborn enough to risk a charge of manslaughter, as opposed to "take and use," might take a chance on holding out for the officer to give up. But if what made the officer's choice expedient was a history of bad race relations that had destroyed confidence in law enforcement on the part of racial minorities, the officer's choice to torture this suspect can be expected to aggravate those problems, which are also matters of life and death for many. Expediency for the officer in such a situation does not begin to justify that choice. If anything, it is an argument against.

One might object that, because of the racial issues, this is just a poorly chosen case for justifying torture. How about an otherwise similar case in which the suspect does not appear to be a member of a racial minority? Apparently, the officer in this case did not even have to rest his judgment on the suspect's looks. He says he found property stolen from the car in the suspect's pockets. We are not told how he knew it was stolen from the car or how he found it in the suspect's pockets, although much rests on those details.

Yet, the general point still holds: with such time pressures when stakes are high, *conditions are highly unfavorable to making good judgment calls*. If there are not serious questions regarding eyewitness testimony, which is as unreliable as it is unfortunately influential, there are apt to be questions regarding the value of other evidence that points to a particular suspect. Rather than providing a reason to torture, shortness of time is more plausibly a reason not to make the kinds of judgment calls that would appear to justify such a decision.

Shortness of time counts against torture, not in favor. It is no excuse. If there is no time for other methods, there may simply be no time to find the bomb (or the baby).

(2) **Relative mercifulness**: the uncooperative interrogee is complicit in an attempt at mass murder, in which victims might suffer as severely as torture victims. In contrast, the interrogator would cause only one person (or a few) pain without death. Therefore, the interrogee deserves, if anything, worse than to be tortured. Could such an interrogee complain?

At least three responses suggest themselves. First, the interrogee is a *suspect* not yet found guilty by tolerable standards of evidence of withholding vital information. Recall that interrogees have no convincing way to demonstrate their ignorance to a torturer. The car thief recorded on videotape might have been a brother, cousin, or look-alike of the man caught, with the same faddish hair, wearing the ubiquitous uniform of jeans and a gaudy T-shirt. He might have been mentally ill or on heavy medication and unable to remember. For interrogees who are misidentified, mentally ill, or on medications that affect memory, where is the mercy? Where is the mercy when many who are ignorant or confused must be tortured to find one who has useful information?

Second, even if some suspects deserve the extremities of torture and could not complain that they were treated worse than they were prepared to treat others, it does not follow that anyone is entitled to administer those deserts. Presumably, Heinrich Himmler, head of Adolf Hitler's SS (*Schutzstaffel*) and overseer of the death camps, concentration camps, and *Einsatzgruppen* (special killing squads), deserved at least to be starved to death or worked to death, if not made to dig his own grave and then beaten to death. He could hardly have complained. It does not follow that a court would have been justified in imposing those penalties. If no one would be entitled to administer such deserts, then a lesser treatment is not merciful. Merciful treatment would have to be more lenient than the treatment that one has a right to administer.[21]

Third, recall that when torture is done secretly, the tortured are vulnerable to being "disappeared," "pumped and dumped." Evidence gained by torture is worthless for criminal convictions but may convince interrogators of the danger of releasing the tortured. Even those who reveal nothing may be perceived to be dangerous as potential witnesses against their torturers. There is no mercy here for torture survivors.

Since torture is not merciful, mercy is no excuse for it.

(3) **Last resort**: kinder methods have failed. The suspect has refused to answer questions or to answer them truthfully. Or is it just that the suspect has refused to say what the interrogator wants to hear? Does the interrogator know how to recognize the value of what the interrogee has said? What counts as *failure of a method*? How does an interrogator know that the method has failed rather than something else? Failure to elicit needed information does not imply a failure of a method. The method may have elicited all the information that any method would elicit. That is a virtual certainty if the suspect lacks the needed information.

What kinder methods were tried first? Bribes? Beatings? Threats milder than torture? Truth serum? "Kinder" here seems to mean only "less harsh." Is it assumed that the harsher the method, the greater the likelihood of success? None of these methods is really kind. All of them appeal to a suspect's weaknesses or vulnerabilities, and at least the first three are as likely to elicit lies as truths. Genuinely kind methods would appeal to the suspect's strengths, gain good will, build trust and confidence. Of course, as military interrogator Alexander's memoir shows, trust can also be exploited in ways that are disastrous for the suspect.

---

[21] In a more general sense, merciful treatment is simply less than one has the *power* to inflict or administer. But that sense of mercy would not offer a moral excuse.

But the suspect whose trust is so exploited is not degraded. If it is one's strengths that are used against one, one can salvage a certain self-respect.

Some will think torture worth a try, even if the likelihood of success is remote. Are we back, then, to the 1 percent doctrine? Suppose torture fails. Was the effort worthwhile? Suppose the torturer unintentionally kills the suspect without learning anything, or the toddler dies anyway, or the bomb fails to detonate, or is a fake, meant only to terrorize. Can a failed torturer leave with the satisfaction of having tried? Anglican Bishop Joseph Butler, a generation older than Beccaría, noted in his critique of psychological egoism (Butler 1983, p. 52) that a failed pursuit of riches leaves only ashes; there is no inner satisfaction in having tried but failed to get rich, whereas failed benevolent endeavors, or a failed pursuit of justice, leaves a partially compensating satisfaction of having tried. When genuinely kind methods fail, one might leave with the satisfaction of having tried. But would failed torture not leave worse than ashes?

That more humane methods have failed (if they have) is no reason to think torture would succeed. That a method is the only one left implies *nothing* about its likelihood of success. Again, there is no reason here in favor of torture.

(4) **Defense of the innocent**: the objective is a worthy one – saving innocent lives. But how innocent are those lives? The toddler in the car (like other children) is, of course, innocent. An odd observation. How could the toddler be guilty? "Innocent" here seems to mean "defenseless." Adult citizens threatened by a bomb may be also defenseless. But, in the sense of "innocence" that refers to an absence of guilt, to claim that a democratic state that defends itself by torture is protecting *the innocent* is to beg the question of the moral permissibility of torture.[22] If self-defense is offered as an *excuse*, the wrongness of torture is conceded – what is right needs no excuse – and thereby the lack of innocence of those who would excuse it. Of course, many in a democratic state may not support their government's torture policies. They may be innocent in the relevant sense, although there is something odd about the supposition that an excuse for torturing is to protect those who do not believe in it or support it.

---

[22] I owe this thought to Clare Chambers, who suggested, in her comments on an earlier draft of this essay (at the British Academy symposium, January 13, 2007), that I was begging the question in asking how innocent we are if we defend ourselves by torture. I mean to urge the facing of that question, not beg it in the construction of excuses.

The question needs to be faced whether a nation, state, or city defended at the cost of torture is worth preserving. There are limits to what is morally permissible, or even morally excusable, in cases of individual self-defense. Likewise, there are limits to what is morally permissible, or even excusable, to defend another or others who may be defenseless. If the cost of torture as an instrument of national defense is to undermine trust within the nation (not to mention the cost of undermining the trust of other nations), how can what is saved be worth the cost? Aristotle, in his discussion of the voluntary and the involuntary in *The Nicomachean Ethics* III:1, held that "some acts, perhaps, we cannot be forced to do, but ought rather to face death after the most fearful sufferings; for the things that 'forced' Euripides' Alcmaeon to slay his mother seem absurd" (Aristotle 1925, p. 49). On the most natural reading, Aristotle is saying that some acts are such that one should die rather than do them. If this is true for *individuals*, are there not also deeds that *nations* should "face the most fearful sufferings" rather than do? Among the likely candidates for deeds that a nation should "face the most fearful sufferings" rather than do, I should think torture would be near the top of the list, along with genocide and mass rape as a weapon of war. If torturing, like killing one's mother, is not among the things to which Aristotle refers, it is hard to imagine what would be. And if torture is an impermissible means of national defense, the innocence of the nation that supports it cannot be an excuse. For that support is not innocent.

Empirical arguments, like most of those presented by Arrigo (2004) and Rejali (2007), that highlight torture's unintended consequences should suffice to persuade even political realists and utilitarians that a policy of torture, lawful or clandestine, is not the way to go, even for the sake of national defense or in other extreme circumstances. Yet those arguments skirt the moral heart of the matter. The philosophical arguments that most persuade me highlight the arrogance of torturers – arrogance regarding what they can know and what they can control as well as arrogance in the values they attach to their own security – and the degradation of democracy as well as the betrayal of both tortured and torturer. This chapter has emphasized the arrogance of torturers and the betrayal and degradation of democracy. The next chapter focuses on what torture does to the individuals who suffer it.

Torture survivor Jean Améry refers in his memoir to the destruction of his "trust in the world" (Améry 1980, p. 28). Betrayal is not confined to immediate victims. Citizens of a democracy, supposedly protected, are betrayed also in the lack of accountability to which torture policies lead. Arrigo's final arguments regarding widespread social corruption speak to this point. Even if actual trust survives, torture is apt to destroy trust*worthiness*. Whether it does is partly an empirical question (under what conditions can a torture policy be maintained? How much secrecy and deception of the citizenry are necessary?) and partly a philosophical one (when is a government worthy of the trust of its citizens?). Loss of trustworthiness is a cost that tends to negate the hoped-for gain of protecting a society or saving lives. If what is protected by torture is no longer worth protecting, then protection is not a reason in favor of torture. That means that the risks of a policy that prohibits torturing some suspects who really may be guilty of withholding vital information is a cost worth bearing for the sake of preserving the only conditions under which trust is likely to be warranted.

It does not follow that methods that use brain rather than brawn, such as Alexander used to find al Zarqawi, are free from all such difficulties. Some of those methods also rely on betrayal. They can (and sometimes do) result in the death of the interrogee (later, in the sentence of a court). Yet, however in need of moral improvement, those methods have six clear advantages, independently of the greater effectiveness claimed for them by the FBI and the US military. The first four have been discussed in this chapter; the last two are elaborated in chapter 8. First, methods such as those used by Alexander are not degrading. Second, there is no good reason to deceive a public about them. Third, evidence so obtained can be used in court. Fourth, there is no reason for interrogators to resort to "pump and dump." Fifth, interrogees have "a fighting chance" to defend themselves, unlike torture victims. Sixth, interrogees released when the interrogator discovers that they were victims of mistaken identity (as in one case that Alexander describes) do not suffer the long-term post-traumatic stress of torture victims. In a case recounted by Alexander in which the interrogee was found to have been identified mistakenly as a suspect, the interrogee spontaneously forgave him, acknowledging that he (Alexander) was just doing his job. A basic level of mutual respect was maintained. Neither was traumatized. How likely is it that a tortured suspect would respond similarly on being released when a torturer discovered a mistaken identity? Is it not more likely that if any are released, they would be forced to sign statements saying they had not been mistreated?

There is no *a priori* argument against torture here. But neither does my case rest solely on empirical beliefs regarding torture's efficacy. It rests heavily on an appeal to values. Torture does not fit with democratic values, procedural justice, due humility regarding what we can know and control, or a balanced view of the importance of our own security. Further moral arguments in the next chapter, which may persuade non-democrats as well, appeal to respect for the humanity of interrogees and consider what distinguishes torture, morally, from other hard treatment.

CHAPTER 8

Ordinary torture

> Twenty-two years later, I am still dangling over the ground by
> dislocated arms, panting, and accusing myself. (Améry 1980, p. 36)

Philosophers who reflect on torture tend to focus almost exclusively on options and choices of potential torturers and their ratifiers, to the relative neglect of the experience of the tortured. That is the approach represented in chapter 7. The focus changes in this chapter to the harm that torture does to its victims. Since torturers and ratifiers are the only free agents in the case, a focus on them might be thought ethically appropriate. Yet the experiences, positions, and agency of the tortured should not be neglected.

It is in terms of harm to victims that the claim has been made that the harsh procedures authorized for use in counterterrorism programs of the United States after 9/11 do not amount to torture.[1] Darius Rejali calls these procedures "clean tortures" (Rejali 2007, p. xvii) since they need not leave marks (although some can and do). When it is said that a procedure is not really torture, the procedure is apt to be presented abstractly rather than considered in contexts where it is combined with other procedures and carried out repeatedly over a long time. It is apt to be presented with no mention of such conditions as continuous solitary confinement or incommunicado detention. Yet, according to the 2007 International Committee of the Red Cross (ICRC) Report on the Treatment of Fourteen "High Value Detainees" in CIA Custody, many forms of ill-treatment have been inflicted repeatedly and in combination over long periods of time on detainees held incommunicado and in continuous solitary confinement.[2]

---

[1] According to Mazzetti and Shane (2009b, p. A13), the Central Intelligence Agency (CIA) approved the harsh interrogation program in 2002, but "nervous CIA officials began to curb its practices much earlier than most Americans know: no one was waterboarded after March 2003, and coercive interrogation methods were shelved altogether in 2005."

[2] Hereafter, this report is referred to in the text as the 2007 ICRC report, to distinguish it from the 2004 ICRC report on the treatment of prisoners in Iraq (discussed in chapter 7). The ICRC 2007 report is available at www.nybooks.com/icrc-report.pdf. Pages cited are for a single-spaced printout using Times New Roman 12.

Detainee Abu Zubaydah suffered a combination of many repeated harsh procedures under such conditions while he was still recovering from surgery for gunshot wounds that were inflicted during his capture (ICRC report 2007, pp. 6, 9, 10, 13–14, 17).

The twelve procedures discussed in the 2007 ICRC report are: suffocation by water,[3] prolonged stress standing, beatings by use of a collar, beating and kicking, confinement in a box, prolonged nudity, sleep deprivation and use of loud music, exposure to cold temperature or cold water, prolonged use of handcuffs and shackles, threats, forced shaving, and deprivation or restricted provision of solid food (ICRC report 2007, p. 2). After examining each method through private interviews with each of the fourteen detainees, and taking into account that detainees were held incommunicado and in continuous solitary confinement, the carefully worded 2007 ICRC report concludes that "the allegations of ill-treatment of the detainees indicate that, in many cases, the ill-treatment to which they were subjected while held in the CIA program, either singly or in combination, constituted torture" (ICRC report 2007, p. 26).

That conclusion is philosophically as well as politically significant. It does not offer "a thin line," as Judge Jay S. Bybee is said to have put it, "between harsh treatment of a high-ranking Al Qaeda terrorist that is not torture and harsh treatment that is" (N. Lewis 2009, p. A12). Rather, it suggests that torture can be the cumulative impact of coordinated procedures, administered under certain environmental conditions to persons in varying conditions of health and fitness. Torturing can be a complex structured activity with a division of labor. If we look only at particular procedures, one by one, we can miss the torture. Listening to the experience of the tortured uncovered that complexity.

By "ordinary torture" I do not mean traditional paradigms of torture. I mean torture of many kinds inflicted routinely or under circumstances that are not extraordinary. Under most such circumstances, a conscientious agent would not be tempted to justify or excuse the use of torture. Oddly enough, wartime tends to be regarded as an extraordinary circumstance.[4] Routine interrogational torture of war captives may be claimed to be exceptional in two respects: in those selected for special treatment ("high value detainees") and in the existence of wartime conditions. Still, when torture becomes routine even in war, it becomes ordinary. And so I

---

[3] Waterboarding by the method of pouring water on a cloth covering the face of the interrogee, as described in chapter 7, note 2.

[4] For most of my life, the US has been engaged in at least one war, not always declared.

include in this chapter consideration of the kinds of experience revealed by the fourteen detainees. The procedures evaluated by the ICRC were used to interrogate suspects believed to be high-ranking al Qaeda operatives. Sessions were not brief and instantly effective, contrary to what was suggested by former CIA officer John Kiriakou, who is reported to have said in December 2007 that after being waterboarded "for probably 30, 35 seconds" Mr. Zubaydah started to cooperate and, from that day on, answered every question (Stelter 2009, p. A1). A declassified Justice Department memo later revealed that Mr. Zubaydah was subjected to multiple sessions of waterboarding, "at least 83 times" (Stelter 2009, p. A1). This is routine.

Further, as Henry Shue notes, torture has many other uses than as a tool of interrogation, not the least of which is terrorism (Shue 1978, pp. 124–43). Torture was widely used in the twentieth century in Chile, Argentina, and elsewhere to intimidate others who were not in custody. Torture can work to coerce, punish, gain revenge, even entertain. It can be a source of information about the effects of certain treatments, substances, or conditions on the body. For revenge, discipline, and coercion, torture has long been a staple of organized crime.[5] Like terrorism, torture can be inexpensive (materially) and so a method of choice for some.

This chapter has three main conclusions. The first is that the 2007 ICRC report is right to judge that use of the procedures it discusses, singly or in combination and under conditions of continuous solitary confinement and incommunicado detention, has amounted to torture. A second conclusion is that the UN definition of torture should be revised to take into account more victims and more of the victims' experience, including extreme stress that is not, literally, painful but is very harmful and the so-called aftermath, which can last a lifetime and shorten a life. A third conclusion is that many common civilian activities and practices, including some widely considered acceptable, impose treatment that should be recognized as torture. These practices include some of what is done to prison inmates, some death penalties, some forms of domestic violence and aggravated rape, many violent hate crimes, and certain commercial, military, and even academic, laboratory experiments on vertebrate animals.

I begin with a survivor's account of the experience of being tortured in interrogation. Only part of what he recounts depends on the fact that he was being interrogated.

---

[5] Its interrogational use by hired thugs, using a female expert, is portrayed in some hard-to-watch scenes in the French film *Tell No One* (2008). Another graphic portrayal, in which the (unauthorized) torturer pursues kidnappers of his daughter, is a scene in the film *Taken* (2008) in which the torturer walks off leaving the electricity on after getting the information he sought.

Until the 1970s, most of these were not generally acknowledged to be rapes. Much torture still goes unacknowledged and is labeled something else: interrogation, punishment, discipline, research, and so on. Many common tortures are not done by public officials on behalf of governments but by private individuals. Torture, as defined by the United Nations, is restricted to the deeds of public officials. Still, that definition is a good place to begin.

2. THE UN DEFINITION

In Beccaría's day, torture was highly regulated by law. It was no secret. Most people seemed no more ashamed of its existence than many are today of the application of the death penalty. People knew torture when they saw it. Its definition was not an issue. But neither clean nor dirty rough interrogation techniques used in the late twentieth and early twenty-first centuries have been public or well publicized, except when exposed as scandal, as in the case of the prison at Abu Ghraib (Danner 2004) and in the 2007 ICRC report on the dark sites.[10]

"Clean" procedures authorized in the CIA's post-9/11 interrogation programs need leave no permanent visible scars or permanent physical injury. Some do not require physical touching. When an interrogee's will is enlisted to maintain stress positions, the procedures have even been called "self-inflicted" (despite coercion to "inflict" them). Because these techniques depart in such ways from classical techniques like *la corda* (used on Beatrice Cenci, described in chapter 7) and the *strappado*, some say they are not torture or call them "torture lite."[11]

The meaning of "torture" raises many questions. How severe must pain be to count as torture? Can it be psychological? Emotional? Must it be inflicted intentionally? What does the relevant intention include? Does the purpose matter? If an interrogator never lays hands on the victim, can it still be torture? A helpful survey of definitional issues is provided in Seumas Miller's *Stanford Encyclopedia of Philosophy* entry on torture (Miller 2008).[12]

---

[10] "Dark sites" are the secret prisons that were maintained by the US for the interrogation of high-value al Qaeda operatives. As one of his first acts as president, President Barack Obama ordered them closed (Shane 2009a).

[11] For memos defending these methods during the G. W. Bush administration, see Greenberg and Dratel (2005).

[12] *The Stanford Encyclopedia* is electronic only. The website for Miller (2008) is http://plato.stanford.edu/entries/torture. Page citations are to a single-spaced printout.

Unlike terrorism, but like genocide, torture is defined in documents passed by the UN and ratified by many nations. Let us take as a point of departure, then, not another philosopher's definition but internationally accepted documents that explicitly ban torture and present it as a violation of human rights. The 1948 Universal Declaration of Human Rights says, "no one shall be subjected to torture or to cruel, inhuman or degrading treatment or punishment"(Glendon 2001, pp. 310–14). The 1975 UN Declaration against Torture defines torture as: "any act by which severe pain or suffering, whether physical or mental, is intentionally inflicted by or at the instigation of a public official on a person for such purposes as obtaining from him or a third person information or a confession, punishing him for an act he has committed, or intimidating him or other persons. It does not include pain or suffering arising only from, inherent in or incidental to, lawful sanctions to the extent consistent with the Standard Minimum Rules for the Treatment of Prisoners," adding, "Torture constitutes an aggravated and deliberate form of cruel, inhuman or degrading treatment or punishment" (Burgers and Danelius 1988, p. 191). The 1984 UN Convention against Torture and other Cruel, Inhuman or Degrading Treatment or Punishment reiterates, in its Article 1, most of the 1975 definition but deletes the words "to the extent consistent with the Standard Minimum Rules for the Treatment of Prisoners," concluding simply, "It does not include pain or suffering arising only from, inherent in or incidental to lawful sanctions" (Burgers and Danelius 1988, pp. 177–90).[13]

Portugal wanted a paragraph stating that certain uses of psychiatry should be regarded as torture. Switzerland wanted a sentence stating that torture "also means medical or scientific experiments that are not justified by a person's state of health and serve no therapeutic purpose" (Burgers and Danelius 1988, p. 42). These proposals were rejected. But the conduct in question might be covered by obligations of the convention's Article 16 regarding "acts of cruel, inhuman or degrading treatment which do not amount to torture as defined in Article 1" (Burgers and Danelius 1988, p. 181).

France argued that "torture" should be defined "intrinsically," without regard to who perpetrates it (Burgers and Danelius 1988, p. 45). France had a point. The restriction to acts of public officials is arbitrary. And yet, as will become clear by the end of the next section, there may have been a good

---

[13] The 1955 Standard Minimum Rules for the Treatment of Prisoners can be found at www.unhchr. ch/html/menu3/b/h_comp34.htm. They are also excerpted in Amnesty International (1984, pp. 252–53).

reason behind that restriction, although the convention could have noted that it does not reflect ordinary usage. As a result of that restriction, the global movement against domestic violence has been unable to rely on the convention. It has had to appeal instead to equal protection rules and argue that women receive less protection from their governments against violence (in general) than men receive (Fineman and Mykitiuk 1994, pp. 323–46).

The 1984 convention's unqualified exclusion of lawful sanctions is outrageous. In his *Genealogy of Morals*, Nietzsche summarizes a history of state punishments, performed in public as spectacles, that were clearly tortures:

Consider the old German punishments; for example, stoning (the sagas already have millstones drop on the head of the guilty), breaking on the wheel (the most characteristic invention and speciality of the German genius in the realm of punishment), piercing with stakes, tearing or trampling apart by horses ("quartering"), boiling of the criminal in oil or wine (still employed in the fourteenth and fifteenth centuries), the popular flaying alive ("cutting straps"), cutting flesh from the chest, and also the practice of smearing the wrongdoer with honey and leaving him in the blazing sun for the flies. (Nietzsche 1969, p. 62)

Torture spectacles carried out as punishments are not just a thing of the past. Consider the 1986 execution in Iran of Soraya M., accused by her husband of adultery. Buried to her neck and shoulders in sand, she was stoned to death by men of her village, starting with her father. She died slowly, as the stones, thrown from a distance, did not always hit or hit squarely. Finally, after determining that she still lived, someone crushed her skull with a stone from above. Her biographer, Iranian journalist Freidoune Sahebjam (kidnapped and tortured by Iranians in 1979 in Paris for an article he published in *Le Monde*; Sahebjam 1990, pp. viii–ix), reports that over a thousand women were stoned to death in Iran between 1979 and 1994 (p. vii).[14] Iran's death penalty torture is more economical than those of many countries. Section 3 of this chapter considers some more expensive death penalties common in the US.

Within the scope that it defines, the 1984 convention rejects torture absolutely. In Article 2 of Part 1, it defines the following obligation of states:

1. Each State Party shall take effective legislative, administrative, judicial or other measures to prevent acts of torture in any territory under its jurisdiction.

---

[14] Sahebjam reports that this ritualized, public execution was authorized by the village mayor. According to Soraya's aunt Zahra (Sahebjam 1990, pp. xii–xv), Soraya was falsely accused by her husband, who had fallen in love with a younger woman. A film *The Stoning of Soraya M.* (DVD; 2009) is based on this book.

2. *No exceptional circumstances whatsoever, whether a state of war or a threat of war, internal political instability or any other public emergency, may be invoked as a justification of torture.*

3. An order from a superior officer or a public authority may not be invoked as justification of torture (Burgers and Danelius 1988, p. 178; emphasis mine).

Given the exclusion of lawful sanctions and the restriction to public officials, this obligation sounds more comprehensive than it is.

If we abstract from the exclusion of state-sanctioned punishments and the restriction to acts of public officials, the convention defines torture as a function of three elements: intention, pain or suffering, and purpose. Its full title, Convention against Torture and Other Cruel, Inhuman and Degrading Treatment or Punishment, implies that torture is also cruel, inhuman, or degrading, although not necessarily all of that by definition. Treatment not perceived as cruel is not apt to be regarded as torture. It is less clear that inhumanity and degradation belong to the concept, although real tortures, like those described in this chapter so far, tend to be both. The 1975 declaration explicitly found torture to be aggravated and deliberate, and there is good reason, as will become apparent, to include those elements in the definition.

Do the convention's three defining elements, together with aggravation and deliberateness, distinguish the "clean" techniques, morally, from torture? Much depends on how the elements are interpreted.

3. APPLYING THE UN DEFINITION TO THE "CLEAN" TECHNIQUES

When many procedures applied to a single individual are authorized or carried out by different individuals, only whoever is responsible for co-ordinating or overseeing them may be in position to foresee and intend the overall result. But what does the relevant intent include? Intent rules out accidents. But should intent be construed narrowly as the aim and the means chosen to achieve it? Or should it be construed more broadly to include collateral harms that are reasonably foreseeable, although they are neither aims nor means? Surgical pain (an example that is not usually torture) is typically collateral, reasonably foreseeable but neither an aim nor a means to surgery's goal. Collateral pain need not be *acc*idental. It is *inc*idental. When incidental pain is foreseeable, should it be construed as intended? A narrow interpretation of intent says no. A broader one says yes. Each interpretation has significant implications for what should count as torture.

The broader interpretation of intent can find post-traumatic stress disorder (PTSD) intentional when it is reasonably foreseeable. PTSD is a collateral harm, neither an end in itself nor a means to the ends of interrogation. The narrower interpretation of intent, restricting it to aims and means, excludes PTSD as not part of the intended suffering. That makes it easy to ignore as not a responsibility of those who torture. PTSD is not captured by anything in the UN definition.

The narrower interpretation of "intentionally inflicted" might initially appear right if one thinks the role of intent is to capture culpability. Yet, more is relevant to culpability than simply the choices of ends and means. Like the use of harmful means, foreseeable collateral harms can be accepted as part of the price of achieving one's ends. That acceptance is a moral choice.

But, one may ask, who is responsible for that price? It depends on the case. Some harms that might be regarded as collateral in relation to what I do are the result of others' choices, and they are responsible, not I (or, not only I, depending on the case). Enemies who shield themselves with innocent hostages, hoping to deter attacks, bear responsibility for that choice and consequently for the fate of the hostages when the strategy fails. It is not clear that the attacker bears any part of that responsibility, depending on what alternatives the attacker had. The attacker need not find the hostages' deaths an acceptable part of the price of the attack, even if, because of others' choices, they do die from the attack. But when foreseeable collateral harms do not result from the choices of others, one can be responsible for them. They become costs one accepts as the price of achieving a certain end by certain means. Someone who steals a car with a baby in the backseat, knowing the baby is in the backseat but interested only in the car (say, for a getaway), is responsible for the fate of the baby. The baby is neither an end nor a means. It is part of the price of stealing the car, which the thief apparently accepts. If the baby was in the car not as a result of anyone's negligence or other wrongdoing, the thief alone is culpable.

Aggravation and deliberateness are also indicators of culpability. Deliberateness is a way of intending or of carrying out an intention (deliberately), not itself either an end or a means. Sometimes "aggravated" is a judgment about one's choice of means (was a weapon used?). But it can be a judgment about circumstances of one's intention (was the victim defenseless?), rather than about means to an end.

A narrow reading of intent (which would restrict the content of an intention to the agent's willed ends and means), then, is not adequate to capture culpability. In the absence of any better reason to read "intent" narrowly, I adopt the broader interpretation, which counts as intentional at least those reasonably foreseeable collateral ("incidental") results that are not the results of others' choices. "Intentional," then, captures what the agent is willing to accept as well as what the agent is willing to do. Both doing and accepting are moral choices. In Kantian language, both belong in the maxim of one's action (regardless what Kant thought), as they indicate one's will in morally relevant ways.

The content of an intent to torture, then, can have the following form. The agent is willing to do act A in order to achieve purpose P, despite the reasonable foreseeability of collateral harm C. Both A and C are intentional, although only P is the aim. The foreseeability of C, however, also needs clarification. It is reasonably foreseeable that some waterboarded victims will drown (collateral harm) and that some injuries (collateral harms) will be inflicted by others on victims whose faces are hidden by hoods. But not all of those harms need be intended, and not just because of others' choices. Many collateral harms are preventable through precautions. Torturers can seek the advice of health care personnel. The services of health care personnel are in fact enlisted for such purposes (ICRC report 2007, section 3, pp. 21–23).[15] The case is otherwise with PTSD. No precautions are apt to make that harm unlikely, short of reducing the severity of treatment to something less than torture. Foreseeable harm that is probably not preventable, even if collateral, can be part of what makes a deed or policy one of torture. Preventable harm that occurs despite all reasonable precautions should not be counted as contributing to the evil of torture; such harm is not intended, even on the broad interpretation. But preventable harm that occurs because precautions were not taken should count; that harm was willingly accepted, like foreseeable harmful results that are not preventable.

Like the classical tortures, the clean techniques inflict suffering that lasts long beyond interrogation without contributing further to interrogation's purpose. When these techniques are called "torture lite," or not really torture, the contrast is with *pain during interrogation* and sometimes with the

---

[15] According to the 2007 ICRC report (section 3, pp. 21–23) the roles of health care personnel, based on interviews with detainees, have been highly problematic, at times serving the interests of interrogators rather than those of interrogees. These observations corroborate Jean Arrigo's concerns (Arrigo 2004) regarding the corruption of professionals.

enduring and visible gross physical injuries (such as broken limbs) of classical tortures. Pain, suffering, and disabilities experienced continuously or
intermittently long after use of the techniques is concluded are ignored in
that contrast. The clean methods may seem, abstractly, relatively humane,
compared to the *strappado* or *la corda* (although even those procedures did
not necessarily leave enduring physical marks). Singly (rather than in combination) and not inflicted repeatedly, many of the clean methods might
inflict less intense pain during interrogation. Sensory deprivation inflicts
no *pain* at all, although the anxiety it produces is reported to be more
severe than that of traditional tortures, and the severe and enduring psychological and emotional harms and behavioral disorders that can result
are reported to be at least as severe in the case of some clean procedures
(McCoy 2006, p. 9).

Post-traumatic harm has been, for at least half a century, a reasonably
foreseeable result of the clean techniques, foreseeable by anyone with
access to the history of how captured US soldiers were treated in the
Korean war. Clean tortures used in the 1950s by communist interrogators included "shackling the Americans to force them to stand for hours,
keeping them in cold cells, disrupting their sleep and limiting access to
food and hygiene" (Shane and Mazzetti 2009, p. A14). The American
military program Survival, Evasion, Resistance, and Escape (SERE) was
created decades ago "to give American pilots and soldiers a sample of the
torture methods used by Communists in the Korean War, methods that
have wrung false confessions from Americans" (Shane and Mazzetti 2009,
p. A14). It appears that the SERE program, and indirectly the 1950s communist methods of interrogation, were sources of procedures used to interrogate top al Qaeda suspects.

The intent of interrogational torture, then, is to use methods that
have long been well known to inflict not just short-term intense distress
but also enduring intolerable harms that contribute nothing to the purpose. Without those enduring harms, torture would not be so naturally
described as "the most horrible event a human being can retain within
himself" (Améry 1980, p. 22). It would not be the atrocity that it is if victims experienced a recovery comparable to what many women experience
after hours, even days, of natural childbirth labor.[16]

The UN definition specifies "pain or suffering inflicted" "for such purposes as …" And so, even if PTSD is reasonably construed as intentional,

---

[16] Not all women who survive do recover from the psychological trauma of a difficult childbirth. By
all reports, my grandmother, who was badly torn during my mother's birth (in 1915), did not.

it is not *inflicted for a purpose*. It is accepted as part of the price of pain or suffering that is inflicted for a purpose. Thus, it eludes the UN definition. It is not counted as part of the torture, even though it is one of the most morally important aspects of torture. If torture were defined to reflect more of the experience of those who undergo it, the relevant intentions would include harm to victims that torturers are willing to accept as consequences of what they do to achieve their purposes.

Severe pain or suffering is the second major element in the convention's definition. This element distinguishes torture from less traumatic painful procedures and also from cruel, inhuman, or degrading treatment that is not painful or even anxiety-provoking. Degrading treatment that is not painful includes certain medical or psychiatric procedures (perhaps the ones Portugal and Switzerland wanted the UN convention to count as tortures) that do not offer a compensating benefit to the persons on whom they are performed. An example is Frances Farmer's lobotomy (noted in chapter 4), alleged to have been performed to make her more controllable in the mental hospital where she was incarcerated (Arnold 1979).[17]

Yet "severe pain" underdescribes what torture victims undergo and does not make perspicuous what is morally serious. As noted in chapter 4, normal pain is useful to the person whose pain it is. It is a warning that something is wrong (one's hand is too close to the fire). Normal pain does not shame or humiliate. Torture does. (Recall Améry's "shrilly squealing piglet at slaughter.") It is meant to break the will of interrogees, who can emerge as broken human beings, not just temporarily defeated ones.

Not everyone is affected in the same ways. It can matter whether one has information to withhold. Had Améry possessed information that his interrogators sought, he might have been able to take a certain pride in withholding it. Henri Alleg did when he was tortured in Algeria by the French, who subjected his body to jolts of electricity (and other tortures, including simulated drowning) in fruitless efforts to get information he actually did possess. He wrote in his memoir that after surviving the first days he "suddenly was proud and happy not to have given way" and "was convinced that I could still hold out if they started again" (Alleg 1958, p. 102). I do not know what long-term harms he sustained. He wrote this only four months after his torture.

---

[17] See chapter 4, note 9. Much of the "treatment" that Farmer endured in the mental hospital at Steilacoom in Washington State fits any plausible definition of torture, even if "intent" is construed narrowly (Farmer 1972).

One survivor (I no longer recall who) speculated that when someone breaks, it is *fear* of pain, not actual pain, that does the work. That hypothesis is close to what researchers discovered in searching for methods to break people without leaving detectable scars. They learned that *stress* is the key. Pain is a source of stress, not necessarily the most effective. Threats, humiliations, and mock executions can be as stressful. Fear may be more stressful than pain.

McCoy's chapters on the history of torture and mind control discuss two twentieth-century innovations in methods of breaking people by uses of stress discovered by psychologists funded by the US government to come up with improved interrogation techniques (McCoy 2006, pp. 5–12, 21–59). One innovation (the so-called "self-inflicted" suffering) engages the will of the interrogee (as in maintaining one's body in a stress position). If someone's will is already engaged in that way, it is more difficult for the person to resist. The other innovation is sensory deprivation (as in hooding or severe isolation), which causes no physical pain but can be more stressful and cause greater psychological trauma.[18]

In order to challenge the position that because sensory deprivation is not painful, it cannot be torture, it is tempting to stretch the meaning of pain to cover all kinds of felt trauma. Sensory deprivation can be traumatic. But pain, interpreted that broadly, becomes a metaphor, which makes it less useful in a definition that is supposed to distinguish torture from other forms of ill-treatment. That may be why the UN convention definition says "pain or suffering," rather than just "pain." But "suffering" is too broad. It covers much that is not plausibly regarded as torture. What one suffers in torture is severe and harmful stress. Often pain is the source of that harmful stress. If severe and harmful stress is what does the work even in classic torture, then harmful stress is more basic to torture than pain. A morally more perspicuous definition of torture, then, might specify "pain or other severe and harmful stress" rather than "pain or suffering."

It might be objected that such a substitution changes the meaning of "torture." It certainly changes how torture is conceived. But it does not change torture if, in fact, it gives a better account of what torture has been all along. Torture is still distinguishable from other hostile techniques of

---

[18] Hooding can combine sensory deprivation with other assaults, including assaults on sensory experience. Harbury presents cases in which hoods were filled with pesticides to cause asphyxiation (Harbury 2005, pp. 72–73). Others have described hoods lined with other substances, ranging from talcum to substances with vile odors.

interrogation, such as truth serum (which relieves rather than imposes stress), however morally objectionable they may be in other ways. But the clean procedures are clearly tortures under such a revised definition. "Self-inflicted" stress positions, harmful sensory deprivation, near-death experiences, mock executions, and threats to family members can be as harmfully stressful as intense pain, if not more so, not only during the application of procedures but in foreseeable long-term effects.

It should be noted that stress positions, such as forced standing, can also produce intensely painful injuries. Calling them "clean tortures" is misleading. On the effects of forced standing with one's hands shackled to the ceiling, Danner quotes psychologists who studied communist interrogation methods:

After 19 to 24 hours of continuous standing, there is an accumulation of fluid in the tissues of the legs. This dependent edema is produced by the extravasation of fluid from the blood vessels. The ankles and feet of the prisoner swell to twice their normal circumference. The edema may rise up the legs as high as the middle of the thighs. The skin becomes tense and intensely painful. Large blisters develop, which break and exude watery serum. (Danner 2009b, p. 51)

Swellings of the feet and legs as a result of being forced to maintain stress positions are also reported in the ICRC interviews with detainees from the dark sites (ICRC report 2007, section 1.3.2, pp. 11–12).

Stress that continues long beyond interrogation is commonly referred to as "the aftermath." Sister Dianna Ortiz, tortured in Guatemala in 1989, says one never heals from torture but at most learns to cope with the aftermath (Harbury 2005, pp. 145–46; see also Ortiz 2004). But listen to Améry: "It still is not over," he writes. "Twenty-two years later I am still dangling over the ground by dislocated arms, panting, and accusing myself" (Améry 1980, p. 36). "At the first blow," he writes, "… trust in the world breaks down"; "it is like a rape, a sexual act without the consent of one of the two partners" (Améry 1980, p. 28); "with the first blow from a policeman's fist, against which there can be no defense and which no helping hand will ward off, a part of our life ends and it can never again be revived" (Améry 1980, p. 29).

How much aftermath there is and the forms it takes may vary with procedures, how long they are used and in what combination under what conditions, what the interrogee believed about the possibility of terminating the stress before death, the general state of the interrogee's health, and other factors, such as being held incommunicado and in solitary confinement. Yet Améry's interrogation was not especially prolonged compared with that of Ortiz's spouse or even that of Alleg, who was tortured for days and then held for a month under the threat of more.[19] Jennifer Harbury summarizes clinical reports on the so-called "aftermath" as follows: insomnia, nightmares, flashbacks, chronic anxiety, inability to trust others, deliberate self-injury, violent behavior, substance abuse, inability to concentrate, depression, paranoia, guilt, suspicion, sexual dysfunction, memory loss, attempts to numb continuing pain by drug or alcohol abuse – symptoms that can last decades or the rest of a life and hasten its end (Harbury 2005, p. 146). This is aftermath only in relation to *interrogation*. It is part of what *torture*, in reality, *is* – prolonged stress that not even torturers can turn off (short of murder) as they can turn off the electricity or the water. The Fox network television serial drama *24*, which features interrogational torture, does real survivors a disservice by sanitizing torture, deceptively compressing the process, and presenting survivors as bouncing back the next day, with no aftereffects other than lingering anger or resentment.

The third item in the UN definition is purpose. Convention drafters debated whether to include purposes, as they could not agree on a definitive list. The result is a compromise, a sample list with no claim to being exhaustive. Philosophical incompleteness here can be remedied by acknowledging that the only purpose conceptually excluded is benefit to recipients who consent rationally and freely (or would if they could). Without such consent, surgery without anesthesia would be torture. With consent, it is not, regardless how painful or stressful.[20] Remarkably, the UN definition does not explicitly mention absence of consent. Perhaps that point seemed obvious. Absence of consent can be presumed in the purposes that it does mention (obtaining information or a confession, punishing, intimidating).

An apparent counter-example to absence of consent is the practice in earlier centuries of undergoing legally administered torture in order to give one's testimony weight in court. The painter Artemisia Gentileschi was put to the thumbscrew in 1612 in testifying that she was raped by Agostino Tassi (Bissell 1999, pp. 14–18). One might argue that the torture was for her benefit, namely, to give her testimony credence. But the rule

---

[19] Alleg reports the following conversation in his presence: "'So he doesn't want to talk?' one of the civilians said. 'We have time,' said the major. 'They're all like that at the beginning. We'll take a month, two months, three months, but he'll talk'" (Alleg 1958, p. 88).

[20] My great-grandmother endured an operation on the kitchen table to remove her gallbladder and gallstones with only whiskey for anesthesia. Two generations later, people still talked about her screams. But she consented. I never heard of her experiencing anything like what we now call PTSD. She lived a long time after.

that an alleged rape victim's testimony not be credited without torture is for the protection of the accused, not for the benefit of victims. Further, it is unclear how readily Artemisia submitted to torture. Her father, who took the case to court, was concerned not only about her rape but also about a property dispute with Tassi.

The full title of the UN torture convention implies that torture is "cruel, inhuman or degrading." These judgments are not explicitly included in its definition. In debates over "torture lite," much has been made of the contrast between procedures that are merely cruel, inhuman, or degrading and procedures that amount to torture. Judge Jay S. Bybee referred to "the thin line" that separates torture from other harsh treatment (N. Lewis 2009, p. A12). Yet, from considerations so far, it appears that the "lines" are multiple and thick, not thin. Cruel, inhuman, and degrading treatment becomes torture not simply by passing an arbitrary line on a continuum of increasing pain but through complex, prolonged, and varied experiences of severely harmful stress to which disorientation and environmental factors contribute.

Although cruelty, inhumanity, and degradation do not distinguish torture from some other harsh treatment (such as involuntary lobotomies), it is worth pausing over these three concepts, which do tend to apply to real tortures. Cruelty, inhumanity, and degradation contribute in distinctive ways to the harmful stress of torture. Cruelty can be deliberate, reckless, or callous. It can be unresponsive to or coldly exploitative of vulnerabilities. It need not be sadistic. "Inhumane" usually refers to lack of compassion, a form of cruelty. "Inhuman" is not the same but suggests "monstrous" or "indecent," failures to observe even minimal decorum. Typically aesthetically repellent, what is inhuman tends to be shocking. It deviates from expectations even in cruelty (when it is cruel, which it need not be). Aristotle, who seems to lack a conception of evil, has a conception of the inhuman: "brutish" vices, which surpass ordinary vice and encompass habits that range from nailbiting to cannibalism (Aristotle 1925, pp. 159, 171). "Brutish" is an unfortunate term, as brutes' behavior tends to be decent (compared to much that humans do to them) when they are not mistreated. Améry experienced his torture as inhuman.

To degrade, as noted in chapter 4, is to reduce in rank or diminish in capacity or value. Treatment of human beings is called degrading only when the degree is severe. Degrading treatment disables, disfigures, or diminishes. Or it subjects to contempt characteristics in virtue of which those degraded deserve respect. We are degraded by failures to treat us as capable of rational choice. We are degraded by treatment that exploits or manipulates our capacities for rationality in ways to which we could not reasonably consent. But we are degraded more by treatment that actually diminishes or destroys those capacities and treatment that diminishes or destroys our capacities for trust, hope, or sympathy or makes us appear, even physically, less than human. A corpse cannot suffer cruelty but can be degraded.

The distinct meanings of "cruel," "inhuman," and "degrading" are illustrated in Shakespeare's play *Titus Andronicus*, probably inspired by the story of Atreus in ancient times. Atreus sought revenge by murdering Thyestes's sons, turning their corpses into a pie, and feeding the pie to Thyestes (Pausanius 1979, vol. 1, p. 172, n. 208). Shakespeare's character Titus Andronicus similarly seeks revenge by serving the Empress Tamora a pie made from the flesh of her murdered sons, who had raped and mutilated his daughter Lavinia (Shakespeare 1984, pp. 183–88).[21] The rapists' intent was to degrade Lavinia. Her father (Titus), after murdering the rapists, degrades their corpses in making the pie and is not only cruel but inhuman to serve that pie to their mother. Her sons, however, not only raped but mutilated Lavinia, cutting her tongue out and her hands off to prevent her telling. That was cruel, inhuman, *and* degrading, despite the pragmatic intent. It was also torture, as was Titus's revenge. Lavinia uses a stick held in her mouth to write the rapists' names in the dust. Shakespeare had an uncanny sense of retribution.

Such cruelty, inhumanity, and degradation are not entirely a thing of the past or of fiction. In 1978 Lawrence Singleton raped teenaged Mary Vincent in California and then chopped off her arms (but left her tongue) and left her naked in a ditch to die (Taylor 2002). That was diabolical torture (on the Nero paradigm), evil treatment for an evil end. Mary Vincent survived to testify against him. He was convicted but continued his criminal career upon his release from prison.[22]

If the UN definition was revised to (1) center harmful stress rather than pain, (2) make explicit the absence of a purpose of benefiting recipients who consent rationally and freely (or would if they could), (3) interpret the intent of torture so as to include willingness to accept reasonably foreseeable harmful stress or to ignore its possibility, and (4) make explicit that the source of torture can be multiple procedures the effects of which can be aggravated by repetition, by the physical or psychological condition of

---

[21] This play is the basis of Julie Taymor's film *Titus* (2000).

[22] Singleton (also a teen) served half of a fourteen-year sentence for this crime. In 1997 he was sentenced to death for murder in Florida. He died of cancer in 2001. See Taylor (2002).

the person to whom they are applied, and by environmental conditions, then the resulting definition would not distinguish the clean procedures from classic interrogational torture. The advantage of the clean procedures over horsewhipping an interrogee who is suspended naked with dislocated shoulders is not moral progress. Given the current UN definition, the advantage is an increase in plausible deniability. But that advantage is not a result of the absence of marks on the bodies of the tortured. Some of the clean procedures do leave marks, and some of the classic ones did not. Plausible deniability is largely a result of loopholes in the UN definition. Revising the definition could remove that advantage.

If the revised definition does not distinguish the clean procedures from classical tortures, it also does not yet distinguish torture from other injuries that are comparably stressful but are genuinely not torture. As Shue noted, severe injuries inflicted in military combat might satisfy all of the criteria discussed so far (Shue 1978). Many combat injuries are as harmfully stressful, reasonably foreseeable, and they fail to benefit consenting recipients. They can be cruel, inhuman, degrading, deliberate, and aggravated by environmental conditions. They often lead to "shell shock," a form of PTSD. But they are not necessarily torture (even though torture *can* be inflicted on battlefields). Something is lost in setting aside the UN convention's restriction to acts by public officials, which implies a profoundly asymmetrical relationship between torturer and tortured. In place of that restriction, something more general is needed to capture the asymmetry of that relationship.

A distinctive evil of torture emerges when we look not only at what torturers do and what the tortured suffer but at the relation between torturer and tortured. That relation is an aggravation not made explicit in the UN definition but possibly captured, in part, by the restriction to public officials. It is critical to distinguishing torture from otherwise comparable combat injuries. Shue identifies the aggravating factor as the victim's defenselessness against the assailant (Shue 1978, p. 130). The defenselessness of the victim is matched by the torturer's relative invulnerability, yielding a severely imbalanced power relationship. This relationship is what makes torture morally worse than equally painful or harmfully stressful injuries incurred by armed soldiers. Defenselessness aggravates any deliberate assault and is utterly central to torture's cruelty. Defenselessness has degrees. In torture, they represent degrees of hopelessness. Before capture, soldiers have a fighting chance. After capture, they are vulnerable to torture. This is when they are supposed to be protected by IHL.

In response to the objection that interrogees are not really defenseless because they can protect themselves by providing information, Shue points out that ignorant interrogees have no such option. The only "defense" of those who are not ignorant may be the betrayal and self-betrayal of ingratiating themselves with parties who, as Shue notes, can violate with impunity any agreements they make with those who are at their mercy. But, as Shue argues, an option that requires one to do what one believes is wrong is no option at all for a conscientious individual (Shue 1978, pp. 135–36). Those tortured not for information but for other purposes, such as punishment or to terrorize others, lack even such apparent options. Shue puts it well: "torture begins only after the fight is – for the victim – finished. Only losers are tortured … now that the torture victim has exhausted all means of defense and is powerless before the victors, a fresh assault begins … In this respect torture is indeed not analogous to the killing in battle of a healthy and well-armed foe" (Shue 1978, p. 130). Soraya M., buried in sand to her neck and shoulders, illustrates the point perfectly.

The UN definition's restriction to acts by public officials captures a power imbalance. Institutions can give officials power to render others defenseless. Yet other sources of power can do that, too. Multiple perpetrators have the power of combination. Disparities of physical power (muscle strength, size, weight, skill, freedom of movement, and access to weapons) and mental power (knowledge, experience, level of alertness, and access to mind-altering drugs) are exploitable to create impotence in others. Bound victims are physically impotent. The sleep-deprived are mentally impotent. Building into the definition of torture the defenselessness of the victim obviates any need to restrict the concept of torture to acts by public officials. And so I would include that defenselessness as a fifth modification of the UN definition, additional to the four mentioned above regarding intent, stress, consent, and collateral harm.

The definition of torture so modified applies not only to clean and dirty interrogational procedures by governments and criminals but also to tortures found in ordinary civilian life, many of which are not criminal.

4. FIVE KINDS OF ORDINARY, MOSTLY CIVILIAN, TORTURE

Five kinds of ordinary cruelty that include much unacknowledged torture are: (1) aggravated and forcible rapes, including gang rapes and rapes of women in wheelchairs,[23] (2) lynchings and other hate crimes by mobs or

---

[23] The Chimera Self-Defense program for women offers special self-defense training for women who are physically challenged. See www.danecountyrcc.com/chimera/ for the Madison, WI group. Chicago has many Chimera Self-Defense sites.

gangs against victims often tied up or in other ways rendered impotent, (3) domestic abuse and family violence, including cruelty to small children, infirm elders, and animal companions, (4) many lawful death sentences carried out on forcibly restrained fully conscious convicted offenders, and (5) painful research and testing on caged and restrained vertebrate animals by scientific experimenters, consumer research agents, military personnel, even educators. In the first three cases, perpetrators are formally liable to criminal punishment, although in the US relatively few are convicted. In the fourth case, there need be no crime. In the fifth, researchers exposed for violating codes receive at worst a fine, or they lose benefits, such as grants. Most escape with impunity. Some are rewarded with paychecks. These five categories do not exhaust ordinary civilian torture. But they make the point that vast amounts of torture remain publicly unacknowledged. Not all conduct in these five categories is torture. My claim, like the analogous claim of the 2007 ICRC report, is that much of it is.

I begin with rape, not because it is the worst but because it illustrates a change in public perception. Susan Brownmiller's 1975 study *Against Our Will* included a chapter on war rape (Brownmiller 1975, pp. 31–113). Nearly two decades later, Justice Richard J. Goldstone, chief prosecutor of the UN International Criminal Tribunals for the former Yugoslavia and Rwanda, acknowledged that rape as a weapon of war is torture, that mass rape is a crime against humanity, and that the practice has been engaged in as policy, not simply by aberrant individuals acting on their own initiatives (Human Rights Watch 1996, pp. 30 ff.). The same features that make war rape torture apply to much civilian rape, including forcible rape in prisons, rapes of children, and rapes of homeless women.[24] Menachem Amir found in his study of over 600 rapes in Philadelphia that 43 percent were perpetrated by multiple assailants (Amir 1971, p. 143). Inez García (chapter 5) was raped by multiple assailants, one of whom stood guard.

One of slavery's most profound evils (least noted by philosophers but greatly responsible for abolitionist sentiment) is slaves' vulnerability to torture, including rape. In ancient times, much torture of slaves was lawful and routine. Ancient Greek and Roman law allowed owners to torture slaves for information even merely as witnesses. Roman law held that

[24] On fraternity gang rape, see Sanday (1990). See philosophers Jeffner Allen (1986, pp. 27–59) and Brison (2002) for autobiographical reflections on surviving aggravated rape and near-murder. See Sebold's account of her brutally violent rape as a first-year university student (Sebold 1999, pp. 5–27). Police told Sebold she was lucky (hence, the title of her memoir, *Lucky*), because the last woman raped in the same area was killed. On informally tolerating rape as a tool of prison discipline, see Conover (2000).

slaves' testimony was worthless *unless* extracted under torture (Peters 1985, pp. 11–39; Ruthven 1978, pp. 23–42; Williams 1911, pp. 73–74). Except for treason, social status determined who was torturable.

Part of the legacy of slavery is descendants' continuing vulnerability to torture. Long after the Emancipation Proclamation (1862), African Americans continued to be vulnerable to unlawful but widely tolerated torture by ordinary white citizens and law enforcement officers. Between 1882 and 1968, at least 3,445 African Americans suffered the terroristic torture of lynching. Many were publicly burned alive (Wells-Barnett 1970, 1987). Not only the lynched were defenseless but, also, terrorized black communities had no defense against hooded assailants who might include law enforcement officers.[25] Mob lynching is rarer now. But racist torture continues, despite improved accountability. The 1991 bludgeoning of Rodney King by police in Lake View Terrace, California – fifty-six blows with metal batons by multiple officers while King was on the ground, unarmed – was torture, although the officers were exonerated of criminal wrongdoing by a white jury in Simi Valley.[26] The 1997 sodomizing of Haitian immigrant Abner Louima with a broken broom handle by New York City police officer Justin Volpe (Lawrence 2000, p. 169) and the 1998 dragging murder of James Byrd by three white supremacists in Texas (King 2002) were torture. Byrd's and Louima's torturers were not exonerated. But their crimes are more often reported as beating, dragging, and sodomizing than as torture. Some of the hate crimes perpetrated against lesbian, gay, and transgender people are torture. Some are lynchings, such as the 1998 murder of Matthew Shepard, beaten by multiple assailants, tied to a fencepost, and left to die (Loffreda 2000, pp. ix, 1–5).

Less public are the tortures of violent domestic cruelty, a global issue (Fineman and Mykitiuk 1994, pp. 323–34).[27] Because the *percentage* of family members gravely harmed by domestic violence is small, it is easy not to appreciate how numerous the victims are and how serious the issue is. According to 1990s statistics for the US, battering is the largest source of injury to women (more than car accidents, rapes, and muggings

---

[25] Lynching statistics provided by the archives at Tuskegee Institute can be found at www.law.umkc.edu/faculty/projects/ftrials/shipp/lynchstats.html. During the same period, 1,297 white people were lynched in the US. The statistics are only for documented cases.

[26] The edited videotape aired on television omitted a three-second segment showing Rodney King charging police officer Laurence Powell, which, apparently, influenced the Simi Valley jury, enabling them to interpret police response as self-defense (Cannon 1997, pp. 20–50).

[27] For detailed accounts of cases of domestic violence that include torture, see Millett (1979); McNulty (1980); Johnson (1990); Ferrato (1991) (a photography book of female survivors, with commentary); Herman (1992); Jones (1994); Pelzer (1995); Silverman (1996); and Sipe and Hale (1996).

combined); a quarter of violent crime is wife assault; one in six marriages has a pattern of abuse; 12 percent of murders are spousal killings; every eleven days a woman is murdered by her husband, boyfriend, or live-in lover; at least 70 percent of men who batter their wives also abuse their children physically; and the FBI estimates that 90 percent of domestic violence is unreported (Women's Action Coalition 1993, pp. 55–58; sources p. 58). The website "A Safe Place" (copyright "2001–2009") gives further statistics, indicating that matters have not improved: "7% of women (3.9 million) are abused by their partners … every 9 seconds a woman is physically abused by her husband … from 7% to 26% of pregnant women are abused … domestic violence is repetitive in nature … 42% of murdered women are killed by their intimate partners," and so on.[28] Many statistics include abuse less serious than torture. But much domestic abuse sends survivors to hospital emergency rooms.

Torture in domestic cruelty is apt to be both terrorist and interrogational. Activists call it "battering," a blanket term for everything from verbal abuse to murder. "Battering" has become a stand-in term for severe cruelties that are not literally beatings: burning, cutting, stabbing, choking, and the twisting and dislocation of limbs; prolonged confinement in small spaces; deprivation of food, water, bathroom privileges, and freedom to move one's limbs from a painful position; deprivation of medications and such necessary physical aids as wheelchairs, creating potentially lethal dangers; throwing against walls and down stairs; terroristic driving; running over with cars; and murdering animal companions (often torturing the animal). "Battered" often describes victims accurately enough, even when "battering" does not literally describe the mode of assault. Yet feminist activists reject the term "battered woman" on the grounds that it suggests that victims are certain kinds of women, as though they were responsible, and takes the focus off the abuser, who is. And so, "battering" has come to be a comprehensive term that includes even verbal put-downs, property destruction, and abuse of a partner's credit cards, which are not torture. Still, much of the burning, cutting, and so forth of defenseless victims is torture. In her very practical and useful book *Next Time She'll Be Dead*, investigative journalist Ann Jones correlates domestic battering's punitive and terroristic methods, item by item, with the methods in the chart on coercion from the AI 1973 *Report on Torture* (Jones 1994, pp. 81–105; Amnesty International 1973, p. 173). Partners who have scruples

[28] www.asafeplaceforhelp.org/batteredwomenstatistics.html.

against retaliating are easily rendered defenseless. Many are held in servitude under credible threats of murder. When escape is attempted or help sought, violence escalates, often to murder, one very good reason to "stay."

Those who have not experienced or witnessed domestic abuse firsthand may wonder whether intimate partners are *defenseless* against domestic violence to the degree requisite for torture. Ordinarily, they are not tied up naked on a table or hoisted on a pulley with their hands tied behind their backs.

In the context of domesticity, such restraints are unnecessary to disable a partner, elder, or child. Torturers of small children and infirm elders tend to be adults in their physical prime or teenagers.[29] Many nursing home residents are bedridden. Some are mentally challenged. Older children use their greater physical strength, knowledge, and authority to torture younger ones, just as those who torture animals tend to pick on tiny ones, such as frogs, and on injured ones. Power disparities need not, of course, lead to torture, or no infant would survive. But when there is already abuse or the probability of it, gross power disparities aggravate the likelihood of torture by making it easy to disable victims. Given intimate access and trust, an intimate partner of either sex is easily disabled by a partner who is willing to use weapons and take advantage of the other's scruples against doing likewise. If scruples against retaliating count against a victim's defenselessness in domestic violence, then the refusal, as a matter of conscience, to divulge information that could terminate torture should likewise count against the defenselessness of an interrogee who *is* tied up naked on a table. Shue's point that a defense that one finds immoral is not available to a conscientious individual applies here as well.

Women, encouraged to bond with more powerful men, are commonly at a disadvantage against assaultive partners with respect to physical size, muscle strength, combat skills, training in and access to physical means of defense, and emotional preparedness to use available means effectively, not to mention legal and economic disadvantages that many face or disadvantages added by pregnancy and childcare responsibilities. Again, such power differentials do not create abuse. They do make it easy for able-bodied men who are so inclined to disable a partner.

If the use in statistical reports of terms like "domestic abuse" and "family violence" masks torture by categorizing it together with noisy quarrels,

---

[29] See Cauffiel (1993) on the Alpine Manor nursing home murders in Grand Rapids, MI, by young women employees who suffocated patients in their beds, apparently for a lark.

verbal put-downs, and mutual combat, the terms "punishment" and "discipline" likewise mask the torture of children and elders in private homes, nursing facilities, and schools and, similarly, the torture of soldiers by superior officers and of prison inmates by other inmates and by guards. In his *Encyclopedia Britannica* entry on torture, Williams writes, "torture as a part of the punishment may be regarded as including every kind of bodily or mental pain beyond what is necessary for the safe custody of the offender (with or without forced labour) or the destruction of his life" (Williams 1911, vol. xxvii, p. 727). Although that statement needs qualification, in prisons the stage is set for torture. Inmates are rendered physically defenseless on admission, caged, and governed by severely restrictive rules. Some are subjected to bright lights that are never turned off. Guards, in contrast, are mobile, trained, given discretion, equipped for self-defense and communication, and able to assist each other and control the conditions of their own sleep. With such disparities in place, abuse readily escalates to torture. Recall that in Zimbardo's SPE, most of the guards slid without coaching into such abuse of prisoners that the experiment was terminated early (Haney, Banks, and Zimbardo 1973, pp. 69–97; Zimbardo 2007, pp. 23–194).

The opposition of relative invulnerability to defenselessness holds for many punishments. Yet not all are torture. Curtailment of freedom need not cause pain, intolerable suffering, or severe stress. It need not be cruel, inhuman, or degrading. Those punished are less likely to feel betrayed when punishment is retributive, with limits set in advance, and conforms to expectations. Much of what prisoners actually experience, however, does not conform to expectations. In an essay on torture in US prisons, Jamie Fellner details authorized and unauthorized tortures (Roth, Worden, and Bernstein 2005, pp. 173–83). One authorized policy that has potential for torture, which Fellner calls "a prime example of the mistreatment of inmates," is prolonged solitary confinement of mentally ill prisoners. Most of Fellner's examples are violent: "When Florida inmate Frank Valdez died in 1999, every rib in his body was broken, his corpse bore the imprint of boot marks, and his testicles were badly swollen. Correctional officers admitted having struggled with him but denied they had used excessive force. They claimed most of his injuries had been 'self-inflicted'" (Roth, Worden, and Bernstein 2005, p. 177). Fellner notes that "both men and women prisoners also face staff rape and sexual abuse from staff and other prisoners" (Roth, Worden, and Bernstein 2005, p. 174).

Such reports make me reluctant, in criticizing the death penalty, to rely on the argument that imprisonment is a less severe penalty than death, although in some prisons it probably is. Gary Gilmore (chapter 1), who at the age of thirty-five insisted that he be executed in accord with his sentence, was incarcerated most of his life since he was fifteen in prisons in Oregon and Illinois. Such reports as Fellner cites also suggest limitations of the argument that imprisonment, unlike the death penalty, is not irreversible. Some harms that prisoners suffer are irreversible and not just because lost years are not recoverable. Some prisoners are murdered. Serial murderer Jeffrey Dahmer, for example, was murdered in a Wisconsin prison not forty miles from where I live.

How common is torture in US prisons? Fellner reports that "there are no national or even state-specific statistics on this kind of staff abuse of inmates. Prisons systems have little incentive to gather such statistics, and no laws require them to do so" (Roth, Worden, and Bernstein 2005, p. 174). Prison inmates' vulnerability to torture can be greater than that of many victims of domestic violence, a special irony for those who are in prison because of the ways in which they fought back against an abusive partner.

State-sponsored executions do not always conform to expectations, either. Although torture is not openly endorsed in US executions today, some executions are horribly bungled. As with staff abuse, we do not know the extent. The public is not likely to hear unless an investigative journalist goes after the story. Ethel Rosenberg's electrocution, which did get publicity, took almost five minutes (Radosh and Milton 1983, pp. 418–19). If the bungling is unintentional, it is not torture. But if precautions are either knowingly or through negligence inadequately enforced, it becomes reasonably foreseeable that there will be such "accidents," as openings are created for executioners to aggravate deliberately the sufferings of the condemned.

Torture may be routine even in normally successful executions, if the methods used are known to produce an extremely painful death. The condemned are first rendered defenseless. Many are bound on a table or to a chair or with hands shackled and a rope around their necks. In all but lethal injection, they remain fully conscious to the end. Questions have been raised about the drug cocktail used in lethal injection: how often do subjects suffer excruciating pain that they are unable to communicate? Every method of execution employed in the US during my lifetime, save lethal injection, has been publicly defended at the time of its use as "instantaneous," and all are defended as either "painless" or "almost painless." Yet research tends to produce evidence to the contrary. Nor is it clear that "painless" is the intention in ordinary executions other than lethal injection. Writing my dissertation on punishment in the 1960s, I was astonished to learn that the condemned who faint are revived for their executions. Why, I wondered, if we are to be reassured that the execution is "instantaneous" and "almost painless"? The reason philosophers tended to give, that it is disrespectful to kill rational beings while they are unaware, is ludicrous, given how long prisoners on death row have been fully aware. To the question, "why not administer death painlessly?" the more honest popular response was, "It's supposed to hurt; after all, it's punishment!" That was also a common objection then to the idea of execution by lethal injection.

The UN definition restricts torture to what is inflicted "on a person." That seems to exclude non-human animals, which are not commonly regarded as persons. From a moral point of view, that exclusion is arbitrary. Even though torture can do things to human beings that it cannot do to other animals, there are enough similarities between humans and other vertebrate animals to make the case that they, too, are vulnerable to torture. Many gains sought through the torture of animals are grotesquely disproportionate to what the animals are made to suffer. Tortures to which dogs are subjected in the testing of military weaponry (Newkirk 1992, pp. 107–37) risk being diabolical, evil treatment for evil ends.

Many vertebrate animals are routinely subject to treatment that is, if anything, worse than the ordinary tortures human beings undergo. Animals used in laboratory experiments and testing procedures are caged and rendered physically defenseless. Scientists, educators, military personnel, and testers of commercial products conduct tests and studies (often grant-funded) that subject animals to extreme pain and other extreme stress for purposes that in no way benefit the animals and often yield meagre benefit, if any, to human beings (Singer 2002, pp. 25–94). It would be no more sensible for the animals to consent if they could than for human beings to consent to be subjected to such treatment.

In experiments and tests, the purposes are different from what they usually are when human beings are tortured, although humans, too, have been tortured experimentally, at Dachau by Nazis, for example, and in China during WW II by Japanese military unit 731. In experiments, foreseeable pain is apt to be incidental or result from neglect or callousness. On the broad understanding of "intent," the animals are tortured. Their pain is accepted by testers and experimenters as part of the price of the test or experiment, even when it contributes nothing to the aim. Animal liberationists' main concern has been to liberate animals from torture in laboratories and in agribusiness. People for the Ethical Treatment of Animals (PETA) and the Animal Liberation Front (ALF) have been animals' AI.

Until publicly exposed by PETA in 1984 in a videotape edited from tapes kept in his lab, Dr. Thomas Genarelli at the University of Pennsylvania received research grants to inflict head injuries on baboons, ostensibly to learn how better to treat human victims of brain damage from whiplash in car accidents. Ingrid Newkirk writes in *Free the Animals!* (Newkirk 1992, p. 183):

Dr. Genarelli and his research crew used dental cement to seal monkeys' heads into metal helmets. A pneumatic device violently "accelerated" the head at varying angles and degrees of force up to 3,000 g's [3,000 times the force of gravity]. According to NASA, a force of only 15 g's can kill a human being.

Deborah Blum, describing that tape in *The Monkey Wars* (Blum 1994, pp. 117–18), writes:

Obviously, the laboratory workers weren't just "documenting" the research. Posing before the camera, young scientists held dazed baboons in silly "say cheese" poses; dangled them by crippled limbs, laughed when they struggled. Propping up one brain-damaged animal, whose paws quivered uncontrollably, researchers turned the camera on him and began a voice over: "Friends! Romans! Countrymen! (laughter) Look, he wants to shake hands. Come on ... He says, 'You're gonna rescue me from this, aren't you? Aren't you?'"

This cruelty violates even standard codes for the treatment of animals in research. But PETA and the ALF have been concerned not just about code violations but about standards themselves and their loopholes and about the design of research projects, such as Genarelli's.[30] Experiments that were war crimes when performed on human prisoners at the Dachau concentration camp have since been performed on pigs in England and on dogs in the US in military testing (Mitscherlich and Mielke 1949, pp. 4–41;

---

[30] "Animal Welfare Act" (www.idausa.org/facts/awafacts.html), a website sponsored by the organization In Defense of Animals (San Rafael, CA), with information on how to obtain a copy of the Act, summarizes in a page what the Animal Welfare Act does not do for animals in the US. For example, it "does not protect animals during an experiment, regardless of how painful or even unnecessary it is." That Act (originally the Laboratory Animal Welfare Act, passed in 1966) and its amendments, administered by the Animal and Plant Inspection Service of the US Department of Agriculture, is one of two mechanisms of control regarding the treatment of some laboratory animals in the US (Orlans 1993, pp. 50–51). The other is the set of voluntary guidelines, Guide to the Care and Use of Laboratory Animals (www.nap.edu/openbook.php?record_id=5140) together with the Public Health Service (PHS) Policy for Humane Care and Use of Laboratory Animals, published by National Institutes of Health. The 2002 revision of the PHS Policy is available at http://grants.nih.gov/grants/olaw/references/PHSPolicyLabAnimals.pdf.

Newkirk 1992, pp. 107–37; Singer 2002, pp. 83–84). Many animal experiments fail to take animal pain seriously rather than aim to cause them pain as either end or means. But if it was torture at Dachau when human prisoners' pain was not taken seriously, it is torture for the imprisoned pigs and dogs.[31]

An example of failure to take animal pain seriously is the inhumanly cruel Draize test, in which corrosive substances are applied to the eyeballs of conscious immobilized rabbits to determine the level of corrosiveness or toxicity in the substance.[32] In the US, anesthesia is not required, although sometimes a topical is used during the application "provided it does not interfere with the test" (Singer 2002, p. 55). It is difficult to fathom the mind that devised that test. On the narrow reading of intent, which does not count incidental suffering, the Draize test is not torture. But neither is cruel sexual abuse of children, when their suffering is incidental to, rather than a source of or a means to, the abuser's pleasure.

With the broad reading of intent, deliberate infliction of procedures that are severely painful or stressful on defenseless animals can be torture regardless of whether the pain or stress is an end, means, or collateral effect. "Deliberate" is an apt characterization in the case of the Draize test. Lab workers deliberately, even meticulously, prepare the restrained rabbits' eyes. Researchers design the tests very deliberately, knowing the result for the animal.

The five kinds of ordinary torture just surveyed cannot be written off as the work of a few deranged minds. Social complicity in all of them is widespread and takes many forms. It is often lawful and not a source of moral shame or stigma. Currently lawful complicitous support for the death penalty in the US includes the participation by health care personnel who certify the fitness or competence of the condemned to be executed, just as other health care personnel have certified the fitness of interrogees to be subjected to harsh interrogation procedures. Currently lawful complicitous support for animal torture in the US includes traffic in products saleable only on condition that they are tested by practices that in fact torture the animals. Some products not tested on animals are marked in

---

[31] For descriptions of the high-altitude and immersion experiments performed, ostensibly for military purposes, on human prisoners at Dachau, see Mitscherlich and Mielke (1949, pp. 23–91). For descriptions of medical experiments performed by Japanese military on Chinese civilians between 1932 and 1945, see Harris (1994, pp. 1–112), and Tanaka (1996, pp. 135–65).

[32] The test is named after John J. Draize, toxicologist in the US Food and Drug Administration, who created it in 1944 to test *cosmetics*. Since then it has been used to test many substances, including bleach, shampoo, ink, and oven cleaner (Singer 2002, pp. 54–55).

the US "cruelty-free." It would be a sign of moral progress to be able to mark, instead, products that are so tested as "torture-certified."

5. WHAT BENTHAM'S DEFINITION MISSES

Bentham's reflections on torture, cited by Dershowitz (Dershowitz 2002, pp. 42–43), were written during the 1770s and '80s (Twining and Twining 1973, pp. 306–56), when torture was being phased out of European criminal procedure. Arguing that sometimes torture can be easier to justify than punishment, Bentham elaborated regulations that would restrict its state-sanctioned use to extreme situations. Given a choice between abolishing state-sanctioned torture or endorsing its (then) existing use, he would abolish it. But given an option to reserve state-sanctioned coercive torture for crises, he would reserve it. His position is understandable, given how he defined torture.

"Torture," says Bentham, "is where a person is made to suffer any violent pain of body in order to compel him to do something or to desist from doing something which done or desisted from the penal application is immediately made to cease" (Twining and Twining 1973, p. 309). Although he thinks of torture only as coercive (not, say, as revenge), he says this definition gives the most extensive sense of the term. Despite his contrast of torture with (presumably ordinary) punishment, he also thinks of torture as essentially punitive:

> Torture or other compulsory applications may be considered as a continual application of successive punishments for a continual repetition of offences: the offence of the first moment consisting in the not doing the thing required at that moment, and so on. The delinquent ceases to be punished when he ceases to offend. (Twining and Twining 1973, p. 324)

He produces the example of a nurse whipping or even pinching a child to get it to stop (or start) doing something (Twining and Twining 1973, p. 310).

Whipping a child can be torture. Many find that an argument against whipping rather than for torture.[33] But the pinching example and Bentham's definition suggest that he did not think torture (in the "most

---

[33] For public policy on child abuse, Kathleen Malley-Morrison and Denise A. Hines recommend that "the United States should follow in the footsteps of the European Union and identify corporal punishment of children as a violation of their human rights." They also recommend that "the United States should not treat corporal punishment, psychological aggression, and neglect as criminal offenses but should invest more in social service solutions to problems and to [sic]

extensive sense") need be severe. He did see the potential for escalation and abuse, which led him eventually to reject routine torture.

Still, Bentham is right that the nurse example shares with coercive torture a certain advantage over ordinary punishment. Torture inflicted in advance as a coercive measure is pre-emptive. Ordinary punishment comes only *after* an offense has been committed. Torture, Bentham thinks, secures compliance quickly (an optimistic view, we have seen). It can be a long time, he notes, before ordinary punishment, such as confinement, is so intolerable that compliance is preferable, whereas "one stroke of the rack" may get a person to answer "in a moment." And torture, he thinks, ceases with compliance (again, optimistic). With other punishments, "in order to make sure of applying as much as is necessary you must commonly run a risque of applying considerably more" whereas "of Torture there need never be a grain more applied than what is necessary" (Twining and Twining 1973, p. 311). No mention of aftermath.

Bentham reasons by a calculus of pain. He ignores the defenselessness of the tortured and the destruction of hope and trust. Dershowitz, following Bentham, treats torture as simply causing temporary intense physical pain by such acts as pushing needles under fingernails.

But interrogational torture's harm is not reducible to pain during the interrogation, except when the victim dies or is killed immediately after, as is commonly done with tortured animals. Both humans and other animals can experience betrayal as well as pain. But human beings also experience distinctively human forms of harmful stress. To ignore the relationship between torturer and tortured is to miss torture's blows to hope, trust, and self-respect. Not even a Nietzsche would be strengthened by such blows.[34] Tortured human beings, though defenseless, need not be passive but can become desperately active in seeking to accommodate torturers. To overlook how low the tortured can sink in their own eyes trying to meet demands is to miss torture's blows to self-respect. Crueler than

---

evaluation and reporting of the results of those efforts" (Tonry 2009, p. 157). For an example of European activism against the corporal punishment of children, see the following website for the 1999 Irish Campaign to abolish corporal punishment of children in Europe and to challenge legal acceptance of such punishment: http://ec.europa.eu/justice_home/daphnetoolkit/files/others/europe_violence/5.1.pdf (accessed July 21, 2009).

[34] Nietzsche suffered migraine and other severe bodily pain (not from torture). His attitude toward the universe was characteristically agonistic. Expressing a personal commitment, he wrote, "*Out of life's school of war*: What does not destroy me makes me stronger" (Nietzsche 1976, p. 467); ["Aus der Kriegsschule des Lebens: Was mich nicht umbringt, macht mich stärker" (Nietzsche 1967–77, vol. VI, p. 60)]. Reading that personal commitment as the empirical generalization that whatever does not kill one (anyone) makes one stronger is naive and unjust to Nietzsche.

pain are memories of choosing against one's principles and values, accusing oneself and loved ones in order to ingratiate oneself with persons one despises, becoming complicit in projects one regards as evil, being broken as a human being. Orwell got it right in *Nineteen Eighty-Four* (1949). In Room 101 Winston Smith betrays the person he loved. Torture tends to diminish those it does not kill. Many who, like Alleg, do not give in do not survive, either. Others, like Améry, who betray no one because they cannot, suspect, as Améry did, that they would have, if they could have.

Unlike Winston Smith, whose capacity for love was degraded into servile attachment to his abuser, Améry did not become attached to his torturers. Unable to comply with their demands, he had no occasion for servile gratitude for their rewards for his cooperation. In 1974, he attempted suicide unsuccessfully. In 1978, the year after his memoir was reissued, he succeeded in a hotel room in what he preferred to call a "voluntary death" (Gilman and Sipes 1997, p. 775; Améry 1999).

Severe damage to morale, to self-respect, and to one's capacities for trust, hope, and sympathy – what one psychologist calls "soul murder" (Shengold 1989) – are the greatest harms suffered by many survivors. Not easily factored into a calculus of pain, they promise fragile and highly problematic social relations. They make probable the depression of despair, inadequate care of the self, and premature death. A popular argument is that since pain is temporary and death forever, being killed is worse than being tortured, even if under torture one would wish for death. That conclusion is not obvious when one considers the so-called aftermath. A torturer who kills probably does more wrong than one who "merely" tortures (depending on the nature of the torture). But even when that is so, being deprived of life may not be a worse harm for the person who is tortured.

CHAPTER 9

Genocide is social death

If the slave no longer belonged to a community, if he had no social
existence outside of his master, then what was he? The initial
response in almost all slaveholding societies was to define the slave
as a socially dead person. (Patterson 1982, p. 38)

I. PROLOGUE

Social death is not necessarily genocide. But genocide is social death.
Social death has many sources – slavery, banishment, disfigurement, illness, even self-chosen isolation. It can be an evil or not, depending on the
harm it does and whether it results from inexcusable wrongs. Self-chosen
isolation ordinarily leaves open many possibilities for reconnecting. Even
when isolation is not self-chosen, a person who is shunned is not ordinarily
cut off from a shared language, history, traditions, and the like. Genocide
is an extreme of social death.

The intentional production of social death in a people or community is
the central evil of genocide. That is so not only when a genocide is mainly
cultural but even when it is homicidal on a massive scale. Social death
distinguishes the evil of genocide, morally, from the evils of other mass
murders. Even genocidal murder can be understood as an extreme means
to the primary goal of social death. Social vitality exists through relationships, contemporary and intergenerational, that create contexts and
identities that give meaning and shape to our lives. Some of those relationships are with kin, friends, and coworkers. Others are less personal
and mediated by basic social institutions – economic, political, religious,
educational, and so on. Loss of social vitality comes with the loss of such
connections. A life robbed of the meanings created by social contexts and
identities need not be entirely meaningless, if not all of a life's meanings
depend on specifically *social* vitality. Spiritual vitality may sustain some.
Nevertheless, loss of social vitality is a profound loss. Not all mass murders

have as part of their apparent aim or intent to inflict such a loss. The 1995 Oklahoma City bombing by Timothy McVeigh, for example, did not. It was an atrocity, but not a genocide. Not all mass murders that do have the aim of robbing individuals of their social vitality are successful in doing so. The Czechoslovakian Jews of Terezin from the "family camp" at Auschwitz who walked into the gas chambers singing the Czech national anthem and the *Hatikva* clung to their social as well as spiritual vitality to the very end (Müller 1979, pp. 102–11). Nevertheless, the Nazi genocide robbed them of descendants who might have shared it.

Putting social death at the center of genocide takes the focus off body counts, individual careers cut short, and mourners. It puts the focus instead on relationships, connections, and foundational institutions that create community and set the context that gave meaning to careers and goals, lives and deaths. If social death is central, the term "cultural genocide" is redundant and misleading. It is redundant if social death implies cultural death as well. It is misleading insofar as "cultural genocide" suggests that some genocides do not include cultural death.

Putting social death at the center explains and clarifies the position, controversial among genocide scholars, that genocidal acts are not necessarily homicidal. Forcibly sterilizing the women or the men of a targeted group, or forcibly separating children from their parents for re-education to assimilate them into another group, can be genocidal in both aim and effect. Policies of kidnapping and transporting children have been deliberately intended to achieve the destruction of the native social identities of American Indian children and of the mixed-race children of the "stolen generations" in Australia.[1] It might seem to observers that transported children simply undergo a change in their social identity, not that they lose social vitality. Change without degradation may be the intent; defenders of those policies seem to have regarded the change as an upgrade. Yet, parents' social vitality is to a great extent a casualty of the children's forced re-education. And in reality, transported children often fail to make a satisfying transition. Nevertheless, since it is at least possible for children to acquire and embrace a new social identity, the question arises whether, on a definition of genocide that does not require homicide, a meaningful distinction can be drawn between genocide and socio-cultural assimilation that is not genocidal. I defer that issue to chapter 10, where it arises naturally in reflecting on genocidal rape aimed at forced impregnation.

---

[1] Two films portray the plight of stolen children in Australia. One, *Rabbit-Proof Fence* (2002), is based on the true story of a woman who, as a child, escaped twice and was twice recaptured, walking hundreds of miles to return home. The other is the epic, *Australia* (2008).

The Nazi genocide was not only a program of mass murder but an assault on Jewish social vitality. That assault had stages. In Western Europe it began with social restrictions, such as curfews and mandatory badges. It escalated through a series of exclusions from ordinary social activities, schools, professions, and jobs, to denying access to bank accounts, confiscating property, and denying protection against criminal assault. The Nazi genocide was not simply the final slaughter. It was the whole process. Assaults on Jewish social vitality were experienced not only by those eventually "resettled in the East" but also by hidden children who survived, some passing as Christians.[2] Many hidden children were forced to stay indoors and away from windows, cut off from a normal childhood, normal education, friendships with peers, and the physical activities of normal play. Some were sent to England by parents unable to accompany them who did not survive.[3]

Other genocides have likewise had a progression of stages, reducing social vitality before extinguishing it. In the town of Celinac in northern Bosnia non-Serbs were given "special status" prior to expelling them or concentrating them in camps. A curfew was imposed from 4 p.m. to 6 a.m. Non-Serbs were prohibited from (1) meeting in cafés, restaurants, or other public places, (2) bathing or swimming in the nearby rivers, (3) hunting or fishing, (4) moving to another town without permission, (5) carrying a weapon, (6) driving or traveling by car, and the list goes on (Power 2002, p. 250). In Rwanda, the Hutu newspaper *Kangura* published in December 1990 a list of "Ten Commandments of the Hutu," governing relations between Hutu and Tutsi. They included such statements as that any Hutu who marries, befriends, or employs as a secretary or concubine a Tutsi woman shall be considered a traitor, and likewise for any Hutu who makes a business partnership with a Tutsi, invests money in a Tutsi enterprise, or lends to or borrows money from a Tutsi, and that list goes on as well (Powers 2002, pp. 338–39). Genocides can have not only many stages but many forms. Mass sterilization, for example, can be genocidal, not simply a prelude to genocide.

For a long time I thought, with historian Steven T. Katz, that the Nazi genocide was unique in at least the following respect: even Jews who fled Germany to other countries in Western Europe and Jews who had converted to Christianity (or whose parents or even grandparents had done so)

---

[2] "Resettlement in the East" was a Nazi euphemism for transportation from Western Europe to the death camps in Poland.

[3] Lore Segal's apparently autobiographical novel *Other People's Houses* (1973) tells the story of a child sent to England who worked as a servant in others' homes – for her, houses.

were hunted down and murdered, although, for many, their social identities were not, or no longer, Jewish (Katz 1994, pp. 27–63). A well-known convert to Christianity hunted down at her convent in the Netherlands and sent to Auschwitz where she died in 1942 is the philosopher Edith Stein. She had converted in 1922, although she never rejected her Jewish identity.[4] It was not only Nazis who engaged in such pursuit, however. At the end of WW I many Armenians who had fled to Russia were hunted down also and murdered by Talat Pasha's Committee of Union and Progress (CUP). Historian Ben Kiernan quotes allied German military attaché von Lossow as saying of this CUP campaign that it involved "the total extermination of Armenians in Transcaucasia also"; he reports that von Lossow added, "Talat's government party wants to destroy all Armenians, not only in Turkey, but also outside Turkey" (Kiernan 2007, p. 414). Such pursuits make a certain perverted sense if the rationale is to extinguish all possibility of later generations reinvigorating the old identity and seeking revenge. Edith Stein would have left no biological descendants, but she would no doubt have taught others respect for Judaism. To eliminate revenge in a future generation, criminal organizations also sometimes eliminate an entire family, including children and infants. Genocide carries that kind of reasoning to an extreme.

Unlike Edith Stein, some Armenians were able to save their lives by religious conversion. The powerlessness of Jews to save their lives by conversion or through the conversion of their parents or grandparents remains a factor that distinguishes the Holocaust from the Armenian genocide. It may not distinguish the Holocaust as clearly from the 1994 Rwandan genocide, to the extent that Tutsis could not save themselves by becoming Hutus or by citing Hutu ancestors. But Tutsis who fled across borders were less zealously pursued than were Jews fleeing Hitler's regime. At the level of such specifics, it is difficult to generalize about genocides and to find truly distinguishing characteristics of particular genocides.

A genocide is not necessarily part of a larger war, although it is sometimes executed under the cover of a larger war. The Armenian genocide was perpetrated in the midst of WW I and the Holocaust in the midst of WW II. James W. Nickel notes in an essay on several ways to get rid of groups that genocide can be regarded as itself "a kind of war on a people" (Jokić 2001, p. 165), a one-sided war. Lucy Dawidowicz so regards it in her history, *The War against the Jews* (Dawidowicz 1975). Yet calling genocide an unjust

---

[4] Stein was a student of and later assistant to Edmund Husserl. Her doctoral dissertation on empathy was published in 1917 (Stein 1964). For sensitive and informative reflections on Stein (and on three of her well-known European Jewish female contemporaries who also died in the Holocaust), see Brenner (1997, pp. 59–95, 123–29).

war grossly understates the case. Genocide is not simply unjust. It is an evil. When it becomes an end in itself, it is diabolical. Like torture, genocide is one-sided. Like torture victims, the majority of genocide victims are defenseless – women, children, the elderly, the sick, the disabled. Able-bodied men and boys are rendered defenseless before their murder. Just as torture victims are tied up naked on a table or in other ways made defenseless before they are assaulted, genocide victims have been disarmed, herded into small spaces, made to strip and sometimes, to dig their own graves. Or they have been victims of surprise lethal attacks in the night or at holiday celebrations, when they are especially vulnerable. Insofar as a genocide inexcusably inflicts intolerable suffering and stress on defenseless victims, it is not just comparable to torture: it is quite literally mass torture. The Nazi death camps (as well as many of the concentration camps) and the 1990s rape/death camps in the former Yugoslavia were clearly sites of mass torture. Unarmed machete victims in Rwanda were tortured to death or left to die after torture. Much of the horror aroused by reports of genocides stems from the tortures that victims suffer. But what makes a particular genocide a mass torture is not the same as what makes it a genocide.

John Rawls opens his first treatise with the observation that "Justice is the first virtue of social institutions, as truth is of systems of thought" (Rawls 1999a, p. 3). He continues, "A theory however elegant and economical must be rejected or revised if it is untrue; likewise laws and institutions no matter how efficient and well-arranged must be reformed or abolished if they are unjust" (Rawls 1999a, p. 3). Like critics who find these claims overstated, Rawls goes on to note that although "these propositions seem to express our intuitive conviction of the primacy of justice," "no doubt they are expressed too strongly" (Rawls 1999a, p. 4). Not every injustice is intolerably harmful. Reforms are not always worth the expense. Yet Rawls's claim about the need to reform or abolish unjust institutions gets plausibility from the case of injustices that are also *evils*. Had Rawls written that no matter how efficient and well arranged, laws and institutions must be reformed or abolished if they are *evils*, he would not have overstated the case. Wartime injustices are apt to fall into this category. Certainly genocide does.

2. THE CONCEPT OF GENOCIDE AND PHILOSOPHICAL REFLECTION ON GENOCIDE

"Genocide" is a hybrid term that combines the Greek word *genos*, for race or tribe, with the Latin *cide*, for killing. It was coined by Polish-Jewish attorney and scholar Raphael Lemkin (1900–59). Lemkin came to the US as a refugee in 1941. He taught at Duke and Yale universities, served in the United States War Department, and advised Supreme Court Justice Robert H. Jackson at the International Military Tribunal (IMT) in Nuremberg. As early as 1933 he campaigned for an international convention to outlaw what he came to call genocide (Lemkin 1944; Charny 1999, vol. II, p. 402). When he was a student at the University of Lvov, he was outraged to learn from one of his professors that Talat Pasha could not have been charged under any law for the 1915 massacre of Armenians (Power 2002, pp. 1, 17, 19). Pasha, the former Turkish interior minister, was assassinated on March 21, 1921 by Armenian survivor Soghomon Tehglirian (who was legally acquitted later by a court). Tehglirian did it because there was then no possibility of charging anyone for the kinds of crimes Pasha had committed against the Armenian people. *Piracy* was an international crime. But no international crime covered what we now call genocide. "Certainly human beings and their cultures are more important than a ship and its cargo," argued Lemkin (Power 2002, p. 48).

Lemkin's persistence finally resulted in the United Nations Convention on the Prevention and Punishment of the Crime of Genocide of December 9, 1948 (one day before the UN adopted the Universal Declaration of Human Rights).[5] Under Article VI of the Genocide Convention, perpetrators can be tried either in the state where the crime was committed or by "such international penal tribunal as may have jurisdiction with respect to those contracting parties which shall have accepted its jurisdiction" (Power 2002, p. 63). As it turned out, Article VI provided a loophole for ratifiers, including the US, which at the time of this writing has not accepted the jurisdiction of the International Criminal Court (ICC) .

Although the Genocide Convention has long been widely cited, it was not acted upon in international courts until the 1990s. The first state to bring a case to an international court under the convention was Bosnia-Herzegovina in 1993. In September 1998 the Rwanda tribunal gave the first verdict interpreting the Genocide Convention when it found Jean-Paul Akayesu guilty on nine out of fifteen counts of genocide, crimes against humanity, and violations of the Geneva Convention for his roles in the Rwandan genocide of 1994, and Jean Kambanda, Rwanda's former prime minister, was given a sentence of life imprisonment for six counts of genocide and crimes against humanity (Charny 1999, vol.II, p. 577; Gutman and Rieff 1999, p. 153).

[5] For the text of the UN Convention on the Prevention and Punishment of the Crime of Genocide, see Power (2002, pp. 62–63); Charny (1999, vol. II, pp. 578–80); or the website www.hrweb.org/legal/genocide.html. For the text of the Universal Declaration of Human Rights see Charny (1999, vol.II, pp. 572–74) or www.un.org/en/documents/udhr/.

Forty years elapsed before the US ratified the Genocide Convention. By then, ninety-seven other members of the UN had done so. Wisconsin Senator William Proxmire, inspired by Lemkin's campaign, gave a new speech to the US Senate in favor of ratification every day that the Senate was in session for nineteen years, from 1967 to 1986, a total of 3,211 speeches (Power 2002, p. 306). When President Harry Truman sent the Genocide Convention to the Senate in 1949, it was rejected as "a 'sell-out' to the communists" (Charny 1999, vol. II, p. 597). The Senate finally ratified it with the required legislation in 1988, when President Ronald Reagan asked it to do so, but with "two reservations, five understandings, and one declaration" attached as integral parts. One understanding was "That with regard to the reference to the international penal tribunal in Article VI of the Convention, the U.S. declares that it reserves the right to effect its participation in any such tribunal only by a treaty entered into specifically for that purpose with the advice and consent of the Senate" (Charny 1999, vol. II, p. 597–98). Behind the resistance of the US to ratification and that disabling "understanding" are worries about questions regarding the US in Vietnam and questions regarding its bombings of Japan in 1945.

The *term* "genocide" and explicit international recognition of the concept are thus relatively new, less than three-quarters of a century. Although the Armenian genocide was a major motivator for Lemkin, the Holocaust is more widely cited today as a paradigm of genocide. Turkey continues to deny that the Armenian massacres were genocidal. In 1939 Hitler asked, in a meeting with his military chiefs, "Who today still speaks of the Armenians?" (Power 2002, p. 23). The Nazis had learned from the Young Turks, as the Young Turks had learned from the Germans, who committed in 1904 what historian Ben Kiernan calls "the opening genocide of the twentieth century" against the Herero people of what is today South Africa (Kiernan 2007, pp. 364–454). And the Germans in South Africa took as precedents for their treatment of indigenous Africans the European-American exterminations of Indians in the Americas.

Although the attempt to hold perpetrators accountable is new, Lemkin and many others find the *practice* of genocide ancient. In their sociological survey, Frank Chalk and Kurt Jonassohn discuss instances of apparent genocide that range from the Athenians' annihilation of the people of the island of Melos in the fifth century BCE (recorded by Thucydides) and the ravaging of Carthage by Romans in 146 BCE (also listed by Lemkin as the first of his historical examples of wars of extermination) through mass killings in Bangladesh, Cambodia, and East Timor in the second half of the twentieth century (Chalk and Jonassohn 1990). Kiernan's historical survey adds Japanese imperialism in East Asia, Maoism in China, and genocides in Rwanda, Iraq, Bosnia, and Darfur (Kiernan 2007, pp. 455–538, 554–606). Controversies are ongoing over whether to count as genocidal some annihilations of indigenous peoples in the Americas and in Australia, who also succumbed in vast numbers to diseases from Spain and Britain. Controversial also is whether to count as genocidal Stalin's induced mass starvation of Russian peasants in the 1930s and whether to count the war conducted by the US in Vietnam.

The literature of comparative genocide, which historian Peter Novick calls "comparative atrocitology" (Novick 1999), includes to date relatively few book-length treatments of genocide by philosophers. In contrast there are voluminous contributions from sociology, literature, and history. Four notable exceptions in philosophy are Berel Lang, *Act and Idea in the Nazi Genocide* (1990), Laurence Mordekhai Thomas, *Vessels of Evil: American Slavery and the Holocaust* (1993), David H. Jones, *Moral Responsibility in the Holocaust* (1999), and Arne Johan Vetlesen, *Evil and Human Agency: Understanding Collective Evildoing* (2005). The first three of these focus on the Nazi genocide. But chapter 1 of Lang's *Act and Idea* is a thoughtful exploration of intent in defining genocide (Lang 1990, pp. 3–29). Vetlesen takes up ethnic cleansing in the former Yugoslavia, as well as the Holocaust, and discusses the logic of genocide (Vetlesen 2005, pp. 145–219). Most philosophical essays on genocide have appeared since the 1980s and are included in anthologies, mostly interdisciplinary, that tend to focus on the Holocaust.[6] One noteworthy essay, James Nickel's "Moral Dimensions of Four Ways of Getting Rid of Groups," is buried in a volume on war crimes and collective wrongdoing (Jokić 2001).

A notable earlier philosophical essay is Jean-Paul Sartre's monograph, *On Genocide* (Sartre 1968). It was written for the Sartre–Russell International War Crimes Tribunal, which convened to consider war crimes by the US in Vietnam. In 1974 Hugo Adam Bedau, best known for his decades-long philosophical campaign against the death penalty, published a long and thoughtful response essay, "Genocide in Vietnam?" (Held, Morgenbesser, and Nagel 1974, pp. 5–46). Relying on a fairly narrow understanding of intent, that essay defends the US against the suspicion that it committed genocide in Vietnam. It argues that since

---

[6] A philosophical collection that treats the concept of genocide more generally is Roth (2005). A philosophical collection on many genocides is Card and Marsoobian (2007). Among anthologies that include philosophical essays with a focus on the Holocaust are Garrard and Scarre (2003); Rosenberg and Myers (1988); and many volumes coedited by John K. Roth (e.g. Rittner and Roth, 1993; Roth and Berenbaum 1989; Rubenstein and Roth 2003).

the intent, understood as the *aim*, was not to exterminate a people, even if that was nearly a consequence, US action in Vietnam was not a genocide. The broader understanding of intent defended in chapter 8, which includes not only ends and means but also willingness to pursue them in ways that do reasonably foreseeable harm, suggests that the issue of the US in Vietnam is not so easily resolved.

Of interdisciplinary anthologies that include philosophical essays, notable is Alan S. Rosenbaum's anthology *Is the Holocaust Unique? Perspectives on Comparative Genocide,* now in its third edition (Rosenbaum 2009). That volume includes discussions of the Nazi assault on Jews and Romani, the Atlantic slave trade, the Turkish slaughter of Armenians in 1915, Stalin's induced famine, the Rwandan genocide, Japanese atrocities during WW II, and atrocities committed in Cambodia from 1975 to 1979 under the direction of Pol Pot. Legal scholar Martha Minow reflects philosophically in two books (Minow 1998, 2002) on responses by governments to mass atrocity, including genocides. Jonathan Glover's *Humanity: A Moral History of the Twentieth Century* (Glover 2000) is an impressively ambitious philosophical survey of evils, including reflections on Rwanda, Stalin, and Nazism.

There are some organizations that sponsor conferences or sessions at conferences that philosophers attend. The Institute for Genocide Studies and the Association of Genocide Scholars, which holds conventions, attract an interdisciplinary group of scholars. The Society for the Philosophic Study of Genocide and the Holocaust sponsors sessions at conventions of the Society for Phenomenological and Existential Philosophy and the American Philosophical Association. An interdisciplinary conference, "Lessons and Legacies of the Holocaust," convenes biennially. Although philosophers are now represented in these ways in genocide scholarship, it remains true that historians, psychologists, sociologists, and political scientists are contributing far more than philosophers. Social scientists' contributions are empirically oriented studies of origins, contributing causes, effects, monitoring, and prevention. Yet philosophical issues run throughout. Those issues include such foundational matters as the meaning of "genocide," a highly contested concept, and its conceptual relationship to other atrocities. There are also philosophical questions about whether perpetrators can be punished in a meaningful way that still respects moral standards. If adequate retribution is morally impossible and deterrence unlikely for the ideologically motivated, then what is the point? If there is nevertheless some point sufficient to justify punishing, then who should be punished, by whom, and how?

I mention issues of accountability only to indicate, and then set aside, some of the philosophical work that needs to be done. My focus in this chapter and the next continues to be the meaning of genocide and its relationships to other atrocities. There are no philosophical debates regarding justifications for genocide. Understood as the murder of a people, genocide is wrong by definition (even though murdering a people need not be done by mass killing). Nevertheless, like terrorism and torture, actual genocides have often been reactive, not spontaneous. As Vetlesen puts it, in many instances "the perpetrator group does exactly what it castigates the target for having done (in some remote or recent past) or for being now about to do against one's own group" (Vetlesen 2005, p. 175). Perpetrators do not call it "genocide." But often enough they do call it "extermination" (Kiernan 2007, pp. 364–90). Military leaders have defended mass exterminations as retaliation or pre-emption, invoking the right of self-defense (Vetlesen 2005, p. 175). In thinking about how to avoid doing evil in response to evil, it is important to think about genocide and become as clear as we can about it, so as to recognize when a proposed response or military measure, such as use of a weapon of mass destruction (WMD), would be, or would risk, genocide. When it is unclear whether an action is genocidal, questions of justification can and do arise. Chapter 10 considers ethnic cleansing, forced cultural assimilation, and a certain use of a WMD with such questions in mind.

3. THE MURDER OF GROUPS

Controversies over the meaning of "genocide" lead naturally to the questions of whether genocide is ethically, politically, or legally different from non-genocidal mass murder. At stake, for practical purposes, is whether it is important to add the category of genocide to already existing crimes against humanity and war crimes. Crimes against humanity were important additions to war crimes. Unlike war crimes, crimes against humanity need not be perpetrated during wartime or in connection with a war. They can also be committed against nationals of the same state. But given that murder of civilians is already a war crime and a human rights violation, the question arises whether making genocide a distinct crime captures anything that other crimes omit. Morally, the question is whether there is a distinct wrong here.

The easy answer is that genocide targets a group whereas non-genocidal mass murders just target many individuals. But that contrast needs clarification. Since groups are made up of many individuals, how does eliminating a group differ from eliminating many individuals? Why are the 1995 bombing in Oklahoma City by Timothy McVeigh and the bombings of September 11, 2001 (9/11) not genocides? Casualties were massive. Occupants of a bombed building are a kind of group. If the answer is that only certain kinds of groups are possible targets of genocide, the question becomes: what distinguishes those kinds of groups? What distinctive wrong is committed when such a group is destroyed that is not committed when other groups are destroyed?

We might begin to answer the question about 9/11 and Oklahoma City by pointing out that the "genos" behind "genocide" is widely understood today to refer to *a people*. Occupants of those bombed buildings did not constitute a people. A people is not an aggregate. Nor is it only a *structural group*, in Iris Marion Young's sense (discussed in chapters 3 and 4) – a serial collectivity united by the relationships of members to externals, which gives them common interests. Occupants of the Twin Towers in Manhattan might be regarded as a structural group, if only briefly, in that the external threat of the planes, at least after the first one hit and a second was sited, gave them an immediate common interest in escape or in avoiding burning to death. Still, those occupants were not a people. Nor were they simply a portion of the American people (which is more plausible in the case of the Oklahoma City bombing). Occupants of the Twin Towers included people from a great many nations, which could have been partly why those towers were targeted.

A people is a *social group* in Young's sense, that is, a collectivity united by internal relationships and traditions, such as common language and practices. Relationships that constitute a people include connections of kinship and citizenship as well as cultural and social relationships created by such things as a common literature, cuisine, humor, and by sharing in the creation and maintenance of laws and traditions. These practices and relationships create the social vitality that gives meanings to the lives of members of peoples. The social vitality of the occupants of bombed buildings comes largely from their memberships in other groups.

Cultural and social relationships may or may not be sufficient to enable a particular social group to act. There can be deep conflicts within a people, including conflicting traditions and conflicting interpretations. Harm to a people does not necessarily harm an individual member, whose interests may not coincide with those of the people as a whole. But destruction of a people can harm members, even if not each, in a distinct and fundamental way. To the extent that relationships that define the group are important sources of meaning and identity in the lives of its members, destruction of the group is for them a serious loss. By the same stroke it is a loss of the possibility of such meaning and identity for descendants.

To complicate matters, the target of the Nazi genocide was not defined consistently as either a social group (united by internal relationships) or a structural group (united by relationships to externals) but was something of a hybrid in that it included both people who self-identified as Jewish and people who did not although they bore a variety of relationships to people who did. The apparatus of the Holocaust targeted more than the Jewish people when it defined "Jewish" at least partly in terms of biological ancestry, rather than cultural heritage. A biological group is not a people.[7]

Against this background, it seems apt that the philosopher Ludwig Wittgenstein came up with the idea of "family resemblance" concepts. Wittgenstein was raised Catholic. But his ancestors were found to include converts from Judaism. Consequently, he had to flee the Nazis. It would be difficult to find a better paradigm of a family resemblance concept, especially after Hitler, than the concept "Jewish."[8] Even those who self-identify as Jewish appear to constitute many peoples, given the multiplicity of native languages and diaspora cultures. If diaspora Jews constitute a family of peoples, the Nazi genocide targeted both the family and a multiplicity of friends and relatives. Still, not all individuals were endangered in the same way. Those who identified as Jewish were threatened with a special loss insofar as Judaism and Jewish culture(s), not just individual Jews, were threatened. The Roma also were threatened with that kind of loss. Converts to Christianity and descendants of converts were stripped of social relationships that shaped and animated their daily lives and so suffered a degree of social death. But those who no longer (or never had) self-identified as Jewish were not threatened by genocide with the deeper, intergenerational loss of meaning for their lives and deaths that threatened those who did identify as Jewish.

Men who were identified as homosexuals and either killed for that reason or forced to wear the "pink triangle" in the Nazi concentration camps suffered some of the losses imposed by a genocide if they were members of gay communities.[9] When gay communities are destroyed, members lose the social vitality that shaped and animated their lives in

---

[7] There is another sense in which some say the Holocaust targeted more than the Jewish people. Some, like Dawidowicz (1975), apply the term "Holocaust" specifically to Hitler's war against the Jews; others apply the term "Holocaust" to the larger Third Reich project of exterminating peoples labeled "non-Aryan," including the Roma.

[8] On Wittgenstein's Jewish ancestry, see Monk (1990, pp. 4–8) and Waugh (2008, pp. 15–16).

[9] On the men who wore pink triangle badges, see Heger (1980) and Plant (1986).

the context of a larger social world that had rejected them. Does that loss constitute a gay *genocide*? Nickel considers the case of forcibly "re-educated" homosexuals to be analogous to that of the forced assimilation of cultural groups, which he sees as a way of "getting rid of groups" that is not ordinarily genocidal (Jokić 2001, p. 169).[10] But the men of the pink triangles were persecuted and ostracized, not re-educated. They resemble victims of a genocide to the extent that their lives had first or most importantly gained positive meaning from the gay communities to which they belonged. Yet those communities were far younger, transitory, in flux, and inevitably less richly textured and layered than communities constituted by sharers of a natural language, religion, and multi-generational traditions. Gay communities are like many political communities (some *are* political communities), pockets of resistance to prevailing norms. Yet those communities were only part of what gave shape and meanings to the lives of their members, who had many communities of origin, even if the gay part was experienced by many as the only *good* part. Gay communities can have a life-saving impact on those who are otherwise cultural rejects, as members reject homophobic aspects of the dominant culture. Although many who engaged in same-sex intimacies then as now did not belong to gay communities and some were even married, the men most likely to be rounded up and sent to camps were those who met at gay bars or gay parties or were activists.[11] Wittgenstein's idea of a family resemblance is helpful for thinking about the extent to which and ways in which the idea of a gay genocide makes sense (or does not). Destruction of gay communities is not a paradigm of genocide. But it bears relevant similarities and so, when the assault is systematic, might find a place in the extended family of genocidal assaults.

In chapter 5 it was argued that the Columbine High School massacre of 1999 in Colorado was not an instance of terrorism, even though the shooters intended to bomb the school, which would have killed hundreds in addition to the twelve students and the teacher that they in fact killed before killing themselves. I deferred to this chapter the question whether that massacre was genocidal. It certainly aimed to destroy a group that was not a mere aggregate (students, faculty, and staff of Columbine High School) and, as much as possible, the material foundations of that group (the physical facilities of Columbine High). Whether it was an attempt

[10] Chapter 10 takes up the issue of whether forced assimilation can be genocidal.
[11] Although there were lesbians in the camps, they did not wear pink triangles. They were there for other reasons, such as that they were identified as Jewish or as resisters.

at genocide depends on the nature, extent, and depth of the social vitality created by the ties uniting those who spent so much time in that high school. What contribution did that vitality make to the meanings of their lives? In favor of counting the massacre as genocidal are the facts that almost all the social life of many high-school students takes place either in high school or with friends from high school, much of the social lives of its faculty are closely tied to their work there as well, and high-school culture is passed along, to some extent, from generation to generation. To the question, "Who are you?" the response might well be "I'm a student at Columbine High" or "I'm a teacher at Columbine High." Against counting that slaughter as genocidal are the facts that a high school "generation" is only (for many of us, fortunately) four years out of a student's lifetime, and even during those years, family, religious affiliation, or ethnicity are apt to be as socially vital or more so. The employment and degree of involvement for faculty may be longer or shorter, according to their choices. Unlike gay communities, high schools are not ordinarily places to which people flee for security, though they are often enough places from which students (if not also faculty) wish they could flee.

Questions about which kinds of groups are potential targets of genocide bring to the fore the implicit assumption that the group destroyed was not itself an evil. Recall the Murder, Inc. problem from chapter 4. Criminal organizations, such as Murder, Inc., pose a problem for ethical theories that hold that there is a presumption against destroying any entity that is capable of thriving or flourishing. Since criminal organizations are capable of thriving – that is, they can grow and be strong, even robust (although "flourishing" may be inapt for a group that bears flowers of evil) – such theories would establish a presumption against destroying them. Yet that is absurd. A similar issue arises for the theory of genocide as social death. Without the tacit understanding that the group destroyed by a genocide contributed at least a tolerably decent kind of meaning to the lives of its members, what is to prevent the forcible disbanding of such groups as the Ku Klux Klan (KKK) or Murder, Inc. from falling within the meaning of genocide? Conceivably, those organizations give as much meaning to the lives of their members as gay communities have given theirs. Members may find their activities within the organization to be the best parts of their lives. They, too, might feel rescued by membership and the acceptance it confers. Why was de-nazification, then, not a form of genocide? If the men with the pink triangles were victims of something like a genocide, why should the "family" of genocidal assaults not be extended to include also criminal organizations dismantled by law enforcement?

A sufficient answer lies in the tacit assumption that groups that are possible victims of genocide are not themselves evils. The meanings that a group contributes to the lives and deaths of its members must be tolerably decent. Of course, most social groups are apt to have both good and bad features. Sociologist Kathleen Blee interviewed women in Indiana who had belonged to the KKK in the 1920s. They told her that the Klan served as a locus for social interaction of like-minded people (Blee 1991, p. 1). But destruction of the KKK as an organization would no more deserve a place in an extended family of genocidal atrocities than would destruction of Murder, Inc., not even if former members' lives would shrivel without the organization. Forcibly imposed social death of a group is not genocidal if the group itself is an evil. The judgment that a group is an evil must be understood as the judgment that what basically defines the group is evil, that evil practices are so essential to it that they could not be eliminated without eliminating the group.

The judgment that there is something relevantly similar to a genocidal loss in the destruction of gay communities but not in destroying criminal organizations like Murder, Inc. appears to rest on the prior judgment that gay communities are not evils, whereas Murder, Inc. is. Provided that human rights are respected, forcibly disbanding or impoverishing an evil group so that it can no longer function is not an evil. Killing members simply because they are members ordinarily would be an evil, although membership can entail paying dues that finance crimes, and initiation into some groups requires the new member to commit a capital crime. Still, individuals can and ought to be convicted on evidence of their roles in specific crimes, not simply on evidence of their relationship to an evil group.

The hypothesis that genocide is possible only against groups that are not themselves evils brings out a certain disanalogy between the concept of genocide as murder of a people and the concept of murder as applied to the wrongful killing of an individual. In order for killing a human being to be murder, it does not matter whether the victim was evil. What matters is that the killing was not authorized or done in self-defense. Murder of an evil person is still murder. But destroying an evil group is not murdering that group.

Genocide does not presuppose that *no one* in the target group is evil. It is sufficient that the group is on the whole, or basically, not an evil. When the Southern Poverty Law Center (SPLC) uses lawsuits to bankrupt white supremacist groups in the US, it is not committing genocide. This is not simply because the SPLC acts within the law. Nazis also operated through institutions of law, passing the Nuremberg Laws in 1935, for example. Rather, the reason seems to be a judgment about the moral status of the group destroyed, that it was an evil.

At the root of the idea that the destruction of an evil group is not an evil, whereas the murder of an evil individual is still murder, might be the following difference between evil individuals and evils groups. Human beings are not defined by principles they espouse or the values they hold at any given time. We are defined in part by capacities that give us the potential for insight and deep character change. We can make ourselves better. In contrast, evil groups are organizations that are defined by their basic principles, and the basic principles of some organizations do not provide a basis for moral reform within the organization. Laws that make killing even an evil person murder seem to presuppose that all human beings are bearers of a certain value, that we all have, as Kant thought, the *capacity* for good.[12] Perhaps, likewise, for the destruction of a group to count as a genocide, that group must have, as a group, capacities for self-correction and moral improvement. Destroying a group that lacks such capacities, then, would not be genocide. A group defined by evil principles that lacked such capacities would be an unredeemable evil. The Third Reich appears to have been such a group. Members of the German Resistance tried to bring about changes from within the Third Reich that would have been improvements, for example, in the famous July 20, 1944 attempt to assassinate Hitler and Himmler.[13] But they failed. There was no effective mechanism, such as impeachment, for moral improvement from within.

Like the individual who is capable of deep character change, some organizations and other groups, such as states, have built into their structures mechanisms for change that give them potentialities for moral reform. They, too, can make themselves better. Such a structure provides an argument for the view that even a bad organization or state, like a bad person, can be the bearer of a value that deserves respect. This seems true, for example, of states that (currently) have bad administrations but decent constitutions that have not been disabled. It may be likewise true of some organized religions and other long-standing cultural groups. But such

---

[12] Even if Kant was wrong to think that all human beings have that capacity, the presumption that everyone does might still underlie the decision to treat even the murder of an evil human being as an evil.

[13] The July 20 plot is the subject of two films in the first decade of the twenty-first century, the feature, *Valkyrie* (2008) with Tom Cruise as Colonel Claus von Stauffenberg (who positions the bomb that failed to kill either Hitler or Himmler) and a documentary, *Operation Valkyrie: The Stauffenberg Plot to Kill Hitler* (2004), which is more informative than the feature film.

organizations as the KKK and Murder, Inc. appear to have evil purposes so integral to their nature that without those purposes there is insufficient reason for the organizations to exist.

Perhaps the basis for regarding even the murder of an evil person as an evil is simpler and more pragmatic. A state that allows its citizens, residents, or transients to kill others (whatever their character) without authorization, except in self-defense, cannot provide basic security for its members. The good in question is simply basic security, not a characteristic or capacity of individuals. Yet the value of that security rests on its being necessary for the realization of human good. The presupposition seems to be either that all human beings have the potential to contribute to that realization, in virtue of the human capacities for evaluation and self-correction, or that there is no non-arbitrary way to determine that some individuals lack those capacities (or no way to do so that is not intolerably vulnerable to abuse). The analogous presupposition of genocide's wrongness would be that a world that tolerates the destruction of certain kinds of human groups is not a world that can secure the potentiality for realizing human good.

I am reminded of W. E. B. DuBois's 1897 essay "The Conservation of Races," in which he argues against assimilation as an ideal.[14] His view was that "the history of the world is the history, not of individuals, but of groups" (DuBois 1970, p. 75) and that a race is "a vast family of human beings, generally of common blood and language, always of common history, traditions, and impulses, who are both voluntarily and involuntarily striving together for the accomplishment of certain more or less vividly conceived ideals of life" (DuBois 1970, pp. 75–76). Races, for DuBois, were distinguishable more importantly by their spiritual characteristics, ideals, and ways of life than by gross physical differences, such as skin color or hair texture. DuBois's races are peoples, or perhaps families of peoples. He saw each such group as striving in its own particular way "to develop for civilization its particular message, its particular ideal" (DuBois 1970, p. 78). A presupposition of the evil of genocide might be that ethnic, racial, national, religious, and relevantly similar groups need to be protected in order to secure the potential for development of the goods of civilization or humanity. There is no such need to protect evil organizations such as Murder, Inc.

A similar thought is found in Lemkin's *Axis Rule*. He writes, "The world represents only so much culture and intellectual vigor as are created by

---

[14] I am indebted to Lucius Outlaw for calling my attention to this essay long ago in his own essay, "On W. E. B. Du Bois' 'The Conservation of Races'"(Bell and Blumenfeld 1995, pp. 79–102).

its component national groups. Essentially the idea of a nation signifies constructive cooperation and original contributions, based upon genuine traditions ... The destruction of a nation, therefore, results in the loss of its future contributions to the world" (Lemkin 1944, p. 91). One might add, "and most likely a loss of the histories of its past contributions, which are part of their meaning, as well." "Nations," for Lemkin in this observation, play the role of "races" for DuBois. Like DuBois's races, Lemkin's nations are peoples. Elsewhere, Lemkin does not restrict the relevant groups to nations.

The concept of genocide is disanalogous to the concept of homicide in at least two ways. First, genocide need not succeed in eliminating an entire group. On the most widely accepted definitions, it need not kill anyone. But homicide must succeed in actually killing someone. An intended homicide that does not succeed is only an attempt, which carries a less severe penalty. A genocide that fails to eliminate an entire group is still a genocide. There is nevertheless room for a distinction between genocide and attempted genocide. Attempts are included in the Genocide Convention's list of punishable acts. An attempted genocide might consist of the implementation of only some early stages of a genocidal plan. But even in paradigmatically successful instances, where there is clear evidence that the intention was to eliminate everyone and all stages of a complex genocidal plan are carried out, there are usually some survivors.

A second disanalogy is that homicide can be justified, whereas genocide cannot. Homicide is not necessarily unlawful or even immoral – in self-defense, for example – whereas genocide is in principle incapable of justification. The murder of a people (genocide) is, like the murder of an individual, wrong by definition. What "murder" conveys in both cases is an unjustifiable destruction of vitality.

In sum, if social death is central to genocide, the concept of genocide does capture something that was not already captured by existing war crimes and crimes against humanity. Relationships internal to a group – cultural, political, economic, educational, familial, linguistic, religious – that turn what might otherwise be an aggregate into a community are destroyed or seriously degraded. The harm members suffer is a loss of context and identity that gave meaning and shape to their lives and would have given meaning to their deaths. That loss is not captured by previously existing war crimes or crimes against humanity. There is, further, a loss to humanity in the destruction of human potential, a matter to which I return in section 4.

4. THE UN DEFINITION OF "GENOCIDE"

The definition of "genocide" is in such flux that the Association of Genocide Scholars asks members on its information page (printed in a members' directory) to specify which definition of "genocide" they use in their work. The most widely cited definition is that of Article II in the 1948 UN Convention on the Prevention and Punishment of the Crime of Genocide:

In the present Convention, genocide means any of the following acts committed with the intent to destroy, in whole or in part, a nation, ethnical [sic], racial or religious group, as such:

(a) Killing members of the group;

(b) Causing serious bodily or mental harm to members of the group;

(c) Deliberately inflicting on the group conditions of life calculated to bring about its physical destruction in whole or in part;

(d) Imposing measures intended to prevent births within the group;

(e) Forcibly transferring children of the group to another group. (Charny 1999, vol. II, p. 578)

Article III lists the following acts as punishable:

(a) Genocide;

(b) Conspiracy to commit genocide;

(c) Direct and public incitement to commit genocide;

(d) Attempt to commit genocide;

(e) Complicity in genocide. (Charny 1999, vol. II, pp. 578–79).

Every clause in the UN definition is controversial. Much hinges on how each is interpreted and on whether the lists are taken to be exhaustive.

Israel Charny and others criticize the UN definition for not recognizing *political* groups, such as the Communist Party, as possible targets of genocide. The issue is not whether political groups are plausibly regarded as peoples. Some religious groups, such as the Amish, are plausibly regarded as peoples. Others are not. Yet targeting any religious group for extermination is apt to be acknowledged as genocidal. Theoretically, the issue is whether group membership is central enough to the social vitality of members that destruction of the group would threaten them with a profound loss of (tolerably decent) meaning for their lives. Practically, the issue is what kinds of mass killings should subject their perpetrators to the penalties and other provisions of the Genocide Convention.

Political groups were in fact recognized in an earlier draft of the Genocide Convention. Chalk and Jonassohn recognize political groups in their historical survey (Chalk and Jonassohn 1990). Some scholars prefer the term "politicide" for the murder of political groups and reserve the term "genocide" for the annihilation of groups into which one is (ordinarily) born – racial, ethnic, national, or religious. Yet one is not necessarily born into one's current national or religious group, although either one's current membership or a former one can prove fatal. Further, politics plays a role in some people's lives comparable to that of religion in the lives of others. When a political group is targeted, many people are killed sheerly for their connections with the group, not for anything they have done as individuals. For such reasons, the distinction between "genocide" and "politicide" has seemed arbitrary to many critics. A natural question is, of course, where to draw the line if political groups are recognized as possible victims of genocide. But line-drawing is not an issue peculiar to the matter of political groups.

The last three clauses of the UN definition – conditions of life intended to destroy the group "in whole or in part," preventing births within a group, and forcibly transferring children – count as genocidal many policies aimed at cultural destruction or at the degradation of social practices and relationships even though the destructive policies are not homicidal. Nickel regards forced re-education as an assimilationist alternative to genocide, a different way of "getting rid of groups" (Jokić 2001, pp. 163–75). It appears that Lemkin's rationale for wanting to include such practices was to enable international agencies to catch and stop a genocide before it reached the stage of mass killing. Yet that rationale is not explicit in the Genocide Convention's definition. According to that definition, preventing births or forcibly transferring children could themselves be genocides, which makes a certain sense in terms of the social death of a group.

Sterilization and contraception are not the only ways of preventing births. Segregation of the sexes and bans on marriage have been recognized as ways of doing that as well. Destroying family ties can also do that and is a commonly intended consequence of war rape. Although Lemkin regarded deeds that destroy fundamental social relations as both ethnocidal and genocidal, some critics prefer to call them simply ethnocides (or cultural genocides) and reserve the term "genocide" (unqualified) for events that include mass death. Perhaps underlying the wish to draw that distinction is the judgment that physical death is more extreme, at least for the individual, and therefore worse than social death. That physical death is worse, or even more extreme, is not obvious, however, but deserves scrutiny. I return to that view in section 5.

Even clauses (a) and (b) of the UN definition, which specify killing group members or causing them serious bodily or mental harm, are vague. How many must be killed? How grave must bodily or mental harm be? Must it be disabling? (How disabling?) Irreversible? The US Congress worried over the numbers requisite to constitute a genocide. Finally, as one of the "understandings" with which it ratified the convention, the Congress interpreted "in part" as "in substantial part" (Charny 1999, vol. II, p. 597). To the question about mental harm, the US Congress answered, in one of its "understandings," that the relevant mental harm must be "permanent impairment of mental faculties through drugs, torture or similar techniques" (Charny 1999, vol. II, p. 597).

Although most scholars agree on including intention in the definition of genocide, there is no consensus regarding the required content or scope of the intention. The same kind of issue arises here as was encountered in chapter 8 regarding the UN definition of torture: how inclusive is the relevant intent? Is it restricted to ends and means? Or can it include willingness to inflict reasonably foreseeable harms that are incidental? For genocide, the question is whether the relevant intention is restricted to the destruction of a group *as an aim* (one natural understanding of "as such," as Bedau seems to assume in his defense of the US against the charge of genocide in Vietnam) or even as a means to a further aim, or whether it is sufficient that the group was knowingly destroyed as a foreseeable consequence of the pursuit of some other aim. Must the full extent of the destruction even be foreseeable, if the policy of which it is a consequence is already clearly an evil?

Charny defends a broad construction of intent (Andreopoulos 1994, pp. 64–94). He objects to a claim analogous to Bedau's claims about the US in Vietnam made by critics who hold that Stalin's induced peasant famine of the 1930s was not a genocide because his intent (read: aim) was to obtain enough grain to trade for industrial materials for the Soviet Union, rather than to kill the millions who died from this policy. One might have expected the controversy to be over whether the peasants count as a people (or a community, in the relevant sense). Yet, apparently, it is clearer to some critics that the peasants were a people than that their annihilation was intended. Charny argues that because Stalin foresaw the fatal consequences of his grain policies, those policies were genocidal. As in common philosophical criticisms of the "doctrine of the double effect," Charny appears to reject as ethically insignificant a distinction between intending and "merely foreseeing," at least in this kind of case. In doing so, he is philosophically on good ground.

The controversial doctrine of the double effect has been relied on by the Catholic Church to justify certain acts that would otherwise be wrongful killings (Becker 2001, vol. 1, pp. 418–20). In the case of Stalin and the peasants, however, the question is not whether Stalin was justified but whether he was guilty of genocide. It is basically a question of the extent of his responsibility and the depth of his culpability. Is he responsible and culpable for deaths that were reasonably foreseeable results of his acts if those deaths were neither his aim nor a means to his aims? The doctrine of the double effect maintains that when those conditions are met, one is not responsible and not culpable, provided that one's aims and the means one chooses to implement them are not themselves wrong. Making use of that doctrine, the Church has found that one is responsible and culpable for fetal death that results from abortion to save the mother, because killing the fetus is interpreted as a means. But, at the same time, it has found that one is not culpable for fetal death resulting from the removal of a cancerous uterus, because in that case, fetal death is not interpreted as either an aim or a means but merely as a consequence of the surgery.

Many find the distinction between fetal death from abortion and fetal death from removal of a cancerous uterus troubling and far from clear. Why is the death of a fetus from abortion not also only a consequence? The aim could be redescribed as "to remove the fetus from the mother's body in order to save the mother," rather than "to kill the fetus to save the mother," and at least when the fetus need not be destroyed in the very process of removal, one might argue that death due to extrauterine nonviability is not a means to saving the mother's life, either. My argument is more fundamental: if one can foresee the harm that will result from one's act and one chooses to do it anyway, one is accepting that harm as part of the price of one's deed, at least in cases where the harm does not also depend on choices made by others. One may not like the fact that such harm results, and one might never have chosen to cause such harm as either an end or a means. Nevertheless, one accepts it, and that is a moral choice. Acceptance makes one responsible.

Critics who do not want to count Stalin's starvation of the peasants as a genocide seem to hold that if the peasants' deaths were not instrumental toward Stalin's goal but only a side effect, then the foreseeability of those deaths is not enough to make Stalin's policy genocidal, any more than foreseeability of fetal death in the case of the cancerous uterus makes the hysterectomy a murder. Charny appears to hold that, on the contrary,

foreseeability of the peasants' mass death in this context is enough to constitute genocidal intent. To put the point in terms of the broad construction of intent for which I argued in chapter 8, even if the peasants' mass
death was intended neither in itself nor instrumentally, it was intended –
that is, it was willingly accepted. I think Charny is right on this point. If
those mass deaths from starvation did not constitute a genocide, that was
not because although they were foreseeable, they were neither an end nor
a means.

Some controversies focus on whether the intent was "to destroy a group
as such." One might argue with Bedau, drawing on Lang's discussion of
the intent issues (Lang 1990, pp. 3–29), that the intent is "to destroy a
group as such" when it is not just accidental that the group is destroyed
in the process of pursuing a further end. This interpretation also allows
incidental harm to count as intentional. Thus, if it was not just accidental
that the peasant class was destroyed in the process of Stalin's pursuit of
grain to trade for industrial materials, he could be said to have destroyed
the peasants "as such," even if peasant starvation played no more causal
role in producing the grain than fetal death plays in removing a cancerous
uterus. Alternatively, some argue that the words "as such" do not belong
in the definition because, ethically, it does not matter whether a group is
deliberately destroyed "as such" or simply deliberately destroyed. Chalk
and Jonassohn appear to take this view (Chalk and Jonassohn 1990).

Historian Steven Katz maintains in *The Holocaust in Historical Context*
that the mass deaths of Native peoples in the Americas in the sixteenth
century "was the iatrogenic consequence of conquest (i.e., the overwhelming majority of deaths was due to disease not premeditated murder)" (Katz
1994, p. 91; cf. Rosenbaum 2009, pp. 55–74). David Stannard, Professor of
American Studies at the University of Hawaii, and historian Ben Kiernan
point out that many tribes were in fact not wiped out by disease but
were deliberately slaughtered, down to the last man, woman, and child,
although many of these slaughters occurred after the sixteenth century
(Rosenbaum 2009, pp. 295–340; cf. Stannard 1992, pp. 57–146; Kiernan
2007, pp. 213–363).

The idea that American Indians *as a group* were not targets of genocide
fails to distinguish the many peoples included in that "group." American
Indians are no more a single people or community than are Black Africans.
No commonalities of language, occupation, religion, or tradition unite
them. They are a group only in the structural sense or the aggregative
sense. As a structural group, the many Native peoples of the Americas
did acquire a common interest in protection against Europeans and their

descendants. Even if destroyers myopically saw only "Indians," that inability to discriminate did not produce ties that define a social group but only revealed a failure to notice an absence of the kinds of ties that would have been required to define a comprehensive social group. Native peoples in the Americas did not all meet the same fates. Some did succumb to genocide, not just disease.

Further, some appear to have succumbed to both. There is at least indirect evidence that some smallpox epidemics among North American Indians were not accidental (although, again, these epidemics are later than the sixteenth century). A 1763 correspondence between General Sir Jeffrey Amherst and Colonel Henry Bouquet includes a postscript from Amherst saying "Could it not be contrived to send the *Small Pox* among those disaffected tribes of Indians? We must on this occasion use every stratagem in our power to reduce them" (Parkman 1994, vol. II, p. 39), to which Bouquet replies, "I will try to inoculate the – – [sic] with some blankets that may fall into their hands, and take care not to get the disease myself" (Parkman 1994, vol. II, p. 40; the blank space is in the original quotation). To this Amherst replies, "You will do well to inoculate the Indians by means of blankets as well as to try every other method that can serve to extirpate this execrable race" (Parkman 1994, vol. II, p. 40). In *The Conspiracy of Pontiac* historian Francis Parkman says, "There is no direct evidence that Bouquet carried into effect the shameful plan of infecting the Indians though, a few months after, the smallpox was known to have made havoc among the tribes of the Ohio" (Parkman 1994, vol. II, p. 40). C. Hale Sipe reports, in his account of the Pontiac wars, that in June of that same year, "Captain Escuyer, commandant of Fort Pitt, noted in his journal '… we gave them two blankets and a handkerchief out of the smallpox hospital. I hope it will have the desired effect'" (Sipe 1929, p. 424). Reflecting on this history, Lenore A. Stiffarm writes, "It did. The disease spread rapidly among the Mingo, Delaware, Shawnee, and other nations of the Ohio River Valley, killing perhaps 100,000 people and bringing about the collapse of Pontiac's military alliance" (Jaimes 1992, p. 32). She lists other epidemics that may also have resulted from using smallpox as a biological weapon.

Even if the extent of the deaths caused by biological warfare was not entirely foreseeable, enough was foreseeable that users of such weapons could appreciate and intend the genocidal potential. Part of the controversy regarding American Indians is empirical: to what extent were fatal epidemics accidental (not just incidental)? But part, also, is philosophical disagreement regarding the interpretation of intent. If perpetrators of biological warfare could know that the intolerably destructive consequences had an uncontrollable extent, it does not matter, ethically, whether they could foresee the full extent. They could have known enough to appreciate that there was a risk of destroying entire peoples.

That history suggests yet a further question regarding "genocidal intent." Should *willingly taking the risk* of annihilating a people by performing any of the acts enumerated in the UN definition of genocide be enough to constitute genocidal intent? That genocidal intent need not succeed suggests that willingness to take such a risk might be within a fair interpretation of genocidal intent. The idea that one is responsible for what one accepts as well as for what one does also suggests that one can be responsible for accepting a risk. Yet the punishable acts enumerated in the Genocide Convention do not include culpable risk-taking, although they do include attempts and conspiracies.

It remains to elucidate further the specific ethical import of genocide and how that import helps to determine the scope of the concept of genocide.

5. THE SPECIFIC EVIL OF GENOCIDE

Genocide is a paradigm of what Avishai Margalit calls a special sense of "indecent" in that genocide not only destroys victims but first *humiliates* them by deliberately inflicting an "utter loss of freedom and control over one's vital interests" (Margalit 1996, p. 115). Vital interests can be transgenerational and thus survive one's death. Before death, genocide victims are ordinarily deprived of control over vital transgenerational interests as well as control over more immediate vital interests. They may be literally stripped naked, robbed of their last possessions, lied to about the most vital matters, witness to the murder of family, friends, and neighbors, made to participate in their own murder. If female, they are especially likely also to be violated sexually. Victims have been killed with no regard for lingering suffering or exposure. They and their corpses are routinely treated with utter disrespect. These violations of basic human rights account for much of the moral opprobrium attaching to the concept of genocide. They are the most visible and publicized atrocities associated with genocides. Nickel cites "the intentional and malicious killing of innocent people" and "large-scale violations of very important human rights" in stating what is wrong with genocide, the wrongness of which he finds so obvious that it scarcely needs to be stated (Jokić 2001, p. 165).

What "intentional and malicious killing of innocent people" and "large-scale violations of very important human rights" do not convey, however, is the combined effect of many such crimes on a people and the appreciation that this combined effect is the result of a complex plan with many stages. Chapter 10 explores further the idea of such a plan.

Social vitality is interpersonal. An individual can experience social death without others experiencing it, too. But for an individual to have social vitality, others must have it. I borrow the concept of social death from Orlando Patterson's work on slavery (Patterson 1982, pp. 5–9). Patterson argues that slavery, as historically a substitute for slaughter of the conquered in war, simply substituted one kind of death for another, social death for mass homicide. Slaves in the Americas who descended from kidnapped Africans were born socially dead, cut off from intergenerational social connections in both directions, past and future. They were, as he put it, natally alienated. In genocides, survivors experience a social death, to a degree and for a time. Some later become revitalized in new ways; others do not. Descendants of genocide survivors, like descendants of slaves who were kidnapped, may be "natally alienated," no longer able to pass along and build upon the traditions, cultural developments (including languages), and projects of earlier generations. In the previous section, the question arose briefly whether physical death was worse for the individual than social death. Both are extremes. But they are extremes of different kinds. The harm of social death is not necessarily less extreme, even for the individual. Further, social death can aggravate physical death by making it indecent, removing all respectful and caring ritual, social connections, and social contexts that can make dying bearable and make one's death meaningful. It should not be assumed that physical death is worse. Whether it is may depend on the degree of social death in question and the possibilities for revitalization. When a whole people dies socially, prospects for survivors may be grim. I return to this question again in the final chapter.

The view that the special evil of genocide is social death is controversial. African American and Jewish philosopher Laurence Mordekhai Thomas argues that in contrast to American slavery, which natally alienated slaves, the Holocaust did not natally alienate Jews (Thomas 1993, pp. 150–57). Slaves were born severed from most normal social and cultural ties that connect people with both earlier and later generations. Most Holocaust victims were not born natally alienated, and enough of a saving remnant survived to reconstitute and reinvigorate Jewish culture. Thomas does not explicitly generalize about genocide and natal alienation. He makes this judgment in regard to the particular genocide of the Holocaust. Yet, the apparent implication is that a genocide no more successful than the

Holocaust (an accepted paradigm of genocide) is not natally alienating, because enough victims survive and enough potential victims escape that they are able to preserve the group's cultural traditions. But the reasons Thomas finds that the Holocaust was not natally alienating point toward the even stronger conclusion that the Holocaust did not produce social death.

Thomas's analyses of patterns of evil in American slavery and the Holocaust are philosophically groundbreaking and have been helpful to me in thinking about these topics. Yet I want to problematize his reasoning here. Natal alienation is a special case of social death, not the only case. Natally alienated individuals are born without certain basic social and cultural connections. The connections Thomas cites are with a culture, language, history, traditions, rituals, social practices, and the like. He seems not to be thinking of immediate family and community ties, ties that individuals have to other particular individuals. Thomas finds members of an ethnic group natally alienated when the cultural practices into which they are born "forcibly prevent most of them from fully participating in, and thus having a secure knowledge of, their historical-cultural traditions" (Thomas 1993, p. 150). He notes that after seven generations of slavery, memories of one's ancestral culture are totally lost, which is plausible.

Patterson, however, describes natal alienation as "the loss of ties of birth in both ascending and descending generations." He continues, "It also has the important nuance of a loss of native status, of deracination." Natally alienated slaves are without socially supported ties to either parents or children and without "attachment to groups or localities other than those chosen … by the master" (Patterson 1982, p. 7). The "socially supported" part is important. Slaves do form bonds with parents and children, supported by other slaves. But there is little stability in support by slaves who are powerless to prevent the break-up of families by owners.

Patterson used the term "natal alienation" for the extreme case of being born to social death, with individual socially supported connections, past and future, cut off at the very outset of life from all but one's oppressors. Hereditary slavery as practiced in slave-holding states of the US through most of the nineteenth century yields a paradigm of natal alienation in this sense. Slaves kidnapped from Africa were ripped from their families and cultures, and chained with others who spoke diverse languages. Their social vitality was immediately and severely reduced, but they were not natally alienated. Their descendants were *born* to social death (natally alienated). As a consequence of being cut off from kin, slaves lose cultural ties and heritage.[15] But the first step is to destroy ties with family and community, to ex-communicate them from society, as Patterson puts it (Patterson 1982, p. 5). In Rawlsian terms, slaves are first excluded from the benefits and protections of the institutions that form the basic structure of the society into which they are born or thrown and in the context of which they can look forward to living out their lives (see Rawls 1999a, pp. 6–10 on "the basic structure of society"). Loss of cultural heritage follows. Natal alienation might be a clue to descent from genocide survivors (although not proof, insofar as genocide depends also on intent).

Thomas recognizes that alienation is not "all or nothing." A lost cultural heritage can be rediscovered, or partially recovered, later or in other places. Those who were alienated from some cultures may become somewhat integrated into others. Still, he denies that the Holocaust natally alienated Jews *from Judaism* as slaves were natally alienated from African religions and cultures "because the central tenets of Judaism – the defining traditions of Judaism – endured in spite of Hitler's every intention to the contrary" (Thomas 1993, p. 153).

The question, however, should be not simply whether the traditions survived but whether individual Jewish victims were able to sustain their connections to those traditions. Sustaining the connections meaningfully requires a family or community setting for observance. Many Jews escaped social death because of where they lived (in the US or Australia for example) and because the Axis powers were contained and defeated. Those who escaped were able to maintain Jewish traditions with which survivors might conceivably connect or reconnect. But many were unable to connect or reconnect with Jewish traditions. Some found family members after the war. Some created new families. Many did not. Many lost entire families, their entire villages, and the way of life embodied in the shtetl (village). Some could not produce children because of atrocities performed on them in the camps. Many survivors lost access to communal memories embodied in such cultural institutions as libraries and synagogues.

Responding to the observation that entire communities of Jews were destroyed and that the Yiddish language is on the way out, Thomas argues that members of those communities were destroyed not "as such" (not as

---

[15] At least, they lose a *knowledge* of their ties to a cultural heritage. That they may nevertheless continue to observe traditions the origins of which they are unaware is suggested by the case of the descendants of crypto-Jews (Jews forced into secrecy by the Inquisition) in southwestern states of the US who have only recently discovered that some of their customs have Jewish origins and meanings. The lack of socially protected stability in slave families makes it less likely that ancestral customs would have been as well-preserved among slaves in the US.

shtetl Jews, for example) but more simply "as Jews," and that the entire community of Jews was not destroyed.[16] He concludes that "the question must be whether the Holocaust was natally alienating of Jews as such, without regard to any specific community of Jews" (Thomas 1993, p. 153). Yet, social vitality for individuals comes mainly through the specific communities to which they belong, which determine the languages they speak and many of the traditions they observe. Indigenous Americans may have been murdered by killers who saw only "Indians," not Iroquois, Sauk, or Arapaho. But survivors of massacred tribes experienced social death even though other tribes (other "Indians") survived.

Some European Jews survived the Holocaust only by passing as Christians. Passing can yield a degraded social vitality. Hidden children taken in by strangers and raised to be Christians sometimes discovered their Jewish heritage only later, if at all. If survivors are welcomed into the societies in which they survive, Thomas does not consider them alienated. Even those who pass as members of another religion need not be entirely socially dead, despite alienation from their religion of origin. Still, if they were originally connected in a vital way with their inherited religion and they then experience no vital connection to the new one, they do suffer a degree of social death. For those who survive physically, knowledge and memory of what is lost are insufficient for social vitality. Those who cannot participate in social forms they remember do not have vitality through them but only the memory of it. Further, from 1933 to 1945 Jewish children in Europe were born to a condition that became progressively more *natally* alienating. Contrary to the apparent implication of Thomas's view, social death seems to me central to the Nazi's Final Solution, at least as important to what is evil about it as the mass physical murder and physical torture.

Genocide not only intentionally strips individuals of the ability to participate in social relationships, activities, and traditions, it aims to destroy the possibility of those particular kinds of relationships, activities, and traditions for others in the future. The question was raised in chapter 4 whether evils done to ethnic groups which lack the kind of internal structure that enables a group to act as a group are always best understood only in terms of the harm suffered by individuals in virtue of their group membership. For the most part, that is how I have interpreted the harm of genocide. I have interpreted it as harm to individuals considered as members of groups. And yet, for groups that transcend their current members in both temporal directions, as nations and ethnic groups do, the harm

---

[16] It is commonly estimated that roughly two-thirds of European Jews were killed.

of genocide is not entirely reducible to harms done to the members of one generation. The only *members* who can be harmed are those living now. The dead can no longer be harmed (or, if Aristotle is right, not enough to make the difference between a good life and a bad one; Aristotle 1925, pp. 22–23), and potential members cannot be harmed yet. The very potentiality for future members can be destroyed, but the only *members* harmed by that destruction are current members.

If it is granted that the group, considered as an entity that spans many generations and has the potentiality for many more, can be harmed in ways that are not reducible to harm to its living members, does that harm to the group have ethical significance? Can it be intolerable? An evil? Has the group a vitality of its own that is not reducible to the vitality of its living members? This kind of question returns in the next and final chapter.

CHAPTER 10

Genocide by forced impregnation

How can rape, forced pregnancy, and resultant childbirths, the
production of new persons, be genocide, the annihilation of a
people? (Allen 1996, p. 92)

I. A PARADOX

It was argued in chapter 6 that rape can be terrorist and in chapter 8 that it
can be torture. Drawing on the understanding of genocide as social death,
this chapter examines the idea that mass rape, even when aimed at forced
pregnancy and births, can be a strategy of genocide. It is not difficult to see
how rape can be a terrorist practice and at the same time torture. It may be
less obvious that mass rape can be genocidal, especially when it is aimed at
mass impregnation. International documents mention rape explicitly as a
violation of human rights. The Fourth Geneva Convention of 1949 states,
"Women shall be especially protected against any attack on their honour,
in particular against rape, enforced prostitution, or any form of indecent
assault" (Human Rights Watch 1996, p. 30, n. 46). The International
Committee of the Red Cross (ICRC) considers rape to be among the grave
breaches specified by that convention (Human Rights Watch 1996, p. 30,
n. 46). In 1995 Justice Richard Goldstone, Prosecutor for the International
Criminal Tribunal for the Former Yugoslavia (ICTY), affirmed that rape
can constitute torture (Human Rights Watch 1996, p. 32). The ICTY
at The Hague and the International Criminal Tribunal for Rwanda
(ICTR) at Arusha explicitly include rape among crimes against humanity
(Gutman and Rieff 1999, p. 108). War rape is clearly on record as a violation of International Humanitarian Law (IHL). But the 1948 United
Nations Genocide Convention does not mention rape or forced pregnancy
in its list of acts that can be committed with genocidal intent.

In a short but powerful book, *Rape Warfare: The Hidden Genocide in
Bosnia-Herzegovina and Croatia*, Beverly Allen, teacher of languages and

literature at Syracuse University, argues that several rape policies employed by Serb military forces in the early 1990s wars in Bosnia-Herzegovina and Croatia are genocidal (Allen 1996). Allen learned of the rape/death camps in Bosnia-Herzegovina and Croatia from a former student, a woman of Croatian descent, who showed her translations of testimonies of dozens of Bosnian and Croatian women who had survived two things: "*rape/death camps* and what we later came to recognize as *genocidal rape*" (Allen 1996, p. xi). One of the Serbian policies was to enforce pregnancies resulting from the rape of Muslim women by Serb soldiers. Women were raped until they became pregnant, held prisoner until abortion was no longer safe, and then released.

It struck Allen initially as ludicrous that Serbs could try to "kill off the Bosnian-Herzegovinian and Croatian peoples by producing more of them, by fathering babies." "The equation, more babies equals genocide," she writes, "is a glaring example of faulty logic" (Allen 1996, p. xiii). That equation is at least paradoxical. To dispel the paradox, she imaginatively reconstructs a reasoning process and its assumptions, by which Serb officers might have concluded that they were forcing Muslim women to have Serbian children. Yet, she realizes that this belief does not make good sense, given the children's dual biological ancestry and the cultural upbringing awaiting those who survive. More interesting than how Serb officers might have reasoned is the question of how their policy could in fact *be* genocidal. What they thought is relevant to whether they had genocidal intent. Yet, not everything they thought is to the point. The paradox that most basically troubles Allen is captured in the question heading this chapter. How could a policy of mass rape aimed at producing new persons *be* genocidal?

Allen's paradox calls for further clarification of the concept of genocide and consideration of how any kind of mass rape policy can be genocidal. Drawing on Raphael Lemkin's understanding of genocide, which differs from that of the UN Genocide Convention, and building on Allen's insight that rape aimed at enforced pregnancy uses sperm as a weapon of biological warfare, this chapter concludes that the paradoxical Serb rape policy could indeed be part of a genocidal plan, and that in order to make the case, there is no need to rely on the idea that Serb policy-makers or rapists might have thought they were producing Serbian children.

2. THE BRANA PLAN FOR ETHNIC CLEANSING

There is good evidence that Serb policies of systematic rape had a military intent. That intent was to force Muslims to leave Bosnia. Allen's research supports and corroborates testimonies and reports to that effect that were offered a few years earlier in Alexandra Stiglmayer's *Mass Rape: The War against Women in Bosnia-Herzegovina* (Stiglmayer 1994). Allen bases her own report on accounts by Italian journalists who saw photographs of minutes of meetings at which documents were ratified that set out plans known as the Ram plan and the Brana plan. She names officers who authored the plans (Allen 1996, p. 56). "Ram," she writes, means "loom," "thus the Serb military policy will weave its way from many angles across Bosnia and Croatia." "Brana," she writes, means "dam," "thus, the Serb military policy will 'dam up' the Muslim population, keep it elsewhere" (pp. 57–58). She quotes journalist Giuseppe Zaccaria, who summarized the minutes of a meeting of Serb army officers in a Belgrade suburb in 1991, noting that the officers adopted an explicit policy in the Brana plan to target women and children as the most vulnerable part of the Muslim religious and social structure. He quotes from the minutes of that meeting:

Our analysis of the behavior of the Muslim communities demonstrates that the morale, will, and bellicose nature of their groups can be undermined *only if we aim our action at the point where the religious and social structure is most fragile. We refer to the women, especially adolescents, and to the children.* Decisive intervention on these social figures would spread confusion among the communities, thus causing first of all fear and then panic, leading to a probable [Muslim] retreat from the territories involved in war activity. (Allen 1996, p. 57; the emphasis and brackets are Allen's)

That military officers endorsed this plan is a basis for distinguishing the Serbian rapes – morally, politically, and militarily – from retaliatory rapes committed by Bosnians and others. Not all war rapes are authorized or committed with the same intent. Not all aim, as policy, to undermine the "morale, will, and bellicose nature" of a target group. Some are revenge. Some are permitted as rewards for soldiers or encouraged for bonding among soldiers. Yet it may not be clear that the aim described at the meeting, which was to undermine the will to fight in Bosnian Muslims and thereby cause a probable *retreat*, is actually genocidal.

What did Serbian officers mean when they identified children and women, especially adolescents, as the most vulnerable point in the social and religious structures of Muslim communities? Two answers suggest themselves. The simplest and most obvious is that women and children are usually unarmed. They are probably not trained to fight. They are vulnerable in that they could not put up much effective resistance. But, then, why would the officers say, "especially adolescents"? One might expect adolescents to be better able to put up resistance than younger children or older women. And why would Serb officers locate this fragility of Muslim communities in its "religious and social structure"? A more complex answer to the question of why the vulnerability of Muslim communities was identified in this way is that the relevant vulnerable point was, first of all, the religious and social concerns of Muslim men for the women and children of their families, especially their concerns for adolescent women not yet married (presumed virgins). The entire community was vulnerable to being manipulated through these concerns. Adolescent women were an especially vulnerable part of the community. They had something to lose that was considered precious to the future of the community. They were no doubt vulnerable in the first sense as well. That is, they were probably also for the most part unarmed and relatively untrained in physical defense.

Allen identifies three forms that the Serbian army mass rapes took in three different kinds of localities. In the first locale, military forces "enter a village, take several women of varying ages from their homes, rape them in public view, and depart." Several days later, soldiers from the army "arrive and offer the now-terrified residents safe passage away from the village on the condition they never return" (Allen 1996, pp. vii, 62). In the second locale, persons held in "concentration camps are chosen at random to be raped, often as part of torture preceding death" (Allen 1996, p. 63). These tortures and murders are used to terrorize. In the third locale, women are imprisoned in rape/death camps and raped "systematically for extended periods of time" either as torture preceding death or as torture leading to forced pregnancy. Pregnant victims are then "raped consistently until such time as their pregnancies have progressed beyond the possibility of a safe abortion," at which time they are released (Allen 1996, pp. vii, 62). This last case, with the goal of pregnancies that will come full term and yield births, gives rise to Allen's paradox. "Genocidal rape aimed at enforced pregnancy," she writes, "would seem to be a peculiarly Serb contribution to the history of atrocity" (Allen 1996, p. 92).

Serbian military officers understood the Brana plan as ethnic cleansing. That use of the term "cleansing" is grating. Masking a dirty project with the word "cleansing" is a perfect instance of Orwellian "doublethink" (Orwell 1949) or code in the spirit of Nazi language rules, like "Final Solution," "Special Treatment," and "Resettlement in the East" (Arendt 1965, p. 85). As James W. Nickel notes, "In principle, ethnic cleansing could proceed by paying all of the members a group enough money to induce them to emigrate" (Jokić 2001, p. 166). (Has that ever been done?) "Ethnic homogeneity enforced by violence" is a more honest description of actual practice. But "ethnic cleansing" has already entered reference works and seems here to stay.

Nickel distinguishes ethnic cleansing of a territory from expulsive secession, "which moves the border rather than the people and thus abandons the territory" (Jokić 2001, p. 166). In ethnic cleansing, borders remain the same, but people are expelled. Reluctantly, Nickel entertains the possibility of justifiable ethnic cleansing, renamed "forced relocation," when it is "carried out to achieve the goal of ... peace through ethnic partition" (Jokić 2001, p. 167). I share Nickel's reluctance. Even "forced relocation" calls to mind the ethnic cleansing of the western coastal states of the US during WW II when Japanese immigrants, residents, and citizens were put into designated camps, called "relocation camps."

Of the term "ethnic cleansing" Catharine MacKinnon writes, "This is a euphemism for genocide" (Stiglmayer 1994, p. 73). "Ethnic cleansing" is certainly a euphemism. But is it a euphemism for genocide? Perhaps MacKinnon was not generalizing but only commenting on the Serbian case. Nickel recognizes both genocidal and non-genocidal forms of ethnic cleansing but regards a policy as non-genocidal if it does not aim at mass killing. On the understanding of genocide proposed in chapter 9, a policy is genocidal if it aims at destroying (or foreseeably destroys) an ethnic, national, religious, or other appropriately defined group. If that can be done without mass killing, then ethnic cleansing by means of expulsion can, in principle, also be genocidal. There was also mass killing of Bosnian Muslims. But were the rape policies aimed at ethnic cleansing part of a genocide?

A 1993 report to the Security Council by the UN Commission of Experts defines "ethnic cleansing" as "rendering an area ethnically homogenous by using force or intimidation to remove persons of given groups from the area" (Gutman and Rieff 1999, p. 136). Its characteristic method is terror created through "killing, destruction, threat, and humiliation" (Gutman and Rieff 1999, p. 136). Removal of an ethnic group from a territory need not be genocidal if there is a decent chance that those expelled will survive to become re-established as basically the same group at other locations. Many Jews expelled by Christian rulers from Western Europe between the end of the thirteenth century and the end of the fifteenth migrated to new lands, from North Africa to the Middle East, Poland, even China, where they established communities that endured for centuries, some to the present day. Many also died during those expulsions, much was lost, and the communities altered in becoming embedded in new cultural contexts.

Abstractly considered, it would seem that destroying a group goes beyond expelling it. But the process of expulsion can be highly destructive, depending on such factors as what those expelled are permitted to take, how much time they are allowed to sell immovable property (if allowed to sell) and to pack belongings, as well as such further matters as travel conditions, available routes, modes of transport, and whether they have protection while traveling or, on the contrary, are vulnerable, as the Armenians were in 1915, to murder, even planned mass murders, and to lethal environmental conditions.[1]

Spain's expulsions of the Jews in 1492 and later of the Moriscos, a Muslim group, in 1609 are not commonly cited by historians as genocides. Yet many Spanish Jews and many of the Moriscos were in fact killed during these purges. Entire communities were destroyed. There is a good case for regarding these purges as ethnically, not just religiously, motivated, despite the possibilities held out to some for conversion (Netanyahu 2001; Lea 1901). Conversion was a precarious choice during the Inquisition, which zealously sniffed out heretics and extracted confessions under torture.

And so questions arise regarding the characterization of any of the Serbian rape policies as genocidal. If the point was to intimidate Muslim populations into leaving Bosnia, are those policies any more genocidal than Spain's expulsions of the Moriscos and earlier the Jews? Or, are *all* of these policies genocidal? The expulsions of the Armenians are commonly so regarded today by most genocide scholars, including Lemkin, and by almost everyone else except, formally, the governments of Turkey and (at the time of writing) the US. Allen does not take up this issue. Her focus is the enforced pregnancy policy. But an answer to the question of how forcible expulsion and mass rape aimed at expulsion can be genocidal is helpful for answering the question how rape aimed at enforced pregnancy can be.

3. HOW CAN EXPULSION AND MASS RAPE AIMED AT EXPULSION BE GENOCIDAL?

Allen characterizes as genocidal all three of the forms of military rape that she describes and claims they fit the definition of the 1948 UN Genocide Convention. Yet it is not clear that they do fit under any of the acts enumerated in that convention's definition. Recall that the convention defined genocide as "any of the following acts committed with the intent to destroy, in whole, or in part, a nation, ethnical, racial or religious group, as

---

[1] Nickel notes these factors that complicate expulsions as elements that make a particular ethnic cleansing wrong. But he does not regard the expulsions as genocidal as long as they fall short of mass killing. For a history of the Armenian genocide, see Balakian (2003).

such: (a) killing members of the group; (b) causing serious bodily or mental harm to members of the group; (c) deliberately inflicting on the group conditions of life calculated to bring about its physical destruction in whole or in part; (d) imposing measures intended to prevent births within the group; (e) forcibly transferring children of the group to another group" (Charny 1999, vol. ii, p. 578). So worded, the definition does not require that the intent succeed in destroying a group, even in part. Yet intolerable harm can be done if any of the enumerated acts is carried out. Any committed with the requisite intent is sufficient to ground a charge of genocide. The definition does not say explicitly that these are the only acts that might ground that charge. But neither does it provide a general principled way to identify other acts that might do so.

Invoking the UN definition, Allen asserts that "All forms of genocidal rape constitute the crime of genocide as described in Article II of the 1948 United Nations Convention on the Prevention and Punishment of the Crime of Genocide" (Allen 1996, pp. viii, 63). There certainly were many killings of Muslims (clause (a)). Rapes by Serbs caused mental and bodily harm to surviving Muslim women and girls (clause (b)). But were those rapes committed with the intent to destroy, in whole or in part, Bosnian Muslims as a group? Put that way, the Brana plan seems very close to clause (c), "deliberately inflicting on the group conditions of life calculated to bring about its physical destruction in whole or in part." The Brana plan aimed deliberately to inflict conditions of life calculated to "spread confusion among the communities" (Allen 1996, p. 57, quoting the minutes of the meeting of Serb officers), to demoralize and destroy the will to fight, and to motivate flight.

But was the intent of the Brana plan to *destroy* Bosnian Muslims as a group? Or was it the more limited project of *expelling* them and undermining their will to fight? If the destruction of a group is a clearly foreseeable consequence of measures taken to disable and expel, it will not quite do to say that destruction was unintended. The definition could, and I think should, be revised to accommodate that point. Instead of saying simply "with intent to destroy, in whole or in part," that definition could be revised to say "either with intent to destroy, or with the reasonably foreseeable consequence of destroying, in whole or in part, a nation, ethnical, racial or religious group."[2] Whether such a revision would be an

---

[2] Such a revision would be the simplest way to indicate, without getting into controversies over the meaning of "intent," that reasonably foreseeable consequences willingly brought about can be culpably genocidal.

improvement is one of the controversies that surround the convention's definition of genocide.

But *is* it reasonably foreseeable that dispersal, demoralization, and confusion will result in physical destruction of the group? "Physical destruction" sounds to many readers (for example, to genocide scholar and sociologist Helen Fein) like mass murder or massive interference with biological reproduction (Hinton 2002, pp. 74–90). There were mass murders; mass graves have been excavated. But the definition recognizes explicitly other ways to destroy a community physically than by killing or hindering biological reproduction. That recognition opens the door to acknowledging still other factors that can contribute to such destruction. When a nation forcibly expels a group rapidly, it inevitably forces the group to abandon significant property. Those forced to flee may never be able to recreate the physical bases of their communities or reconstruct institutions and historical and other public records that defined so much of their communal life, all of which require a material basis. That has been the predicament of many expelled groups, including the Armenians, the Moriscos, and the expelled Spanish Jews. That kind of loss deeply erodes the life of the group.

Is just anything, then, that erodes the life of a group genocidal? Or must the destruction be of a certain degree, extent, or of particular sorts? A helpful way to approach that issue is found in Lemkin's work. In his 1944 book *Axis Rule in Occupied Europe*, Lemkin understands the term "genocide" ordinarily "to signify *a coordinated plan* of different actions aiming at the destruction of essential foundations of the life of national groups, with the aim of annihilating the groups themselves" (Lemkin 1944, p. 79; emphasis mine). Elsewhere in *Axis Rule* he adds racial or ethnic and religious groups as potential targets of genocide. Most genocides, he notes, do not happen overnight. The coordinated plan and the different actions to which Lemkin refers are implemented in stages by many agents.

Lemkin's approach strikes me as differing from that of the Genocide Convention in a significant respect. Unlike the convention, Lemkin does not understand genocide as consisting in any of a set of enumerable acts, *each* of which might have the intent to destroy a group "in whole or in part." Rather, Lemkin understands genocide as an overarching *plan*, and it is to the plan, rather than to specific kinds of action taken to implement it, that the requisite intent attaches. If the plan and its implementation are collective, so is the relevant intent. Genocide takes place over a period of time, utilizing many techniques that together – like the many procedures of interrogation applied to detainees at the dark sites – produce an intolerably harmful effect. That effect can be an intended destruction of a group. Activities that further such a plan take their genocidal character from that of the plan to which they contribute. Thus, military rape as a weapon can become genocidal when it is part of or foreseeably contributes to a larger plan that has a genocidal aim. The question then becomes how it can make such a contribution. Why would mass rape not threaten to undermine rather than contribute to such a plan, at least when victims are not systematically murdered after they are raped?

Lemkin enumerates and discusses several techniques of genocide under the headings of the political, social, economic, biological, physical, religious, and moral. These are what he means by "the essential foundations of the life of national groups" that a genocidal plan aims to destroy (Lemkin 1944, p. 79). He illustrates each of these kinds of techniques with Hitler's actual policies in various countries of occupied Europe (Lemkin 1944, pp. 79–90). A genocidal plan, as he understands it, might be put into effect more or less fully. Thus, Lemkin recognizes degrees and stages of genocide. Understood against the background of Lemkin's discussion, "in whole or in part" in the UN definition of genocide might be construed to refer not basically to the *portion of a group* that is affected, which is how it is generally interpreted and may have been the convention's intent. More fundamentally, and more plausibly, "in whole or in part" could be taken to refer to the "essential foundations" that Lemkin cites, dimensions along which the group is attacked – political, social, economic, biological, physical, religious, and moral dimensions – and to the stages of a genocidal plan that include such dimensions. When these foundations of the life of a group are attacked ("in whole or in part"), members of the group generally, not just a larger or smaller portion of it, can be expected to suffer.

A critic may wonder whether Lemkin's approach is too loose. Is that approach, which recognizes non-homicidal genocidal policies, in danger of counting too much as genocidal and thereby lessening the special moral gravity of the concept of genocide? What is the role in genocide of intentional mass killings? On the point about killing, Lemkin is less than clear. His motivation for including as genocidal many acts not themselves homicidal seems to be to enable intervention before matters reach the stage of mass killing, to identify a genocide-in-the-making and stop the process before it is too late. Yet the question remains whether mass killing is necessarily even the end point of a genocidal trajectory. Must a genocidal multistage process have an *intended*, even reasonably foreseeable, termination in mass killing?

Fein worries about metaphorical uses of the term "genocide" and complains that the concept is in danger of becoming banalized by being applied to such things as race-mixing (Hinton 2002, p. 74). She argues that we should distinguish genocide from non-genocidal assimilation, even when assimilation is forcibly imposed. She points out that Hitler's plans for peoples who were genetically related to Germans (such as the Dutch, Luxembourgers, and Norwegians) differed significantly from his plans for non-Germanic peoples (such as Poles and Jews) (Hinton 2002, pp. 76–77). She regards the plans for German-related peoples as *not* genocidal on the grounds that they involved an assimilationist policy of "Germanizing" through the imposition of techniques that Lemkin calls political, social, and economic, and through such cultural measures as requiring the speaking of German and prohibiting the teaching of other languages in the schools. In contrast, Hitler regarded Poles and Jews as un-Germanizable. Only their soil, he said, could be Germanized, not the people.

Lemkin, however, regards "Germanizing" as a euphemism for a "functional aspect of the main generic notion of genocide" (Lemkin 1944, p. 80). Germanizing fits what he regards as the second of a two-phase genocidal process. "Genocide has two phases," he writes, "one, destruction of the national pattern of the oppressed group; the other, the imposition of the national pattern of the oppressor. This imposition, in turn, may be made upon the oppressed population which is allowed to remain, or upon the territory alone, after removal of the population and the colonization of the area by the oppressor's own nationals" (Lemkin 1944, p. 79). On this view of genocide, the Dutch under the Nazi occupation were targets of non-homicidal genocide. In pondering whether Lemkin's or Fein's is a better way to understand genocide, the question naturally arises once again: what is at stake in the insistence that genocides have a mass homicidal intent? Is there an underlying assumption that non-homicidal policies are less extreme or that they do less harm? I return to that issue after a closer look at "in whole or in part" and two ways to interpret that phrase.

4. "IN WHOLE OR IN PART"

The question of possible overinclusiveness arises for the Genocide Convention's definition not only in regard to the five kinds of non-homicidal acts that it lists but also in regard to the words "in whole or in part." These words are commonly understood (for example, by the US Congress in its ratification) to refer to a portion or the whole of the target *population*. On that interpretation, individual members are parts of all of the groups to which they belong. Any intentional killing of even a single individual destroys part of all those groups. Of course, not all intentional killing is motivated by hostility based on the victim's group identity. Killings that do not target victims based on their group identity would not be intended to destroy a group even in part. But if all killings that do target victims based on their group identity are admitted to be instances of the destruction of a group "in part," then, it appears that on a very literal reading of the UN definition, all hate crime murders are genocidal acts. That result is overinclusive. It does risk banalizing the concept of genocide. Hence, the question arises how large the part must be for harm to a group to count as genocidal. Ten percent (literally, decimating)? Twenty? Fifty? More than fifty percent?

To avoid overinclusiveness and also to avoid having to draw an inevitably arbitrary line, the US Congress and others have interpreted "in part" as "in substantial part." "In substantial part" seems to mean "a substantial portion of the group." One or a few hate crime murders, then, would not be a genocide. Vagueness, of course, remains in the term "substantial," and that is deliberate. That vagueness has been exploited politically by countries that choose not to get involved, as the US chose not to get involved in 1994 during the massive killings in Rwanda. The plea of ignorance of how many were being killed makes sense of the claim that it was not clear that what was occurring there was a genocide if "in part" is read as "in substantial part," meaning a large portion of the group. It appears that what persuaded many that Rwanda was indeed the site of a genocide were the sheer numbers of Tutsis and moderate Hutus murdered by Hutu extremists, which ranged from 500,000 by the estimates of Human Rights Watch to 800,000 or more by the estimates of the UN (Landesman 2002, p. 85).

In contrast, what we might call "the Lemkin approach" (even though Lemkin did not participate in drawing up the Genocide Convention) need not have mass killings even as an intended termination point. Lemkin's approach suggests interpreting "in whole or in part" not in terms of numbers killed but in terms of the many essential foundations of the life of the group (economic, political, religious, and so forth) that are seriously eroded or destroyed. A genocide, then, substantially destroys ties that bind individuals into a people, including the kinds of ties that tend to outlive individual members and give meaning and shape to the group. The intended termination of a genocidal plan is the destruction of a people as a people, as its foundations are ruined, with a concomitant destruction of social vitality in the lives of survivors. Massive enough killings suffice. But they are not always necessary.

So understood, the target of a genocidal plan is not simply a population. The target is, more specifically, the *ties* – economic, political, religious, and so forth – that turn a population into a community or a people. These relationships require activities that genocidal plans prohibit or make impossible, typically in an escalating fashion, until little if any social activity remains. As the process goes on, the lives of individuals contract, although the population may not. Capacities for interaction atrophy. What remains approaches a living death, at least, social death.

There is a certain ambiguity in the concept of social death. Does "social death" refer to the death of a social *group*? Or to the destruction of social vitality in its *members*? Is there, ultimately, a difference? And if so, does the death of a social group matter, to the extent that it is not reducible to the destruction of social vitality in its members? These issues were encountered at the end of chapter 9, where I deferred further discussion to this chapter. They are relevant to the question of whether non-homicidal destruction of a group is less harmful than mass homicides would have been. Worries about banalizing the concept of genocide suggest that the idea that non-homicidal measures are less harmful is what motivates the insistence by Fein, Nickel, and others that genocides are necessarily homicidal.

In chapter 9 I noted that, because the only group members who can be harmed are the living (not potential members, who may never exist, and not past members who no longer live), when a group's history and potentialities transcend the lives of its current members, the harm done in the destruction of that group is not reducible to effects on its current members. By destruction of a group's history I do not mean, of course, the destruction of past facts. I have in mind, rather, the destruction or gross distortion of records and representations of the group's past. Appeal to the loss of substantial histories and potentialities is a factor that distinguishes genocides in which the group destroyed is a well-established nation or ethnic group with long and rich cultural traditions from the slaughter of political groups and of gay communities. It is at least partly on the basis of that distinction that some would resist the idea that political groups and gay communities are among the kinds of groups against which genocide can be committed. On the family resemblance approach to the concept of genocide, it is at least a reason for regarding those groups as outside the "immediate family," outside the paradigm instances.

But, then, one may wonder, does the destruction of the histories and potentialities of an ethnic group have any ethical import independently of how it affects the living? Arendt argued that genocide is not only a crime against a particular human group but "a crime against mankind," which violates "an altogether different order and an altogether different community" (Arendt 1965, p. 272). The living who are affected are not only members of the group against whom a genocide is perpetrated. Destruction of an ethnic group harms humanity more generally. But how are we to understand the humanity that is harmed? Is it only a community of the living? Humanity, like an ethnic group, also has histories and potentialities. Some of those are destroyed when an ethnic group is destroyed. Insofar as those histories and potentialities are not simply distributable to living individuals, can their destruction be intolerable? An evil? Do ethnic groups have lives of their own? Does humanity?

Humanity is not just a community of living human beings but a species. Perhaps ethnic groups are like ecosystems (and species) in that although they are not exactly living beings, they are living systems. They have amazing resilience. Perhaps ethnic groups could be regarded as a kind of ecosystem. Although humanity can and continually does survive the murder (and other disappearances) of ethnic groups (and of ecosystems of many kinds), it seems in principle possible that some such murders could be such that humanity would be unable to recover, or unable to recover at a decent level. The inexcusable infliction of such a loss would be a very great evil, and the harm that is partly constitutive of it would not be capturable by what the individuals of any single generation suffer. Even the inexcusable infliction of a loss that was very substantial, although not so severe that humanity would be unable to recover, might be a very great evil. It could result in the social death of groups as developing agents in a global community. That could be a worse evil than a particular homicidal genocide.

Still, I do not rely on the idea of the death of a group as something distinct from the destruction of social vitality in its members in order to make the case that genocide is social death, that it need not be homicidal, and that a non-homicidal genocide can be worse for those who survive it than a homicidal genocide would have been. But it remains to clarify how social death can be a greater harm than physiological death for the individual. To do so, it is helpful to consider, first, how Lemkin's approach to the idea of genocide provides natural ways to distinguish between genocidal and non-genocidal hate crimes and between genocidal and non-genocidal cultural assimilations. The two concluding sections of this chapter consider more fully how the non-homicidal genocidal assaults of the rape-aimed-at-enforced-pregnancy policy could be more harmful to individual victims than a massively homicidal genocide might have been.

5. HATE CRIMES AND ASSIMILATIONS

On what I call "the Lemkin approach" to understanding "in whole or in part," there is still room for dispute about whether an assault on the ties that define a community or a people rises to the level of genocide and about what the intent of the assault is.[3] Degrees of genocide, on the Lemkin approach, are determined by the depth, extent, and irreparability of the degradation and destruction of the social and cultural foundations of the group. The genocidal significance of mass murders is determined by their impact on those foundations.

Hate crime murders are easily terrorist, and many are also tortures. But they do not, as a rule, specifically target communal ties. They are less likely to be part of an overarching plan for destroying a group. Many simply target individuals, arbitrarily selected as representative of a group, with the object of intimidating others into keeping a low profile or staying out of certain geographical (or cultural) areas. Many are one-off crimes expressive of hatred. The 1998 murder of twenty-one-year-old gay university student Matthew Shepard in Laramie, Wyoming did not specifically target the ties that constitute a gay community. But it may have deterred members of gay communities from patronizing the bar where Shepard encountered his murderers. And it could have been intended to keep them away.[4]

Not even all mass murders and expulsions motivated by hatred of groups have the power to strip victims of the social identities that give meaning to their lives and would ordinarily give meaning to their deaths. The 9/11 bombings and the Oklahoma City bombing lacked that power. Those who would maintain that the Spanish expulsions of the Moriscos and the Jews or the Turkish expulsions of the Armenians were not genocidal could be expected to hold that these expulsions did not foreseeably destroy or substantially degrade the economic, political, and other social relationships that defined and animated those groups, that they did not foreseeably rob group members and their descendants of social identities that for centuries had given meaning and shape to the lives of Jews, Muslims, or Armenians. Conversely, those who would maintain that these expulsions *were* genocidal could be expected to argue that indeed they did.

---

[3] Although I refer to Lemkin's approach to genocide, I here refer to "the Lemkin approach" to "in whole or in part," rather than "Lemkin's approach" because I am not aware that Lemkin ever explicitly commented on the words "in whole or in part" in the convention's definition. He was not a part of that convention, although he was greatly influential in bringing it about.

[4] For the story of Matt Shepard's murder and the aftermath, see Loffreda (2000).

Fein's worry about distinguishing genocide from cultural assimilation or race-mixing points to a continuing philosophical problem for definitions of genocide that do not make homicide essential to that concept. Assimilation of groups through voluntary intermarriage results in destruction of the groups *as they were originally*. Does that mean that, in the language of the Genocide Convention, each is destroyed "as such"? Even if assimilation is forced by one group on another, as in the case of the Sabine women (Livy 1960, pp. 27–32), if the assimilation is successful, people do not become socially dead. If a forced assimilation is implemented with some respect for individuals (as in Livy's recounting of the treatment of the Sabine women), social vitality need not be a casualty. Multiple histories and potentialities might conceivably become integrated with an enriched result all around. In that case, everyone changes and "assimilation" is a misleading term, insofar as it suggests one-sidedness. But the issue remains. There is not a double genocide here if social vitality is not a casualty of the process. Such possibilities distinguish the idea of cultural mixing, even if imposed, from that of genocide. Social identities change. But cultural histories and potentialities might, in principle, be enhanced, not diminished. Such is, of course, the rhetoric of the "melting pot" in the US.

And yet, forced assimilation is often not successful. It does not always leave members of both groups with new forms of social vitality. Nickel notes this fact and uses it to argue against the practice of forced assimilation. To the argument that it is only natural for cultures to change as people mingle together, he responds with impeccable logic that this fact "does not make forced assimilation or deliberate cultural destruction permissible, any more than the fact that it is normal and natural for humans to die makes murder permissible" (Jokić 2001, p. 169). But he continues to regard forced assimilation as non-genocidal when it is unaccompanied by mass slaughter.

Yet, what is wrong with forced assimilation is not simply that it is often unsuccessful. The intended result has sometimes been only a partial assimilation to produce a subservient class, as when the stolen generations of mixed-race Australian Aboriginal children were trained for service to Australians of European descent.[5] The film *Rabbit-Proof Fence* (2002) gives a brief view of this process in a school to which the kidnapped children were sent for such training. Further, the self-perceptions of many do not

---

[5] The 2007 UN Declaration on the Rights of Indigenous Peoples condemns such practices (www. un.org/esa/socdev/unpfii/en/drip.html).

track the change in their socially perceived identities. As with expulsion, much can depend on how the assimilation proceeds, whether it is resisted, and if it is resisted, how resistance is met, and so forth. Transportation and re-education of children of an oppressed group might have as an intended goal a more thorough-going assimilation than that of children of the stolen generations in Australia. But if children are prohibited from speaking their native language and communicating with their families of origin, instead of enabled to become bilingual and to maintain and enrich their family connections, the oppressive tactics could be stages in a genocidal plan for the groups into which they were born. Not all members of the group are transported, only the children. Parents, grandparents, and others from whom the children are kidnapped are left with radically diminished social vitality and no hope for the future. Of those transported, some individuals may assimilate successfully. Many do not. Those not successfully assimilated whose efforts at resistance are also unsuccessful, as is largely the case for the protagonist of the film *Rabbit-Proof Fence* (2002), suffer a loss of social meaning to their lives, which they may be unable to replace with new meanings that would happily reinvigorate their lives. A common result of forced assimilation is to leave victims and their descendants feeling with good cause that they belong nowhere. It is not obvious that they are harmed less than they would have been by a genocidal slaughter. It can be better to die with self-respect and dignity than to live without them, if there is no hope of their recovery.

The case of forced assimilation shows that Lemkin's more complex approach to the concept of genocide is not so generous that it banalizes the concept. The idea of social death is implicit in his understanding of genocide as an intended cumulative impact of many forms of social assault. On Lemkin's approach, whether forced assimilation is genocidal depends on its foreseeable trajectory. Where is it going? Is it a stage in a plan that, if successful, will destroy a people? If so, will it do so in a way that leaves the social vitality of individuals robust, even though the vitality takes new forms? Even if not, the genocidal destruction need not terminate in mass murder. If there is some redundancy in the claim that the ancients who slaughtered all the males of a conquered people and then enslaved the remaining women and children committed both mass murder and genocide, it is an informative redundancy. The question of a genocidal trajectory becomes important politically for those who might be obligated to intervene to stop the process before it is too late. Potential interveners who look only for intent to commit mass murder will miss many attempts to destroy a people.

When systematic rape of women and girls of all ages and all conditions, including disability and advanced pregnancy, is among the measures taken to motivate flight, there is a likelihood that the target people will be irreparably demoralized. It is foreseeable not only that many victims will die but also that many survivors will suffer lifelong post-traumatic stress disorder (PTSD). That result can be expected to impede the formation of future families and to have traumatic effects on families that do form. Rapes done publicly can be expected to leave indelible memories and lifelong shame in victims and observers. Rape humiliates. Public, unremitting, irreparable, deep humiliation is among the techniques of genocide.

Lemkin's idea of genocide as an overall plan carried out in stages and with a variety of techniques is useful, then, for explaining how military rape with multiple specific purposes can become genocidal. The escalating forms of terrorism – from the humiliation of public rape to torture preceding murder to exerting control over the future of communities by tampering with the production of the next generation – can all be techniques employed in a plan that has the clearly foreseeable consequence, if not also the explicit aim, of destroying vitality in a people. Vitality destroyed in order to destroy a people's will to fight (as in the Brana plan) can also destroy that people.

6. THE "LOGICAL GLITCH"

Allen finds that genocide by impregnation has, as she puts it, a "logical glitch." To return to the question opening this chapter, "how," she asks, "can rape, forced pregnancy, and resultant childbirths, the production of new persons, be genocide, the annihilation of a people?" (Allen 1996, p. 92). Forced impregnation appears, on the face of it, to have the wrong trajectory, growing rather than diminishing a populace. That appearance is natural enough on the interpretation of "in part" in terms of the sheer number of people left in the target population. But on Lemkin's understanding of genocide, there need be no paradox.

To explain the idea of a genocidal intent in the enforced pregnancy policy, Allen reasons as follows. The intent behind the policy appears to have been to make Bosnian Muslim women bear Serb children. Serb perpetrators, she reasons, may have thought that a generation of children biologically fathered by Serb rapists would change the identity of future generations and thereby alter the identity of formerly Bosnian Muslim communities to something more Serbian. And so, if that policy did have the result of swelling the numbers of a populace, it would not be swelling the numbers of Bosnian Muslims. Some rapists are alleged to have gloated over the "fact" that they were forcing Muslim women to bear "little Chetniks" or Serb children.

Yet, as Allen points out, the child born of military rape contains genes of both biological parents. If it is raised, that child will most likely be raised by its mother, if she survives. If she does not, it will likely be raised by her relatives, friends, or others who share her cultural history. It will consequently take on whatever culture is then hers or theirs. In terms of biological parentage, the child will be as much non-Serb as Serb. The child's culture and social identity will almost certainly not be Serbian. The upshot is that this reconstructed rationale for the Serbian military rapes does not make good sense. Yet Allen suggests that this line of thought may nevertheless have been the rationale animating the policy of rape aimed at enforced pregnancy. People are not always logical.

Is there, however, non-faulty reasoning that could make the forced impregnation policy appear to its perpetrators coherent with a genocidal plan? One response, which Allen seems to find offensive, is that forcibly impregnated Muslim women would be rejected by their families and communities as ruined. With so many women ruined, communities would collapse. Susan Brownmiller, in her groundbreaking chapter on war rape in *Against Our Will*, cites reports that in 1971 "more than 200,000 Bengali women had been raped by Pakistani soldiers" and that "by tradition, no Moslem husband would take back a wife who had been touched by another man, even if she had been subdued by force" (Brownmiller 1975, pp. 78–79). Thus it appears that forced pregnancies could become genocidal partly because of misogynist cruelties of the culture to which the women belong.

Even if Brownmiller was right about 1970s mores in Bangladesh, Allen finds that kind of rationale insensitive to 1990s Muslim communities targeted in Bosnia-Herzegovina. Yet such attitudes are not altogether a thing of the past. Landesman notes, for example, in writing about rapes in the 1994 Rwandan genocide, that "In Rwandan society it is almost impossible for a woman who is known to have been raped to marry." He mentions the case of a Rwandan woman, engaged to be married, who testified at Arusha against Pauline Nyiramasuhuko, the former national minister of family and women's affairs, who is accused of repeatedly inciting Hutu soldiers to rape Tutsi women. The woman's fiancé broke the engagement upon hearing of her testimony (Landesman 2002, p. 89). Even if such attitudes were offensive to contemporary Muslim communities, Serb rapists might have believed that Muslims held those attitudes. Or the rapists might have projected their own attitudes onto Muslims. Even so, social rejections of raped women would not yet explain the significance of a policy of enforced *pregnancy*, as opposed simply to a policy of rape.

Allen's own solution relies on the fact that the genocide convention requires only that the enumerated acts be committed with a certain *intent*, not that the intent succeed. An incoherent intent cannot succeed. But the existence of such an intent is not impossible and might be sufficient for a policy to count as genocidal. "This illogic is possible," she argues, "only because the policy's authors erase all identity characteristics of the mother other than that as [sic] a sexual container" and, again, "The Serb policy erases the victim's cultural identity and treats her as nothing more than a kind of biological box" (Allen 1996, p. 87). Allen supposes that in perpetrators' eyes, Muslim women and girls were only receptacles for Serb sperm, good only for birthing the children of Serb rapists. As mere receptacles, they must have reasoned, the only identity transmittable to progeny would be that of Serb rapists.

Yet, if it is a problem to rely on rapists' false beliefs regarding misogynous Muslim cruelty, it should also be a problem to rely on their false beliefs regarding biological reproduction. A better explanation of the genocidal nature of these policies would not rely on the ignorance or stupidity of the rapists. A better explanation is available. It comes close to Allen's hypothesis about how rapists perceived their victims but does not rely on their prejudices or distortions in their perceptions. The prolonged torture of repeated rape, combined with enforcement of pregnancy by rapists whose biological children victims were forced to bear, could be expected to *dehumanize* the women and girls who endured it. Rapists did not simply and falsely "erase" the cultural identity of their victims. They *stripped* their victims of social vitality. Torture over months to ensure pregnancies not safely terminable might end for the woman in an especially horrifying social death. To borrow and expand Hannah Arendt's imagery from her account of "total domination" in the death camps, it might turn the women and girls who survived physically into little more than gestating corpses (Arendt 2000, pp. 119–45),[6] in Allen's language, "a kind of biological box" or "sexual container" – only, to underline the horror, one might add "living" – a "living biological box or sexual container." Even after birthing, a survivor might not experience herself or be perceived by others as a potential wife, mother, or any other recognized kind of family member. Such a past is

---

[6] Arendt uses the expression "living corpses" (Arendt 2000, p. 132).

hard to live down. Unless she is unusually creative and resilient, as well as lucky in finding support from others, she may find it overwhelmingly difficult to recover social vitality.[7]

Ordinarily, the production of new life is a source of pride for family and community. In this case, the child and its biological mother are potentially constant reminders of shame, humiliation, impotence, and defeat. The production of new life has become an instrument of social death. Even if Bosnian Muslim families would not blame or desert a raped woman or the child of rape, there may be no stable way to integrate that child and its biological mother into the life of a Muslim family or community. Neither female survivors nor the husbands of survivors who are married can be expected to welcome the parenting of children so produced, although some may do the best they can. The production of a generation of children of rape who grow up alongside children who were old enough to have witnessed war rape and to know what it means is a profound assault on the community.

There is no need to rely on faulty logic in authors and executors of the Brana plan to explain its genocidal intent. Whether rapists thought they were producing little Serbs is irrelevant. What counts is the attack on the social meanings of the lives of the women and girls they tortured and on the social vitality of their communities.

Even on an understanding of genocide that interprets "in part" as "a portion of the population," the policy of war rape aimed at enforced pregnancy can fit naturally into a plan that has a genocidal trajectory. Repeated brutal rapes, even without pregnancy, can cause sufficient trauma that survivors may not welcome future sexual relationships. Adding enforced pregnancy could be expected to compound the trauma and impose far-reaching burdens on the community, for which it has no preparation. Together, policies of rape and enforced pregnancy might be expected to have a long-range aim and foreseeable consequence of substantially decreasing, rather than increasing, even the numbers in a target population.

Allen does not explicitly make these arguments. But they can be supported by her radical and insightful claim that when military rape is used to produce and enforce pregnancy, *sperm* becomes a weapon of *biological warfare*. There need be no logical glitches in that concept.

---

[7] Some of the women raped in Bosnia-Herzegovina joined the army to fight back (Stiglmayer 1994, pp. 91–93, 98–99). Some, such as those whose testimonies Allen read, survived to record their experiences and publicize the records.

7. SPERM AS A BIOLOGICAL WEAPON

That enforced pregnancy uses sperm as a biological weapon makes perfect sense of the Brana plan as genocidal. Allen presents this idea, which helps to clear up her paradox, in a chapter on remedies (Allen 1996, pp. 103–32) rather than in her chapter called "Analysis" (Allen 1996: pp. 87–101). Her reason for that placement might be the existence of international conventions against biological weapons, which could be invoked in response to genocidal rape. The Geneva Protocol of 1925 prohibits bacteriological warfare (Hashmi and Lee 2004, p. 52). The Convention on the Prohibition of the Production, Development and Stockpiling of Bacteriological (Biological) and Toxin Weapons and on Their Destruction (BWC), concluded in 1972 (Hashmi and Lee 2004, p. 53), might be invoked in response to genocidal rape aimed at enforced pregnancy, if the case can be made that such a policy uses sperm as a biological weapon.[8] Although the BWC is focused on the destruction of certain weapons and on prohibiting their development, production, and stockpiling, its opening lines include the words "The States Parties to this Convention ... determined for the sake of all mankind, to exclude completely the possibility of bacteriological (biological) agents and toxins being *used* as weapons" (emphasis mine). It is an interesting question how to exclude completely the possible *use* of sperm as a biological weapon.

Allen seems ambivalent between two views. One is that "the *faulty logic* of Serb policy views sperm in genocidal rape precisely as an agent of biological warfare" (Allen 1996, p. 129; my emphasis). The other is that, Serb logic aside, she can "begin to show how serious genocidal rape is, and how universal a menace it might be, by determining, as [she encourages] the judges of the United Nations International Criminal Tribunal to do, that it *is* a crime of *biological warfare*" (Allen 1996, p. 123; emphasis Allen's). Perhaps the two views are reconcilable if the first one means that Serb rapists lacked a logical understanding of how the weapon works. At any rate, suppose we go with the second view, namely, that genocidal rape aimed at enforced pregnancy can and should be viewed as a crime of biological warfare.

The idea of sperm as a biological weapon presents certain puzzles. Biological warfare is usually understood as the military use of bacteriological or viral organisms that make people sick fairly quickly with diseases so contagious that they spread rapidly through a population. The

---

[8] See www.opbw.org/convention/conv.html for the full text of the BWC.

alleged distribution of blankets infected with the smallpox virus, noted in chapter 9, is an example. The diseases tend to produce death, permanent disability, or disfigurement, making it impossible for the target people to defend itself. But sperm does not behave like bacteria or viruses, although, like the blankets, it can be a vehicle for either. We would not say that it was blankets that became a WMD; rather, the WMD was smallpox, apparently transmitted by blankets. Some mass rape in war has in fact been intended to transmit lethal disease to the raped woman as well as to any child she may carry. Rwanda's President Paul Kagame is quoted by Landesman as saying, "We knew that the government was bringing AIDS patients out of the hospitals specifically to form battalions of rapists" (Landesman 2002, p. 116). Such a use of sperm to transmit the AIDS virus would be an instance of biological warfare as it is understood in the UN interpretation of the BWC. But the WMD would be the AIDS virus, not the sperm that carried it, although mass rape by infected men could be genocidal. In the policy of rape aimed at enforced pregnancy, sperm is not the carrier of a weapon. It becomes the weapon.

Our understanding of biological weaponry is evolving. The Geneva Protocol of 1925 was titled "Protocol for the Prohibition of the Use in War of Asphyxiating, Poisonous, or Other Gases and of *Bacteriological* Methods of Warfare" (emphasis mine). In 1969 the UN General Assembly interpreted that protocol as applying to "any *biological* [not just specifically bacteriological] agents of warfare ... which are intended to cause disease or death in man, animals or plants and which depend for their effects on their ability to multiply in the person, animal or plant attacked" (Hashmi and Lee 2004, p. 52; emphasis and brackets mine). The change from "bacteriological" to "biological" came about because of the discovery of viruses and other agents that can multiply in a host. Allen's proposal that sperm is used as a biological weapon in mass war rape aimed at enforced pregnancy requires certain further but natural extensions of the understanding of biological weapons.

Sperm, although biological, does not by itself multiply in the body of its host. But when it fertilizes an egg, the resulting embryo grows and invades the woman's body. Its cells multiply. A forced pregnancy also has exponentially growing social and psychological impacts on everyone close to the pregnant woman. Pregnancy need not cause disease or death, although it can and does. It need not produce disability or disfigurement. It can, but there are surer ways to get those results. Without carrying the HIV virus or other socially transmitted disease (STD), sperm can be used to poison a woman's social vitality and to poison a people socially and psychologically.

It need not harm the reproductive system. But, as Allen observes correctly, it does use that biological system against the people. The point of causing disease or death by the use of biological weaponry is to sap the spirit of the target population and undermine its capacity for defense. Sperm used for forced impregnation can produce that effect. A population that cannot defend itself is vulnerable to genocide. Although the biological agent (bacterial, viral, or sperm) is physical, the ways its use impedes defense are psychological and social as well.

Sperm was not the only weapon used in the Brana plan. Much of the harm was done by the torture of rape, especially when it was done publicly, independently of any resulting pregnancy. But sperm was a key weapon in the enforced pregnancy policy. And the two worked together – rape and enforced pregnancy – to produce harms that neither alone would have sufficed to produce. It was because the enforced pregnancy resulted from rape by Serbian soldiers that it was as harmful as it was.

Thus, like disease, death, and disablement, enforced pregnancy resulting from rape has the potential to destroy a people's morale, especially if inflicted on the youth of a community, who represent its future. If the objective is to undermine the will to fight, mass rape and enforced pregnancy can serve that end as effectively as infectious disease, with less danger to those who use the weapon. Classically, soldiers are motivated to fight to protect their homes, families, and the futures of their communities. If families become direct targets, what is left to protect? What can sustain the will to fight? Direct attack on civilian women and children was explicitly designed to motivate men to cease fighting and leave the area as the only way to protect what remained of their families and their ability to shape their futures. The cost of achieving that domination and expulsion by mass rape was genocidal, the likely destruction of social vitality in a people. In Hitler's Final Solution, genocide finally became an end in itself (thereby, diabolical), as it was known to have become counterproductive to Germany's (other) war efforts. In Bosnia-Herzegovina, committing genocide became the price the Serb military was willing to pay to achieve the goal of ethnic cleansing. Although not one evil for the sake of another, it was one evil as the price of another. Perhaps that deserves to be considered diabolical, also.

Advanced pregnancy also physically impedes a woman from defending herself or anyone else and makes her a significant physical burden to anyone who tries to defend or protect her. Such reduced physical capacities for defense are not sufficient to ground a charge of genocide. But in this context they, too, are on the right trajectory. They contribute in the "right" way. They speak directly to the point of biological weapons. Sperm is being used against a target population to impede its capacities to defend itself, physical as well as social and psychological.

One might object to calling sperm a biological weapon on the grounds that agents of biological warfare, historically, have not had acceptable peacetime uses – the smallpox virus, for example.[9] Smallpox virus has, so far as I know, no good uses, other than to inoculate against smallpox (which, without that virus, would be unnecessary). But sperm is required for procreation. Calling sperm a weapon of biological warfare, especially of genocidal biological warfare, might sound shocking to some, as it puts a substance necessary for reproduction, which many associate with love-making, into the same category as smallpox or the plague and the poison gases used during WW I and in Iran.[10] Historically, biological weapons, like the poison gases, have been weapons of mass destruction (WMD). Hence, the concern to prohibit their use. WMD make genocide easier and more likely. Consequently, many would like to see WMD destroyed. To prevent use of sperm as such a weapon might seem to require sterilizing soldiers. Some might, for that reason, resist the labeling of sperm as a weapon of biological warfare.

It is tempting to respond that a biological weapon need not be a WMD and that sperm is an example of a biological weapon that is not. However, sperm has been used not only as a biological weapon but also as an instrument of genocide, in which case it arguably does become a WMD, even if not a weapon of mass killing and even if only in combination with other weapons. Further, for women and girls victimized by the Brana plan, sperm may no longer have good connotations or hold the potential for welcome new life. The fact is that sperm has been used not only to produce welcome new life but also to ruin lives. It is vitally important that people globally, especially women and girls, know and appreciate that human sperm has been so used, that it does not serve only benign purposes.

Also, it is not true that all agents of biological and chemical warfare have only wartime uses. Zyklon B, used to kill in the gas chambers at Auschwitz, has been used as a pesticide during peacetime. Some Holocaust deniers maintain to this day, despite overwhelming evidence to the contrary, that poisonous gases were used at Auschwitz only as pesticides for

---

[9] Ann Cudd raised this issue in response to a paper in which I tried out some of these ideas at the Spindel Conference at the University of Memphis in 2007.

[10] Some might suspect that only a lesbian would be tempted to classify sperm as a biological weapon.

disinfecting clothing (Lipstadt 1993, pp. 157–82).[11] Rachel Carson points out that the growth of industries for the production of chemicals with in-secticidal properties "is a child of the Second World War," that in develop-ing agents of chemical warfare, "some were found to be lethal to insects," and that this discovery "did not come about by chance: insects were widely used to test chemicals as agents of death for men" (Carson 1962, p. 16). Many pesticides originated as weapons of war. Thanks to Carson's research, many of these pesticides today have gravely negative connota-tions for many of us.[12] Even in small doses, some are very toxic to people, more so than to rats and insects (Lipstadt 1993, p. 168). Still, they have had major peacetime uses. Other substances used to promote life (to grow crops, for example) have been used as weapons of war. The bomb used by the "Sterling Hall Four" to blow up the Army/Math Research Center on my campus on August 24, 1970 was made from fertilizer.[13]

Not everything that can be used as a weapon should be destroyed. Given the weapons used in the 9/11 bombings, should we now destroy box cutters and large aircraft? There should be no need to sterilize soldiers to prevent war rape. Still, even if only in fantasy, sterilization is not an obvi-ously morally inappropriate penalty (even if *ultimately* inappropriate) for soldiers who do it, or for officers who order or condone it, and who are properly convicted of having done so.[14]

Allen observes that the military appeal of biological weapons is that they can destroy a people, or a people's will to fight, without destroying the inhabited territory. She also notes some of the classic dangers of bac-teria and viruses, which explain why they are not used oftener. Even if they do not destroy a territory, the irreversible and relatively uncontainable

---

[11] The overwhelming evidence includes Claude Lanzmann's nine-hour film *Shoah* (1985), which interviews many who were adults in Poland between 1942 and 1945 about what they witnessed, did, knew, and smelled. *Shoah*'s interviewees include Filip Müller, who survived three years as a worker in the gas chambers at Auschwitz (Müller 1979). Alain Renais's film *Night and Fog* (1955) includes footage from the liberation of Buchenwald, visited in person by US President Dwight D. Eisenhower, in case anyone would try to deny the facts in the future, even though Buchenwald was not designated as a death camp. Countless survivor memoirs give mutually corroborating but independent reports on "life" and death in the camps. For detailed responses to Holocaust denial, see Lipstadt (1993); Shermer and Grobman (2000); and Vidal-Naquet (1992).

[12] Some years ago, I persuaded a local supermarket to relocate their pesticides from the aisle that also contained kosher foods.

[13] For the story of the bombing of the Army/Math Research Center and its aftermath, see Bates (1992).

[14] On advantages and disadvantages of castration as a penalty for rapists (and related issues), see Card (2002, pp. 129–38). Most of the same points apply to sterilization. Immanuel Kant appears to favor castration for "rape and pederasty" (Kant 1996a, p. 498); at any rate, he raises no objec-tion when he notes that these are the penalties imposed for those crimes, rather than penalties that would be retributive in kind.

dispersal of organisms of biological warfare may make that territory un-inhabitable for a long time. Disease-causing biological organisms are not fine-tunable weapons that can be made to target specific individuals. They are not easily controlled once unleashed in a population. Finally, there is the danger of blowback: the wind can literally blow the organisms back into the faces of those who would use them.

As a biological weapon, sperm has many of the advantages of bacteria and viruses without their disadvantages. Unlike bacteria and viruses, sperm is easily containable, storable, preservable, and deliverable by means of men's bodies. It is generated spontaneously and needs no special equipment. It is in those respects economical. If rape and enforced pregnancy are effective in terrorizing a people into evacuating a territory, sperm as a weapon does not risk making the territory uninhabitable, at least not the way bacteria and viruses could.[15] Unlike poison gases and viruses, sperm can be delivered with perfect accuracy to a specific target. Even if it does not result in pregnancy, the delivery itself can inflict substantial harm. Finally, there is no danger of "blowback," or so it might seem. A Croatian woman noted, however, that even though the rapists cannot be impregnated, a generation of rape children might grow up to seek revenge. Allen adds: on whom they would be motivated to seek revenge will depend on how they are raised (Allen 1996, p. 132). There could be blowback, after all.

In fact, Allen notes, many of the impregnated women attempt third-trimester abortions. Some commit suicide. Some kill the newborn. Others walk out of the hospital room leaving the newborn behind. Some try to find someone less traumatized to raise it (Allen 1996, p. 99). By such means, they thwart some of the intent of the enforced pregnancy policy. But the intent nevertheless makes sense and does not cease to be genocidal for lack of success. Further, in accord with Lemkin's idea that genocide is an overall plan involving many strategies, the Brana plan was not the only strategy implemented by the Serbs in its project of ethnic cleansing.

A plausible answer to Allen's paradoxical question, "How can rape, forced pregnancy, and resultant childbirths, the production of new persons, be genocide, the annihilation of a people?" (Allen 1996, p. 92) is found by combining Lemkin's idea that genocide is a complex project with multiple stages that attack a community along many dimensions, with

---

[15] War rape might provoke a people to destroy immovable property as they leave, as some evicted tenants and victims of mortgage foreclosure in the US have trashed their apartments and houses before vacating.

Allen's idea that rape aimed at producing enforced pregnancy is a form of biological warfare that can bring social death to victims. This policy was only part of a complex plan that had a genocidal intent. The Brana plan can thus be seen to be genocidal without relying on the idea of producing Serbian children, even if some rapists thought they were doing that or joked about the idea. It is enough that military rape aimed at enforced pregnancy uses sperm as a biological weapon to contribute to an overall plan intended to destroy social vitality in a people.

Bibliography

Abbey, Edward. 1975. *The Monkey Wrench Gang*. Philadelphia: Lippincott.

Abbott, Geoffrey. 2005. *Execution: The Guillotine, the Pendulum, the Thousand Cuts, the Spanish Donkey, and 66 Other Ways of Putting Someone to Death*. New York: St. Martin's Press.

Alexander, Matthew (pseudonym) with John R. Bruning. 2008. *How to Break a Terrorist: The U.S. Interrogators Who Used Brains, Not Brutality, to Take Down the Deadliest Man in Iraq*. New York: Free Press.

Alleg, Henri. 1958. *The Question*. (No translator identified). Introduction by Jean-Paul Sartre. New York: George Braziller.

Allen, Beverly. 1996. *Rape Warfare: The Hidden Genocide in Bosnia-Herzegovina and Croatia*. Minneapolis: University of Minnesota Press.

Allen, Jeffner. 1986. *Lesbian Philosophy: Explorations*. Palo Alto, CA: Institute of Lesbian Studies.

Allen, Paula Gunn. 1986. *The Sacred Hoop: Recovering the Feminine in American Indian Traditions*. Boston: Beacon.

Améry, Jean. 1964. *Preface to the Future: Culture in a Consumer Society*. Trans. Palmer Hilty. New York: Ungar.

    1980. *At the Mind's Limits: Contemplations by a Survivor on Auschwitz and Its Realities*. Trans. from German by Sidney Rosenfeld and Stella P. Rosenfeld. Bloomington and Indianapolis: Indiana University Press.

    1984. *Radical Humanism*. Ed. and trans. Sidney Rosenfeld and Stella P. Rosenfeld. Bloomington: Indiana University Press.

    1994. *On Aging: Revolt and Resignation*. Trans. John D. Barlow. Bloomington: Indiana University Press.

    1999. *On Suicide: A Discourse on Voluntary Death*. Trans. John D. Barlow. Bloomington: Indiana University Press.

Amir, Menachem. 1971. *Patterns in Forcible Rape*. Chicago: University of Chicago Press.

Amnesty International. 1973. *Report on Torture*. New York: Farrar, Straus, and Giroux.

    1984. *Torture in the Eighties: An Amnesty International Report*. London: Amnesty International Publications.

Anderson, James C. 1993. "Species Equality and the Foundations of Moral Theory," *Environmental Values* 2:4, 347–75.

Anderson-Gold, Sharon and Pablo Muchnik, eds. 2009. *Kant's Anatomy of Evil.* New York: Cambridge University Press.

Andreopoulos, George, ed. 1994. *Genocide: Conceptual and Historical Dimensions.* Philadelphia: University of Pennsylvania Press.

Arendt, Hannah. 1965. *Eichmann in Jerusalem: A Report on the Banality of Evil.* Rev. and enlarged edn. New York: Penguin.

2000. *The Portable Hannah Arendt.* Ed. Peter Baehr. New York: Penguin.

Aristotle. 1925. *The Nicomachean Ethics.* Trans. David Ross. Oxford: Oxford University Press.

1947. *Basic Works of Aristotle.* Ed. Richard McKeon. New York: Random House.

Arnold, William. 1979. *Frances Farmer: Shadowland.* New York: Jove/HBJ.

Arrigo, Jean Maria. 2004. "A Utilitarian Argument against Torture Interrogation of Terrorists," *Science and Engineering Ethics* **10**:3, 1–30.

Attfield, Robin. 1982. "The Good of Trees," *Journal of Value Inquiry* **15**, 35–54.

Aust, Stefan. 2009. *Baader-Meinhof: The Inside Story of the R.A.F.* Trans. Anthea Bell. New York: Oxford University Press.

Austin, J. L. 1961. *Philosophical Papers.* Oxford: Clarendon Press.

Balakian, Peter. 2003. *The Burning Tigris: The Armenian Genocide and America's Response.* New York: HarperCollins.

Bar On, Bat-Ami. 2002. *The Subject of Violence: Arendtean Exercises in Understanding.* Lanham, MD: Rowman and Littlefield.

Baron, Marcia. 2007. "Excuses, Excuses," *Criminal Law and Philosophy: An International Journal for Philosophy of Crime, Criminal Law and Punishment* **1**:1, 21–39.

Bates, Tom. 1992. *Rads: The 1970 Bombing of the Army Math Research Center at the University of Wisconsin and Its Aftermath.* New York: HarperCollins.

Baumeister, Roy. 1997. *Evil: Inside Human Violence and Cruelty.* New York: W. H. Freeman and Co.

Beauvoir, Simone de. 1949. *Le Deuxième Sexe*, 2 vols. Paris: Gallimard.

1953. *The Second Sex.* Ed. and trans. H. M. Parshley. London: Jonathan Cape.

Beccaría, Cesare. 1963. *On Crimes and Punishments.* Trans. Henry Paolucci. Indianapolis: Bobbs-Merrill.

Becker, Lawrence C., ed. with Charlotte B. Becker. 2001. *Encyclopedia of Ethics.* Second edn., 3 vols. New York: Garland.

Bedau, Hugo Adam and Paul Cassell, eds. 2004. *Debating the Death Penalty: Should America Have Capital Punishment?* Oxford: Oxford University Press.

Begg, Moazzam with Victoria Brittain. 2006. *Enemy Combatant: My Imprisonment at Guantánamo, Bagram, and Kandahar.* New York: The New Press.

Bell, Linda A. and David Blumenfeld, eds. 1995. *Overcoming Racism and Sexism.* Lanham, MD: Rowman and Littlefield.

Benn, S. I. 1985. "Wickedness," *Ethics* **95**, 795–810.

Bentham, Jeremy. 1948. *Introduction to the Principles of Morals and Legislation.* New York: Hafner.

Berkowitz, Leonard. 1999. "Evil is More than Banal: Situationism and the Concept of Evil," *Personality and Social Psychology Review* **3**:3, 246–53.
(Unpublished). "The Problem of Evil in Contemporary Social Psychology."

Bernstein, Richard. 2002. *Radical Evil: A Philosophical Interrogation.* Cambridge: Polity Press.
2005. *The Abuse of Evil: The Corruption of Politics and Religion since 9/11.* Cambridge: Polity Press.

Bissell, R. Ward. 1999. *Artemisia Gentileschi and the Authority of Art.* University Park, PA: Pennsylvania State University Press.

Blass, Thomas, ed. 2000. *Obedience to Authority: Current Perspectives on the Milgram Paradigm.* London: Lawrence Erlbaum Associates.

Blau, Peter M., ed. 1975. *Approaches to the Study of Social Structure.* New York: Free Press.

Blee, Kathleen. 1991. *Women of the Klan: Racism and Gender in the 1920s.* Berkeley: University of California Press.

Blum, Deborah. 1994. *The Monkey Wars.* New York: Oxford University.

Bowden, Mark. 1999. *Black Hawk Down.* New York: Atlantic Monthly Press.

Bratman, Michael E. 1999. *Faces of Intention: Selected Essays on Intention and Agency.* Cambridge: Cambridge University Press.

Braudy, Susan. 2003. *Family Circle: The Boudins and the Aristocracy of the Left.* New York: Knopf.

Brenner, Rachel. 1997. *Writing as Resistance: Four Women Confronting the Holocaust.* University Park, PA: Pennsylvania State University Press.

Brison, Susan. 2002. *Aftermath: Violence and the Remaking of a Self.* Princeton, NJ: Princeton University Press.

Brown, Brooks and Rob Merritt. 2002. *No Easy Answers: The Truth behind Death at Columbine.* New York: Lantern Books.

Brownmiller, Susan. 1975. *Against Our Will: Men, Women, and Rape.* New York: Simon & Schuster.

Burgers, J. Herman and Hans Danelius. 1988. *The United Nations Convention against Torture: A Handbook on the Convention against Torture and Other Cruel, Inhuman or Degrading Treatment or Punishment.* Dordrecht: Martinus Nijhoff Publishers.

Burleigh, Michael. 2009. *Blood and Rage: A Cultural History of Terrorism.* New York: Harper.

Butler, Joseph. 1983. *Five Sermons.* Ed. Stephen L. Darwall. Indianapolis: Hackett.

Cannon, Lou. 1997. *Official Negligence: How Rodney King and the Riots Changed Los Angeles and the LAPD.* New York: Random House.

Card, Claudia. 1962. "Some Aspects of the Problems of Punishment." Unpublished BA thesis. University of Wisconsin, Madison.
1969. "Retributive Justice in Legal Punishment." Unpublished PhD dissertation. Harvard University, Cambridge, MA.
1991a. "Rape as a Terrorist Institution." In Frey and Morris (1991), 296–313.
1995. *Lesbian Choices.* New York: Columbia University Press.

1996. *The Unnatural Lottery: Character and Moral Luck*. Philadelphia: Temple University Press.

2001. "Is Penalty Enhancement a Sound Idea?" *Law and Philosophy* **20**:2, 195–214.

2002. *The Atrocity Paradigm: A Theory of Evil*. New York: Oxford University Press.

Card, Claudia, ed. 1991b. *Feminist Ethics*. Lawrence, KA: University Press of Kansas.

1999. *On Feminist Ethics and Politics*. Lawrence, KA: University Press of Kansas.

2003. *The Cambridge Companion to Simone de Beauvoir*. Cambridge: Cambridge University Press.

Card, Claudia and Armen T. Marsoobian, eds. 2007. *Genocide's Aftermath: Responsibility and Repair*. Malden, MA: Blackwell.

Carlyle, Thomas. 1937. *The French Revolution*, 3 vols. London: J. Fraser.

Carruthers, Peter. 1992. *The Animals Issue: Moral Theory in Practice*. Cambridge: Cambridge University Press.

Carson, Rachel, 1962. *Silent Spring*. Boston: Houghton Mifflin.

Cauffiel, Lowell. 1993. *Forever and Five Days*. New York: Kensington.

Chalk, Frank, and Kurt Jonassohn, eds. 1990. *The History and Sociology of Genocide: Analyses and Case Studies*. New Haven: Yale University Press.

Charny, Israel (Editor in Chief). 1999. *Encyclopedia of Genocide*, 2 vols. Santa Barbara, CA: ABS-CLIO, Inc.

Clark, Lorenne M. G. and Debra J. Lewis. 1977. *Rape: The Price of Coercive Sexuality*. Toronto: The Women's Press.

Clausewitz, Carl von. 1982. *On War*. London: Penguin.

Cole, Philip. 2006. *The Myth of Evil*. Edinburgh: Edinburgh University Press.

Conover, Ted. 2000. *Newjack: Guarding Sing Sing*. New York: Random House.

Conroy, John. 2000. *Unspeakable Acts, Ordinary People: The Dynamics of Torture*. New York: Knopf.

Cullen, Dave. 2009. *Columbine*. New York: Twelve.

Cuomo, Chris J. 1998. *Feminism and Ecological Communities: An Ethics of Flourishing*. London: Routledge.

Daly, Mary. 1978. *Gyn/Ecology: The Metaethics of Radical Feminism*. Boston: Beacon.

Danner, Mark. 2004. *Torture and Truth: America, Abu Ghraib, and the War on Terror*. New York: New York Review Books.

2009a. "U.S. Torture: Voices from the Black Sites," *The New York Review of Books* April 9, 69–77.

2009b. "The Red Cross Torture Report: What It Means," *The New York Review of Books* April 30, 48–56.

Davis, Angela. 1981. *Women, Race, and Class*. New York: Vintage.

Dawidowicz, Lucy S. 1975. *The War against the Jews, 1933–1945*. New York: Holt, Rinehart, and Winston.

De Grazia, Sebastian. 1989. *Machiavelli in Hell*. Princeton, NJ: Princeton University Press.

De Kock, Eugene, as told to Jeremy Gordin. 1998. *A Long Night's Damage: Working for the Apartheid State*. Saxonwold, Republic of South Africa: Contra Press.

De Sade, Marquis. 1966. *The 120 Days of Sodom, and Other Writings*. Compiled and trans. Austryn Wainhouse and Richard Seaver. New York: Grove Press.

De Waal, Frans. 1989. *Peacemaking among Primates*. Cambridge, MA: Harvard University Press.

1996. *Good Natured: The Origins of Right and Wrong in Humans and Other Animals*. Cambridge, MA: Harvard University Press.

Dershowitz, Alan. 2002. *Why Terrorism Works: Understanding the Threat, Responding to the Challenge*. New Haven: Yale University Press.

2006. *Preemption: A Knife that Cuts Both Ways*. New York: Norton.

DesAutels, Peggy and Margaret Urban Walker, eds. 2004. *Moral Psychology: Feminist Ethics and Social Theory*. Lanham, MD: Rowman and Littlefield.

Dostoevsky, Fyodor. 1950. *The Brothers Karamazov*. Trans. Constance Garnett. New York: Modern Library.

DuBois, W. E. B. 1969. *The Souls of Black Folk*. New York: New American Library.

1970. *W. E. B. Du Bois Speaks: Speeches and Addresses 1890–1919*. New York: Pathfinder.

Duff, Anthony. 2007. "Excuses, Moral and Legal: A Comment on Marcia Baron's 'Excuses, Excuses'," *Criminal Law and Philosophy: An International Journal for Philosophy of Crime, Criminal Law and Punishment* 1:1, 49–55.

Durant, Will and Ariel Durant. 1975. *The Age of Napoleon*. New York: Simon & Schuster.

Ehrenreich, Barbara and Deidre English. 1978. *For Her Own Good: 150 Years of the Experts' Advice to Women*. Garden City, NY: Anchor Press.

Eisnitz, Gail. 1997. *Slaughterhouse: The Shocking Story of Greed, Neglect, and Inhumane Treatment Inside the U.S. Meat Industry*. Amherst, NY: Prometheus.

El-Hai, Jack. 2005. *The Lobotomist: A Maverick Medical Genius and His Tragic Quest to Rid the World of Mental Illness*. Hoboken, NJ: John Wiley and Sons.

Estrich, Susan. 1987. *Real Rape*. Cambridge, MA: Harvard University Press.

Ezorsky, Gertrude, ed. 1972. *Philosophical Perspectives on Punishment*. Albany, NY: State University of New York Press.

Faludi, Susan. 1991. *Backlash*. New York: Crown.

Farmer, Frances. 1972. *Will There Really Be a Morning?* New York: Dell.

Feinberg, Joel. 1970. *Doing and Deserving*. Princeton, NJ: Princeton University Press.

1984. *Harm to Others*. New York: Oxford University Press.

Ferguson, Ann. 2009. *Dancing with Iris: The Philosophy of Iris Marion Young.* New York: Oxford University Press.

Ferrato, Donna. 1991. *Living with the Enemy.* New York: Aperture.

Fineman, Martha Albertson and Roxanne Mykitiuk, eds. 1994. *The Public Nature of Private Violence: The Discovery of Domestic Abuse.* New York: Routledge.

Foreman, Dave. 1991. *Confessions of an Eco-Warrior.* New York: Harmony Books.

Foreman, Dave and Bill Haywood, eds. 1993. *A Field Guide to Monkeywrenching.* Chicago: Abzug Press.

Francione, Gary. 1995. *Animals, Property, and the Law.* Philadelphia: Temple University Press.

  1996. *Rain without Thunder: The Ideology of the Animal Rights Movement* Philadelphia: Temple University Press.

French, Peter A., ed. 1972. *Individual and Collective Responsibility: The Massacre at My Lai.* Cambridge, MA: Shenkman.

Frey, R. G. and Christopher W. Morris, eds. 1991. *Violence, Terrorism, and Justice.* Cambridge: Cambridge University Press.

Fromm, Erich. 1973. *The Anatomy of Human Destructiveness.* New York: Holt, Rinehart, and Winston.

Frye, Marilyn. 1983. *The Politics of Reality: Essays in Feminist Theory.* Trumansburg, NY: The Crossing Press.

  1992. *Willful Virgin: Essays in Feminism 1976–1992.* Freedom, CA: The Crossing Press.

Garner, Bryan A. (Editor in Chief). 2004. *Black's Law Dictionary.* Eighth edn. St. Paul, MN: Thomson/West.

Garrard, Eve and Geoffrey Scarre, eds. 2003. *Moral Philosophy and the Holocaust.* Burlington, VT: Ashgate.

Gentry, Curt. 1992. *J. Edgar Hoover: The Man and the Secrets.* New York: Plume.

Gilbert, Margaret. 1989. *On Social Facts.* Princeton, NJ: Princeton University Press.

  1996. *Living Together: Rationality, Sociality, and Obligation.* Lanham, MD: Rowman and Littlefield.

Gilligan, Carol. 1982. *In a Different Voice: Psychological Theory and Women's Development.* Cambridge, MA: Harvard University Press.

Gilman, Sander L. and Jack Sipes, eds. 1997. *Yale Companion to Jewish Writing and Thought in German Culture, 1096–1996.* New Haven: Yale University Press.

Gilmore, Mikal, 1994. *Shot in the Heart.* New York: Doubleday.

Glendon, Mary Ann. 2000. *Sociality and Responsibility.* Lanham, MD: Rowman and Littlefield.

  2001. *A World Made New: Eleanor Roosevelt and the Universal Declaration of Human Rights.* New York: Random House.

Global Outlook: The Magazine of 9/11 Truth. 2005. No. 10. See www.globaloutlook.ca.

Glover, Jonathan. 2000. *Humanity: A Moral History of the Twentieth Century.* New Haven: Yale University Press.

Goldman, Emma. 1931. *Living My Life*, 2 vols. New York: Knopf.
1969. *Anarchism and Other Essays*. New York: Dover.
Goodpaster, Kenneth. 1978. "On Being Morally Considerable," *Journal of Philosophy* **75**:6, 308–25.
Grant, Ruth, ed. 2006. *Naming Evil, Judging Evil*. Chicago: University of Chicago Press.
Grayling, A. C. 2006. *Among the Dead Cities: The History and Moral Legacy of the WWII Bombing of Civilians in Germany and Japan*. New York: Walker and Company.
Greenberg, Karen J., ed. 2006. *The Torture Debate in America*. Cambridge: Cambridge University Press.
Greenberg, Karen J. and Joshua L. Dratel, eds. 2005. *The Torture Papers: The Road to Abu Ghraib*. Cambridge: Cambridge University Press.
Griffin, David Ray. 2004. *The New Pearl Harbor: Disturbing Questions about the Bush Administration and 9/11*. Northampton, MA: Olive Branch Press.
Griffin, James. 2008. *On Human Rights*. Oxford: Oxford University Press.
Grisham, John. 2006. *The Innocent Man: Murder and Injustice in a Small Town*. New York: Doubleday.
Gutman, Roy and David Rieff, eds. 1999. *Crimes of War: What the Public Should Know*. New York: Norton.
Haney, Craig, Curtis Banks, and Philip Zimbardo. 1973. "Interpersonal Dynamics in a Simulated Prison," *International Journal of Criminology and Penology* **1**, 69–97.
Harbury, Jennifer K. 2005. *Truth, Torture, and the American Way: The History and Consequences of U.S. Involvement in Torture*. Boston: Beacon.
Hare, Richard. 1979. "On Terrorism," *Journal of Value Inquiry* **13**, 240–49.
Harris, Sheldon. 1994. *Factories of Death : Japanese Secret Biological Warfare, 1932–45, and the American Cover-up*. London and New York: Routledge.
Harrison, Kathryn. 1997. *The Kiss*. New York: Random House.
2008. *While They Slept: An Inquiry into the Murder of a Family*. New York: Random House.
Hart, H. L. A. 1961. *The Concept of Law*. Oxford: Clarendon Press.
Hashmi, Sohail H. and Steven P. Lee, eds. 2004. *Ethics and Weapons of Mass Destruction: Religious and Secular Perspectives*. Cambridge: Cambridge University Press.
Hausman, Daniel. 2008. "Protecting Groups from Genetic Research," *Bioethics* **22**:3, 157–65.
Hearst, Patricia Campbell with Alvin Moscow. 1988. *Patty Hearst: Her Own Story*. New York: Avon.
Heger, Heinz. 1980. *The Men with the Pink Triangle*. Trans. David Fernbach. Boston, MA: Alyson Publications.
Held, Virginia, Sidney Morgenbesser, and Thomas Nagel, eds. 1974. *Philosophy, Morality, and International Affairs*. New York: Oxford University Press
Herman, Barbara. 1993. *The Practice of Moral Judgment*. Cambridge, MA: Harvard University Press.

2007. *Moral Literacy*. Cambridge, MA: Harvard University Press.

Herman, Judith Lewis. 1992. *Trauma and Recovery*. New York: Basic Books.

Hinton, Alexander Laban, ed. 2002. *Genocide: An Anthropological Reader*. Malden, MA: Blackwell.

Hobbes, Thomas. 1950. *Leviathan*. New York: Dutton.

Hoffman, B. 2002. "A Nasty Business," *Atlantic Monthly* January, 49–52.

Holy Bible, Revised Standard Version. 1952. New York: Thomas Nelson and Sons.

Horder, Jeremy. 2004. *Excusing Crime*. Oxford: Oxford University Press.

2007. "Excuses in Law and in Morality: A Response to Marcia Baron," *Criminal Law and Philosophy: An International Journal for Philosophy of Crime, Criminal Law and Punishment* 1:1, 41–47.

Horwitz, Sari and Michael E. Ruane. 2003. *Sniper: Inside the Hunt for the Killers Who Terrorized the Nation*. New York: Random House.

Howie, John, ed. 1987. *Ethical Principles and Practice*. Carbondale and Edwardsville, IL: Southern Illinois University Press.

Hughes, J. Donald. 1983. *American Indian Ecology*. El Paso: University of Texas.

Human Rights Watch/Africa, Human Rights Watch Women's Rights Project, Fédération Internationale des Ligues des Droits de l'Homme. 1996. *Shattered Lives: Sexual Violence during the Rwandan Genocide and Its Aftermath*. New York: Human Rights Watch.

Institoris, Henricus and Jacobus Sprenger. 2006. *Malleus Maleficarum*, 2 vols. English and Latin. Ed. and trans. Christopher S. Mackay. Cambridge: Cambridge University Press.

Jack, Belinda. 2005. *Beatrice's Spell: The Enduring Legend of Beatrice Cenci*. New York: Other Press.

Jaimes, M. Annette, ed. 1992. *The State of Native America: Genocide, Colonization, and Resistance*. Boston: South End.

James, Stanlie M. and Claire C. Robertson, eds. 2002. *Genital Cutting and Transnational Sisterhood: Disputing U.S. Polemics*. Urbana and Chicago: University of Illinois Press.

Jaspers, Karl. 1947. *The Question of German Guilt*. Trans. E. B. Ashton. New York: Dial Press.

Johnson, Joyce. 1990. *What Lisa Knew: The Truths and Lies of the Steinberg Case*. New York: Putnam.

Johnson, Lawrence, 1991. *A Morally Deep World: An Essay on Moral Significance and Environmental Ethics*. Cambridge: Cambridge University Press.

Jokić, Aleksandar, ed. 2001. *War Crimes and Collective Wrongdoing: A Reader*. Malden, MA: Blackwell.

Jones, Ann. 1994. *Next Time She'll Be Dead: Battering and How to Stop It*. Boston: Beacon.

Jones, David H. 1999. *Moral Responsibility in the Holocaust: A Study in the Ethics of Character*. Lanham, MD: Rowman and Littlefield.

Kaczynski, Theodore J. 1995. *The Unabomber Manifesto: Industrial Society and Its Future* by "FC." Berkeley, CA: Jolly Roger Press.

Kaldor, Mary. 2001. *New and Old Wars: Organized Violence in a Global Era, with an Afterword.* Stanford, CA: Stanford University Press.

Kant, Immanuel. 1930. *Lectures on Ethics.* Trans. Louis Infield. New York: Century.

1996a. *Practical Philosophy.* Trans. Mary J. Gregor. Cambridge: Cambridge University Press.

1996b. *Religion and Rational Theology.* Trans. Allen W. Wood and George di Giovanni. Cambridge: Cambridge University Press.

Katz, Steven. 1994. *The Holocaust in Historical Context*, vol. 1, *Mass Death before the Modern Age.* New York: Oxford University Press.

Kekes, John. 2005. *Roots of Evil.* Ithaca: Cornell University Press.

Kiernan, Ben. 2007. *Blood and Soil: A World History of Genocide and Extermination from Sparta to Darfur.* New Haven: Yale University Press.

King, Joyce. 2002. *Hate Crime: The Story of a Dragging in Texas.* New York: Pantheon.

Kittay, Eva Feder and Diana T. Meyers, eds. 1987. *Women and Moral Theory.* Totowa, NJ: Rowman and Littlefield.

Koedt, Anne, Ellen Levine, and Anita Rapone, eds. 1973. *Radical Feminism.* New York: Quadrangle.

Kraut, Richard. 2007. *What Is Good and Why: The Ethics of Well-Being.* Cambridge, MA: Harvard University Press.

Kutz, Christopher. 2000. *Complicity: Ethics and Law for a Collective Age.* Cambridge: Cambridge University Press.

2007. "Causeless Complicity," *Criminal Law and Philosophy* 1, 289–305.

Lackey, Douglas P. 1989. *The Ethics of War and Peace.* Englewood Cliffs, NJ: Prentice Hall.

Lafferty, Shelagh Marie. 1991. *Policy Analysis Exercise, Analysis of Newspaper Coverage of Rape 1989–1990.* Cambridge, MA: Harvard University, Kennedy School of Government.

Landesman, Peter. 2002. "A Woman's Work," *New York Times Magazine*, September 15, 82–89, 116, 125, 130, 132, 134.

Lang, Berel. 1990. *Act and Idea in the Nazi Genocide.* Chicago: University of Chicago Press.

Langbein, John H. 1977. *Torture and the Law of Proof.* Chicago: University of Chicago Press.

Laqueur, Walter. 2001. *A History of Terrorism.* With new introduction. New Brunswick: Transaction.

Lara, María Pía. 2007. *Narrating Evil: A Postmetaphysical Theory of Reflective Judgment.* New York: Columbia University Press.

Lawrence, Frederick M. 1999. *Punishing Hate: Bias Crimes under American Law.* Cambridge, MA: Harvard University Press.

Lawrence, Regina G. 2000. *The Politics of Force: Media and the Construction of Police Brutality.* Berkeley: University of California Press.

Lea, Henry Charles. 1901. *The Moriscos of Spain: Their Conversion and Expulsion.* Philadelphia; Lea Brothers and Co.; unabridged facsimile edition Elibron Classics, 2006.

Leicht, Justus. 2004. "The Daschner Case and the Rehabilitation of Torture in Germany," *The World Socialist*, online at www.wsws.org/articles/2004/dec2004/tort-d13.shtml.

Lemkin, Raphael. 1944. *Axis Rule in Occupied Europe: Laws of Occupation, Analysis of Government, Proposals for Redress.* Washington DC: Carnegie Endowment for International Peace, Division of International Law.

Leopold, Aldo. 1966. *A Sand County Almanac.* New York: Ballantine.

Levi, Primo. 1989. *The Drowned and the Saved.* Trans. Raymond Rosenthal. New York: Vintage.

Levin, Michael. 1972. "The Case for Torture," *Newsweek* June 7, 434–35.

Levinson, Sanford. 2004. *Torture: A Collection.* New York: Oxford University Press.

Lewis, Jim. 2009. "Behind Bars … Sort Of," *New York Times Magazine* June 14, 48–53.

Lewis, Neil A. 2009. "Official Defends Signing Interrogation Memos," *The New York Times* April 29, A12.

Lifton, Robert J. 1986. *The Nazi Doctors: Medical Killing and the Psychology of Genocide.* New York: Basic Books.

Lipstadt, Deborah. 1993. *Denying the Holocaust: The Growing Assault on Truth and Memory.* New York: Free Press.

Livy. 1960. *The Early History of Rome: Books I–V of The History of Rome from Its Foundation.* Trans. Aubrey de Sélincourt. Baltimore, MD: Penguin.

Loffreda, Beth. 2000. *Losing Matt Shepard: Life and Politics in the Aftermath of Anti-Gay Murder.* New York: Columbia University Press.

Lovelock, J. E. 1979. *Gaia: A New Look at Life on Earth.* New York: Oxford University Press.

Luban, David. 2002. "The War on Terrorism and the End of Human Rights," *Philosophy and Public Policy Quarterly* **22**:3, 9–14.

    2005. "Torture, American-Style: This Debate Comes Down to Words vs. Deeds," *Washington Post* November 27, B1.

Luce, R. Duncan and Howard Raiffa. 1957. *Games and Decisions: Introduction and Critical Survey.* New York: Wiley.

Mabbott, J. D. 1949. "Punishment," *Mind* n.s. **48**,152–67.

Mackey, Chris and Greg Miller. 2004. *The Interrogators: Inside the Secret War against Al Qaeda.* New York and Boston: Little, Brown and Company.

Mailer, Norman. 1979. *The Executioner's Song.* Boston: Little, Brown and Company.

Margalit, Avishai. 1996. *The Decent Society.* Trans. Naomi Goldblum. Cambridge, MA: Harvard University Press.

Marx, Karl. 1967. *Capital: A Critique of Political Economy*, 3 vols. Ed. Frederick Engels. Trans. from 3rd German edn. by Samuel Moore and Edward Aveling. New York: International Publishers.

May, Larry. 1987. *The Morality of Groups: Collective Responsibility, Group-Based Harm, and Corporate Rights.* Notre Dame, IN: University of Notre Dame Press.

    1992. *Sharing Responsibility.* Chicago: University of Chicago Press.

1996. *The Socially Responsive Self: Social Theory and Professional Ethics.* Chicago: University of Chicago Press.

2005. *Crimes against Humanity: A Normative Account.* Cambridge: Cambridge University Press.

2007. *War Crimes and Just War.* Cambridge: Cambridge University Press.

2008. *Aggression and Crimes against Peace.* Cambridge: Cambridge University Press.

May, Larry and Stacey Hoffman, eds. 1991. *Collective Responsibility: Five Decades of Debate in Theoretical and Applied Ethics.* Savage, MD: Rowman and Littlefield.

Mazzetti, Mark. 2009. "Release of C.I.A. Interrogation Memos May Open the Door to More Revelations," *The New York Times* April 18, A7.

Mazzetti, Mark and Scott Shane. 2009a. "Memos Spell Out Brutal C.I.A. Mode of Interrogation," *The New York Times,* April 17, A1, A10.

2009b. "Debates Over Interrogation Methods Sharply Divided the Bush White House," *The New York Times* May 4, A13.

McCoy, Alfred. 2006. *A Question of Torture: CIA Interrogation, from the Cold War to the War on Terror.* New York: Henry Holt and Co.

McDougall, Susan with Pat Harris. 2003. *The Woman Who Wouldn't Talk.* New York: Carroll & Graf.

McLean, Bethany and Peter Elkin. 2004. *The Smartest Guys in the Room: The Amazing Rise and Scandalous Fall of Enron.* Updated edn. New York: Portfolio.

McNulty, Faith. 1980. *The Burning Bed.* New York: Harcourt Brace Jovanovich.

Medea, Andra and Kathleen Thompson. 1974. *Against Rape: A Survival Manual.* New York: Farrar, Straus, and Giroux.

Melzer, Milton. 1993. *Slavery: A World History.* New York: Da Capo.

Merriam-Webster's Collegiate Dictionary. 1993. 10th edn. Springfield, MA: Merriam-Webster, Inc.

Milgram, Stanley. 1974. *Obedience to Authority: An Experimental View.* New York: Harper and Row.

Mill, John Stuart. 2002. *Basic Writings of John Stuart Mill.* Introduction by J. B. Schneewind. Notes and Commentary by Dale E. Miller. New York: Modern Library.

Miller, Madeline S. and J. Lane Miller. 1961. *Harper's Bible Dictionary.* New York: Harper and Row.

Miller, Seumas. 2008. "Torture," *The Stanford Encyclopedia of Philosophy.* Ed. Edward N. Nalta. Online at http://plato.stanford.edu/entries/torture and http://plato.stanford.edu/entries/torture/notes.html.

Millett, Kate. 1979. *The Basement: Meditations on a Human Sacrifice.* New York: Simon & Schuster.

Minow, Martha. 1998. *Between Vengeance and Forgiveness: Facing History after Genocide and Mass Violence.* Boston: Beacon.

Minow, Martha, ed. 2002. *Breaking the Cycles of Hatred: Memory, Law, and Repair.* Princeton, NJ and Oxford: Princeton University Press.

Mitscherlich, Alexander and Fred Mielke. 1949. *The Death Doctors*. Trans. James Cleugh. London: Elek Books.

Moline, Jon. 1986. "Aldo Leopold and the Moral Community," *Environmental Ethics* **8**:2, 99–120.

Monk, Ray. 1990. *Ludwig Wittgenstein: The Duty of Genius*. New York: Free Press.

Moore, Solomon. 2009. "Study of Rape in Prisons Counts 60,500 Attacks," *The New York Times* June 23, A17.

Morton, Adam. 2004. *On Evil*. New York: Routledge.

Müller, Filip. 1979. *Eyewitness Auschwitz: Three Years in the Gas Chambers*. Ed. and trans. Susanne Flatauer. New York: Stein and Day.

Naess, Arne. 1979. "Self-Realization in Mixed Communities of Humans, Bears, Sheep, and Wolves," *Inquiry* **22**, 231–41.

Nagel, Thomas. 1979. *Mortal Questions*. Cambridge: Cambridge University Press.

National Commission on Terrorist Attacks upon the United States. 2004. *The 9/11 Commission Report: Final Report of the National Commission on Terrorist Attacks upon the United States*. New York: Norton.

Neihardt, John. 1932. *Black Elk Speaks: Being the Life Story of a Holy Man of the Oglala Sioux*. New York: Morrow.

Netanyahu, Benzion. 2001. *Origins of the Inquisition in Fifteenth-Century Spain*. 2nd edn. New York: New York Review Books.

Newkirk, Ingrid. 1992. *Free the Animals! The Untold Story of the U.S. Animal Liberation Front and Its Founder, "Valerie."* Chicago: Noble Press.

Nietzsche, Friedrich. 1967–77. *Sämtliche Werke: Kritische Studienausgabe in 15 Bänden*. Ed. Giorgio Colli and Mazzino Montinari. Berlin and New York: Walter de Gruyter.

   1969. *On the Genealogy of Morals and Ecce Homo*. Ed. and trans. Walter Kaufmann and R. J. Hollingdale. New York: Vintage.

   1976. *The Portable Nietzsche*. Ed. and trans. Walter Kaufmann. New York: Penguin.

Norlock, Kathryn. 2004. "Environmental Evils and the Atrocity Paradigm," *Ethics and the Environment* **9**:1, 85–93.

Novick, Peter. 1999. *The Holocaust in American Life*. Boston: Houghton Mifflin.

Nussbaum, Martha and Jonathan Glover, eds. 1995. *Women, Culture and Development: A Study of Human Capabilities*. Oxford: Oxford University Press.

Nussbaum, Martha and Amartya Sen, eds. 1993. *The Quality of Life*. Oxford: Oxford University Press.

O'Brien, William V. 1981. *The Conduct of Just and Limited War*. New York: Praeger.

Orlans, Barbara. 1993. *In the Name of Science: Issues in Responsible Animal Experimentation*. New York: Oxford University Press.

Ortiz, Dianna with Patricia Davis. 2004. *The Blindfold's Eyes: My Journey from Torture to Truth*. Maryknoll, NY: Orbis Books.

Orwell, George. 1949. *Nineteen Eighty-Four*. New York: Harcourt, Brace, Jovanovich.

Pagels, Elaine. 1995. *The Origin of Satan*. New York: Random House.

Parfit, Derek. 1984. *Reasons and Persons*. Oxford: Clarendon Press.

Parkman, Francis. 1994. *The Conspiracy of Pontiac and the Indian War after the Conquest of Canada*, 2 vols. Vol. ii, *From the Spring of 1763 to the Death of Pontiac*. Lincoln: University of Nebraska Press. First published 1851.

Patterson, Orlando. 1982. *Slavery and Social Death: A Comparative Study*. Cambridge, MA: Harvard University Press.

Pausanias. 1979. *Guide to Greece*, 2 vols. New York: Penguin.

Pelzer, Dave. 1995. *A Child Called "It."* Deerfield Beach, FL: Health Communications, Inc.

Pepperberg, Irene M. 2002. *The Alex Studies: Cognitive and Communicative Abilities of Gray Parrots*. Cambridge, MA: Harvard University Press.

   2008. *Alex & Me: How a Scientist and a Parrot Uncovered a Hidden World of Animal Intelligence – and Formed a Deep Bond in the Process*. New York: Collins.

Peters, Edward. 1985. *Torture*. New York: Basil Blackwell.

Plant, Richard. 1986. *The Pink Triangle: The Nazi War against Homosexuals*. New York: Holt.

Plato. 1961. *The Collected Dialogues of Plato, Including the Letters*. Ed. Edith Hamilton and Huntington Cairns. New York: Pantheon.

Poussaint, Alvin. 1972. *Why Blacks Kill Blacks*. New York: Emerson Hall.

Power, Samantha. 2002. *"A Problem from Hell": America and the Age of Genocide*. New York: Basic Books.

Puzo, Mario. 1978. *The Godfather*. New York: New American Library.

Radosh, Ronald and Joyce Milton. 1983. *The Rosenberg File: A Search for the Truth*. New York: Holt, Rinehart, and Winston.

Rawls, John. 1999a. *A Theory of Justice*. Rev. edn. Cambridge, MA: Harvard University Press.

   1999b. *Collected Papers*. Ed. Samuel Freeman. Cambridge, MA: Harvard University Press.

Regan, Tom. 1983. *The Case for Animal Rights*. Berkeley: University of California Press.

Regan, Tom and Peter Singer, eds. 1976. *Animal Rights and Human Obligations*. Englewood Cliffs, NJ: Prentice-Hall.

Reitan, Eric. 2001. "Rape as an Essentially Contested Concept," *Hypatia* **16**:2, 43–66.

   (Unpublished). "Defining Terrorism."

Rejali, Darius. 2007. *Torture and Democracy*. Princeton, NJ: Princeton University Press.

Reynolds, David S. 2005. *John Brown, Abolitionist: The Man Who Killed Slavery, Sparked the Civil War, and Seeded Civil Rights*. New York: Knopf.

Rich, Adrienne. 1979. *On Lies, Secrets, and Silence: Selected Prose 1966 – 1978*. New York: Norton.

1980. "Compulsory Heterosexuality and Lesbian Existence," *Signs: A Journal of Women in Culture and Society* **5**:4, 631–60.

Rittner, Carol and John K. Roth, eds. 1993. *Different Voices: Women and the Holocaust*. New York: Paragon House.

Roberts, Monty. 1996. *The Man Who Listens to Horses*. London: Hutchinson.

Robinson, Nehemiah. 1960. *The Genocide Convention: A Commentary*. New York: Institute of Jewish Affairs, World Jewish Congress.

Rosenbaum, Alan S., ed. 2009. *Is the Holocaust Unique? Perspectives on Comparative Genocide*. Boulder, CO: Westview.

Rosenberg, Alan and Gerald E. Myers, eds. 1988. *Echoes from the Holocaust: Philosophical Reflections on a Dark Time*. Philadelphia: Temple University Press.

Rosenberg, David and Michael Lieberman. 1999. *Hate Crimes Laws*. [No place of publication given] Anti-Defamation League.

Ross, W. D. 1980. *The Right and the Good*. Oxford: Clarendon Press [1930].

Roth, John K., ed. 2005. *Genocide and Human Rights: A Philosophical Guide*. New York: Palgrave Macmillan.

Roth, John K. and Michael Berenbaum, eds. 1989. *Holocaust: Religious and Philosophical Implications*. New York: Paragon House.

Roth, Kenneth, Minky Worden, and Amy D. Bernstein, eds. 2005. *Torture: Does It Make Us Safer? Is It Ever OK? A Human Rights Perspective*. New York and London: Human Rights Watch.

Rousseau, Jean-Jacques. 1950. *The Social Contract* and *Discourses*. Trans. G. D. H. Cole. New York: Dutton.

Rubenstein, Richard L. and John K. Roth, eds. 2003. *Approaches to Auschwitz: The Holocaust Legacy*. Louisville, KY: Westminster John Knox Press.

Ruthven, Malise. 1978. *Torture: The Grand Conspiracy*. London: Weidenfeld and Nicolson.

Sahebjam, Freidoune. 1990. *The Stoning of Soraya M*. Trans. Richard Seaver. New York: Arcade Publishing.

Salter, Kenneth W. 1976. *The Trial of Inez García*. Berkeley, CA: Editorial Justa Publications Inc.

Sanday, Peggy Reeves. 1990. *Fraternity Gang Rape: Sex, Brotherhood, and Privilege on Campus*. New York: New York University Press.

Sartre, Jean-Paul. 1960. *Critique de la raison dialectique. Tome I: Théorie des ensembles pratiques*. Paris: Librairie Gallimard.

1968. *On Genocide*. Boston: Beacon.

1976. *Critique of Dialectical Reason I: Theory of Practical Ensembles*. Vol. 1 of 2 vols. Trans. Alan Sheridan-Smith. London: NLB.

Sayre, Kenneth. 1976. *Cybernetics and the Philosophy of Mind*. New York: Humanities Press.

Scheffler, Samuel. 2006. "Is Terrorism Morally Distinctive?" *Journal of Political Philosophy* **14**:1, 1–17.

Scheler, Max. 1954. *The Nature of Sympathy*. Trans. Peter Heath. London: Routledge and Kegan Paul.

Schlosser, Eric. 2001. *Fast Food Nation: The Dark Side of the All-American Meal*. Boston: Houghton Mifflin.

Schott, Robin May, ed. 2007. *Feminist Philosophy and the Problem of Evil*. Bloomington, IN: Indiana University Press.

Schulz, William F., ed. 2007. *The Phenomenon of Torture: Readings and Commentary*. Philadelphia: University of Pennsylvania Press.

Sebold, Alice. 1999. *Lucky*. New York: Scribner.

Segal, Lore. 1973. *Other People's Houses*. New York: New American Library.

Senesh, Hannah. 2004. *Hannah Senesh: Her Life and Diary, The First Complete Edition*. Woodstock, VT: Jewish Lights.

Shakespeare, William. 1984. *Titus Andronicus*. Ed. Eugene M. Waith. Oxford: Oxford University Press.

Shane, Scott. 2009a. "Obama Orders Secret Prisons and Detention Camps Closed," *The New York Times* January 23, available online at www.nytimes.com/2009/01/23/us/politics/23GITMOCND.html.

　　2009b. "C.I.A. to Close Secret Prisons, Scenes of Harsh Interrogations," *The New York Times* April 18, A1, A9.

Shane, Scott and Mark Mazzetti. 2009. "In Adopting Harsh Tactics, No Inquiry into Past Use: Interrogations Based on Torture Methods Chinese Communists Used in '50s," *The New York Times* April 22, A1, A14.

Shengold, Leonard. 1989. *Soul Murder: The Effects of Childhood Abuse and Deprivation*. New Haven: Yale University Press.

Shermer, Michael and Alex Grobman. 2000. *Denying History: Who Says the Holocaust Never Happened and Why Do They Say It?* Berkeley: University of California Press.

Shue, Henry. 1978. "Torture," *Philosophy and Public Affairs* 7:2, 124–43.

　　2005. "Torture in Dreamland: Disposing of the Ticking Bomb," *Case Western Reserve Journal of International Law* 37, 231–39.

Sierra Club v. Morton, Secretary of the Interior, *et al.* 1972. 405 U.S. 727.

Silverman, Sue William. 1996. *Because I Remember Terror, Father, I Remember You*. Athens, GA: University of Georgia Press.

Singer, Marcus G. 2004. "The Concept of Evil," *Philosophy* **79**, 185–214.

Singer, Peter. 2002. *Animal Liberation*. 2nd edn., rev. New York: HarperCollins.

Sipe, Beth and Evelyn J. Hale. 1996. *I Am Not Your Victim*. Thousand Oaks, CA: Sage.

Sipe, C. Hale. 1929. *The Indian Wars of Pennsylvania*. Harrisburg, PA: Telegraph Press.

Smith, Adam. 1937. *An Inquiry into the Nature and Causes of the Wealth of Nations*. Ed. Edwin Cannan. New York: Modern Library.

Sontag, Susan. 2007. *At the Same Time: Essays and Speeches*. Ed. Paolo Dilonardo and Anne Jump. New York: Farrar, Straus, and Giroux.

Der Spiegel magazine. Reporters, Writers, and Editors. 2001. *Inside 9/11: What Really Happened*. Trans. Paul De Angelis and Elisabeth Koestner with contributions from Margot Dembo and Christopher Sultan. New York: St. Martin's Press.

Spiegel, Marjorie. 1996. *The Dreaded Comparison: Human and Animal Slavery.* New York: Mirror Books.

Stannard, David E. 1992. *American Holocaust: The Conquest of the New World.* New York: Oxford University Press.

Stein, Edith. 1964. *On the Problem of Empathy.* Trans. Waltraut Stein. The Hague: Nijhoff.

Stelter, Brian. 2009. "How ABC Interview Shaped a Torture Debate," *The New York Times* April 28, A1, A15.

Sterba, James, ed. 2003. *Terrorism and International Justice.* New York: Oxford University Press.

Stevenson, Robert Louis. 1991. *The Complete Shorter Fiction.* New York: Carroll & Graf.

Stiehm, Judith. 1981. *Bring Me Men and Women: Mandated Change at the U.S. Air Force Academy.* Berkeley: University of California Press.

    1989. *Arms and the Enlisted Woman.* Philadelphia: Temple University Press.

    2006. *Champions for Peace: Women Winners of the Nobel Peace Prize.* Lanham, MD: Rowman and Littlefield.

Stiehm, Judith, ed. 1983. *Women and Men's Wars.* Oxford: Pergamon Press.

Stiglmayer, Alexandra, ed. 1994. *Mass Rape: The War against Women in Bosnia-Herzegovina.* Trans. Marion Faber. Lincoln: University of Nebraska Press.

Stone, Christopher. 1974. *Should Trees Have Standing? Toward Legal Rights for Natural Objects.* Los Altos, CA: William Kaufmann, Inc.

Suskind, Ron. 2006. *The One Percent Doctrine: Deep Inside America's Pursuit of Its Enemies Since 9/11.* New York: Simon & Schuster.

Sussman, David. 2005a. "Defining Torture," *Case Western Reserve Journal of International Law* **37**, 231–39.

    2005b. "What's Wrong with Torture?" *Philosophy and Public Affairs* **33**:1, 1–33.

Tanaka, Yuki. 1996. *Hidden Horrors: Japanese War Crimes in World War II.* Boulder, CO: Westview Press.

Taylor, Michael. 2002. "Lawrence Singleton, Despised Rapist, Dies; He Chopped Off Teenager's Arms in 1978," *San Francisco Chronicle* January 1, available online at www.sfgate.com/cgi-bin/article.cgi?f=/c/a/2002/01/01/MN225792. DTL&type=printable.

Taylor, Paul W. 1986. *Respect for Nature: A Theory of Environmental Ethics.* Princeton, NJ: Princeton University Press.

Taylor, Telford. 1992. *Anatomy of the Nuremberg Trials.* New York: Knopf.

Tec, Nechama. 1993. *Defiance: The Bielski Partisans.* New York: Oxford University Press.

Thomas, Laurence Mordekhai. 1993. *Vessels of Evil: American Slavery and the Holocaust.* Philadelphia: Temple University Press.

Tithecott, Richard. 1997. *Of Men and Monsters: Jeffrey Dahmer and the Construction of the Serial Killer.* Madison, WI: University of Wisconsin Press.

Tonry, Michael, ed. 2009. *The Oxford Handbook of Crime and Public Policy.* Oxford: Oxford University Press.

The Torah: The Five Books of Moses. 1962. Philadelphia: The Jewish Publication Society.

Tuomela, Raimo. 1995. *The Importance of Us: A Philosophical Study of Basic Social Notions.* Stanford, CA: Stanford University Press.

2002. *The Philosophy of Social Practices: A Collective Acceptance View.* Cambridge: Cambridge University Press.

Turkus, Burton B. and Sid Feder. 1951. *Murder, Inc.* New York: Manor Books.

Twining W. L. and P. E. Twining. 1973. "Bentham on Torture," *Northern Ireland Legal Quarterly* **24**:3, 306–56.

VanDeVeer, Donald. 1979. "Interspecific Justice," *Inquiry* **22**:1–2, 55–70.

Vetlesen, Arne Johan. 2005. *Evil and Human Agency: Understanding Collective Evildoing.* Cambridge: Cambridge University Press.

Vetterling-Braggin, Mary, Frederick A. Elliston, and Jane English, eds. 1977. *Feminism and Philosophy.* Totowa, NJ: Littlefield, Adams and Co.

Vidal-Naquet, Pierre. 1992. *Assassins of Memory: Essays on the Denial of the Holocaust.* Trans. Jeffrey Mehlman. New York: Columbia University Press.

Walzer, Michael. 1973. "Political Action: The Problem of Dirty Hands," *Philosophy and Public Affairs* **2**:2, 160–80.

1977. *Just and Unjust Wars: A Moral Argument with Historical Illustrations.* New York: Basic Books.

Waugh, Alexander. 2008. *The House of Wittgenstein: A Family at War.* New York: Doubleday.

Wellman, Carl. 1979. "On Terrorism Itself," *Journal of Value Inquiry* **13**, 250–58.

Wells-Barnett, Ida. 1970. *Crusade for Justice.* Chicago: University of Chicago Press.

1987. *On Lynchings: Southern Horrors, A Red Record, and Mob Rule in New Orleans.* Salem, NH: Ayer Co.

Wenz, Peter. 1988. *Environmental Justice.* Albany, NY: State University of New York Press.

Wiesenthal, Simon. 1997. *The Sunflower: On the Possibilities and Limits of Forgiveness.* Rev. and expanded edn. Trans. H. A. Pichler. New York: Schocken.

Williams, James. 1911. "Torture," *Encyclopedia Britannica.* Eleventh edn., 33 vols. Cambridge: Cambridge University Press, vol. XXVII, 72–79.

Wittgenstein, Ludwig. 1958. *Philosophical Investigations.* Trans. G. E. M. Anscombe. Oxford: Blackwell.

Wittig, Monique. 1992. *The Straight Mind and Other Essays.* Boston: Beacon.

Wolfendale, Jessica. 2006. "Training Torturers: A Critique of the 'Ticking Bomb' Argument," *Social Theory and Practice* **32**:2, 269–87.

Women's Action Coalition. 1993. *WAC STATS: Facts about Women.* New York: New Press.

Wood, Jim. 1976. *The Rape of Inez García.* New York: G. P. Putnam's Sons.

Yancy, George, ed. 2002. *The Philosophical I: Personal Reflections on Life in Philosophy.* Lanham, MD: Rowman and Littlefield.

Young, Iris Marion. 1990. *Justice and the Politics of Difference*. Princeton, NJ: Princeton University Press.

1994. "Gender as Seriality," *Signs: A Journal of Women in Culture and Society* **19**:3, 713–38.

1997. *Intersecting Voices: Dilemmas of Gender, Political Philosophy, and Policy*. Princeton, NJ: Princeton University Press.

2000. *Inclusion and Democracy*. Oxford: Oxford University Press.

2007. *Global Challenges: War, Self-Determination and Responsibility for Justice*. Cambridge: Polity Press.

Zimbardo, Philip. 2007. *The Lucifer Effect: Understanding How Good People Turn Evil*. New York: Random House.

Films referred to

Information on years of release to theaters (or television) and on DVD, studio, and directors is as complete as I could make it. Films are cited in the text by year of release to theaters (or television) only. For *Hanna's War*, I cannot find a studio or details on any DVD release, but I found a website about that film, which I include here.

Australia. 2008 (DVD 2009). Feature film. Twentieth Century Fox. Dir. Baz Luhrmann.

Come and Get It. 1936 (DVDs 1999, 2005). Feature film. Samuel Goldwyn. Dir. Howard Hawks, Richard Rosson, William Wyler.

Danton. 1982 (DVD 2009). Feature film. Gaumont. Dir. Andrzej Wajda.

Defiance. 2008 (DVD 2009). Feature film. Paramount. Dir. Edward Zwick.

Enron: The Smartest Guys in the Room. 2005 (DVD 2006). Documentary film. Magnolia. Dir. Alex Gibney.

The Executioner's Song. 1982 (DVD 2002). Feature film. Paramount. Dir. Lawrence Schiller.

Fast Food Nation. 2006 (DVD 2007). Feature film. Twentieth Century Fox. Dir. Richard Linklater.

Food, Inc. 2009 (DVD 2009). Documentary film. Magnolia. Dir. Robert Kenner.

Goya's Ghosts. 2006 (DVD 2008). Feature film. Sony Pictures. Dir. Milos Forman.

Hanna's War. 1988 (VHS 1988). Feature film. Dir. Menahem Golan. See: www.imdb.com/title/tt0095275/.

Hotel Rwanda. 2004 (DVD 2005). Feature film. Metro-Goldwyn-Mayer. Dir. Terry George.

Loose Change Final Cut. 2007 (DVD 2007). Documentary film. Louder Than Words Productions. Dir. Dylan Avery.

Milk. 2008 (DVD 2009). Feature film. Universal Studios. Dir. Gus Van Sant.

Murder, Inc. 1960 (DVD 2006). Feature film. Twentieth Century Fox. Dir. Stuart Rosenberg and Burt Balaban.

Night and Fog. 1955 (DVD 2003). Documentary. French with English subtitles. Dir. Alain Renais.

Operation Valkyrie: The Stauffenberg Plot to Kill Hitler. 2004 (DVD 2009). 2 discs. Documentary Film. Koch Vision. Dir. Jean-Pierre Isbouts.

Paradise Now. 2005 (DVD 2006). Feature film. Warner Home Video. Arabic with English subtitles. Dir. Hany Abbu-Assad.

Psycho. 1960 (DVD 1998). Feature Film. Universal Studios. Dir. Alfred Hitchcock.

Public Enemies. 2009 (DVD 2009). Feature Film. Universal Pictures. Dir. Michael Mann.

Rabbit-Proof Fence. 2002 (DVD 2003). Feature film. Miramax Home Entertainment. Dir. Phillip Noyce.

Rhythm on the Range. 1936 (DVD 2003). Feature film. Universal Studios. Dir. Norman Taurog.

Shoah. 1985 (DVD 2003). 4 discs. Documentary. New Yorker Video. Dir. Claude Lanzmann.

Shot in the Heart. 2001 (DVD 2002). Feature film. HBO Home Video. Dir. Agnieszka Holland.

Sleeping with the Enemy. 1991 (DVD 2003). Feature film. Twentieth Century Fox. Dir. Joseph Ruben.

Son of Fury. 1942 (DVD 2007). Feature film. Twentieth Century Fox. Dir. John Cromwell.

The Sopranos, Season 6, Part 2. 2007 (DVD 2007). 4 discs. HBO Home Video. Dir. Tim Van Patten and Alan Taylor.

The Stoning of Soraya M. 2008 (DVD 2009). Feature film. Mpower [sic] Pictures. Dir. Cyrus Nowrasteh.

Taken. 2008 (DVD 2009). Feature film. Twentieth Century Fox. Dir. Pierre Morel.

Taxi to the Dark Side. 2007 (DVD 2008). Documentary film. Velocity / Thinkfilm. Dir. Alex Gibney.

Tell No One. 2008 (DVD 2009). Feature film. French with English subtitles. Dir. Guillaume Canet.

Titus. 2000 (DVD 2006). Feature film. Twentieth Century Fox. Dir. Julie Taymor.

Toast of New York. 1937 (DVD 2009). Feature film. Warner Brothers. Dir. Rowland V. Lee.

Valkyrie. 2008 (DVD 2009). Feature film. United Artists. Dir. Bryan Singer.

The War at Home. 1979 (DVD 2003). Documentary film. Dir. Glenn Silber and Barry Alexander Brown.

The Weather Underground. 2003 (DVD 2004). Documentary film. Dir. Bill Seigel and Sam Green (11).

What Ever Happened to Baby Jane? 1962 (DVD 2006). Feature film. Warner Home Video. Dir. Robert Aldrich.

Websites for international documents

Campaign to Abolish Corporal Punishment of Children in Europe and to Challenge Legal Acceptance of Such Punishment:

http://ec.europa.eu/justice_home/daphnetoolkit/files/others/europe_violence/5.1.pdf (accessed July 21, 2009)

Charter of Fundamental Rights of the European Union (EU) (December 7, 2000):

www.europarl.europa.eu/charter/pdf/text_En.pdf (accessed July 2, 2009)

EU Guidelines on the Death Penalty: revised and updated version (updated 2008):

www.consilium.europa.eu/uedocs/cmsUpload/10015.en08.pdf (accessed July 2, 2009)

International Committee of the Red Cross (ICRC) Report on the Treatment by the Coalition Forces of Prisoners of War and Other Protected Persons by the Geneva Conventions in Iraq during Arrest, Internment, and Interrogation (February 2004):

International Covenant on Civil and Political Rights (1976): www1.umn.edu/humanrts/instree/b3ccpr.htm

www.globalsecurity.org/military/library/report/2004/icrc_report_iraq_feb2004.htm (accessed July 2, 2009)

ICRC Report on the Treatment of Fourteen "High Value Detainees" in CIA Custody (2007):

www.nybooks.com/icrc-report.pdf (accessed July 2, 2009)

United Nations (UN) Convention against Torture and Other Cruel, Inhuman or Degrading Treatment or Punishment (1984):

http://velvetrevolution.us/torture_lawyers/docs/UN_Convention_on_Torture.pdf (accessed July 2, 2009)

UN Convention on the Prevention and Punishment of the Crime of Genocide (1948):

www.hrweb.org/legal/genocide.html (accessed July 2, 2009)

UN Convention on the Rights of the Child (1990):

www2.ohchr.org/english/law/pdf/crc.pdf (accessed on July 21, 2009)

UN Declaration on the Rights of Indigenous Peoples (2007):

www.un.org/esa/socdev/unpfii/en/drip.html (accessed July 6, 2009)

Universal Declaration of Human Rights (1948):

www.un.org/en/documents/udhr/ (accessed July 2, 2009)

Index

Abu Ghraib, 12, 210
act
  genocidal acts, 277
  problem of relevant act-descriptions, 49
Afganistan, 181
aftermath of torture, 219
agent, agency
  agency component of evils, 5, 11
  agency perspective, 9
  collective agency, 62
  conspicuous agents vs. ratifiers, 75
  moral, 54, 55, 89
    destruction of capacity for moral agency, 38, 57
  non-human agents of evil, 89
  non-state agent, 129, 136, 137, 138, 141
  of corporations, 112, 114
  of individuals, 75
  of life, 112
  of oppressors, 79
  of terrorism, 127, 138
  of terrorist organizations, 139
  of torture victims, 205
  under oppression, 72
Akayesu, Jean-Paul, 242
al Qaeda, 139, 173, 197, 206, 210, 216
al Zarqawi, Abu Musab, 192, 203
Alexander, Matthew (pseud.), 192, 193, 200, 203
Alleg, Henri, 217, 220, 236
Allen, Beverly, 267–83, 284, 287
  paradox, 267, 268, 283
  solution to "logical glitch", 285
  sperm as biological weapon, 286
American Indian, Native American
  as marginalized, 74
  ethics, 92, 111
  exterminations, 243
  liberation movement, 76
  peoples, 259
  question of genocide, 259, 260

social death, 265
transported children, 238
Améry, Jean, 202, 205, 208–09, 217–20, 221, 236
Amherst, Sir Jeffrey, 260
Amir, Menachem, 225
Amnesty International (AI), 164, 188, 211, 232
Anderson, James, 108
animals, 94
  animal companions, 143, 225
  Animal Liberation Front (ALF), 168, 232
  laboratory experiments, 207, 225, 231–33
  People for the Ethical Treatment of Animals (PETA), 232
  torture of dogs in testing military weaponry, 231
anti-Semitism, anti-Semitic, 47, 116
Arendt, Hannah, 9, 20, 90, 279, 285
  camps compared to Hell, 60
  living corpses, 38, 285
  on evil as fungus, 38
  on radical evil, 38, 46, 47
  on thinking, 47, 70
Aristizabel, Hector, 27, 180
Aristotle, 98, 104, 108
  on brutish vices, 221
  on excuses, 16, 19
  on friendship, 51
  on justice, 19
  on self-movement, 99, 107, 108
  on the living affecting the dead, 266
  on the voluntary, 202
Arrigo, Jean Maria, 178, 179, 183, 187, 196, 202, 215
  three causal models of torture, 179–82
assimilation, 253
  forced, 281, 282
  misleading term for integration, 281
  partial, 281
  voluntary, 281